EVELYN WAUGH, WRITER

Photograph by Karsh (Woodfin Camp & Associates)

EVELYN WAUGH, WRITER

ROBERT MURRAY DAVIS

PILGRIM BOOKS
NORMAN, OKLAHOMA

By Robert Murray Davis

The Novel: Modern Essays in Criticism
Evelyn Waugh
John Steinbeck
Evelyn Waugh, Writer
Modern British Short Novels
Evelyn Waugh: A Checklist of Primary and Secondary Material
Donald Barthelme: A Bibliography
A Catalog of the Evelyn Waugh
    Collection at the Humanities
    Research Center, University of
    Texas-Austin
Evelyn Waugh, Apprentice

Davis, Robert Murray.
    Evelyn Waugh, writer.

    Includes bibliographic references and index.
    1. Waugh, Evelyn, 1903-1966—Criticism and interpretation. I.
Title.
PPR6045.A97Z64 1981   823'.912   81-1098
ISBN 0-937664-00-6   AACR2

Published by Pilgrim Press Books
P.O. Box 2399, Norman, Okla. 73070
Copyright © 1981 By Robert Murray Davis
Manufactured in the U.S.A. First Edition. All rights reserved
ISBN 0-937664-00-6

For Barbara Hillyer Davis

"Revision is just as important as any other part of writing and must be done con amore."

Waugh to Nancy Mitford

". . . you may, must study them to see the changes."

Waugh to Laura on three versions of *Brideshead Revisited*

Contents

Preface to the
Second Printing

Revising a book about revisions would be self-reflexive beyond even postmodern standards if practical considerations did not make extensive changes unfeasible. As it is, I can say that I have corrected errors of typography, fact, and grammar, but I have left untouched infelicities of style and have refrained from inserting references to recently collected or newly published material by and about Waugh which I had used in the first edition but which I could only cite in relatively inaccessible sources. Nor, though I try to take account of it in this preface, have I interpolated new material into the body of the work.

What I did is far less interesting than what, given the collective wisdom of reviewers of the first edition and the industry of fellow editors and critics, I might have done. This is not the place to discuss in detail the state of reviewing or to survey Waugh scholarship since 1981, but both areas obviously affect a reconsideration of my work.

It can be said that the reviewers gave me plenty to think about. Most were kinder than I expected, perhaps than I deserved. But they were hardly unanimous. One called the book a triumph; another judged it a partial failure; still another even more annoyingly failed to render any judgment at all. One lamented that more detail could not be given even from extant material (let alone, as another pointed out, material lost to the waste-basket); another declared that the book could, without losing anything of value, be cut by half. One regarded the mixture of biography, criticism, and textual history as a wholly new and admirable kind of scholarship; several others regretted that the book did not satisfy more traditional generic requirements. Some thought that the book established Waugh's claims to serious consideration; another sympathized at the waste of my ingenuity on a mere craftsman. Some assumed that the book was a collection of previously published articles; another praised my long commitment to Waugh studies and pointed the way to my retirement. If I were to listen to the more captious, I would have to write a completely different kind of book for this edition, but that seems hardly feasible.

Evelyn Waugh, Writer

Two book-length studies have appeared since the publication of *Evelyn Waugh, Writer*. Ian Littlewood's *The Writings of Evelyn Waugh*[1] pays little attention to previous scholarship, and because his book is primarily critical, his approach does not affect mine. But both Jeffrey Heath and I might have profited from seeing each other's books. His *The Picturesque Prison: Evelyn Waugh and His Writing*[2] demonstrates an awareness of textual histories and notes what happened to the manuscripts of *Vile Bodies* and *Put Out More Flags*—Waugh gave them, respectively, to Bryan and Diana Guinness and to Sir Robert Abdy—but he is far more interested in the major conflict he sees between Waugh's delight in the "lush places" which his secular imagination constructed as refuges from the oppressions of the external world and the recognition by Waugh— "the heresimach, the guardian of civilized values"—that "unlimited secular freedom is a spiritual dungeon." In considerable detail (some of it wrenched from context) and with a good deal of ingenuity (some of it rather strained), Heath goes on to argue that Waugh used his novels as means of exorcising aspects of his own character, in the first four novels operating on the figurative level, using "even the most minor details [to] unexpectedly imitate the underlying shape." He is interested in inner patterns, I in outer ones, but his approach could obviously be used to interpret some of the evidence I presented in this study, since the cast of a mind is more likely to be revealed in the heat of composition than in cooler reflection, and future biographers might wish to examine carefully Waugh's revisions.

Of the many articles published since I completed the manuscript of the first edition, the majority approach Waugh from perspectives so different from mine that neither their cases nor mine are much affected. However, a half-dozen scholarly articles offer new light on some of the books I discuss. Most fascinating for the student of Waugh's biography is the Hursts' "Bromide Poisoning in *The Ordeal of Gilbert Pinfold*,[3] which discovers classic symptoms in most of Pinfold's hallucinations. The Hursts do not appear to know that D. G. Rossetti experienced some of the same symptoms, that Waugh described them in his biography, and that Waugh drew the comparison as his Pinfold delusions were beginning,[4] but this does not make less valuable the blend of medical and literary analysis which they bring to a novel that has rarely been discussed in any terms.

1. (Oxford: Blackwell, 1982; Totowa, NJ: Barnes & Noble, 1983).
2. (Kingston and Montreal: McGill-Queen's University Press, 1982).
3. Mary Jane Hurst and Daniel Hurst, M.D., "Bromide Poisoning in *The Ordeal of Gilbert Pinfold*," *Evelyn Waugh Newsletter*, 16 (Autumn 1982), 1–4.
4. *The Letters of Evelyn Waugh*, ed. Mark Amory (London: Weidenfeld and Nicolson, 1980; New Haven and New York: Ticknor & Fields, 1980; Penguin Books, 1982), p. 418. I cite the Ticknor & Fields edition.

The Los Angeles background of *The Loved One* is now clearer because of James J. Lynch's *"The Loved One* and the *Art Guide of Forest Lawn,"*[5] which demonstrates the influence on the detail and style of the novel of the souvenir which Waugh carried home to England. Also valuable for students of the novel is Donald Greene's "Evelyn Waugh's Hollywood,"[6] which provides a map keyed to the novel and testifies to Waugh's sharpness of observation. Those who want a different view of the composition and textual history of the novel and are masochistic enough to want to know more about the movie version should see Philip Stratford's "Evelyn Waugh and 'The Loved One.' "[7]

Some additional background for *Black Mischief* is provided in Donat Gallagher's "Black Majesty and Press Mischief"[8] and in my study of the manuscript of *Remote People,*[9] but neither affects the analysis of the novel's composition or my reading of it.

Besides these augmentations, there are more substantial publications which give the reader access to background material in much more convenient form. The most important of these is Donat Gallagher's edition of *The Essays, Articles and Reviews of Evelyn Waugh.*[10] Expanded from the rather exiguous *A Little Order* (1977) because of the publicity surrounding the publication of Waugh's letters and the Granada Television version of *Brideshead Revisited,* this volume not only includes 237 pieces by Waugh (up from *A Little Order*'s 55) but an index of proper names, titles, and topics; an eleven-page "Chronological List of Occasional Writings not Printed in This Volume"; and about fifty pages of editorial commentary. This editorial material is itself a major contribution to Waugh studies. Throughout the volume, Gallagher explains financial and rhetorical influences that may have prompted Waugh to write the way he did. For example, Gallagher is able to see Waugh's "youth journalism" not only in the light of *Vile Bodies* but in the context of the kinds of literary and other journalism being practiced at the time. The analysis of British attitudes towards Abyssinia both in 1930 and 1936 enables Gallagher to move the discussion away from the somewhat circular and at this pont stultifying argument over the degree, extent, or

5. *Evelyn Waugh Newsletter,* 17 (Winter 1983), 1–5.

6. *Evelyn Waugh Newsletter,* 16 (Winter 1982), 1–4.

7. *Encounter,* 51 (September 1978), 46–51. The article appeared before my book went to press but dealt with material I had already covered and did not have the advantage of consulting the manuscript.

8. *London Magazine,* 22 (October 1982), 26–38.

9. "Towards a Mature Style: The Manuscript of Waugh's *Remote People," Analytical and Enumerative Bibliography,* 7, nos. 1–2 (1983), 3–15.

10. London: Methuen, 1983. Boston: Little, Brown, 1984.

kind of Waugh's protofascism to a more balanced historical discussion. Waugh's opposition to Tito and to Hooperism seems less Neanderthal when seen in the context of Catholic outrage at the betrayal of Poland and other Catholic countries into the hands of their persecutors and of concerted attacks on the English upper classes by those who hoped to use war sentiment to effect revolutionary social change in England. And a knowlege of Catholic journalism and lay attitudes in the 1940's enables Gallagher to point out the extent to which Waugh revealed his independence of orthodox piety, if not doctrine, and thereby to explain Waugh's intransigence at the changes effected by the Second Vatican Council.

Less impressive in bulk and importance is *Evelyn Waugh, Apprentice*,[11] which collects forty-one items of Waugh's juvenile and uncollected work, twenty-seven of them printed for the first time. Since these materials were available when I worked on the first edition, their publication does not affect my case, but Waugh enthusiasts unable to travel to the Humanities Research Center in Austin may be pleased to encounter some of them for the first time and to see the youthful Waugh sharpening his skills in fiction, verse, and drama. A few of Waugh's schoolboy poems were published in the *Diaries*; "Charles Ryder's Schooldays," Waugh's postwar attempt to turn his diaries into fiction, was published for the first time in 1982;[12] and *PRB: An Essay on the Pre-Raphaelite Brotherhood*, originally published in 1926, was reissued in 1982.[13]

There is a body of work, published and unpublished, which would perhaps modify and certainly augment my account of Waugh's composition of his novels: his letters. As I noted in the preface to the first edition, the *Letters* edited by Mark Amory appeared after my book was in proof, and I was able to change errors of fact or to rectify significant omissions. Since Amory selected 840 letters from about 4,500—and some that he knew about were not available—it is clear that letters yet unpublished and undiscovered will be a major source of modifications and augmentations to my account. Of course, I had seen and taken account of the more than 1,000 letters to A. D. Peters and others at the Humanities Research Center which Amory chose not to publish, but that leaves more than 2,500 *known* items I have not seen.

Some indication of what might be expected came from my rereading of the *Letters* and of my own work. There were gratifyingly few errors of fact or interpretation to correct, but there were dozens of places in which I

11. Ed. Robert Murray Davis (Norman, OK: Pilgrim Books, 1985).

12. *Times Literary Supplement*, 5 March 1982, pp. 255–258.

13. Westerham, Kent: Dalrymple Press, 1982. Preface by Christopher Sykes; Postscript by Christopher Wood.

might, if resetting and rephotographing were free, have incorporated Waugh's testimony about the progress of a book, the situations or people on which it was based, or his often very candid response to what he was writing.

Thus I could now place a bit more precisely the composition of parts of *Rossetti* (*Letters*, p. 25), *Decline and Fall* (pp. 25, 27), *Black Mischief* (pp. 51, 55), and *Scoop* (p. 100). He notes that *A Handful of Dust* is at "first about sponger," identified by Amory as Murrough O'Brien (p. 83 and n.), discusses the difficulty in dealing "with normal people instead of eccentrics" (p. 84), and defends against Henry Yorke's criticism the fantastic ending as "a 'conceit' in the Webster manner" and "justifiable symbolism" (p. 88).

Waugh's comments on later novels are even more useful for the critic. Writing to Nancy Mitford about *Brideshead Revisited*, he said that God, not Waugh, was on Lady Marchmain's side and that Charles Ryder "was a bad painter. Well he was as bad at painting as Osbert [Sitwell] is at writing" (p. 196). And in retrospect he identifies the "aesthetic bugger who sometimes turns up in my novels under various names"—Anthony Blanche in *Brideshead*—as "⅔ Brian [Howard] ⅓ Harold Acton. People think it was all Harold, who is a much sweeter and saner man" (p. 506).

As the letters to Peters and to Laura indicate, Waugh had begun by the composition of *Brideshead* to discuss his work in progress much more openly. Though he never again went into the kind of detail he had with *Brideshead*, he seems to refer more frequently to work in progress, grumbling about the dullness of *Men at Arms* and confessing that he sent it to his publisher even though it was "all falling to bits. But I was going mad trying to get it right so off I sent it" (p. 365). He liked *Officers and Gentlemen* much better, adding, "The reviewers don't, fuck them" (p. 444). And he told Anthony Powell that Guy Crouchback, the central figure in the *Sword of Honor* trilogy, "is a prig. But he is a virtuous, brave prig" (p. 443). He had very clearly in mind the material for the final volume, *Unconditional Surrender*, giving a thorough outline to Maurice Bowra in 1955 (p. 444).

These are only a few of the modifications which could be made from material presently available, and further discoveries are bound to increase our knowledge of Waugh's life, habits of work, and texts. Paul Doyle is completing a heavily annotated glossary of names and allusions in Waugh's novels which will modify if not revolutionize our perception of Waugh's ironic perspective; each of the few pages I have seen provides material which could profitably be incorporated in my study. Donat Gallagher is well into his study of the intellectual, social, and historical backgrounds of Waugh's non-fiction, and this extensive study will obviously throw light on the thematic and perhaps even the technical concerns of the fiction. Martin Stannard has examined the manuscript of *Vile Bodies* in an admittedly journalistic piece, [14] and Dr. J. A. McDonnell is working on an annotated edition of the novel which will include a discussion of Waugh's changes for the printed version. A growing body of theory about the composition and revision of texts can throw more light on the evidence than the glimmers of my pragmatic approach have been able to do. Beyond that, critics like Leszek Kolek[15] and Virgil Nemoianu[16] have begun to apply postmodern critical theories to the novels and to the work as a whole.

When I finished work on the final manuscript of the first edition almost eight years ago, I hoped and perhaps believed that I had said the last word on Waugh. It is now easier to see how vain that hope was, to be able to trust the process of scholarship, to accept with humility the criticisms and extensions that other scholars have made of my work, and to find some gratification at the new and higher valuation of Evelyn Waugh as writer—and perhaps some pride in whatever small part I have had in that revaluation.

Robert Murray Davis
Norman, December, 1985

14. "The mystery of the missing manuscript," *Times Higher Education Supplement*, 1 June 1984, p. 13.

15. " 'Uncinematic Devices' in Evelyn Waugh's *A Handful of Dust*," *Literature in Wissenschaft und Unterricht* (Kiel, W. Germany), 15 (December 1982), 353–365. See also his dissertation, *Evelyn Waugh's Writings: From Joke to Comic Fiction* (Lublin: Uniwersytet Marii Curie-Skłodowskiej Wydział Humanistyczny, 1985), which concentrates on *A Handful of Dust*.

16. "Evelyn Waugh and the Motley Society," *Clio*, 12 (Spring 1983), 233–243.

Preface to
First Edition

For the reader accustomed to critical studies and to biographies, an explanation is in order. Although this book uses biographical material, it is not a biography. Although critical conclusions are frequently presented and critical assumptions are everywhere implicit, this is neither a critical study in the usual sense nor a book about theory, even theory of composition or revision. Rather, as the title implies, it is as thorough as possible a study of Evelyn Waugh as a working writer, as a maker in the sense in which Sir Philip Sidney and others use the term. One assumption, of course, is that Waugh deserves this kind of scrutiny. Another is that by observing the process we can better understand the result. A third is that one can find pleasure and instruction in watching a master at work.

This is the first study of Waugh to make extensive use of the Evelyn Waugh collection in the Humanities Research Center at the University of Texas—Austin to give a comprehensive view of Waugh's career. I have drawn material from his diaries, his letters, the files of his literary agent, his marginalia, his rare or unpublished juvenilia, his fugitive materials unavailable to previous students of Waugh, and manuscript materials from all the novels except *Vile Bodies* and *Put Out More Flags,* which were not available and which therefore could not be included in this book. These and other kinds of evidence serve to establish the personal and intellectual contexts from which the major novels grew and to reveal the process by which Waugh arrived at major decisions about external structure, about the invention and ordering of plot, about the creation and alteration of character for thematic purposes, about verbal and symbolic motifs, and about adjustments to tone and rhythm all the way from individual sentences to scenes, sections, and, in his consistent practice of revising the conclusion after finishing the manuscript, of novels as artistic wholes.

It is important, I think, to emphasize and to demonstrate the labor that Waugh put into his novels because, although he is widely regarded as a master of English prose, many assume that his books came easily to him. Waugh sometimes gave implicit support to the misconception, as in his view that his education at Lancing College "was the preparation for one trade only; that of an English prose writer,"[1] and he wondered that few of his contemporaries took advantage of the training. Boys of his social class were expected to do a good deal of writing in prose as well as verse, Latin as well as English, and to his training in the classics Waugh attributed his perception "that a sentence is a logical construction and that words have basic inalienable meanings, departure from which is either conscious metaphor or inexcusable vulgarity."[2] Throughout his life he continued to apply to prose by his friends, his enemies, and himself the standards and attitude of an exacting schoolmaster,[3] telling Frank Pakenham, for example, that "I wasn't shocked at a politician writing like that, but at a don's. [*Born to Believe*] might be work of a second year undergraduate at BNC [Brasenose College]."[4] In fact, Waugh tended to regard himself less as a novelist than as a writer of prose, for he regarded fiction "not as the investigation of character but as an exercise in the use of language."[5] Very probably he influenced the choice of his epitaph: "Evelyn Waugh: Writer."[6]

Of course, few of Waugh's contemporaries at Lancing had grown up in a home like his, where words were both business and recreation. Arthur Waugh, his father, was addicted to amateur theatricals and to reading aloud from the more obvious English classics; he was also director of Chapman and Hall, the publishing company, and a man of letters in his own rather minor right. Alec Waugh, Evelyn's older brother, published his bestselling *The Loom of Youth* at the age of eighteen and a series of less spectacularly successful books ended only in 1981. Writers of both generations frequented the Waugh house in Hampstead. As a schoolboy, Waugh viewed these figures with some reservations; he had very little regard of any kind for his father and little professional respect for his brother. Throughout his years at Lancing and at Oxford, the younger Waugh

1. Evelyn Waugh, *A Little Learning* (Boston: Little, Brown and Co., 1964), p. 140.
2. *Ibid.,* p. 139.
3. See my "How Waugh Cut Merton," *Month* 6 (April, 1973):150-53, for an extended discussion of Waugh's editorial prowess. Anglophiles will be pleased to learn that the editor of *Month,* Peter Hebblethwaite, S.J., cut part of my original manuscript.
4. Evelyn Waugh, *The Diaries of Evelyn Waugh,* ed. Michael Davie (Boston: Little, Brown and Co., [1977]), p. 704, September 28, 1952.
5. Julian Jebb, "The Art of Fiction XXX: Evelyn Waugh," *Paris Review,* no. 30 (Summer-Fall, 1963), p. 79.
6. Alfred Borrello, "A Visit to Combe Florey: Evelyn Waugh's Home," *Evelyn Waugh Newsletter* 2 (Winter, 1968): 3.
7. See my "Evelyn Waugh's Juvenilia," *Evelyn Waugh Newsletter* 10 (Winter, 1976): 1-7, which deals largely with unpublished work, and the dissertation of Charles E. Linck, Jr., "The Development of Evelyn Waugh's Career: 1903-1939" (University of Kansas, 1962), which deals with published writings and drawings.

wrote a good deal,[7] and meetings with his brother stimulated him to write or to plan to write, but only when he was fired from his schoolmaster's job did he make the overt decision "to set about being a man of letters."[8]

He had postponed the decision, he confessed at the height of his fame, because "I am lazy and [writing] is intensely hard work," and he finally made it because "I wanted to be a man of the world and I took to writing as I might have taken to archaeology or diplomacy or any other profession as a means of coming to terms with the world." By 1946, he saw writing "as an end in itself."[9] Waugh exaggerated his ability to pursue another career; anyone who knows much about Waugh's character would be hard put to envision him as even a cold-war diplomat. More important, even in his Lancing years one can discern the beginnings of an obsession caused by the fact "there are always words going around in my head; some people think in pictures, some in ideas. I think entirely in words."[10] In adolescence he worried about the effect of concentrated study on his style[11]—at Oxford he removed the cause of worry —and while slogging through his prize poem in Spenserian stanzas, he confessed to his diary that "I feel that I must write prose or burst."[12] Looking at his attempts to do other kinds of work, one could plausibly argue that if he had not become a writer he would have been nothing.

He did become a writer, of course, and testimony to his diligence as well as his talent is given by the manuscripts now in the University of Texas—Austin. Most of them are bound in increasingly expensive materials; some—the war trilogy and *Scoop*—were revised so heavily that he enclosed the loose pages in specially constructed boxes with imitation bindings; one—the autobiography—was so chaotic that its various drafts were simply tied up and placed in file folders. Waugh wrote in black or blue ink on the recto of lined foolscap—often torn neatly at the fold—and used red ink to indicate insertions or corrections. Brief emendations were written between lines of the text; Waugh sometimes interrupted a sequence to expand on an earlier idea, drew a neat line to the point of insertion, and continued as before. Longer insertions were written overleaf or on the verso of the previous page. Words or phrases rejected during the heat of first drafting were struck out heavily—this practice accounts for the large number of conjectural readings in my quotations from manuscript. Canceled material a few lines long was boxed and struck through with parallel diagonal lines; longer cancellations, prob-

8. Waugh, *Diaries,* p. 281, February 21, 1927.
9. Evelyn Waugh, "Fan-Fare," *Life* 20 (April 8, 1946):54,56.
10. Jebb, "The Art of Fiction XXX: Evelyn Waugh," p. 80.
11. Waugh, *Diaries,* p. 144, October 31 and November 7, 1921.
12. *Ibid.,* p. 123, April 2, 1921.

ably rejected during the latter stages of revision, were indicated by a single diagonal line.

The revised manuscript went in batches a chapter or so long to the long-suffering typist, who had to deal not only with the neatly marked insertions but with Waugh's handwriting, which became more illegible as he grew older. Mrs. Waugh's testimony supplements evidence in the Texas collection that two typescripts were made, "both of which he corrected individually by hand. The second was then cannibalized and inserted, whenever needed, into the first copy"[13] or, especially in Waugh's postwar novels, into the manuscript itself. From the proof copies I have seen, Waugh must have made it a practice of revising in the clear typescript, galley proofs, and page proofs. Sometimes he revised between editions—in the case of *Brideshead Revisited,* at almost every opportunity.

Yet the obsession that caused Gilbert Pinfold to "find the sentences he had written during the day running in his head," so that "he would again and again climb out of bed, pad down to the library, make a minute correction, return to his room, lie in the dark dazzled by the pattern of vocables,"[14] had a happy effect not only for Waugh's readers but for the author himself. "Style alone," he argued in a passage contemporary with the gestation of *The Ordeal of Gilbert Pinfold,* "can keep [the writer] from being bored with his own work."[15] The "elegance and variety of contrivance" he imputed to his own work was, as the following chapters demonstrate, the result of his discovery of his design not only through accesses of inspiration about structure but through the myriad minute corrections he made from line to line, word to word.

Waugh might have disapproved with the concrete form of this study, but he would hardly have quarreled with the idea behind it. As his collation of George Grossmith's *The Diary of a Nobody* shows, he was interested in the effect of revision. Furthermore, he took justifiable pride in the discipline by which he attained "lucidity, elegance, individuality," to him the major "elements of style,"[16] and while his major motive in assembling manuscript and other materials to sell to the University of Texas may have been, as he wrote to his brother Alec, [17] a desire to provide for his old age, the care with which he collated and annotated the manuscripts indicates that he expected them to be used and that he was concerned with the users' needs.

13. Borrello, "A Visit to Combe Florey," p. 2.
14. Evelyn Waugh, *The Ordeal of Gilbert Pinfold* (London: Chapman and Hall, 1957), p. 11.
15. "Literary Style in England and America," *Books on Trial* 14 (October, 1955): 66.
16. *Ibid.,* p. 65.
17. Undated letter [1965?] to Alec Waugh, Humanities Research Center, University of Texas–Austin.

In using the Texas collection and other materials, I have assumed that Evelyn Waugh is important enough to allow me to expect that the reader has a fairly thorough knowledge of his work; that the reader will be interested in the ways in which the novels came to be written and assumed their final form, including the many small changes by which Waugh achieved his style; and that the close examination of complex stages of revision will deepen our understanding of Waugh's achievement.

In hopes of attaining this end, I have used a large body of material not available to the authors of previous books on Waugh's art: the published diaries and the full manuscript version; the files of A. D. Peters, Waugh's literary agent; and the manuscripts of all of the novels except *Vile Bodies* and *Put Out More Flags,* neither of which is in the collection in Austin and neither of which, therefore, is discussed in this book. *The Letters of Evelyn Waugh,* edited by Mark Amory, appeared after my book was in proof; except for a few corrections of fact, which I have made in the text, information from the *Letters* has been incorporated in the notes.[18] Furthermore, I have consulted a large body of Waugh's nonfiction, especially ephemeral articles and reviews, not previously identified. Perhaps more important, I have attempted to see the material diachronically rather than synchronically: too often in the past, other critics and I have tended to impose a spurious unity of outlook on Waugh's religious, political, and aesthetic views. Although this is not a biography or an intellectual history, it does deal with Waugh's major concerns during the periods when he was composing his novels.

Waugh wrote a good deal of nonfiction, but I have examined only *Rossetti,* his first book, at any length because I think his novels more important, and I make this exception because in that book one can see Waugh making the transition from gifted amateur to professional writer. I have, however, consulted the manuscripts of *Edmund Campion,* the biography of Monsignor Ronald Knox, *Tourist in Africa, A Little Learning,* and a great many shorter works, all at the Humanities Research Center of the University of Texas and all described in my catalogue;[19] and that of *Remote People,* now in the Berg Collection of the New York Public Library. None offers markedly different

18. The Humanities Research Center also has the manuscripts of *Scott-King's Modern Europe* and *Love Among the Ruins.* Because these relatively minor works confirm rather than add to knowledge of Waugh's habits of composition, I have chosen to discuss them elsewhere. See my "Shaping a World: The Textual History of *Love Among the Ruins,"* *Analytical and Enumerative Bibliography* 1 (Spring, 1977):137-54, and *"Scott-King's Modern Europe:* A Textual History," *Evelyn Waugh Newsletter* 12 (Winter, 1978). *The Letters of Evelyn Waugh,* ed. Mark Amory (New Haven and New York: Ticknor & Fields, 1980), includes some letters from the Texas collections and a great many more.

19. Robert Murray Davis, *A Catalogue of the Evelyn Waugh Collection at the Humanities Research Center, University of Texas-Austin* (Troy, N.Y.: Whitston Publishing Co., 1981).

kinds of evidence about Waugh's habits of composition. Students interested in Waugh's nonfiction will find illuminating the work of D. S. Gallagher.

As this statement concedes, no scholar can hope to do everything. In twenty years of working on Waugh, I have accumulated many debts. Ricardo Quintana and Alvin Whitley of the University of Wisconsin, directed my early efforts. Other students of Waugh have been a continual source of enlightenment: Paul A. Doyle originated serious study of Waugh in the United States; Charles E. Linck, Jr., discovered material previously inaccessible to Americans for his doctoral dissertation and later work; D. S. Gallagher is almost preternaturally adept at digging out obscure materials and generous in sharing them; Nicholas Joost was the most gifted copy editor I have encountered. Two of the most acute critics of Waugh, Marston LaFrance—the wittiest student of Waugh—and D. Paul Farr, did not live to complete their work. All of these and many others, here and abroad, have created a remarkable friendly atmosphere in which to work.

Practical help was rendered by the staff of the Humanities Research Center in Austin, with most of the burden falling on Lois Bell Garcia, friend to scholars and invaluable head of the Reading Room. Funds for travel and materials have been provided by the American Philosophical Society, by the Research Council and the College of Arts and Sciences in the University of Oklahoma, and, under the leadership of Victor Elconin, by the English Department of the University of Oklahoma.

Unpublished material by Evelyn Waugh is reprinted by permission of A. D. Peters & Co. Ltd.; it is located at the Humanities Reseach Center, The University of Texas at Austin. Parts of chapters two, seven, nine, and ten contain revised versions of the following articles: "The Early Work of Evelyn Waugh: The Formation of a Method," *Texas Studies in Literature and Language,* Vol. VII, No. 1, Spring 1965; " 'Clarifying and Enriching': Waugh's Changing Conception of Anthony Blanche," *Papers of the Bibliographical Society of America,* Vol. LXXII, Third Quarter 1978; "The Serial Version of *Brideshead Revisited,*" *Twentieth Century Literature,* Vol. XV, 1969; and "*The Loved One:* Text and Context," *Texas Quarterly,* Vol.XV, No. 4, Winter 1972. I am grateful to the editors of these journals for permission to reprint this material.

Barbara Hillyer Davis read and criticized every draft at every stage.

Robert Murray Davis
Norman, Oklahoma
1981

Note on Citations

In order to give some indication of the extent and significance of Waugh's corrections without attempting to reproduce manuscript material or to use a bewildering and costly variety of typefaces, I have adopted the following symbols:

( ) enclose deleted material.

/ / enclose inserted material

(( )) enclose deletions within a deletion.

// // enclose insertions within insertions.

The revisions are sometimes more complex than these symbols can indicate; in those cases, I have used parallel or successive texts or other means indicated in the context. Waugh's spelling, punctuation, and capitalization in manuscript have generally been retained.

The final authorially supervised text of Waugh's novels is in most cases the Uniform Edition published by Chapman and Hall between 1960 and (posthumously, of course) 1967. However, I have occasionally cited other texts, giving the reasons for doing so in the notes.

EVELYN WAUGH,
WRITER

1

Becoming
a Man
of Letters:
Rossetti

With characteristic self-deprecation, Waugh called his first book "hurried and bad," refused to let it be reissued, and made the publisher's commission as well as his composition seem perfunctory. Thirty-five years after the event he told Julian Jebb that he went to his Oxford friend Anthony Powell at Duckworth's, pleaded starvation, and received an offer of fifty pounds "for a brief life of Rossetti. I was delighted as fifty pounds was quite a lot then. I dashed off and dashed it off."[1] In fact, as the evidence in the Waugh archives and the book itself show, he was far less casual in his approach, and *Rossetti: His Life and Works* has an honorable place among modern studies of Rossetti.[2] More significant, in the process of writing the book he not only achieved a coherent theory of the nature and value of art but made the transition from amateur to professional writer.

Heredity as well as environment could have occasioned his interest in the Pre-Raphaelites. One of his great-aunts had married Thomas Woolner; two more, successively, had married William Holman Hunt.[3] Even though at this period Waugh deprecated most of his father's tastes, Arthur Waugh, self-described as "incorrigibly Victorian" and interested in paintings for their subjects, may have fostered his son's interests; books by and about the Pre-Raphaelites were in his library, and in fact he published Holman Hunt's *Pre-Raphaelitism and the Pre-Raphaelite Brotherhood.* However it began, the younger Waugh's interest was manifest as early as 1919, when he hoped to

1. Julian Jebb, "The Art of Fiction XXX: Evelyn Waugh," *Paris Review,* no. 30 (Summer-Fall 1963), p. 76.

2. Evelyn Waugh, *Rossetti: His Life and Works* (London: Duckworth, 1928). Page references are given parenthetically in the text.

3. Judging from Evelyn Waugh, *A Little Learning* (Boston: Little, Brown and Co., 1964), pp. 64, 67, and from Diana Holman Hunt's *My Grandfather: His Wives and Loves* (New York: W.W. Norton and Company, 1969), the Waugh and Holman Hunt families were not otherwise close. But see "The Only Pre-Raphaelite," *Spectator* 205 (October 14, 1960):567.

read a paper on "'the Failure of the Pre-Raphaelites' to the Art group of the Dilettanti."[4]

The next surviving mention of the Pre-Raphaelites comes six years later under far different circumstances. Like events of more moment, it was the result of a fall—from a barroom window as Waugh tried to escape fellow actors in a Terence Greenidge film.[5] Immobilized on his father's sofa for three days with a twisted ankle, Waugh was soon "deep in the study of the Pre-Raphaelites. I want to write a book about them." A few days later, back at Aston Clinton, he noted that "during the last week I have lived with them night and day," fitting the books to his mood: with the exuberant, confident Holman Hunt in the morning; with the irrepressible John Millais later on; and finally, "when firelight and rum and loneliness have done their worst, with Rossetti, soaked in chloral."

The printed sources available to Waugh cannot at this time be traced in full. By the standards of current scholarship they were not extensive, and, judging from the acknowledgments in *Rossetti,* Waugh selected heavily from those available.[6] Even at this stage, however, his approach was far from casual. Extensive and sometimes delightful evidence of his interest is preserved in his library, which contains five of the books mentioned, three of them with marginal annotations and one of those in turn, Holman Hunt's, what amounts to a running commentary. Waugh's note in his copy, "Aston Clinton November 1925,"[7] indicates that he read it during the flush of his initial enthusiasm, and the annotations help define more clearly the direction of his interest. Although in his diary he adopted an anonymous critic's phrase in the first three words when he called Hunt "the only Pre-Raphaelite —untiring, fearless, conscientious,"[8] he was far from blind to Hunt's limita-

4. Evelyn Waugh, *The Diaries of Evelyn Waugh,* ed. Michael Davie (Boston: Little, Brown and Co., 1977), p. 35 (November 1919).

5. Evelyn Waugh, *Diaries,* pp. 232–33 (before November 6, 1925).

6. See Waugh's "Rossetti's Wife," *Spectator* 149 (October 8, 1923): 449. This review of Violet Hunt's *The Wife of Rossetti* discusses "the importance of this personal acquaintance and tireless investigation" because of the official sources' "consistent and ludicrous reluctance . . . to impute such human qualities as undistinguished birth and personal animosity" to the subjects. William Michael Rossetti's official biography Waugh terms "a model of subterfuge."

7. William Holman Hunt, *Pre-Raphaelitism and the Pre-Raphaelite Brotherhood,* 2d ed., 2 vols. (London: Chapman and Hall, 1913). Waugh's copy is in the Humanities Research Center, University of Texas—Austin, which houses Waugh's library. Further references are given parenthetically to volume and page. In "The Only Pre-Raphaelite," Waugh says that the second Mrs. Hunt paid for this edition.

8. He uses the phrase again in "The Only Pre-Raphaelite," a review of Diana Holman Hunt's *My Grandmothers and I.*

tions, both psychological and aesthetic. In young Waugh's view, Hunt was egotistical, stubborn, possibly disingenuous, and certainly prolix. He was also badly educated and a sloppy thinker with confused ideas about nature, an inability to make useful or even meaningful distinctions, and a hopeless incapacity to distinguish between objective and subjective responses. His social sense was also defective: he thought George Meredith "a well-bred Englishman"; Waugh notes that "he was the son of a tailor" (2:187).

Waugh's sense of the ridiculous was especially excited by Hunt's account of Millais and his family. Several times he wrote "Marvellous" in the margin, and at the beginning of the chapter delineating the early relationship of Millais and Hunt, Waugh summarized his response: "Delicious picture of life at 88 Gower Street. How impossible Millais is from the very first and how he shows through Hunt's affectionate description." Equally diverting to Waugh was Hunt's account of Millais's visit to a phrenologist, who found no indications of artistic talent (1:184–85).[9]

In other annotations, Waugh notes contradictions, makes cross references to other materials, and introduces alien aesthetic systems such as those of Eric Gill, Byzantine art, Impressionism, and concepts of form based on sculpture. Next to Hunt's statement that the first artistic impulse came from an attempt to present the beautiful, Waugh countered with: "I should say [?] rather that there were two distinct impulses—ornament and the desire to communicate an intellectual concept (picture writing). These two only became fused in a much later stage. e.g. Egyptian art of the best period" (2:335). These notes indicate that from the very first Waugh's interest was aesthetic as well as dramatic, that he saw, as he did in the biography of Rossetti, that the Brethren were interesting not only because they were lively personalities but also because their work raised as conspicuously as their theories failed to solve a number of interesting aesthetic questions.

Waugh's reading had no immediate results, for renewed mobility and parties at Oxford soon distracted him. Not until July, 1926, when Alastair Graham asked him to write something to be printed on his private press, did Waugh set to work. Using the notes he had taken the previous year, he finished the essay, after four and a half days, on July 23. "I think it quite good," he wrote in his diary, and so did his father. If not "quite good," the booklet is the longest complete work of Waugh's youth, it attempts to achieve a balance between action and analysis, and it shows that Waugh was, haltingly, beginning to find his own voice as a writer of English prose.

9. *P.R.B.: An Essay on the Pre-Raphaelite Brotherhood, 1847–1854* (London: Privately printed by Alastair Graham, 1926); see p. 1 for the use of Hunt's account.

P.R.B.: An Essay on the Pre-Raphaelite Brotherhood; 1847–1854, covered a far shorter time span than *Rossetti* would and focused on the changing fortune and evolving theories of Millais, Holman Hunt, and Rossetti. Even so, it was a good deal of material to cover in twenty-five pages. Waugh's attempt to provide a dramatic framework looks rather like the joke about formula fiction in which "'You son of a bitch!' cried the Queen," is the perfect opening line because it combines sex, violence and high social class. Waugh's beginning is only a little less striking: "I call upon you, Hunt, as a witness of this bad behavior to his mother." Mrs. Millais is indignant because her son has for the first time locked his studio door to discuss revolutionary aesthetic theories—in the portentous year 1847—with Holman Hunt. Unfortunately, Waugh then had to introduce his two principal actors, glance at his scene to present the family's attitude, try to define Pre-Raphaelitism by negation, including the anomalies in the list of Immortals, and present the positive definition, first, of "a revolutionary movement against technically bad painting"—which must then be described—and, second, of "a spiritual change in the attitude of the artist towards his work; a change which is repeatedly indicated by the phrase 'truth to Nature'"—for which slippery term a working definition or definitions must be sought. Only then, after a side glance of a little less than a page at the movement's supposed "Medievalism," is Waugh ready after nine pages of background to return, with, "but these things were all in the future," to the dramatic present and to close the chapter with the jaunty Millais playing backgammon with one hand and beating time to music with the other.

Chapter 2 also attempts to disguise summary by opening dramatically before giving a long retrospect and prospect, but the flaw is less noticeable because Waugh did not attempt to frame the chapter with an interrupted scene. The third and final chapter shows that Waugh was misapplying theory rather than simply erring: it begins with Mrs. Millais's dismayed response to the torrent of critical abuse of the paintings Hunt and Millais sent to the 1850 Royal Academy exhibition, which, in dramatic terms, has not yet occurred.

P.R.B., then, is the work of a not very accomplished apprentice—or, as the list of errata indicates, of two, printer as well as author. The most obviously encouraging thing about it is that the faults are large and glaring; any moderately competent teacher of prose composition could provide clear and explicit directions for revising and greatly improving it. Less obvious but more hopeful are the signs that the itch to write prose he had felt while composing his prize poem at Lancing was permanent and benign: the sense of rhythm, balance, and climax to a sentence or paragraph; the ability to create irony through devastating understatement; the ability to make precise and telling discriminations; the courage to be flamboyant when ostentation is required.

In later life Waugh tried, with success proportionate to the degree of editorial control he was allowed, to improve the writing of priests like Thomas Merton and politicians like Frank Pakenham.[10] He certainly improved his own writing, not only between 1926 and 1927 but between first and final draft of everything he wrote. Since he was an excellent self-critic, it is useful to note what he saved from the pamphlet to put in *Rossetti* and the nuances he introduced in the later work. Thus the passages identical in the two works are less interesting than those that diverge in slight but important fashion. For example, in summarizing the state of English art in 1847, he allowed himself a purple patch:

> The genius of Turner, like one of his own tremendous sunsets, was gradually sinking in clouds of obscured glory. Etty, an infirm old man, sometimes toiled with infinite labor to the life school in Trafalgar Square, but he had for many years now allowed his tardily and hard-won success to seduce him from the superb technique which had alone excused the essential vulgarity of his taste, and with trembling hand he debauched his incomparable flesh tints with greens and violets and ultramarine. [pp. 5–6]

By the time Waugh finished *Rossetti,* he had made the passage even better. He expanded the perspective to include Landseer, Dyce, Maclise, Egg, Constable, and Wilkie, putting Turner in series and moving the simile about sunsets after "sinking" to sharpen the comparison and substituting "late-won" for "tardily and hard-won" both to economize and to avoid the chime.[11] Moreover, he led up to rather than away from what he regarded in *P.R.B.* as the death of "the last of the old school of English painters of any considerable qualities" and in *Rossetti* as "the tragic death in 1846 of the last of the great classical painters, [which] seemed to epitomize the barrenness and brutality of the age"[12]—the suicide of Benjamin Robert Haydon. And in the book he had matured enough to realize that a panoramic summary

10. See my "How Waugh Cut Merton," *Month* 6 (April, 1973): 150–53; and Lord Pakenham's introduction to his *Five Lives* (London: Hutchinson, 1964), pp. 14–15.

11. The passage from *Rossetti,* p. 20, reads in part:
"Turner was seventy-one years old, sinking like one of his own tremendous sunsets in clouds of obscured glory; Etty, an infirm old man, sometimes toiled up with infinite labour to the life school in Trafalgar Square, but had for many years now allowed his late-won success to seduce him from the superb technique which alone excused his essential vulgarity of taste, and with an unsteady hand he debauched his incomparable flesh tints with greens and violets and ultramarine."

12. Waugh, *Rossetti,* p. 20. In the book Waugh cites William Bell Scott's *Autobiographical Notes.* It is possible that he had not read Scott before writing *P.R.B.*

could be as dramatic as an artificially constructed scene. The *P.R.B.* passage is buried in the middle of Chapter 1; the *Rossetti* passage begins Chapter 2 in full confidence that the state of English art in 1847—like the history of Azania or Ishmaelia or England or Neutralia in later work—could be as interesting as royal bastardy. In short, despite his reputation as an anti-intellectual, Waugh knew by 1928 that generalizations about human activity could be made interesting.

So, of course, could details—especially by a writer who all his life was to tread confidently the invisible line that wavers between comedy and satire. The Pre-Raphaelite pantheon was an obvious comic target in 1926, but a year later he improved his treatment considerably, doubling the examples in the third class and more than doubling the list of those who "satisfy the examiners": from the original "Michael Angelo, Pheidias, Flaxman, Leigh Hunt, Milton and many others, whose names are now wholly forgotten" (p. 5) to "Isaiah, Phidias, Flaxman, Joan of Arc, Michael Angelo, Leigh Hunt, Christopher Columbus, Titian, and Haydon" (p. 38), an even more preposterous mélange of eras, nationalities, and occupations. Elsewhere Waugh demonstrated that he could let the detail speak for itself. In *P.R.B.,* Millais's *"Lorenzo and Isabella* was bought by three fashionable tailors for £150 and a suit of clothes—the smartest Millais had yet had" (p. 19). Having already drawn the implicit contrast between Millais's picture and Hunt's—which had been praised by Bulwer Lytton and sold through the good offices of Augustus Egg — Waugh decided in 1927 to let the specific contrast stand by itself and refrained from comment on the suit. He preserved, however, altered in minor but significant detail, the dramatic scene with which he ended *P.R.B.* and Chapter 2 of *Rossetti.* Millais and Rossetti are bidding farewell to Holman Hunt, and Rossetti gives him a copy of *The Girlhood of the Virgin,* inscribed with a touching quotation promising that their shared experience will be forgotten only at death. *P.R.B.* continues:

> Not to be outdone, Millais disappeared to the station buffet and returned, just as the train was starting, with a generous bag of sandwiches for the journey.
>
> "So now the whole round table is dissolved," quoted Rossetti sadly as the train steamed out of the station. [p. 25]

For Waugh the contrast between art idealized into quest and the prosaic concern for food epitomizes the two men. In 1927 he changed "disappeared" to "hurried" to increase the sense of Millais's bustling busyness, deleted "for the journey" as superfluous, and ended the sentence "with a large bag of sandwiches and buns" (p. 62). "Large" is more neutral than "generous," and buns afford an even more incongruous contrast to the Round Table than do sandwiches.

Although Waugh had managed to end *P.R.B.* effectively and could legitimately regard with favor the results of his work, his pleasure in the book soon gave way to various distractions. During the following months he visited first Scotland and Paris with Graham and then Tours with a party including Richard Plunkett Greene, spent dissolute nights in London, and returned in the rain to his teaching job on September 27, the weather accorded to his mood. Almost immediately he received proofs and discovered that "between writing and proof reading I have greatly lost interest in it," and the typographical errors that could not be expunged reconciled him to the booksellers' refusal to stock it when it appeared in November. No one reviewed it because one of Waugh's pupils forgot to mail review copies, but Waugh apparently did nothing to remedy the oversight.[13]

Still, the pamphlet did, to Waugh's pleasure, look like a book. Furthermore, he had been paid for "The Balance," and the prospect of future reward led him to seek a commission from Kegan Paul for an essay on "Noah: Or the Future of Intoxication." He began the essay, which he termed "mannered and literary," with considerable enthusiasm on November 10, but his energies waned in early December, when he confessed himself "tired of words,"[14] and, distracted by plans for a trip to Athens, he finished it hurriedly. It was rejected, and, judging from his mixed reaction, regret at losing the money and recognition that it was not good work,[15] he probably destroyed it. Late in February, 1927, he was consoled by Hugh Chesterman's request for a story to be published in his *New Decameron* series. The following day Waugh was sacked on the spot and concluded despondently that "the time has arrived to set about being a man of letters."[16]

Like most of his other resolutions during this period, this one was not immediately carried out. He did write "A House of Gentlefolks" almost immediately, but by April 7 he was still undecided whether to take a job on the *London Daily Express* "or write a biography that Duckworth show some interest in."[17] The interest was generated in part by Anthony Powell's introduction of Waugh to Thomas Balston of Duckworth's, in part by *P.R.B.,* offered as evidence of Waugh's capability, and in part by the impending Rossetti centenary. Fortunately, Waugh kept his options open, for on May 23, a few weeks after he had received and spent the publisher's advance, he was fired from the *Express.*

13. Waugh, *Diaries*, pp. 266–71 (October 2–November 22, 1926).
14. *Ibid.*, p. 272 (December 6, 1926).
15. *Ibid.*, p. 280 (January 24, 1927).
16. *Ibid.*, p. 281 (February 21, 1927).
17. *Ibid.*, p. 284 (April 7, 1927). The entry notes further that Waugh had met "such a nice girl called Evelyn Gardner."

9

From the "May 7, 1927" he wrote in his copy of William Michael Rossetti's *Ruskin, Rossetti, and Pre-Raphaelitism,* it appears that he had already begun overt preparations for the biography. Rossetti's book seems to be a major cause of Waugh's new respect for Ruskin, whom he had dismissed in *P.R.B.* as having intuitive taste analogous to his wine-merchant father's but no principles: Ruskin's practical advice to Rossetti is often noted; one general judgment is called "Shrewd" in the margin (p. 30), and Ruskin's view that Rossetti was essentially selfish is in large part adopted by Waugh.[18] He had other resources as well: wide and thoughtful viewing and reading; a developing theoretical framework in which to place his observations; and some knowledge of and even more respect for the materials in which the Pre-Raphaelites worked. Upon these varied resources Waugh exercised his growing powers of organization and his increasingly flexible prose style.

One major difference between *P.R.B.* and *Rossetti* is that Waugh's interest was in the first primarily narrative whereas in the second he was concerned not only to illuminate character but to deal with the aesthetic issues raised by Rossetti's paintings. To define more clearly if not answer these questions, Waugh made use of theoretical knowledge that he had been acquiring casually during the twenties. Roger Fry's *Vision and Design* he kept until the end of his life, and Waugh found a good deal he could agree with in its pages, including a refusal, which both shared with Rossetti, to make perspective a standard of judgment; allowance for, in fact praise of, representational elements in art; and a link between "emotional elements of design" and the "essential condition of our physical existence." Fry's praise of some pieces of African sculpture as "greater . . . than anything we produced even in the Middle Ages"[19] probably alienated Waugh, however, and Fry's *Flemish Art,* which Waugh lent to his early mentor Francis Crease, seemed to him too narrow in theory and sympathy.[20] At any rate, in *Rossetti,* Fry's name was used as a shorthand term for the limitations of all modern aesthetics.

To find an alternative, Waugh turned to what for readers of his later blasts against the modern world seem very odd sources. They are less prominently announced but no less marked than his biographical sources.

---

18. William Michael Rossetti, *Ruskin, Rossetti, Preraphaelitism: Papers 1854 to 1862* (London: G. Allen, 1899). See also Waugh's praise of Ruskin in his Preface to Francis Crease, *Thirty-four Decorative Designs* (London: privately printed, 1927), pp. v–viii; and in Evelyn Waugh, "English Letter Writers," *Bookman* (London) 73 (March, 1926): 328.

19. Roger Fry, *Vision and Design* (London: Chatto & Windus, 1920), p. 66. Waugh saw the exhibition on June 24, 1927.

20. Waugh, *Diaries,* p. 288 (August 24, 1927).

One of them, Hubert Waley's *The Revival of Aesthetics*,[21] he cited in the final chapter. I. A. Richards's *Principles of Literary Criticism*[22] he did not mention at all, but he annotated his copy, either on first reading or during the trip to France in 1926, and both his annotations and his theoretical approach in *Rossetti* testify to the book's importance to his developing aesthetic theories.

Waley's and Richards's theories have much in common. Both reject absolutes in favor of inductive methods based upon psychology; and both reject —Richards the more firmly — the concepts of the "aesthetic emotion," with the corollary values placed on intensity, and of the autonomy of the work of art that Richards traces to A. C. Bradley. In short, they repudiate major theorists of modernist and specifically Bloomsbury aesthetics—Benedetto Croce, Henri Bergson, G. E. Moore, Clive Bell — on the grounds that they have misunderstood the mind's functioning and have therefore defined too narrowly the response to art—but are sympathetic to the gestalt psychologists, especially Kurt Koffka. The rejection as well as the allegiance stems from their refusal to distinguish between the experience of art and any other form of experience and between the artist and other kinds of human being. In effect, art is too important in organizing and stabilizing impulses to have limited, even if privileged, status. It should not be surprising, therefore, that both see the essential function of art as communicative[23] and, though it follows less obviously, representational. For Waugh's purposes, even more important was their agreement on the connection of empathy (Richards) or emotion (Waley) with unconscious kinesthetic response, therefore motion, therefore time.

Most immediately useful to Waugh was the theoretical basis for rejecting dominant tendencies in criticism, especially those that posit an "aesthetic emotion" and hold that "artistic perception begins with an appreciation of the reality of form, and becomes creative as it begins to associate forms with each other in *necessary,* and therefore agreeable, relationships; a work of art is a statement of such relationships or of a coherent sequence of such relationships" *(Rossetti,* p. 222). This theory, which cannot admit Rossetti's paintings to the realm of art but finds room for primitive sculpture, Waugh

21. Hubert Waley, *The Revival of Aesthetics,* no. 15 of the Hogarth Essays. (London: Hogarth Press, 1926).

22. I. A. Richards, *Principles of Literary Criticism* (London: K. Paul, Trench, Trubner and Co., 1925 [1924]).

23. Richards goes so far as to argue that "a large part of the distinctive features of the mind are due to its being an instrument for communication" and that "an experience . . . takes the form it does largely because it may have to be communicated" (p. 25).

regarded as too severely limiting. To find an alternative, he turned to Richards, where he found and marked a passage in which Richards conceded that looking at pictures only to see what they are "about" is a mistake but denied that "representative elements" are always extraneous. While some great paintings have little or no representational element, "others equally great can be cited in which the contribution to the whole response made through representation is not less than that made more directly through form and colour. . . . there is no reason why representative and formal factors in an experience should conflict . . . . The psychology of 'unique aesthetic emotions' and 'pure art values' upon which the contrary view relies is merely a caprice of the fancy" (p. 159). Initially Waugh used this theory to argue that painting as well as poetry should "be allowed to traffick with other emotions besides the aesthetic emotion," making room for Rossetti and other nineteenth-century painters currently in disfavor and perhaps reflecting Richards's view that "representation in painting corresponds to thought in poetry" (p. 160).

Useful in different fashion was Richards's view, also marked by Waugh, that "too great insistence upon the quality of momentary *consciousness* which the arts occasion has become in recent times a prevalent critical blunder" and that "the after-effects, the permanent modifications in the structure of the mind, which works of art can produce, have been over-looked" (p. 132). Initially Waugh used the theory not only to counter Roger Fry and like-minded theorists but also in tangential fashion to question Rossetti's and in fact any romantic's view of the world. To the casual view that life is "one damned thing after another" and the intellectual view that it is "the solemn perception of process" Waugh contrasted

> the romantic outlook [which] sees life as a series of glowing and un-related systems, in which the component parts are explicable and true only in terms of themselves, in which the stars are just as big and as near as they look, and *"rien n'est vrai que le pittoresque."*
>
> It is this insistence on the picturesque that divides, though rather un-certainly, the mystical from the romantic habit of mind. [p. 52]

Although Waugh was willing to admit, as he did of Rossetti's *Beata Beatrix,* that "there are manifestations of the human spirit that transcend the ma-terials in which they are discernible," he was on the whole as skeptical as Richards about special, self-contained experiences. Rossetti's limitations as man and artist Waugh traced not only to his lack of "any adequate aesthetic system" (p. 130) but also to his cast of mind, which reacted "to every stim-ulus of sensual impression . . . and [concerned] itself exclusively with the relations existing between events and bodies capable of giving such impressions" (p. 156). He marked and shared Richards's view that "there are plenty of ecstatic instants which are valueless" (p. 132). Twenty years later, reading the autobiography of Saint Thérèse of Liseux, he doubted that the mystical exaltation was any more valid than the countervailing despondency.[24]

Waugh distrusted ecstatic moments not so much because they were private and subjective as because they were incommunicable. He was inclined to doubt the legitimacy of Rossetti's "attempt to express purely unaesthetic emotion in terms of an abstraction of facial expression," comparing the results to cinema close-ups in their use of symbols. The argument is not pursued, the unaesthetic emotions not specified; Waugh was content to raise the issue "whether such emotions are a proper subject for art and whether such devices may legitimately be used to express them" (pp. 209, 210).

If the artist is to communicate, Waugh learned or rediscovered in Richards, his experience must "tally with that of those with whom he communicates." Any differences from the norm "will be confined to the newest, the most plastic, the least fixed part of the mind, the parts for which reorganization is most easy" (pp. 196–197). Since "finer organization is the most successful way of relieving strain," the artist may have social and evolutionary value as well as local, temporary, and minor value. Furthermore, an artist, working *as* an artist, needs not only "the Confucian characteristics of the superior man" and the "courage or audacity, enterprise, goodwill, absence of undue pride or conceit, honesty, humility in its finest sense, humour, tolerance, good health" (p. 180), qualities that aid the recipient of communications as well, but "probity and sincerity *as an artist*" without which the work will be flawed "in its creating impulse" (p. 271). These ideas lie behind Waugh's condemnation—rare in an essentially tolerant book—of Rossetti's refusals, because of his refusal to discipline his desires, to extend himself and paint pictures difficult to sell:

> Instead . . . he attempted to torture his frivolous subjects into expressing all the ideas which he repressed. That is what I mean when I say that he lacked the *moral* stability of a great artist. [p. 98]

At the end of the book Waugh repeats the analysis, adding the view that the "mischievous misconception" of the artist's abnormality, "a sort of spiritual coprophily characteristic of the age," accounted for some of Rossetti's contemporary popularity. Except in isolated moments, Rossetti lacked "that

---

24. Waugh, *Diaries,* p. 676 (April 19, 1947). Sanctity, however, the later Waugh could understand: it was external and concrete in its manifestations.

essential rectitude that underlies the serenity of all really great art." Even his sufferings, and especially his obsessions with magic and suicide, were a sign of his mediocrity and "spiritual inadequacy" (p. 226). Shared vices never guaranteed Waugh's good opinion.

More tantalizing to the student of his novels is Waugh's attention to Richards's and Waley's theories of movement in art. Richards extended his definition of rhythm to include visual art. Conceding that "temporal sequence," though usually present, "is not strictly necessary for rhythm" (p. 138), Waugh then queried in disagreement or incomprehension the statement that "rhythmic elements in a picture or a building may not be successive but simultaneous"—in other words, may have spatial form. Beside the first question he wrote, "It is easier to reduce all spatial to temporal limits than vice versa." Almost casually he seems to be announcing his opposition to a major tenet of modernist aesthetics. The application to painting, particularly in light of Waley's theory of "the element of suggested movement which the human mind tends to import into all questions of shape" (p. 22), is obvious. Waugh's most extensive analysis of form in Rossetti's paintings is based upon the view that their rhythms "are always purely linear. . . . he was untouched by any impulse towards the coherent arrangement of form in space which is now taught in Art Schools as the primary impulse of art" (p. 143). The accompanying diagrams of linear movement in four Rossetti paintings reinforce the generalization. Earlier, analyzing the watercolor *Arthur's Tomb,* he points out:

> It is in many ways a painful picture. Three horizontals constrict the composition until it aches with suppressed resilience. Remove the apple-tree and the whole composition would fly uncontrollably through the frame; the thick, stiff little trunk straps it down and tortures it unendurably. [p. 95]

Because of his emphasis on the translation of inner movement into the work of art, Waley rather than Richards seems to be the source of Waugh's remark that the painting "is important as the only complete expression in Rossetti's art of this stress of constricted energy which is so characteristic of his life."

The distaste for obscurantism that Waugh shared with Richards did not, however, lead Waugh to accept either his methods or his conclusions wholeheartedly. Richards's overt irreligion was not, at this point in Waugh's life, likely to bother him, for, even though he had considered taking Anglican orders early in 1927, his summary of Rossetti's poetic themes indicates that the vocation may not have been firmly grounded in faith. Put baldly, he wrote, Rossetti's conclusion was no more than "the ancient cry of outraged and bewildered humanity confronted with a world not of its own making, and governed by laws outside its comprehension or control." Accompanying this "traditional despair" is an equally "traditional hope": "Still arguing from premises that it knows to be false but dares not abandon, humanity stretches out to some other system" (p. 161). Waugh objected, and would have objected at any stage in his life, not to Richards's atheism but to his optimism.

The annotations to *Principles of Literary Criticism* indicate that Waugh's objections were based on a conception of the mind very different from Richards's. Far from being a Pavlovian, in fact explicitly denying that he was a materialist (and further, that the term has any meaning), Richards nevertheless developed his "account of knowledge in terms merely of the causation of our thoughts" (p. 82), equating the mind with "the nervous system, or rather a part of its activity." Three pages later Waugh noted the distinction between external and mental events, and for the rest of the book devoted considerable energy to an attempt to preserve the primacy and independence of the latter.

Waugh's queries and objections, interspersed with approbation, continue: all reveal his concern to preserve the mind as a more or less independent entity. Temperamentally he found attractive Waley's view that pain rather than pleasure was the more characteristic effect of "contact with the objective world," and Waley's account of the artist working under the impulse of obsession is very similar to Waugh's account of the sleepless Pinfold finding "sentences he had written during the day running in his head, the words shifting and changing colour kaleidoscopically so that he would again and again climb out of bed, pad down to the library, make a minute correction, return to his room, lie in the dark dazzled by the pattern of vocables until obliged once more to descend to the manuscript."[25]

Thus his own experience as well as the idea that movement or rhythm is a central principle in all art made Waley's theory so attractive that Waugh used it to account for Rossetti's inspiration—"the state of mind became automatically translated into visible forms" (p. 224) and to set against the Fry-Bell-Bloomsbury theory that the artist begins with "ideas about form."[26] Waugh the inveterate caricaturist would probably have rejected Waley's

25. Evelyn Waugh, *The Ordeal of Gilbert Pinfold* (London: Chapman and Hall, 1957), p. 11.
26. Although Waugh may not have known the essay, Fry discussed Rossetti's inspiration and achievement in much the terms that Waugh uses, even defending "literary painting" because "it seemed to me unimportant whether the inspiration for harmonious and expressive forms came from the contemplation of the kaleidoscope of external vision or from 'the soul's sphere of infinite images,' " *Burlington Magazine,* quoted in Marina Henderson, *D. G. Rossetti* (New York: St. Martin's Press, 1973), p. 28.

identification of art with emotion and extension of his representational bias to the conclusion that "awareness of distortion destroys aesthetic pleasure by arousing intellectual activity" (p. 31), but Waugh clearly thought that the imagination occupies mysterious and perhaps dangerous territory, and Waley's linking of art with hallucination and dream parallels Waugh's use of them, as in the Brazil section of *A Handful of Dust* or in "that zone of insecurity in the mind where none but the artist dare trespass"[27] as means to insight alternative to and perhaps truer than that of the rational faculties.

Waley's views that the artist gives pleasure by providing temporary freedom "from the fetters of objective oppression," though he is obscure about whether this attribute of mystical experience is analogous to the experience of the artist or audience or both, and that the artist also makes himself useful by foreseeing "the first symptoms of Mind's next move" (p. 36) were also attractive to Waugh. Retreat from complexity obviously appealed to Waugh; his novels are full of evidence, and he once asserted that "the artist's only service to the disintegrated society of today is to create little systems of order of his own."[28] Though he came to detest novelists like D.H. Lawrence or Ernest Hemingway who set up as prophets,[29] he also regarded the artist as a visionary, for, "however aloof he holds himself, [he] is always and specially the creature of the Zeitgeist; however formally antique his tastes, he is in spite of himself of the advance guard. Men of affairs stumble far behind."[30]

These larger issues, however, were for Waugh at all stages of his life less interesting than the details of craftsmanship, on which Richards and Waley are virtually silent. In this respect he was well prepared to write *Rossetti,* for he had intermittently drawn and painted at least since 1908, he had considerable felicity and perhaps talent, and in 1925 he had spent several not conspicuously successful months at Heatherley's Art School.[31] He had soon decided, however, that he was not destined to be an artist:

> I enjoyed making an agreeable arrangement of line and shadow on the paper, but I was totally lacking in that obsession with solid form, the zeal for probing the structure of anatomy and for relating to one another the recessions of plane, which alone could make the long hours before the models exciting.[32]

27. Evelyn Waugh, *The Loved One* (London: Chapman and Hall, 1965), p. 68.
28. "Fan-Fare," *Life* 20 (April 8, 1946):56.
29. Harvey Breit, *The Writer Observed* (Cleveland: World, 1957), p. 149.
30. "Felix Culpa?" *Commonweal* 48 (July 16, 1948):323.
31. For some examples see Alain Blayac, "Evelyn Waugh's Drawings," *Library Chronicle of the University of Texas,* n.s., no. 7 (Spring, 1974), [pp. 42–57].
32. Waugh, *A Little Learning,* p. 211.

In another context the explanation he gave for his failure, particularly interesting in view of his analysis of Rossetti, was that "I had neither the talent nor the application—I didn't have the moral qualities."[33] Yet he did acquire the knowledge necessary for his analysis of Rossetti's paintings, as in the judgment that Rossetti's watercolors depend for unity upon their texture, and for the standards that led him to judge that Rossetti "never had very much respect for the materials in which he worked, none of the craftsman's loving submission to the limitations of medium . . . . Paint, for him, was just so much stuff in which he had to work out the effects he wanted" (p. 50). Putting the matter in impersonal terms, he wrote that, after he saw D. H. Lawrence's "miserable pictures," he "began to understand that a work of art is not a matter of thinking beautiful thoughts or experiencing tender emotions (though these are its raw materials), but of intelligence, skill, taste, proportion, knowledge, discipline and industry; especially discipline."[34]

This love of craftsmanship is central to an understanding of Waugh's responses to a wide range of human activity. To a writer, he told Thomas Merton, "Words should be an intense pleasure just as leather should be to a shoemaker."[35] He frequently spoke of himself as a craftsman to Christopher Sykes and others, and even his view of religion was colored by his delight in seeing a thing well done. As a young man he contrasted favorably the services of the monks at Melloney with belching priests at Glenmalure,[36] and his Easter diary entry, two years to the day before he died, included the observation that "when I first came to the Church I was drawn, not by splendid ceremonies but by the spectacle of the priest as craftsman. He had an important job to do which none but he was qualified for. He and his apprentice stumped up to the altar with their tools and set to work without a glance to those behind them, still less with any intention to make a personal impression on them."[37] This interest may account for his repeated struggles "to escape from my literary destiny into pleasanter but less appropriate work with my hands."[38]

Rossetti was the first product of Waugh's capitulation to his destiny as a writer of English prose; it was also the last stage of his apprenticeship.

33. Jebb, "The Art of Fiction XXX," p. 76.

34. Evelyn Waugh, "Lady Chatterley," *Spectator* 205 (November 18, 1960):771.

35. Breit, *The Writer Observed,* p. 149. For another version of the dictum see Waugh's letter to Father Louis (Merton's name in the Trappist order), August 29, 1949, in Sister M. Thérèse, "Waugh's Letters to Thomas Merton," *Evelyn Waugh Newsletter* 3 (Spring, 1969):2, and *The Letters of Evelyn Waugh,* ed. Mark Amory (New Haven and New York: Ticknor & Fields, 1980), p. 308.

36. Waugh, *Diaries,* p. 127 (July 29–August 30, 1924).

37. *Ibid.,* p. 789 (Easter, 1964).

38. Waugh, *A Little Learning,* p. 90.

Although the manuscript and the book itself refute Waugh's later charge that it was "hurried," it did go quickly. He began writing on July 1, 1927, and in three weeks had produced twelve thousand words, roughly through the account of the violent attack on the Brotherhood in 1850. Of course, he was covering familiar ground, but he was pleased to be making progress and to find the results "fairly amusing."[39] Soon thereafter he was slowed by illness, by the melancholy of Olivia Plunkett-Greene, and by "a tedious and debauched night."[40] To break the pattern, Waugh went to the Abingdon Arms at Beckley on August 13, recovered his health and his spirits, worked daily under the botched Pre-Raphaelite frescoes at the Oxford Union, and by the twenty-third had finished the first three chapters, up to the death of Elizabeth Siddall. Still sanguine, he thought the book "amusing in parts," but he felt that he needed a change to get on with it.

At this point the course of the book becomes less clear. Back at his father's house by the end of August, he received review books from the *Bookman* and, although distracted by the noise and by insomnia, he not only reviewed them but began "a comic novel," probably on September 3. He did not stop working on *Rossetti,* however, and internal evidence in the manuscript indicates that he may have written well into Chapter 8 by September 9, when he visited Sir Hall Caine; in the passages that describe Caine's first meeting with Rossetti (pp. 217–219) Waugh inserted material about Caine's internal responses that he may have obtained from the interview. That would have been fast work even for Waugh, however. At any rate, he was beyond question well into Chapter 7 by October 6, the date of the visit to Kelmscott, for the description of the house and environs in his diary corresponds very closely to the passages inserted in the manuscript.

The difficulty in determining the date of completion is due largely to Waugh's diary entry of mid-September from the Bell, Aston Clinton: he had "finished 20,000 words and felt deeply depressed." Sykes assumes that the work in question is *Decline and Fall,* for which the diary offers no evidence. If, however, the figure refers to the continuation of *Rossetti,* then Waugh was keeping to his schedule of roughly seven thousand words a week, which would have brought him to or near the end of Chapter 6. It is certain that he finished the diagrams of Rossetti's paintings on October 1 and left the Grahams' house, Barford, in mid-October. By this time the manuscript was probably very near completion, for by the twenty-second he was working at the Academy of Carpentry and devoting a great deal of time to Evelyn

39. Waugh, *Diaries,* pp. 285–86 (July 22, 1927).
40. *Ibid.,* p. 286 (August 23, 1927).

Gardner. The fragmentary diaries mention neither novel nor biography until July, 1928, when he was correcting proofs of *Decline and Fall.*

The manuscript of *Rossetti* contains little evidence about the process of composition. The major insertions are the description of Kelmscott (p.183); the rumors about the death of Elizabeth Siddall learned from Hall Caine (p. 110); the passage on the morality of exhuming the poems from her grave (p. 152) written in an anthropological manner that shows that Waugh read the copy of *The Golden Bough* he carried to Arnold House in 1925; and over half of the analysis of Rossetti's poetry (pp. 154–162). Those who crave startling changes of conception or suppressed scandals will be disappointed; those who take pleasure in watching a good writer make himself better by a series of small revisions will find much to delight them. Again and again one can see Waugh retouching—from exclamation:

> What could be more artificial—the presposterous quotation, itself spurious, or the lovely Miss Wilding, in green velvet, delicately posed . . . .

to sharpened comparison:

> What is the more artificial—the honeyed quotation, itself spurious, or the lovely Miss Wilding, delicately posed in green velvet . . . (p. 193).

from a mixture of Latinate and Saxon describing Rossetti's affairs as:

> swift and unscrupulous. He liked the adventure of promiscuity.

to a resounding Latinate series worthy of Gibbon:

> swift and unscrupulous; characterized by insolence of inception, energy of enjoyment, and vagueness of termination; he relished the adventure of promiscuity and of grotesque encounter. [p. 107]

from flat chronology (though he is sensitive to excessive alliteration):

> So the record that began with the / sweet / girlhood of Mary the Virgin ends with / the slow poisoning of / Pia di Tolomei, (gazing) / as she gazes/ out from her prison parapet (over the poisonous Marshes of Maremma) and the pestilential (exal) exhalations of the Maremma Marshes.

to emphatic dislocation:

> La Pia ends the record of his work. It is fitting that his last months should have been occupied with the story of Pia di Tolomei, the imprisoned bride, slowly dying among the pestilent exhalations of the Maremma marshes—the end of a life's work which began with the sweet girlhood of Mary the Virgin. [p. 212]

from conjecture:

> It was probably at Penkhill that he first began drinking large quantities
> of whiskey.

to illuminating detail:

> In the cellars of his hospitable hostess he found a whisky which ap-
> pealed to his sense of taste, and it is from this visit on that his steady
> over-indulgence in spirits dates. [p. 149]

from the banal:

> Charles August Howell, mentioned above, was one of the most prominent
> and fascinating people of his time; it is greatly to be hoped that someone
> who knew him, will write his life before it is forgotten. Oscar Wilde
> once expressed his intention of doing so. He was the complete adventurer,
> prince of a race whose fame is sadly evanescent.

to the sprightly:

> It is greatly to be hoped that, before he is wholly forgotten, someone who
> knew him will write a life of Charles August Howell. His fame, so bril-
> liant and fascinating in his [MS: presence] lifetime, is already very dim;
> he belongs to that (evanescent) race of adventurers / whose / / evane-
> scent / / genius is purely social and / who, unless by some freak of chance
> they become Prime Ministers (of), or, in a better day, the favourites
> of kings, are forgotten almost as soon as the actors and actresses of the
> stage. [p. 119]

Waugh was even learning the most difficult stylistic feat of all: to abandon
a favorite phrase rather than force it into an unsuitable context. He twice
tried to use "sick bird whisperings" of Elizabeth Siddall's poems and finally
settled for "wan" to describe her personality two pages later (p. 58); he
tried three times to fit "predatory masculinity" into the description of
Lancelot's figure in "Arthur's Tomb," finally abandoning it for "all the
sentimental despondence of Malory aflame with masculinity, crouching and
peering under the beetle back of his shield like some obscene and predatory
insect" (p. 94).

There are dozens of other examples of the ordinary construction made inevitable—a mark of Waugh's best and most attentive state of mind. Less
amenable to demonstration but no less instructive are his revisions in the
interest of climax. For example, the series of quotations condemning the
P.R.B. (p. 46) originally ended with those by Thomas Macaulay and Charles

Kingsley. Perceiving that in the vehemence as well as in the importance of the author the Dickens quotation is climactic, Waugh moved it to the final position it had held in *P.R.B.* (p. 20). Later he moved the effect—highly laudatory reviews of *Poems and Ballads*—before the cause—Rossetti's choosing the reviewers—to deflate their language more effectively. After quoting Rossetti's hypnotic sonnet on Lilith, he originally wrote, "What more can one add except that Mrs. Schott sat as the model?" On second thought, perhaps remembering his earlier change from "she did not appear in company" to "there was no company into which she could be introduced without offense" (p. 125), he wrote, more simply and more devastatingly: "Mrs. Schott sat as the model for the picture" (p. 135).

Waugh's improving sense of construction extended to the organization of the book as a whole. At the beginning he announced his dependence on two sources of interest: Rossetti as a character and the aesthetic questions raised by his work. In the final version the second is adumbrated in a single paragraph. The manuscript continues for another two pages, presenting and comparing aesthetic theories, judging that Rossetti's "contented acceptance of confusion marks him down as something less than great" and concluding, rather lamely, that "he is none the less interesting for that" and the execrable transition, "with this brief introduction we can proceed with our narrative." As the book progressed, Waugh must have seen that he had satisfied the theoretical interest before the biographical and that placing Rossetti as a painter was more suited to the conclusion than to the introduction. At any rate, between manuscript and final proofs he canceled this passage, drawing upon but not reproducing it in his conclusion.

One other kind of revision, perhaps the most characteristic, shows that Waugh had crossed the uncertain line that sets off the gifted amateur from the professional. Time and again he would introduce a new topic, cancel what he had written, and give further detail or analysis to support the previous topic. The unfailing mark of the amateur is the desire to get it over with. In restraining himself again and again, Waugh altered a habit that no one can ever fully break.

The resulting book is held in higher esteem by scholars than by its author. In fact, William Fredeman, the major bibliographer of the Pre-Raphaelites, calls it one of the two serious biographies published between 1928 and 1965. The book represented "a healthier approach" because many readers saw it "as an attack on the jargon of modern art criticism by one who was himself an ally of contemporary art." Although the book is not very useful to the student of the Brotherhood, "at least Waugh provides the seeds of a method for a critical biography, in contrast to another, formidable type of writing," presumably represented by the other serious book of this period, Oswald Doughty's *A Victorian Romantic.*[41]

Though Fredeman exaggerates Waugh's allegiance to contemporary painting, this conclusion and his emphasis on genre are occasioned by the book itself. From the first page to the last, Waugh has managed to have the best of both sides of the major contrasts he established. Modernist aesthetics are too narrow, but they work admirably for Impressionist art, and Waugh's analyses of Rossetti's paintings look remarkably like Roger Fry's analyses in *Flemish Art;* his book is neither the kind that makes the corpse into a puppet to amuse the audience in the manner of Lytton Strachey nor the decorous, dehumanized kind that embalms the Victorian era. These dichotomies, with which *Rossetti* begins, are rhetorically masterful, for they assure not only elders like his father (author of "Reticence in Literature") but contemporaries like Harold Acton that this book is not going to offend their tastes. By first classifying himself with "all those young men and women who, in every age, concern themselves with providing the light reading of their more cultured friends" and then condemning the products of this mass, he both flatters his audience and prepares his escape, Houdini-like, from that class. Rossetti is not funny, he continues, but he is interesting enough to make "a plain account of his life and work" itself interesting. In these opening paragraphs, as Sykes observes, can be heard "the confident authority of the voice, such as had not been heard from Evelyn before and was to be a mark of his writing henceforward."[42]

Perhaps this confidence is most notably exercised and expressed in the passages summarizing the standards of the Royal Academy and the character of Oxford in 1853. Unhampered by nuance or qualification, they go about their work of demolition. Thus William Morris found Oxford to be

> very much like the Oxford of Gibbon's time; the President of Magdalen had been elected before the French Revolution and was not receptive of new ideas; the head of his own college, Exeter, never put in an appearance at all; the dons, idler than those of today and more widely ignorant, were no less tedious; hunting and whoring were the only interest of the undergraduates who were not bores; no one seemed to remember having heard the names of Newman or Pusey.

> Oxford culture, as Morris hoped to find it, is a growth of very recent years, and can only be found in those red wastes of Gothic about the

41. William E. Fredeman, *Pre-Raphaelitism: A Bibliographical Study* (Cambridge, Mass.: Harvard University Press, 1965), p. 31.

42. Christopher Sykes, *Evelyn Waugh: A Biography* (Boston: Little, Brown and Co., 1975), p. 80.

Woodstock and the Banbury Roads. They were all fields in Morris's time. [p. 79]

Only the confident control of the passage keeps it from sounding preposterously arrogant. Master of the devastating adjective, Waugh plays off Victorian against modern Oxford, Arnold's Barbarians against the modern apostles of culture, red wastes against fertile fields, himself superior to all. Although he was at least a decade away from the phase in his life in which the old alone seemed good, he is far from a meliorist. The complacency of the reader receives, in the contrast of dons and of cultures, a double inflation and deflation.

This detached superiority was useful in dealing with the less savory aspects of Rossetti's career. Waugh's social attitudes are rather like those of Dr. Fagan in *Decline and Fall:* he can excuse Rossetti for his messiness, his sexual escapades, his greed—almost every failing except that of not being a gentleman. Of the relations between Ruskin and Rossetti he writes: "I do not see any reason to laugh at the older and more generous man; if he was partly a prig, Rossetti was partly a cad" (p. 67), and later he condemns *The Damozel of the San Grail* for the "indefinable taint of ill breeding about it" (p. 196). But a worse failing was that Rossetti let his sloppiness mar his art. These attitudes make an interesting contrast with those found in one of his sources, Ford Madox Hueffer (later Ford) who saw the issue between Ruskin and Rossetti as a conflict of "perhaps an over-sweetening of sensualism" and "undoubtedly a Puritanic overstrenuousness of moral purpose in [Ruskin's] aesthetic teaching," with the result that "Ruskin definitely fell foul of Rossetti's luxuriance; and Rossetti saw that his own magnificence was too precious a thing to be sacrificed for ever to Ruskin's personal feelings." Hueffer concluded that Rossetti "was not cold-blooded enough to be self-conscious, self-analytical enough to be other than prodigal. He wasted his gifts, as he wasted his life, with a fine unconsciousness."[43] To Waugh there was nothing fine about it; he had learned, in the interval between *P.R.B.* and *Rossetti,* to appreciate Ruskin's generosity and perceptiveness. Hueffer's remarks make all the clearer the social and moral contexts in which Waugh operates, just as Richards and Waley help clarify the aesthetic context.

These contexts were not, however, as might be expected of the persona Waugh creates, always conventional. Rossetti's addiction to chloral, taken to combat insomnia, Waugh judges solely on practical grounds. After con-

---

43. Ford Madox Heuffer, *Rossetti: A Critical Essay on His Art* (Chicago: Rand, McNally and Co., n.d.), pp. 33, 84. Waugh used the Duckworth edition, also undated.

sidering the effects of the drug and the alternative, he concludes that when Rossetti "spoke of it openly and sensibly, as one of the necessary things for his work" (p. 171) he judged himself and the situation correctly. Sykes notes the obvious parallels between Waugh's and Rossetti's insomnia and the deleterious effects of chloral (p. 82), but it would be a mistake to conclude (Sykes does not) that Waugh's judgment was swayed by sympathy. Though he calls insomnia "this terrible disease" (p. 148) he puts it in an impersonal context and maintains an objective tone.

Adverse judgments are rendered with the same detachment and judiciousness. Dealing with the moral issues of Rossetti's disinterment of his wife's body to recover his poems—this passage inserted after first draft—Waugh took the anthropological view that

> The taboo of dead bodies that is effective among all but the highest and lowest civilizations is presumably sanitary in origin. There is no reason why one should look upon the grave as more sacred than the dung-heap.

But, he adds, Rossetti so regarded it,

> and it is his reluctance to comply [in the disinterment], coupled with his compliance, that clearly indicates a real degradation in his character. In burying the poems he was, according to his lights, performing a sacramental act, and in digging them up he violated that sacrament, and one can discern no motive for this violation other than frank, disagreeable vanity. [p. 152]

Several years later Waugh asserted in *Remote People* that "a prig is someone who judges other people by his own, rather than by their standards,"[44] but clearly he had been operating on this assumption for some time.

In fact, it helps account for his refusal two pages later in *Rossetti* to condemn or even to be shocked by Rossetti's arranging favorable reviews of the poems he had culpably recovered. Waugh observed that he "was only complying with the universal custom of his and all other ages" and argued that "it would scarcely have been seemly if the work of a poet of such high but limited reputation should have been trusted to hack-writers possibly ignorant of his eminence" (p. 154). It is notable, however, that, heterodox as the sentiments may be, the style is cool, formal, and logical. Waugh is no warmer or more personal as supporter than as critic.

This portrait of Waugh as moralist, though accurate, is only partial, for he allowed himself, if not the antics he condemned in the followers of

---

44. Evelyn Waugh, *Remote People* (London: Duckworth, 1931), p. 51.

Strachey, a good deal of fun. In discussing the postures of the figures in Rossetti's *The Question of the Sphinx,* he indulged his taste for absurdity in "an exceedingly ungraceful half-hour before the looking-glass attempting to get into the same position" as the figure of Youth, finally deciding that it was impossible. More subtly, from the lofty plateau of twenty-three, Waugh gently undercut the pretension of Holman Hunt and Rossetti by changing "a visit to France and Belgium" to "a few weeks of crude and confident observation in France and Belgium. They discerned 'sweetness' in Fra Angelico, 'coarseness' in Rubens, 'power' in Leonardo da Vinci, and 'sympathy for sublime sentiment' in Titian—but no doubt they had a good time" (p. 41). Marking the end of Rossetti's dominance of William Morris's life and thought, Waugh notes that "'Topsy' got engaged to be married, a very salutary change of interest for him." [p. 187]

Like the biographers he disparaged, Waugh refused to be awed by the figures he treated. The Pre-Raphaelite Brotherhood's beginning and end he traced to "people talking in Bloomsbury," and his account of its composition is full of buried irony, as in, "The seventh member, F. G. Stephens, was a pupil of Hunt's brought in for no very clear reason. Later he became an art critic on the *Athenaeum,* where, he says, he found his early artistic training of great value" (p. 35). This seems mild enough, though "he says" is suspicious, unless the reader can remember Waugh's introductory note that he quotes Stephens throughout "in order to show by example the critical chaos in which Rossetti worked." And memories of Wales and reverberations from *Decline and Fall,* which he had already begun planning and perhaps writing as he finished *Rossetti,* stir in Waugh's analyses of the probable cause of Morris's love of the crowded Kelmscott: ". . . his Welsh blood, prompting him to the native cosiness of caves and hovels" (pp.183–184). Youthfulness may explain if not excuse Waugh's transition from a paragraph about Rossetti's sexual indiscretions to one about his domestic arrangements: ". . . he had got, if the phrase may be allowed, into a rut of habitual irregularity" (p.108).

As the qualifying clause indicates, Waugh was consciously working with stylistic effects. He clearly remembered his theory, developed in his essay on the decay of language,[45] that, because everything had been said, words had lost their precision. This seemed to him a particular problem in Chapter 4, covering the years 1862 to 1867, where he was attempting to describe not only the content but also the effect of what to him were Rossetti's major

45. Evelyn Waugh, "The Twilight of Language/for the Dilettanti, Sunday Feb. 13th 1921," unpublished essay now in the Humanities Research Center.

works. His view that *Beata Beatrix* is "the most purely spiritual and devotional work of European Art since the fall of the Byzantine Empire" sounds in isolation like a gush of art jargon, sorting ill with the persona Waugh had created. Aware of this, he added, "This statement is offered as a considered judgment and not as an ecstatic outburst," and went on to reinforce his superiority by condemning viewers who "speak of it coldly in terms of saturation, and planes and plastic values" for constricting their "artistic perceptions to an antlike narrowness" (p. 130).

Eight pages later, describing *Monna Vanna* and *The Beloved*, he used conventional terms in more subtle fashion. Had Rossetti gone blind as he feared he would, Waugh asserted, "he would have passed into the darkness with the knowledge that in these two superb paintings he had enriched his fellow men with the most sumptuous visions of barbaric glory that had ever burst into the grey city of his exile." Once again Waugh insisted that his language was precise—"All these adjectives are used deliberately and for what they are worth"—but this time he was preparing, with the last clause, to make an even finer discrimination and definition. Imagining a Rossetti enthusiast who breathlessly searches for the "words of adequate luxury" which Waugh had just provided, he offered a more sober response in, "We who are less single hearted can echo his phrases word for word, but with a slight and significant shifting of implication."

Then, in one of the shifts of tone characteristic of his best work, Waugh allows his sense of the absurd free play on the enormous sleeve in *Monna Vanna:* "the great swirl of gold and white, prolonged and accentuated by the folds of the dress, stands out from the rest of the body, like the partially inflated envelope of an airship designed by some tipsy Maharaja. At any gust of wind it may again take flight, dandling at its bow the little china hand with its ring and wristlet" (p. 139). To return to earth as the judicious, responsible critic-biographer, Waugh denied that his language is impertinent and justified the analysis by subordinating it to a major criticism of Rossetti in terms usually reserved for praise, his skill and sense of luxury: " . . . his skill was not supreme and his sense of luxury was largely superficial."

Throughout *Rossetti,* Waugh was testing and juxtaposing various styles. To Sykes the deeply purple patches and the borrowed humorous styles are evidence that Waugh had not attained full mastery of his style (pp. 81–82). Perhaps, of isolated instances, Sykes's view is correct, but it ignores the larger and far more important techniques, to be characteristic of his finest work, that Waugh was perfecting: stylistic collage and abrupt shift in tone. He had struggled with these devices in "The Balance," where the machinery for introducing them overwhelmed him, and his interest in literal collage is evident in the Christmas cards he designed in the late 1920s. Some of the borrowed styles were soon abandoned: the periodic construction ending in the Conradian "unfathomable and incommunicable despair" (p. 149); the melodramatic conclusion of a paragraph on the effects of Elizabeth Siddall's death, that Rossetti was left "with a part of his soul dead and festering within him" (p. 112); the eminently Victorian turning away from conjecture—a second thought in manuscript—in "if he had met Janey Morris in 1850, . . . but it is idle to speculate" (p. 58). These styles, each characteristic of some aspect of *Rossetti,* may account for Waugh's later repudiation of it. More important, however, was his discovery of the effect of juxtaposing styles not with laboriously erected machinery, as in "The Balance," but with a seemingly reckless dive. Summarizing the savage critical attacks on the Pre-Raphaelites in 1850, Waugh undercut the charge that they were presumptuous with a three-stage drop in levels of usage from formal to standard to slang:

> They were very young men, daring to set themselves up as superior to the artistic standards of their age. They thought themselves cleverer than Raphael. They wanted to teach their grandmothers to suck eggs. [p. 44]

Even more effective was the juxtaposition of the orotundities of Victorian style to Waugh's curt directness. Hall Caine's affecting description of the burial of Rossetti's poems with Elizabeth Siddall's body, reminiscent of some of the parodies by Mark Twain, is followed by the single sentence that concludes the chapter: "Brown disapproved of the whole business" (p. 111). Earlier Waugh had executed a startling double shift from sententious high Victorian to nursery to sober modern style. First he quoted William Bell Scott's description of the forlorn Haydon at the Westminster Hall Exhibition, which by its very contents told him that he had been rejected. The quotation ends, "Youth can stand much, it takes a great deal to kill at twenty-five, but this veteran, on that day, was one of the most melancholy of spectacles." Waugh added:

> Poor Mr. Toad, deserted by Rat, Badger, and even Mole, with the stoats and the weasels permanently established in his inheritance!
> But this is the man who had defended the Elgin Marbles when Payne Knight and all the fashionable experts denounced them as the work of provincial masons and Roman copyists.

He continued with a eulogy of Haydon, condemning a society that could occasion his death of "neglected vanity" (pp. 21–22). This device, by which the reader is led into an easy response and then given details that make that response seem damningly inadequate, is used locally in all of Waugh's novels and is magnified into a structural principle in *A Handful of Dust.*

It would be easy to distort *Rossetti* in search of other evidence that its author was a budding novelist. There is, for example, Waugh's interest in characters like the irrepressible Millais, worthy of a place in *Decline and Fall;* the gruff and energetic Ford Madox Brown, whose saltiness Waugh used to undercut Pre-Raphaelite excesses of emotion; and Ruskin, for whose mind and virtues Waugh displayed considerable respect. Waugh seems to have been attracted to them, however, primarily as people interesting in themselves and then as material for a biographical rather than a fictional exercise. The process of writing the book did, however, shift Waugh's interest away from the dramatic and mimetic modes notable in "The Balance" and later in *Vile Bodies* to a kind of narrative summary, perhaps because he was writing from sources that used this method. For a writer who came to believe that "drama, speech, and events" were essential elements of narrative, this seems an odd way to begin a career as novelist. *Rossetti* does not convey well the sense of experiential time passing, it contains very little dialogue, and it is only intermittently dramatic and almost never scenic. Yet it allowed Waugh the opportunity to create for himself an authorial voice rather than record the voices of others, and he used this new ability during the final stages of writing *Rossetti* to begin *Decline and Fall.*

2   Becoming a Novelist: *Decline and Fall*

Waugh's feeling that "I must write prose or burst" was given vent between the time he left Oxford and his decision "to set about being a man of letters"[1] not only in the expository mode of *P.R.B.* but earlier and more frequently in narrative prose: "The Temple at Thatch," unfinished and burned; "The Balance," his first professional writing, or at least—since he had been paid for undergraduate work and for designing book jackets for Chapman and Hall —the first he published while nominally self-supporting; and, on the strength of that story, "The Tutor's Tale: A House of Gentlefolks," which was commissioned just before he was sacked from Aston Clinton school for drunkenness and possibly—he could not recall details—for lechery. Neither surviving tale is more than a curiosity, but what he learned in writing them, in writing and helping film *The Scarlet Woman,* and in writing *Rossetti* he used to make *Decline and Fall* an unusually assured and polished first novel.

Waugh gives the impression in *A Little Learning* that Harold Acton's gentle mockery of "The Temple at Thatch" was equal to the loss of a prospective job as a factor in his attempted suicide, but his diary provides evidence that the verdict was not unexpected and in fact accorded with his more critical London mood. As he recalled the story nearly forty years later, it "concerned an undergraduate who inherited a property of which nothing was left except an eighteenth-century classical folly where he set up house and, I think, practiced black magic."[2] Subject and treatment seem to have been the result of Alastair Graham's influence, for the two friends had planned to "build a maze of brick with a really exquisite grotto inside."[3] In July, 1924, Waugh began the story in a manner that Acton, rather like Anthony Blanche remonstrating with Charles Ryder in *Brideshead Revisited* about the debilitating effects of "English charm," described as "Too

1. Evelyn Waugh, *The Diaries of Evelyn Waugh,* ed. Michael Davie (Boston: Little, Brown and Co., 1976), p. 289 (February 21, 1927).
2. Evelyn Waugh, *A Little Learning* (Boston: Little, Brown and Co., 1964), p. 223.
3. Waugh, *Diaries,* p. 162 (June 24, 1924).

English for my taste . . . . Too much nid-nodding over port."[4] Before and during Waugh's stay at Heatherley's Art School, his work with Terence Greenidge—a far different sort of friend, bizarre rather than charming—on *The Scarlet Woman,* and his search for a schoolmaster's job, he worked at the story intermittently, but as early as September he thought it "in serious danger of becoming dull" and a day later wrote that "A suspicion settles on me that it will never be finished." When he left for Wales, he took with him "my drawing things, my clothes, the abortive notes for *The Temple,* Horace Walpole, *Alice in Wonderland, The Golden Bough* and a few other books."[5]

This was the last reference in his diary to the story; not even Acton's response to it or the suicide attempt was recorded. Unlike the autobiography, the diary was not constrained by the theme of the hero's fall in fortune, and in fact Waugh had found a new subject and presumably a new method. By May 5, 1925, he was reading Bertrand Russell's essays, meditating on "the paradoxes of suicide and achievement," working "the scheme for a new book," and trying to buy a revolver from Young, who was to be the model for Captain Grimes. By May 28 he had suddenly decided to make "the first chapter a cinema film and have been working furiously ever since. I honestly think it is going to be rather good." Three months later, having failed to commit suicide, having left Wales, and having secured a job at Aston Clinton, he finished the story, now titled "The Balance," and judged it "odd but, I think, quite good."[6]

Waugh's choice of cinematic form in "The Balance" had obvious causes. As boy and adolescent he was a mere addict rather than a connoisseur of films; diary entries record titles and actors for plays he attended, but movies, whether good or otherwise, were for the most part unidentified, major exceptions being those starring Charles Chaplin or Harold Lloyd. As a reviewer for the *Isis* at Oxford he concentrated largely on acting—in "The Four Horsemen," he praised it "from Mr. Valentino down to the monkey"[7]—and on plot—instead of a hunchback's becoming handsome and marrying the heroine, "he won a lottery and solaced himself with his gorilla, while the heroine married the wicked nobleman. For so much injustice one was grateful."[8] His remarks on technique are brief and not especially illuminating,

4. Waugh, *A Little Learning,* p. 228.

5. Waugh, *Diaries,* pp. 176 (September 3, 1924), 177 (September 7, 1924), 199 (January 23, 1925).

6. *Ibid.,* pp. 212 (May 28, 1925), 218 (August 26, 1925).

7. Evelyn Waugh, "The Super Cinema," *Isis,* March 5, 1924, p. 24.

8. Evelyn Waugh, "Seen in the Dark," *Isis,* January 23, 1924, p. 5.

but two reveal something about his taste. In the same review he found "the real charm of the Cinema . . . in the momentary pictures and situations which appear"; later he praised the director's "amazing flair for choosing good faces" and judged "the photography . . . splendid and in almost all cases the composition excellent. I say in 'almost all cases' because it seemed to me that some of the arrangements have been done before and were rather untidy."[9]

Waugh did not spare his own efforts: at the first screening he was "quite disgusted with the badness of the film" that became *The Scarlet Woman: An Ecclesiastical Melodrama,*[10] but he got drunk enough to console himself.[11] The film reveals little except that the penchant for anarchic Oxonian nonsense did not begin with the Monty Python group. Elsa Lanchester made her film debut as the Protestant woman of easy virtue but steadfast patriotism who foils a Roman Catholic plot to convert the Prince of Wales and conduct a modern Saint Bartholomew's Day Massacre; there is a good deal of slapstick, much of it with strongly homosexual overtones; a great deal of leering and mugging, at which John Sutro and Alec Waugh particularly excel; a wicked portrait of "the Dean of Balliol," played by Evelyn Waugh in a wig and style that have been compared to Harpo Marx's; and a chase scene that owes a great deal to D. W. Griffith.

Though Waugh's subsequent relations with the cinema industry were very uneasy—he was sporadically employed to work on film scripts but seems never to have accepted or been given screen credit—his confessed interest in "drama, speech and events" rather than in psychology made him sympathetic to cinematic technique. Long after his overt experiments with this technique on film and in prose, he discussed at some length its relationship with fictional method:

> . . . no relation is established between writer and reader . . . . Nor is there within the structure of the story an observer through whom the events are recorded and the emotion transmitted. It is as though, out of an infinite length of film, sequences had been cut which, assembled, comprise an experience which is the reader's alone, without any correspondence to the experience of the protagonists. The writer has become director and producer. Indeed, the affinity to the film is everywhere apparent. It is the camera's eye which [follows the character's movements and picks out sig-

9. Evelyn Waugh, "The Super Cinema," *Isis,* March 5, 1924, p. 24.

10. Charles E. Linck, Jr., gives a full account of the film's production and a transcript of the titles and summary of the action in "The Scarlet Woman," *Evelyn Waugh Newsletter* 3 (Autumn, 1969): 1–7.

11. Waugh, *Diaries,* p. 170 (September 1, 1924).

nificant detail]. It is the modern way of telling a story. In Elizabethan drama one can usually discern an artistic sense formed on the dumb-show and the masque. In Henry James's novels scene after scene evolves as though on the stage of a drawing-room comedy. Now it is the cinema which has taught a new habit of narrative. Perhaps it is the only contribution the cinema is destined to make to the arts.[12]

Waugh's undergraduate fiction, except for "Anthony: Who Sought Things That Were Lost," was written in first person and consisted largely of parochial anecdotes. "The Balance," sub-titled "A Yarn of the Good Old Days of Broad Trousers and High Necked Jumpers," shows him working toward but not entirely trusting a technique by which he could present as objectively as possible his own subjective reactions and thus transmute autobiography into fiction. From the devices of the film he adapted techniques by which he was able, sporadically, to achieve authorial distance from the characters and to present selected glimpses of physical action economically and vividly.

The plot of "The Balance"[13] is not particularly remarkable: Adam Doure, an art student recently down from Oxford, has his romance with Imogen Quest broken off as a result of her mother's objection. In rather self-conscious despair he resolves to commit suicide, sells his books to raise money, and goes to Oxford with the object of saying a dignified, Petronian farewell to his friends. However, only Ernest Vaughan, talented but thoroughly debauched, is able to accompany him, and the farewell dinner degenerates into a series of drunken misadventures culminating in the wreck of an impulsively commandeered automobile. Alone in his hotel room, Adam drinks poison—only to vomit profusely and fall asleep. Wandering into the fields near the river on the following morning, he sleeps again; then, looking into the water, he engages his reflection in a rather sophomoric dialogue about the meaning of life. Finally he comes to an understanding of the balance between life and death: the appetite, which is governed by circumstances, determines whether man wishes to live or die.

Of much greater interest than the story is the variety of techniques that Waugh employed to tell it. Each of the four sections is told in a different narrative mode: "Introduction," which shows the attitudes of the Bright Young People toward Adam, is almost wholly in dialogue; "Circumstances," which is by far the longest section, ends with Adam taking poison and uses

---

12. Evelyn Waugh, "Felix Culpa?" *Commonweal* 48 (July 16, 1948):323.

13. Evelyn Waugh, "The Balance," *Georgian Stories, 1926* (London: Chapman and Hall, 1926), pp. 253–91; (New York: G.P. Putnam's Sons, 1926), pp. 279–323. I cite the latter text parenthetically.

the conventions of the silent film that Waugh had learned from reviewing and from *The Scarlet Woman;* "Conclusion," which concludes with Adam's decision to accept the verdict of chance and live, is developed partly by formal exposition of Adam's mental state and partly by his dialogue with himself; and "Continuation," which returns to the gay and thoughtless world of Adam's contemporaries, uses a third-person observer to reflect on the lightly malicious gossip. It is not surprising that Conrad Aiken, while praising the story for its "astonishingly rich portrait of a mind" and predicting that Waugh might "do something very remarkable," made the reservation "if he is not too clever."[14]

Waugh did not get beyond his depth in the first and last sections, where the dialogue clearly presages that of the novels, or in the structure, which like that of *Decline and Fall* shows the central character being separated from an unsuitable world through a counterfeit death. In his most ambitious section, "Circumstances," however, he obviously found that the techniques of the film scenario were inadequate for his purpose, and he added several elements. First, to expand the speaking parts beyond the limits of the caption, he introduced additional lines of dialogue, which, he says in a note, "are deduced by the experienced picture-goers from the gestures of the actors; only those parts which appear in capitals are actual 'captions'" (p.281). Next, to provide some kind of framework for his script and to point up the contrast between his story and stereotyped movie plots, he selected three members of the audience to present the conventional filmgoers' views, recording their comments in italic type. First introduced are Ada and Gladys, two servants, who make obvious comments on the action and try vainly to place the plot in a familiar category: comedy, "society," "murder," or romance. The third spectator, selected for his contrasting views, is a young Cambridge man who desires that the characters talk like ladies and gentlemen, labels without difficulty as "expressionismus" the film's technique, and understands the significance of the action little better than Ada and Gladys.

This machinery is ponderously established, intrusive, and uneconomical, but Waugh did even greater violence to the film convention. Strictly speaking, the characters' internal reactions could not be shown in a film, but Waugh further strained his device to include them—and even added background information in the neutral voice of the detached author.

When Waugh is dealing with dialogue, his devices are fairly successful, though a bit cluttered, as in the luncheon conversation between Adam and Imogen:

14. Conrad Aiken, *Literary Review* 23 (April 9, 1927):4.

She sits down at the table.

"You haven't got to rush back to your school, have you? Because I'm never going to see you again. The most awful thing has happened—you order lunch, Adam. I'm very hungry. I want to eat a *steak-tartare* and I don't want to drink anything." [This dialogue is to be inferred by the film goer.]

Adam orders lunch.

LADY R. SAYS I'M SEEING TOO MUCH OF YOU. ISN'T IT TOO AWFUL?

Gladys is at last quite at home. The film has been classified. Young love is being thwarted by purse-proud parents. [p. 293]

When the story has to deal with a setting, however, the scenario fails to translate into verbal description the swiftness of the film's visual impact, and in fact Waugh sometimes abandons physical detail for generalized evaluation. A good example is the description of Lady Rosemary Quest's house:

An interior is revealed in which the producers have at last made some attempt to satisfy the social expectations of Gladys and Ada. It is true that there is very little marble and no footmen in powder and breeches, but there is nevertheless an undoubted air of grandeur about the high rooms and Louis Seize furniture, and there is a footman. The young man from Cambridge estimates the household at six thousand a year, and though somewhat overgenerous, it is a reasonable guess. Lady Rosemary's collection of Limoges can be seen in the background. [p. 290]

When Waugh is faithful to the limits of his convention, the description is sometimes awkwardly obtrusive. In attempting to give something of the atmosphere of a bookstore, where a minor bit of action takes place, he is forced by his cinematic method to use a great deal of space for description, for analysis, and for a short scene with a wholly irrelevant character (pp. 300–301).

Waugh's attempt to reproduce the effect of the movie amply justifies itself, however, when he uses its characteristic qualities: the ability to translate ideas and attitudes into visual terms, to control the physical distance of the audience from the action, to select only the relevant details, to shift rapidly from scene to scene without formal transition, and to control the speed of the action. Particularly noteworthy in "The Balance" is Waugh's use of Adam's visions of death: first, a realistic view of the effect his suicide will have on his family, "scenes of unspeakable vulgarity involving tears, hysteria, the telephone, the police"; next, "a native village in Africa" from which "a man naked and sick to death . . . draws himself into the jungle to die alone"; and, finally, a "hall, as if in some fevered imagining of Alma Tadema, . . . built of marble, richly illuminated by burning Christians," where in an atmosphere violent and decadent a Roman patrician leisurely takes his life (pp. 298–99). Like a film shot, the second vision is spliced into later action to reveal Adam's growing sense of isolation as he vainly seeks someone with whom to share a last feast (p. 305) and as he lies down to die after drinking the poison (p. 313).[15] While the physical details of the third vision are not repeated, the whole series of squalid episodes of Adam's drunken wanderings through Oxford is implicitly contrasted with the decadent splendor of the Roman's death.

As significant as the visual rendering of thought is the effect of the cinematic device on the narrative style, for Waugh is able to give the sense of drunken confusion without using the character's mind as the center of observation. As a result, he can avoid subjective analysis and speed the pace and rapidity of transition, as in this sequence:

> A public-house in the slums. Adam leans against the settee and pays for innumerable pints of beer for armies of ragged men. Ernest is engrossed in a heated altercation about birth control with a beggar whom he has just defeated at "darts."
>
> Another public-house: Ernest, beset by two panders, is loudly proclaiming the abnormality of his tastes. Adam finds a bottle of gin in his pocket and attempts to give it to a man; his wife interposes; eventually the bottle falls to the floor and is broken.
>
> Adam and Ernest in a taxi; they drive from college to college, being refused admission. Fade out. [p. 309]

At least as effective is the series of scenes in which Adam tries to find a dinner companion (pp. 302–305), for they portray economically a wide variety of Oxford types.

That the story is on the whole a failure can be attributed partly to Waugh's choice of too complicated a variety of narrative methods and partly to his attitude toward the material. Like the circumstances of almost all of Waugh's other central characters, Adam's closely parallel, though they do not reproduce, those of his creator. Like Evelyn Waugh in 1924 and 1925, Adam has left at Oxford a circle of friends whom he misses and from whom he

15. Although I do not use the same terminology, I am indebted for the concepts to Joseph and Harry Feldman, *Dynamics of the Film* (New York: McLeod, 1952); and to Edward Fischer, *The Screen Arts: A Guide to Film and Television Appreciation* (New York: Sheed and Ward, 1960).

feels estranged; like Waugh, he attends a scrubby art school, where he learns very little; like Waugh, he is without means, is separated from the girl with whom he thinks himself in love, seeks to renew Oxford friendships, and fails, in an ignominious anticlimax, to commit suicide. When Waugh wrote "The Balance," he was too close to the emotions of Adam Doure to treat them, especially in "Conclusion," in other than solemn fashion. Moreover, it is difficult to discern any reason besides the claims of autobiography for the art-school scenes. This failure in economy is only one effect of Waugh's incomplete detachment of himself from Adam; the other was the need to justify Adam's difference from his contemporaries and in general to gain sympathy for him. This necessity accounts for the three sections of the story that are outside the film convention (by itself a means of gaining objectivity); for the movie audience, whose incomprehension is intended to deepen the reader's awareness; and for the authorial analysis of Adam's feelings.

"The Tutor's Tale"[16] resembles Waugh's later short stories in being thin and formulaic, but it does represent a different kind of objectivity from that of "The Balance." To narrate the brief emergence from captivity of the supposedly retarded but in fact ingenuous George, Marquess of Stayle and heir to the Duke of Vanbrugh, Waugh resurrected from "The Balance" the character Ernest Vaughan, drunken companion of and foil to Adam Doure and object of Imogen Quest's interest on the story's final page. As tutor to the young man and narrator he is used to set off by his cynicism and experience the dottiness of George's relatives and keepers and George's "fresh and acute critical faculty and a natural fastidiousness which shone through the country bumpkin" (p. 111). As Ernest notes, sometimes "nature, like a lazy author, will round off abruptly into a short story what she obviously intended to be the opening of a novel" (p. 114); George's relatives change their minds about sending him abroad and recall him to imprisonment on the family estate. The story is a great deal lighter in tone than "The Balance"; George looks forward to certain release, and Ernest's calm objectivity keeps the audience from empathizing with wronged innocence.

Perhaps as important as his experiments with point of view is that Waugh had begun to people the imaginative world upon which his early novels would draw. Ernest never recurs, but the names Vanburgh (or Vanbrugh), Philbrick, and others in the comedy-of-manners convention do, and a hint of the characters of the Bright Young People has begun to appear. The clearest indication of Waugh's progress from self-pitying autobiography is

16. Evelyn Waugh, "The Tutor's Tale: A House of Gentlefolks," *The New Decameron: The Fifth Day* (Oxford: Basil Blackwell, 1927), pp. 101-16.

the shift in his use of Imogen Quest. In the undergraduate effort—a term chosen advisedly—"Fragments: They Dine with the Past," the character Imogen never appears, but she pervades the dinner party at which her name is not spoken: ". . . the thought of her was about and between us all; with such shy courtesy did we treat her, who had been Queen, for all who had loved her were gathered there and none dared even speak her name."[17] The character is so vague that she does not have a surname. In "The Balance," despite her portentous name and "rather a lovely head, shingled and superbly poised on its neck" (p. 282), Imogen is an ordinary girl, speaking in the argot of the Bright Young People who appear briefly in *Decline and Fall* and prominently in *Vile Bodies.* In the latter novel the name is again used of an idealized character, but this time in a conscious travesty of literary creation and considered mockery of the social scene: Adam Fenwick-Symes invents her in his gossip column as "the most lovely and popular of the young married set" who becomes "a byword for social inaccessibility—the final goal for all climbers" who envy her set's "uncontrolled dignity of life."[18] In Imogen's first appearance she is a vague figure created to allow young men the indulgence of self-pitying, nostalgic stoicism. In her final appearance she is used to parody the aspiration of her admirers.

Of course, Waugh had always had, as his diaries reveal, a sharp eye for the inherent absurdities of people and institutions. Social snobbery and self-protection were as central to "Edward of Unique Achievement" as they were to the opening pages of *Decline and Fall.* In the undergraduate story Edward murders his dim tutor, Mr. Curtis, and escapes detection when Lord Poxe, who has drunkenly collapsed next to the body, is the obvious suspect. Poxe, however, is let off with a fine of thirteen shillings because of a fifteenth-century precedent and because the Warden's wife, thinking her husband has killed her lover, confesses her misdeeds, whereupon the Warden hastens to conceal the crime. The chief difference between the story and the novel is not subject but point of view. "Edward" is narrated by a first-person observer, uninvolved except with the Warden's wife, and the cynicism is overt.[19] *Decline and Fall* is narrated by an omniscient author so assured that he can descend from mandarin to slang usage and rise again without apology or self-consciousness.

17. Evelyn Waugh, "Fragments: They Dine with the Past," *Cherwell,* September 5, 1923, p. 42; signed "Scaramel."

18. Evelyn Waugh, *Vile Bodies* (London: Chapman and Hall, 1965), pp. 114–15. This is the last edition supervised by Waugh.

19. Evelyn Waugh, "Edward of Unique Achievement," *Cherwell,* August 1, 1923, pp. 14–18.

The composition of *Decline and Fall,* in contrast to that of "The Temple" and "The Balance," was barely recorded in Waugh's diary, but it is clear that he began it in late August or early September, 1927, and that he had written twenty thousand words and felt deeply depressed by the end of September. Since he had not finished *Rossetti,* however, that figure may refer to additional work on the biography. By January, 1928, he had finished about fifty pages, which he read aloud to Dudley Carew, and, "As was his habit in those days, he roared with laughter at his own comic inventions."[20]

The overlapping of *Rossetti* and *Decline and Fall* has, in hindsight, enormous significance for the development of Waugh's art. The authorial voice he had developed for the biography was adapted to fiction and is largely responsible for the astonishingly sure and professional polish of the novel. Of course, Waugh had become more objective about the events of his own past than he had been in "The Balance," but more important were the changes in technique arising from his conception of narrative voice. The major technical weakness of "The Balance" is that settings and people had to be described, and description not only takes longer than photography but has to have a source. Thus the author cannot be wholly effaced unless the story consists of dialogue alone. Since Waugh could not will the narrator out of existence, he abandoned in *Decline and Fall* and later work the pretense of total objectivity and assumed the role of detached analyst.

Waugh's narrator uses the prerogatives of omniscience to provide physical and historical background, to present formal analysis of character, to summarize fixed attitudes and current thoughts, and to speak directly to the audience or, more rarely, to the characters. As a result, the rapid and easy if sometimes startling narrative movement is suited to comedy because, as in the following passage, the reader is kept at a distance from the action:

> Out of the night Lumsden of Strathdrummond swayed across his path like a druidical rocking-stone. Paul tried to pass.
>
> Now it so happened that the tie of Paul's old school bore a marked resemblance to the pale blue and white of the Bollinger Club. The difference of a quarter of an inch in the width of the stripes was not one that Lumsden of Strathdrummond was likely to appreciate.
>
> "Here's an awful man wearing the Boller tie," said the Laird. It is not for nothing that since pre-Christian times his family has exercised chieftainship over unchartered miles of barren moorland.
>
> Mr. Sniggs was looking rather apprehensively at Mr. Postlethwaite.
>
> "They appear to have caught somebody," he said. "I hope they don't

20. Dudley Carew, *A Fragment of Friendship* (London: Everest Books, 1974), p. 82.

do him any serious harm."

"They appear to be tearing off his clothes."[21]

Particularly notable is the double irony in the third paragraph. Waugh first establishes the contrast between Lumsden's jejune dialogue and the historical source of his confidence and then undercuts historical pretensions with "unchartered" and "barren." The rapid shift to the vantage point of Sniggs and Postlethwaite, like montage in cinema, removes reader and narrator from the action, which is filtered through their well-bred callousness. These technical feats were rarer in *Decline and Fall* than in subsequent novels. However, after the social setting and values and the essentially passive nature of Paul Pennyfeather are established, Waugh consciously uses Paul as interlocutor of a series of eccentrics that in writing the novel he lengthened considerably.

The manuscript seems to bear out, by its very appearance, Waugh's recollection that "I had the facility at the age of 25 to sit down at my table, set a few characters on the move, write 3000 words a day, and note with surprise what happened."[22] Of course, the process was not quite that simple, for the manuscript indicates that Waugh wrote the basic text in at least five stages, went back to insert and emend materials to accommodate changes in plot line and to improve structure, and finally took more careful thought about his conclusion after he had moved beyond the manuscript.[23] And in each stage he was altering word, phrase, and sentence in search of the precise denotation, connotation, reflection of character, and shade of rhythm.

Though the manuscript reveals that he was uncertain about details, Waugh probably began the novel with a general idea of the form. Ten years later, writing as an established novelist with a weekly book page, he commented on the plot in which

> a prosaic hero sets out for a brief holiday, falls accidentally into strange company and finds himself transported far beyond his normal horizons and translated into a new character; finally he returns to his humdrum habits.

21. Evelyn Waugh, *Decline and Fall* (London: Chapman and Hall, 1962), pp. 16–17. This edition is the last supervised by Waugh; it restores the readings altered for the first edition of 1928. See Waugh's Preface.

22. Waugh, Preface, *Vile Bodies,* p. 7.

23. Jeffrey Heath, "Waugh's *Decline and Fall* in Manuscript," *English Studies* 55 (December, 1974): 523–30. Heath cites a great deal of material in this very useful article, but he is interested in variant readings as static states rather than as part of a dynamic process. The many minor errors and omissions do not affect his conclusions; since I worked directly from the manuscript, I have not bothered to correct them. Where our transcriptions differ, mine have been verified.

> It is one of the basic stories of the world . . . . it has been treated romantically, farcically, sentimentally, satirically, melodramatically; it never fails if it is well treated.[24]

Except for the initial step, the description fits *Decline and Fall,* in which Paul Pennyfeather, a dim and respectable divinity student at Scone College, Oxford, is callously and unjustly sent down for indecent behavior. Cut off from vocation, family, and financial support, he takes a job in a pretentious and fourth-rate school in Wales where he meets the oddly sorted masters, Grimes the happy pederast and Prendergast the doubting parson; Philbrick the protean butler; and Margot Beste-Chetwynde, mother of one of the boys. She translates him into a higher sphere as her prospective bridegroom, but he inadvertently becomes involved in her white slavery business and, once again the scapegoat, is sent to prison, where he is really content for the first time and where he encounters Grimes, Prendergast, and Philbrick. Margot's prospective husband arranges for a fake death certificate, and at the end of the novel Paul has returned to Scone, where he studies divinity and shuns the turmoil of Margot's world in favor of what seems to be a placid orthodoxy.

Internal form seems to have been less clearly envisioned. The five separate runs of page numbers in the manuscript are evidence that, however long he took, Waugh wrote each batch of manuscript in a concerted effort. The first segment, numbered 1 to 32, carried him through what is now Chapter 7 of Part 1, the preparation for the sports, and he had a fairly clear idea of the immediately ensuing action—the sports themselves, Grimes's exposure, and plans for the party at the hotel—which are dealt with in the sequence numbered 1 to 20. The party itself, Grimes's marriage and disappearance, and the dispersal of the school on holiday occupy the next section. After the relative complexity of the manuscript of Part 1, Parts 2 and 3 are fairly straightforward, each having a separate, consecutive numbering system.

In Part 1, Waugh was still feeling his way along basic plot lines. For example, by page 23 of the first segment Peter Chetwynde (the "Beste" was added after the manuscript stage) comments that his father pays extra for his organ lessons. Not until five pages later is his mother mentioned, and two pages after that Waugh produced the first individuating details about her—rumors that she poisoned her husband. By "The Sports" she is fully characterized, but Waugh may not have decided to involve her in Paul's destiny until he was in the process of writing "Post Mortem." Midway through the chapter Paul and Grimes prepare to leave for the pub. Waugh's first impulse was to get them away at once, after perfunctory assurances

24. "Bonhomie in the Saloon Bar," *Night and Day,* July 22, 1937, p. 24.

that Prendergast can handle prep, but in immediate second thought he canceled the passage and led first into a discussion, initiated by Paul, of Margot's relationship with Chokey and then the appearance of Prendergast, wig askew. While Waugh may already have decided to introduce the subject of Margot later in the chapter—Paul tells Grimes of her invitation to call, and Grimes jokes about his interest in two subsequent passages—the revision is the first mention of the subject and introduces it less directly than the first draft does.

The plot thread concerning Grimes's first wife was almost never spun. As in the final version, she is mentioned casually in two different conversations, but on the occasion of Grimes's marriage to Flossie Fagan, after stating that "Grimes' Irish wife did not turn up to forbid the bans," Waugh initially wrote: "She did, as a matter of fact, arrive about a week later but Grimes gave her two pounds and she went back to Blackpool where she had a position as a waitress." Then, apparently struck with the idea that she could be useful, he broke off illegibly, canceled the passage, and continued as in the final version.

At least one other potential plot development was canceled in revision. Originally, Waugh took pains to emphasize Peter's extraordinary beauty. While he retained Peter's comment that Margot's "men are [MS. all] so awful . . . and [MS. they] tend to get flirtatious with me" (p. 158), the ensuing line occurs only in manuscript: "'It's terrible having a pretty son in these days,' said Mrs. Chetwynde, 'no one ever looks at one when Peter's in the room—except poor [?] old Maltravers.'" On the morning of Paul and Margot's wedding Peter was originally described as "looking absurdly like a male impersonator" before Waugh canceled the passage, and in Peter's final appearance at Paul's rooms at Oxford he was first introduced as having "grown into a singularly good looking young man." Waugh may have had no specific plan to employ Peter's beauty in the plot, but on reflection he must have seen that it created overtones irrelevant to the direction that the story eventually took.

Besides discovering and discarding elements of plot, Waugh was also concerned with two complementary but distinct principles of structure, physical and thematic. The first principle, judging from the manuscript, Waugh probably addressed at or near the end of the manuscript version. Originally he planned to begin with Chapter 1, "Alma Mater," and perhaps to go on adding chapters until he finished. That was the simplest plan. After he finished twenty-six manuscript pages—down to Grimes's "Cheerioh" (p. 56)—he had decided to subdivide the story, for the last line reads "The End of Part I."[25] But the rest of the manuscript is not consistent.

25. Since the next chapter is headed "Part II, Chapter Seven," Waugh must have changed "Chapter One" to "Prologue" at this point and renumbered subsequent chapters accordingly.

Waugh put "The end of Book I" where the printed version has the end of Part I—after Grimes and Philbrick have disappeared and school has dispersed for vacation. On the next manuscript page Waugh cancelled "Book," inserted "Part," and added a stroke to convert II to III. At the end of what is now Part II, Waugh wrote "End of Part III." The account of Paul's trial, which in the final version begins Part III, was headed "Part IV" in manuscript, but this scene was written after the six pages describing his induction at the prison. The first of these original pages, its number altered from 1 to 3, was headed "Part III"; another stroke made it "IIII." The structural variants are easier to chart than to describe:

Manuscript	Novel
Prologue [changed from One]	Prelude
Chapters I-VI	Part I, Chapters I-XIII (the
Part II, Chapter VII and seven	manuscript's VII is in the novel
unnumbered chapters	part of VI)
Part III	Part II
Part IV	Part III
Epilogue	Epilogue

By the time of publication Waugh had obviously decided that, even though the Llanabba sequence occupied over half the book, division by internal unity was more important than mathematical regularity.

Another kind of revision is evident in Waugh's making Philbrick as important as Grimes and Prendergast. Before a series of lengthy insertions, Philbrick is a minor figure, suspected by the boys of walking out with Dr. Fagan's younger daughter, Dingy, offering Grimes and Paul the station-master's sister, and providing the pistol for Lord Tangent's [MS. Water's] wounding. In three insertions he is given a role equal to that of Grimes and Prendergast. The first is his story to Paul, counterpointing Prendy's futile efforts to supervise the preliminary heats of the sports, about his past as burglar and pubkeeper and his recently abandoned design of kidnapping Tangent. Second are the variant biographies recounted by Grimes and Prendergast. Just before what is now Chapter XII—it begins with the dialogue between Paul and Peter, Waugh inserted, after the manuscript's "Chapter   ", "Pages A.B.C." These contain what is now Chapter XI. Then Waugh inserted into the final school chapter the detectives who seek to arrest Philbrick on charges of "false pretenses and impersonation."

Waugh's reason for developing Philbrick—underlining his satire of society's judging by labels—is easier to deduce than the point at which he did so. Unless he recopied the page on which the first insertion was noted for the typist, it was fairly early in the process, for both the lead-in to Philbrick's story, ending, "I think it is without exception the most beautiful story I know" (p. 64), and the transition at the end of it are included in the basic text, not the insertion. If this is the original manuscript page —and Waugh's consecutive numbering supports the inference—then he had either decided to write it as a separate unit or already done so. Because of the two subsequent additions the first inference is more likely. He may not have waited long, however: the fourth of five pages inserted has a cancel draft of the beginning of Chapter VII, and the evidence of his other manuscripts indicates that he picked up paper containing false starts and used it for other purposes fairly soon after setting it aside. Waugh probably wrote the first insert about the time he wrote the material that encloses it, for the paper is of the same size and color;[26] the second and third long inserts are written on paper identical to that of "The Agony of Captain Grimes" through the end of the Llanabba section and therefore were probably composed separately. Whatever interpretation one accepts, Waugh's shaping of his novel as a whole, as well as his decisions about plot elements, was far more sophisticated than he casually testified almost thirty years later.

There is clearer if less concentrated evidence of this craftsmanship elsewhere in the manuscript. Originally Waugh moved directly from Paul's expulsion from Oxford to the scholastic agency. Later, to intensify Paul's isolation and the callousness of accepting social labels like "sent down for indecent behaviour," he inserted the scene with Paul's guardian. Much later, summarizing the preparations for Paul's wedding, he inserted the one-sentence paragraph asking that the guardian's daughter be chosen a bridesmaid to emphasize both the degree of Paul's triumph and the amorality behind his earlier rebuff. It was probably to undercut the practice of judging by labels rather than by reality that Waugh inserted the passage containing Paul's trial at the beginning of Part III.

Individual chapters were subjected to the same kind of structural revision. In the manuscript Sir Humphrey Maltravers is the only guest at the King's Thursday weekend who is mentioned by name, and Margot's courtship of Paul is placed in a separate chapter. Sometime before publication Waugh added the aberrant, trivial Bright Young People not only to serve as a contrast with the stolid Maltravers but also to prepare more carefully for Margot's emergence from "her little bout of veronal, fresh and exquisite as a seventeenth-century lyric" (p. 158), all the more attractive in her middle position between chattering youth and canting age. Moreover, to emphasize

---

26. This paper is about 5 mm. longer than that used for p. 4 of the first run through p. [20] of the third run.

the contrast, Waugh put the materials into a single chapter, later titled "Pervigilium Veneris."

Because the evidence lies before us, Waugh's reshaping of "The Death of a Modern Churchman" is an even more interesting demonstration of his craft. From the beginning of the chapter he planned to introduce a homicidal convict to murder Prendy, but his original title, "The Experiments Continued," was as bland as the first draft of the convict's dialogue after "he's no Christian" (p.209):

> I had a vision. That's what brought me here. It was like this. I'm a grocer by profession—(or) was, you must understand. Well one day I was locking up the shop for the evening when the angel of the lord came in. I didn't recognize him at first. "Just in time, sir," I said, "What can I do for you?" "Take the Book and read" he said. So I took the Book and it opened at the psalms of King David. You know them?" ¶ Yes" said Paul. ¶ "As I looked the angels hand appeared on the book pointing. I looked where it pointed and it read "Blessed is he that taketh her children & casteth them against the stars." "Whose Lord?" I said. Again the hand pointed

The flatness of this passage was immediately evident, for Waugh broke it off, turned over the page, and, with a stronger sense of the comic possibilities of mixing the high and low styles, wrote:

> It was a vision brought me here. An angel clothed in flame, with a crown of flame on his head, crying "Kill and spare not. The kingdom is at hand." Would you like to hear about it? I'll tell you. [Insertion over page begins] I'm a (butcher)/carpenter/ by profession, or at least I was, you understand.'/,—he spoke a curious blend of cockney & biblical English. / 'Not a (slaughterer) /joiner /—a (purveyor of meat) /cabinet maker /. Well one day I was just sweeping out the shop before shutting up when the angel of the Lord came in. I didn't know who it was at first. "Just in time," I said. "What can I do for you?" Then I noticed that all about him there was a red flame and a circle of flame over his head—same as I been telling you. Then he told me how the Lord had numbered his elect and the day of tribulation was at hand. "Kill and Spare not," he says. I'd not been sleeping well for some time before this. I'd been worrying about my soul & whether I was saved. Well all that night I thought of what the angel had told me. I didn't see his meaning, not at first, same as you wouldn't. Then it all came to me /in a flash /. Unworthy that I am, I am the Lord's appointed' said the (butcher) /carpenter /. 'I am the the sword of Israel; I am the lion of the Lord's elect.' [p. 209]

This was obviously more effective than the first draft, and the change from butcher to carpenter made the Governor's scheme to have him work in his cell more practicable if not more sensible, but Waugh obviously felt the need for some kind of preparation. Therefore, he inserted another prisoner, "a little bony figure" to contrast with the "burly man of formidable aspect" with "red hair and beard, and red-rimmed eyes, and vast red hands which twirled convulsively at his sides" (p. 208). The insertion is far longer than the dialogue on pages 206 and 207, for the smaller convict recounts a tale of comic violence occasioned by a series of wrong numbers during a burglary. Before publication Waugh deleted the anecdote.[27] For one thing, it is not very funny; for another, it is too closely parallel to the larger convict's story to form an effective variant. The dialogue that Waugh retained, however, characterizing the smaller convict as an old lag contemptuous of the wig-wearing chaplain and the innovative prison governor and awed by "the Governor's brother" (alias Philbrick), not only exploits already established comic material from another angle but lays a foundation of normal prison life on which to build the bizarre events to follow.

Less extensive revisions are important evidence of Waugh's increasing sensitivity to shades of tone, especially as they affect character. Confronted with the dispute about the race—Clutterbuck ran five laps, the others six— Dr. Fagan, after judging Clutterbuck the winner of the five-furlong race, originally explains: "Ah yes, a difficult race three miles most gruelling. It is a Llanabba custom," said the Doctor, "to run the longer races concurrently. Mr. Pennyfeather should have explained it through his megaphone." While it tempers discretion with deceit, Waugh cut it to avoid an outright lie and superfluous detail and continued with the following, more satisfactory aesthetically as well as morally: "Then they [the other boys]," said the Doctor imperturbably, "are first, second, third, fourth and fifth respectively in the Three Miles."

All the characters are retouched to a high finish in similar revisions, but Waugh's treatment of Grimes is the most vivid example. Grimes is based on a "monotonously pederastic"[28] fellow master at Arnold House who caught Waugh's ear with, "I never give notice . . . . It's always the other way about with me. In fact, old boy, . . . this looks like being the first end of term I've seen for three schools."[29] Grimes leaps to life with a near echo of the phrase (p. 37), and for the rest of the paragraph and the novel Waugh ceaselessly worked to keep his dialogue to that standard. Almost immediately he changed Grimes's

27. See Heath's transcription, pp. 528–29.
28. Waugh, *Diaries,* p. 211 (May 14, 1925).
29. Waugh, *A Little Learning,* p. 228.

analysis of his problem from "temperament and drink" to the more startling (if perhaps redundant) "temperament and sex" and then changed "one" to "the public school man" in Grimes's praise of the "blessed equity in the English social system . . . that ensures the public school man against starvation," using the phrase for the second time in three lines to establish the label more firmly in the reader's mind. In Grimes's description of his imminent conviction, Waugh changed the infinitive in "it's out of the question to courtmartial an old Harrovian" (MS Caustonian) to the more vivid "to shoot" and also avoided a pointless repetition of "courtmartial" from three sentences earlier. In manuscript "Captain Grimes' Story" ends with " 'I've never been really attracted by women,' said Grimes." Accurate but not distinctive, this was replaced by the time of publication with, " 'Women are an enigma,' said Grimes, 'as far as Grimes is concerned.' " Not only does this establish Grimes's habit of referring to himself in third person (a later revision in manuscript continued this idiosyncrasy), but, more subtle in statement and rhythm, it brings the chapter to a more effective close.

Two chapters later Waugh again rescues Grimes from banality by changing "I don't believe one can ever be unhappy for long provided one listens to instinct" to "I don't believe one can ever be unhappy for long provided one does just exactly what one wants to and when one wants to" (p. 45). Not only does the revision accord better with his usual style, but it sets off more effectively the elevated diction in "singularly in harmony with the primitive promptings of humanity" used of the same attitude in the following sentence. And at the beginning of the sports day Waugh reaches for the vulgar sublime by adding "flowers of emerald green and pink" to Flossie's "violet frock . . . the colour of indelible ink on blotting paper" and inserting Grimes's "Have you seen my fiancee's latest confection [1962: creation]— Ascot ain't in it." Also inserted, to replace the flat, "You don't say," was Grimes's exclamation of pious horror, "What a terrible thing," after the assertion that Negroes cannot control their passions. And in the post mortem, in the passage of inserted dialogue discussed earlier, he first diagnosed Margot's relationship with Chokey as "a simple case of fornication." Again, this is accurate but uncharacteristic, since Grimes is a stranger to moral theology. Much more in tune with his attitude is the revision: "a simple case of good old sex" (p. 102).

Of course, Grimes's attitude is in part created as well as revealed by the phrase, and it could be argued that Waugh was discovering rather than simply revising, since every element of a novel is interdependent with the others. Discovery and alteration are certainly evident in several insertions and deletions in the prison sequence. In the process of writing, Waugh seems to have gained a clearer concept of the prison as suited to Paul's asceticism.

To reinforce this theme, later made overt in two separate passages (pp. 200, 221), Waugh inserted into the scene at the reception center Paul's reflection that "the loss of his personal possessions gave him a curiously agreeable sense of irresponsibility." Between the two major passages developing the theme, Paul is offered a newspaper. At first, anticipating perhaps his encountering Margot's picture and the ensuing meditations, Waugh wrote, "There were plenty of things in it to interest Paul." Almost immediately he drew back, changed it to, "There was very little in it to interest Paul," and continued with his reflections that he is content to have escaped contact with the never-ending series of events. This, of course, is crucial in foreshadowing his placid and instantaneous acceptance of his "static" nature and his return to Oxford.

At the same time Waugh was learning not to develop themes too overtly. He was tempted to do so after the first chapter of the prison sequence, which had ended with Paul "writing up on his slate the thoughts which had occurred to him during the day," where the thoughts must have seemed natural enough. Accordingly, he began a new chapter with a transitional title:

Chapter Two. Paul's Meditations (This Chapter may be omitted on the first reading) [Waugh's parentheses]

/1. Who Am I?/

(My name is) /I am / Paul Pennyfeather. For all I know there may be a hundred other people with the same name. I did not choose my name. The name Pennyfeather was preordained for me centuries ago; the name Paul was chosen by my mother, because she had an uncle Paul who had been kind to her as a child. Why was he called Paul? Perhaps for the same reason. What do I mean when I say that I am Paul Pennyfeather? A chain of consequences so obscurely connected and of such (distant) /remote / origins that it is impossible to trace what I mean. Here I am called D.4.12. That means that for twenty-two hours out of twenty-four I can be found in the twelfth cell of the fourth landing of Block D. D.4.12 is the creature of order and purpose. Paul Pennyfeather is the creature of chaos.

This is not quite true. D.4.12 has only (position) /extension / in space. Paul Pennyfeather has (position) /continuity / in time. How does (position) /continuity / in time suggest itself /to the imagination /? In the form of a series of positions in space, (that is) Paul Pennyfeather at Scone, at Llannabba, at King's Thursday etc. that is to say that Paul Pennyfeather is a series of which D.4.12 is an expression. (That too is not quite true. Explain But [?]) Sometimes I am a part and sometimes a whole. It is very perplexing. (Explain /the position of / D.4.12 in the series Paul Pennyfeather).

2. Why Am I Here?

Waugh broke off and cancelled the passage, no doubt recalling that it contradicted his statement in "Interlude in Belgravia" that Paul as a "real person" would be subordinated to "the unusual series of events of which his shadow was witness" (pp. 146, 147). Furthermore, the content and tone are uncharacteristic, for Paul has never before displayed introspective, let alone philosophical tendencies. And, as Heath says, Waugh "must have sensed that such explicit (and rather banal) philosophizing could only damage a satiric technique founded on the tonalities of innuendo and reticence." Heath's contention that "the passage is valuable as a gloss" can be questioned, however. Undoubtedly the novel deals with the problem of identity, but it does so in social and largely negative terms.

Particularly important is the novel's distinction between the legal and the moral. Paul's question of his guardian, "Have I no legal right to any money at all?" (p. 24) was an insertion within an insertion, and more than two hundred pages later the adjective was again inserted in, "'Oh, death, where is thy sting-a-ling-a-ling?' said the surgeon, and with these words and a laboured effort of the pen he terminated the legal life of Paul Pennyfeather" (p. 239). Between the two passages, prompted by the sight of Margot's photograph, which seems intended to convey her essence, Paul does speculate at some length about

> this whole code of ready-made (justice) /honour / that is the still small voice, /trained to command, / of the Englishman all the world over. On the other hand was the undeniable cogency of Peter Beste-Chetwynde's "You can't see Mamma in prison, can you?" The more Paul considered this, the more he perceived it to be the statement of a natural law. . . . he was strengthened in his belief that there was, in fact, and should be, one law for her and another for himself . . . . if the preposterous processes of law had condemned her, then the woman that they actually caught and pinned down would not have been Margot, but some (totally strange) /quite other / person of the same name and somewhat similar appearance. It was impossible to imprison the Margot who had committed the crime. [pp. 220-21]

It is equally impossible for Grimes to be either heterosexual or dead or for Philbrick to be imprisoned in a single role or for Prendergast to be confident and hopeful.

The difference between Prendergast, the clergyman with Doubts, and Pennyfeather, who at the end of the novel placidly awaits ordination, is that Paul has learned that the essential self lies beyond the range of the questionnaires and forms that permeate the novel and that for various people there are various rules of law, natural or unnatural. Professor Otto Silenus gives him a verbal formula with which to judge his experience, that of riders on the wheel that people mistakenly define as life, "the scrambling and excitement and bumps and the effort to get to the middle. And when we do get to the middle, it's just as if we never started." Paul, Silenus asserts, was never meant to get on the wheel because he is static as opposed to dynamic; ". . . we're probably two quite different species spiritually" (pp. 244, 245).

Paul accepts this judgment, repeating it in the Epilogue (p. 251), and after Waugh finished the manuscript, he displayed his rapidly developing ability to reorder and shape his material in the final pages of the published book. To the end of his career he had a tendency to conclude the manuscript hastily; in fact, the final sentence of *A Little Learning* was added by means of a letter to his agent.[30]

The revisions rarely added striking detail about plot or character; they were more important for providing thematic overtones and rhythmic cadence to the ending and to the novel as a whole. This tendency is particularly marked not only at the end of the novel but at the end of Part 3, which deals with Paul's return to Oxford. In manuscript the whole sequence occupies only three paragraphs: his return and his conversation with his scout about the Pennyfeather who preceded him, a summary of his meeting with the Chaplain and Stubbs, and an account of their activities, concluding with:

> Stubbs even induced Paul to join the League of Nations Union and (The [sic] arranged to go for a walking tour in Belgium together, during the next vacation) took him one afternoon / in company with the chaplain and several members of the O.S.C.U. / to visit the criminals in the prison.
>
> "It opens one's mind" said Stubbs, "to see all sides of life."

The final version (pp. 245–248) is considerably expanded. The passage parallel to the manuscript uses dialogue rather than summary, Mr. Sniggs is reintroduced from the Prologue, and Stubbs is developed at greater length, all the way from his ironic introduction as "a grave young man with a quiet voice and carefully formed opinions" to the trip to the prison to visit the criminals there and sing part-songs to them:

30. Letter to A.D. Peters, December 11, 1963, Humanities Research Center, University of Texas—Austin.

"It opens the mind," said Stubbs, "to see all sides of life. How those unfortunate men appreciated our singing!" [p. 247]

The priggish confidence of the added sentences, combined with the view of prisons Waugh has provided, makes Stubbs into a minor comic monstrosity.

Even more significant for the novel's structure is the material introduced thereafter: Paul reads Dr. Fagan's sensational book, *Mother Wales,* the fulfillment of a plan announced during the sports, and puts it next to his copy of Dean Stanley's *Eastern Church,* a title resurrected from the Prologue. Then he encounters the prosperous-looking Philbrick and, having learned "to temper discretion with deceit," passes him off to Stubbs as Arnold Bennett. Finally, he listens to the lecturer in Church history discuss the multiple heresies of the bishop of Bithynia and concludes, "How right they had been to condemn him."

This added material encapsulates the major themes of the novel. Fagan has made his revulsion into something very like art, and, in placing his book next to *Eastern Church,* Paul is recognizing the existence of coherent, coequal, and perhaps contradictory systems of thought. Philbrick is a reminder of the great wheel from which Paul has escaped but which he does not judge; in the juxtaposed lecture, Paul is provided with a system in which he can find rest and in which, though the happy heathen may go unscathed, perverters of the system can be condemned.

No less significant are the additions to the Epilogue. In manuscript it ended, "So Peter went out and Paul settled down /again/ in his chair." By the final version Waugh had added:

So the ascetic Ebionites used to turn towards Jerusalem when they prayed. Paul made a note of it. Quite right to suppress them. Then he turned out the light and went into his bedroom to sleep. [p. 252]

The first three sentences, echoing the end of "Resurrection," illustrated Waugh's unstated theory that anything repeated was more than twice as funny as a single use and emphasize Paul's choice of a closed system of thought, not necessarily better but, for him, more suitable. The passage as a whole implies firmly and definitely that Paul's adventures are safely ended.

3   Noting with Surprise
What Happened:
Black Mischief

Once Waugh decided "to set about being a man of letters,"[1] he passed rapidly through the stage of what Silenus called "the vile becoming." Drawing not only upon his experience but also upon the collective wisdom of the Waugh household, in less than two years after making the reluctant decision, he was able to purvey advice to the beginner: start with a biography of a well-known figure, for not only is the research less tedious, but reviewers will be grateful for the "opportunity for once more printing their nicely turned opinions" about that person. Though the financial rewards will be slim,

> you will collect a whole list of kindly comments which your publisher will be able to print on the back of the wrapper of your next [book]. This should be a novel, preferably a mildly shocking one. Your biography has made you a "man of letters" and established your integrity of purpose. Librarians who see that distinguished critics have spoken respectfully of your work will be slow to ban it.[2]

From that point the writer need only keep himself in the public eye by unusual behavior to secure commissions for articles "because," as he said in *Labels (A Bachelor Abroad,* in the United States), "people read your books, and people read your books because they read your articles in the papers. (This is called a vicious circle by those who have not got into the running.)"[3]

Despite Waugh's statement that by early 1929 "I had only written two very dim books and still regarded myself less as a writer than an out-of-work private schoolmaster,"[4] his diaries and his letters to his agent reveal that

1. Evelyn Waugh, *The Diaries of Evelyn Waugh,* ed. Michael Davie (Boston: Little, Brown and Co., 1976), p. 281 (February 2, 1927).

2. Evelyn Waugh, "Careers for Our Sons: Literature," *Passing Show,* February 2, 1929, p. 116.

3. Evelyn Waugh, *A Bachelor Abroad* (New York: Jonathan Cape and Harrison Smith, 1930), p. 3. The English title, *Labels,* was less ironic.

4. *Ibid.,* p. 27.

he was quite as conscious and almost as cynical in managing his career in fact as he recommended in printed jest. He was quite willing to write "Wyndham Lewis stuff"[5] or anything else for which there was a market. Thus when the *Evening Standard* editors misread "manners" as "mothers" in Waugh's proposal for an article, he dutifully produced "Matter-of-Fact Mothers of the New Age."[6]

His real ambition, however, was to establish himself as a spokesman for youth.[7] This desire was based partly on conviction, as the schoolboy diaries and school and college journalism demonstrate, and partly on the necessity to support his wife. The themes of "The Claim of Youth or Too Young at Forty: Youth Calls to Peter Pans of Middle-Age Who Block the Way,"[8] the article about mothers, and "The War and the Younger Generation"[9] are very similar. In the last he pronounced that "freedom produces sterility. There was nothing left for the younger generation to rebel against, except the widest conceptions of mere decency.... The result in many cases is the perverse and aimless dissipation chronicled daily by the gossip-writers of the Press." To allay the fears of his audience and to establish his own "integrity of purpose," he ended the article with the faint hope that "a small group of young men and women are breaking away from their generation and striving to regain the sense of values that should have been instinctive to them."

Though less lucrative than articles about social movements, speaking for new literary and artistic movements also appealed to Waugh. He defined people who were "'modern' in the best sense" as those "aware of all the vital movements in their art and of the theories on which they are based; at the same time they are free from the snobbism of immediate acceptance of the *avant garde.*"[10] About the same time he made Ronald Firbank's novels the touchstone for those who could appreciate "a wide and vigorous tendency in modern fiction." Waugh's interest in Firbank was primarily technical, and in the following passage what appears to be description is in fact praise:

---

5. Since he wrote later that he preferred being "forceful" to writing like Lewis, he may have been referring to D. B. rather than to Percy. See his letter to A. D. Peters, n.d. [late 1928]. *The Letters of Evelyn Waugh,* ed. Mark Amory (New Haven and New York: Ticknor & Fields, 1980), p. 30.

6. *Evening Standard,* April 8, 1929, p. 7.

7. Letter to W. N. Roughead of Peters's office, ca. 26 November, 1928; letter to Peters, ca. December 13, 1928.

8. *Evening Standard,* January 22, 1929, p. 7.

9. *Spectator* 142 (April 13, 1929): 570–71.

10. Evelyn Waugh, "Illustrated Books," *Observer,* February 17, 1929, p. 9.

His later novels are almost wholly devoid of any attributions of cause to effect; there is the barest minimum of direct description; his compositions are built up, intricately and with a balanced alternation of the wildest extravagance and the most austere economy, with conversational *nuances*. They may be compared to cinema films in which the relation of caption and photograph is directly reversed; occasionally a brief, visual image flashes out to illumine and explain the flickering succession of spoken words.

Except for *Inclinations* and *Caprice*, the final description is by no means accurate, since Firbank very solidly, if impressionistically, established physical background in his later novels. More accurate is Waugh's description of Firbank's dialogue as lacking any exchange of opinion. His art, Waugh says, is purely selective: "From the fashionable chatter of his period, vapid and interminable, he has plucked . . . the particles of his design." In concluding that the present generation owed a debt to Firbank because he "remained objective and emphasized the fact which his contemporaries were neglecting that the novel should be directed for entertainment," Waugh was making a prediction that his next novel would fulfill.[11]

Vile Bodies clearly shows the influence of Firbank's dialogue[12] and repeats many of the themes of Waugh's articles about modern youth. The *Spectator* material about loss of values and purpose is echoed obliquely in Fr. Rothschild's speech about the younger generation's "fatal hunger for permanence" (pp. 131–32). But the novel, which went through eleven impressions in ten months, was the most obvious and most significant embodiment of Waugh's desire to be a spokesman for youth. The impulse was curbed somewhat as he revised typescript—Adam's parenthetical observation "(a million dead and a million unemployed)" after Mrs. Ape's claim to know all about England was deleted before publication—but the omniscient narrator obviously sympathizes with the young and serves as their historian.[13] Moreover, because of Waugh's debt to Firbank, the narrator is far less solidly established than the narrator of *Decline and Fall*. Comments like "It should be remembered in these people's favor that none of them had dined," "The truth is that like so many people of their age and class, Adam and Nina were suffering from being sophisticated about sex before they were at all widely experienced,"[14] and "O Bright Young People" indi-

11. Evelyn Waugh, "Ronald Firbank," *Life and Letters* 2 (March, 1929); 191, 194–96.

12. Waugh admitted as much in the preface to the final collected edition. (London: Chapman and Hall, 1965).

13. See my *"Vile Bodies* in Typescript," *Evelyn Waugh Newsletter* 11 (Winter, 1977): 7–8, for more extensive description of the variants.

14. This line was deleted for the 1937 Chapman and Hall edition and all subsequent English editions; all American editions retain it.

cate the narrator's partial identification with his characters, and his knowing footnotes and asides about their customs, though they establish him as superior to the audience, identify him as participant in as well as observer of their antics. The ungainly shifts from detachment to sympathy are the major weaknesses of the novel.

Its popularity made Waugh a public figure and his nonfiction a desirable commodity for the newspapers, as his exultant diary entries of May 19 and 21, 1930 (pp. 304, 311), much in the tone of Mr. Toad on top, amply demonstrate. In fact, until he left England for Abyssinia in October, he was able to lead a double journalistic life as commentator on fashion, manners, parties, and his own past for the *Daily Mail* and as weekly arbiter of literature for the *Graphic*. The first series was ephemeral, but the second afforded Waugh his first opportunity to think and write about fiction over an extended period.

Since Waugh reviewed, in roughly half of his working time, eighty-four books in eighteen weeks for a popular journal, major technical pronouncements cannot be expected. Waugh gave his readers the benefit of his own practice and reading, however, and those familiar only with the postwar, Pinfoldish Waugh will be startled to find the younger Waugh speaking of Cezanne, Joyce, Lawrence, and even Picasso in more than respectful terms. In fact, turning away from "youth journalism," he maintained that one had to be middle-aged to catch up with the intellectual currents of the period and be really modern.[15] Earlier, having just published *Vile Bodies*, he listed the marks of the modern novelists as "economy, selection, and accuracy; they attempt a literal transcription of dialogue, choosing each extract only for its significance in the structure of the story; they convey their narrative atmosphere and characterization by means of innuendo rather than direct discription."[16] This is very close to his views in the essay on Firbank. In the *Graphic* reviews five months later Waugh expanded considerably his analyses of "technique," by which he seemed to mean the handling of language and especially dialogue, and was devoting more attention to "structure," by which he apparently meant the relationship of parts to the whole. For example, he praised Henry Green's *Living* because, though originally puzzled,

15. Evelyn Waugh, "Let Us Return to the Nineties but Not to Oscar Wilde," *Harper's Bazaar* [London] 3 (November, 1930):51. See also Evelyn Waugh, "Why Glorify Youth?" *Woman's Journal,* March, 1932, p. 107.

16. Evelyn Waugh, " 'Tess'—As a 'Modern' Sees It," *Evening Standard,* January 17, 1930, p. 7.

The more I read it the more I appreciate the structural necessity of all the features which at first disconcerted me.

There are no unrelated bits such as one finds in most books. A danger in novel writing is to make one's immediate effect and then discard the means one employed. Modern novelists taught by Mr. James Joyce are at last realising the importance of re-echoing and remodifying the same themes.[17]

Waugh's knowledge of Joyce may have been less secure than he implied, for he had been reading "a very interesting treatise" on *Ulysses* only two weeks earlier (*Diary*, p. 242). While not exactly new to Waugh, these opinions about what is essentially cinematic montage, coupled with a stronger appreciation of what some would call motifs or image patterns, were to be important for *Black Mischief*. A year earlier he had praised Firbank's use of a series of casual references to construct an outrageous plot. The kind of structure he was now describing, as *Black Mischief* was to prove, was technically more rigorous and thematically more significant. As Waugh pointed out to the cardinal-archbishop of Westminster after the novel was published, in the hand drums and references to cannibalism introduced in the opening chapter and repeated "in another key in the incident of the soldiers eating their boots," Waugh intended "to prepare the reader for the sudden tragedy when barbarism at last emerges from the shadows and usurps the stage."[18]

More immediately important to *Black Mischief*, however, was the experience Waugh gained during his visit to Abyssinia and East Africa. In a manner different from Hemingway, Waugh tended to get rid of his material by writing about it; moreover, his sense of period and his taste for the topical rendered obsolete even material that he had not exploited.[19] In *Vile Bodies* he treated the decline of the Bright Young People in a way that precluded their use as a central subject in new fiction. His experience in late 1930, however, not only gave him a rich vein of new material in the chaotic Abyssinian scene, reminiscent to him of *Alice in Wonderland,* but as a result of his reception into the Roman Catholic Church on September 29, gave him a new attitude towards it.

17. Evelyn Waugh, "A Neglected Masterpiece," *Graphic,* June 14, 1930, p. 588.

18. Evelyn Waugh, "An Open Letter to the Cardinal-Archbishop of Westminster," unpublished, May, 1933; quoted in F. J. Stopp, *Evelyn Waugh: Portrait of an Artist* (Boston: Little, Brown and Co., 1958), p. 32, reprinted in full in *Letters*, pp. 72–78.

19. See, for example, the Dedicatory Letter to the first edition of *Work Suspended* (London: Chapman and Hall, 1942), in which Waugh announces that "the world in which and for which [the novel] was designed, has ceased to exist."

The change in attitude is clearly illustrated by the contrast between the conclusions of *Labels* and *Remote People* (*They Were Still Dancing* in the United States), written about a year apart. In the first Waugh returned to England, having discovered that its customs and institutions seemed, in contrast to those of other countries, less absurd than he thought, to conclude that "there still remains a certain uncontaminated glory in the fact of race, in the very limits and circumscription of language and territorial boundary, so that one does not feel lost and isolated and self-sufficient." Exiles and all sorts of cranks, he thought, have "a deficiency in that whole rich cycle of experience which lies outside personal peculiarities and individual emotions." But this was no permanent consolation to Waugh; the foghorn emitted "a very dismal sound, premonitory, perhaps, of coming trouble, for Fortune is the least capricious of deities, and arranges things in the just and rigid system that no one shall be very happy for very long."[20]

In gathering the material for *Remote People*, on the other hand, Waugh had learned to appreciate the decadent Arab culture of Zanzibar and to lament the passage of "an existing culture which, in spite of its narrowness and inflexibility, was essentially decent and valuable; we have destroyed that . . . and in its place fostered the growth of a mean and dirty culture."[21] In short, Waugh had discovered politics, because "outside Europe one cannot help being a politician if one is at all interested in what one sees; political issues are implicit in everything . . . " (p. 156). He did retain a sense of solidarity with his countrymen, especially those who had settled in the highlands of Kenya, but not everything he saw testified to the wisdom of British foreign policy or of any course of action that placed Europeans in Africa.

A second and more important change in attitude was his conversion, which gave him a more thorough basis than the limits of language, nationality, and territory for not feeling "lost and isolated and self-sufficient." In secular terms his conversion freed him from the insularity of *Labels*. Before he left for Abyssinia, he drew the line not between Catholicism and Protestantism "but between Christianity and Chaos," for "Civilisation—and by this I do not mean talking cinemas and tinned food, nor even surgery and hygienic houses, but the whole moral and artistic organization of Europe—has not in itself the power of survival. It came into being through Christianity, and without it has not significance or power to command allegiance."[22] But, as the conclusion of *Remote People* demonstrates, the idea of Europe could com-

20. Waugh, *A Bachelor Abroad,* pp. 278, 279.

21. Evelyn Waugh, *Remote People* (London: Duckworth, 1931), pp. 167–68.

22. Evelyn Waugh, "Converted to Rome: Why It Happened to Me," *Daily Express,* October 20, 1930, p. 10.

mand his allegiance without his respecting the actuality. The last clause of *Labels* was, "I lunched in London"; all comparisons with Abroad are precluded. The final chapter of *Remote People,* "Third Nightmare," begins, "On the night of my return I dined in London," and continues with a visit to a hot, crowded, noisy, and oppressive supper restaurant, where, after a page of chatter, poor service, and worse wine, Waugh observes, "I was back in the centre of the Empire, and in the spot where, at the moment, 'everyone' was going." In fact, it was "a rowdy cellar, hotter than Zanzibar, noisier than the market at Harar, more reckless of the decencies of hospitality than the taverns of Kabalo or Tabora." The conclusion is wryly understated: "I paid the bill in yellow African gold. It seemed just tribute from the weaker races to their mentors" (p. 240). Here Waugh's irony is unmixed with personal apprehensions or with the severely restrained pity of *Vile Bodies.* That same irony, expressed more artfully in an impersonal voice, was a major element in the formal and thematic success of *Black Mischief.*

Waugh returned from his African trip with four chapters of his travel book ready for the typist and probably with plans to exploit the material in a novel. By mid-August, while putting the final touches on *Remote People,* he planned to write a best-seller and wanted it handled properly, and Diana Cooper testifies that he remained confident through the publication of *Black Mischief.*[23] Lady Dorothy Lygon, however, recalls that Waugh wrote a great deal of the novel at Madresfield, "groaning loudly as he shut himself away in what had been the day nursery every day; sometimes we were pressed into service as models for the line drawings with which he illustrated it." And Waugh's nickname, "Boaz," was used in the novel for the dissolute Viscount whom Basil Seal has executed.[24]

Although the plot of *Black Mischief* was slow to emerge, its outlines are fairly simple. Seth, the Oxford-educated Emperor of Azania, attempts to impose upon his barbaric and diverse peoples the half-understood trappings of European technology and advanced thought two decades out of date. He is abetted by Basil Seal, a raffish, energetic Englishman who enjoys childish and rather cruel games, of which modernizing Azania is the most complex. Seth's efforts collapse into anarchy as much because of their inherent absurdity as because of the opposition of ecclesiastical, military, and tribal interests. Seth is assassinated; Basil's inaptly named girlfriend, Prudence Courteny, becomes the main course at his funeral feast; the French and

23. Diana Cooper, *The Light of Common Day* (Boston: Houghton, Mifflin, 1959), p. 114.

24. Lady Dorothy Lygon, "Madresfield and Brideshead," in *Evelyn Waugh and His World,* ed. David Pryce-Jones (Boston: Little, Brown and Co., 1973), pp. 50, 51.

British impose boring and superficial order; the Azanians continue to live much as they always have; and Basil, somewhat chastened, returns to an England even more depressing than the one he left.

Both Waugh's correspondence with Peters and the manuscript of the novel show that, at least until the end of 1931, his predictions of success were based upon confidence in his ability rather than a coherent plan of the book. The contrast with the *Decline and Fall* manuscript is striking and instructive. There, despite insertions, revisions, and uncertainty about chapter numbers, Waugh was always able to maintain the basic sequence of page numbers during the writing and was, after the earliest stages, working with an end in view. Page after page is very near fair copy, and though half sheets do occur, they are exceptional. Even after being bound, the manuscript of *Black Mischief* is a mess; before that, as Waugh's mother observed, it was "in a very untidy state."[25] Cancellations and insertions abound; half sheets, which usually indicate Waugh's emphatic rejection of material he cut off as well as out or his rewriting of a bridge between previously composed materials, are very nearly the rule.

The contrast may be due in part to Waugh's new way of writing. Portions of the *Decline and Fall* manuscript are suspiciously clear; Waugh may have recopied them. After the first pages of *Black Mischief* he was revising not only manuscript but, as penciled page references indicate, typescript as well. By 1931 he was using the services of Alexander McLachlan, who endured Waugh's handwriting with only sporadic, plaintive queries about the worst illegibilities until his death in 1946. While writing *Black Mischief*, Waugh once insisted on having a typescript no more than a chapter behind the manuscript and in the final pages, as in *Decline and Fall*, did not bother to include material presumably inserted in typescript.

The process of composition was almost as complex as the physical result. In mid-September, two weeks after he had promised to finish the proofs of *Remote People*, Waugh sent Peters the first chapter of his new novel, called "Accession," suggesting that it might be sold as a short story. Though he took time to write for immediate profit, including "some balls for Woman's Journal"[26] and some short stories, by early December the third chapter was in Peters's hands; ten days later Waugh had almost finished the fourth. He realized, however, that this rate of progress could not continue and asked Peters to fend off his new American publisher because "The novel

25. Catherine Waugh to Peters, November 1, 1933.
26. Letter to W. N. Roughead, ca. November 7, 1931. This article was "Why Glorify Youth?" cited above.

won't be ready for publication for many months yet. I will tell him what it is about when I know myself." Even at year's end, casually agreeing that for serialization "the book can be buggered about anyhow," Waugh confessed that he did not know what form the book as a whole was to take. Nothing more about its form or progress is mentioned until mid-April, 1932, when Waugh asked that any chapters—they were the first three—at Peters's office be sent to him at Chagford, and Peters sent one manuscript, perhaps Chapter 4, to McLachlan, reminding him that he had typed the first three chapters "Some time ago."[27] About three weeks later Waugh wrote that the tiresome Americans, who had objected to the title "Accession," could be given the new title, *Black Mischief*, and could have the novel itself in three weeks. He added, "It is extremely good."

And so it is, though one might ask how a novelist could write half a book with no settled or even, perhaps, very clear idea of what was to happen in the second half. The book itself gives some answers to the question, and the manuscript supplies the rest. As Waugh knew when he sent the first chapter to Peters, it could—and, as "Seth," did—stand as a self-contained unit.[28] Like a Greek tragedy, it began near the end of an action: Seth, emperor of Azania, becomes increasingly aware that the decisive battle in the revolution has been fought and that the victorious army—no one knows which—will enter the city the next morning. The atmosphere of intrigue and betrayal is dispelled when Seth's army enters, and readers of the *Life and Letters* version could be amused by his pretensions to modernity, moved by his increasing fear, relieved by his escape, and satisfied by the resolution of the fates of the treacherous Ali and the agile Youkoumian. Some elements looked forward, of course, but in isolation they were so muted that neither Waugh nor Desmond MacCarthy thought it necessary to remove them.

By the end of 1931, Waugh could be indifferent to serial alterations because he must have seen that his first four chapters still formed a self-contained unit. Chapters 2 and 3, using montage on a far wider scale than had Waugh's previous novels, give the reactions to Seth's victory at the British legation in Azania and in London, where the focus is on Basil Seal's preparations to go to Azania, and manage to create contrasting but complementary pictures of British muddle. Chapter 4 brings the characters from each of the first three together at the Emperor's Victory Ball. Leaving it, the Emperor laments the barbarism of his people and longs for one faithful

27. Peters to Alex. McLachlan, April 22, 1932.

28. *Life and Letters* 8 (March, 1932):188–227. Many readings follow the manuscript rather than the novel.

aide, but this movement is stalled by a subtitle, "Six Weeks Passed" [MS Past],[29] followed by a panoramic view of Azanian life and culminating in "Floreat Azania."

Waugh had created three striking pictures of society and a number of idiosyncratic characters, but he had done nothing to set them in motion. He probably knew that Seth's plans for modernizing the country would fail in some ludicrous way and that Basil would somehow be involved, but may have decided little more than that until he began Chapter 5. Then the plot accelerates. Seth's galloping loss of touch with reality; the breach between his minister of modernization, Basil, and his commander-in-chief, General Connolly; and, following Basil's discovery that Seth's Imperial Bank of Azania is in fact a cupboard filled with privately printed banknotes, Basil's consequent loss of confidence "in the permanence of the One Year Plan"—all combine to create a sense of impending upheaval. With the dissidents properly motivated, Waugh devotes Chapter 6 to bringing their plans to fruition with a riot at the Birth Control Pageant. Chapter 7 deals with the chaos created by the new puppet emperor's death from senility, and the eighth and final chapter with the results of European occupation, when universal blandness buries all.

Even in the second half of the book Waugh seems not to have been fully conscious of his direction. Chapter 6 begins with a letter by Dame Mildred Porch, of the Society for the Prevention of Cruelty to Animals, who uncomprehendingly witnesses the growing crisis and its climax, but the preparation for her appearance had to be inserted in the manuscript of Chapter 5, an indication that Waugh may have conceived of her after he was well into the chapter.

More pervasive, though less important for narrative techique, was the minor plot strain linking General Connolly and Mme. Ballon, wife of the French envoy. The first two references to the supposed affair are not in the first draft, and the last two are not in the manuscript at all. This seems to indicate that the idea occurred to Waugh rather late in the process of composition; the first two additions must have been sent to the typist for insertion. (The other references were incorporated in the manuscript of Chapter 5.) Indeed, though this is necessarily speculation, Waugh may have been forced to devise the plot as a way of disposing of Connolly, the last representative of the old Azania, and of closing the novel with the new regime firmly in control.

29. The subtitle is not in the New Uniform Edition (London: Chapman and Hall, 1962), which is cited parenthetically in the text.

The genesis of the plot may well have been a happy accident. On April 4, 1929, Waugh had published an inconsequential story titled "Consequences" in the *Manchester Guardian*. Whether or not A. E. Coppard had seen the story, in early November, 1931, he wrote to Waugh asking him to contribute to a book in which various authors would collaborate, a format that seems to have been very popular in the late twenties and early thirties. The result would be *Consequences: A Complete Story in the Manner of the Old Parlour Game in Nine Chapters Each by a Different Author.*[30] Waugh replied on November 14 that, although he had a great deal of work to do, he was interested, and he asked the names of the other contributors. When the book appeared, the month after *Black Mischief*, they included Elizabeth Bowen and Sean O'Falain (sic), but Waugh had at some point dropped out of the project. Nevertheless, he may have remembered it, for the Connolly-Ballon plot begins with a game of Consequences played at the Victory Ball by the English legation party with the result that *"the amorous Duke of Ukaka met the intoxicated Mme. Ballon in the Palace w. c. He said to her 'Floreat Azania'..."* (p. 112). The French undersecretaries discover the paper, and gossip and allusions sustain the rumor, though it never affects the action, until it becomes a pretext for Connolly's impending expulsion.

Waugh's local revisions, though less striking, offer significant evidence that he was consciously adopting a narrative method quite different from the stylized action and idiosyncratic monologues of *Decline and Fall* and the quick, shallow exploitation of a fashionable jargon in *Vile Bodies*. The two travel books written between the latter and *Black Mischief* may have shown Waugh the value of what James called "solidity of specification," and, of course, his third novel was more like a travel book than its predecessors because Waugh was for the first time placing his readers in unfamiliar settings. The new technique was not, however, easy for Waugh. Again and again he had to check the impulse to move on to the next detail or scene to establish more firmly the setting, object, or atmosphere he had originally proposed to abandon. For example, in describing the English legation's inhabitants and grounds, he at first intended merely to mention Lady Courteney's love of gardening and move directly to the activities of "The Secretary & The Archivist." Immediately after writing the phrase, however, he reconsidered, struck it, and went on to describe the changes her efforts had made on the grounds (pp. 53–54). The poster for the Birth Control Pageant was made more striking in appearance and effect by Waugh's insertion of detail:

30. London: Golden Cockrell Press, 1932.

/On / One side a native hut of hideous squalor, overrun with children of every age /suffering from every physical //incapacity,// crippled, deformed, blind, (and) spotted and insane / (a withered wife, broken by childbearing) /the father prematurely aged by paternity / squatted by an empty cook pot; through the door could be seen (her husband, prematurely aged by paternity, desperately) /his wife, withered and bowed with child bearing desperately/ hoeing at (his) /their/ inadequate crop.

The result of these and dozens of other additions was a novel much more solidly established in space than its predecessors. The same thing can be said of Waugh's handling of time. In *Decline and Fall* he had depended almost entirely on the solar cycle: Paul is expelled in winter, almost married in June, imprisoned for an unspecified time, and reborn into the same name, college, and rooms at the end of a year. Waugh took no more pains than to alter a few details to make the seasons come out right; the framework is simply that, and no real sense of progression is created or needed. *Vile Bodies* had been constructed on similar lines. Its time span was shorter and the divisions made thematically effective, but again we are given little more than one event succeeding another.[31] *Black Mischief* creates, in a fashion new to Waugh's fiction, a genuine sense of physical and historical process. So that it might do so, Waugh was forced to imagine and render far more completely than in his first two novels the means by which his fictional world came into being, and that involved considerable augmentation of detail. At first, Waugh described the growth of Debra Dowa, capital of Azania and principal setting of the novel, fairly briefly, then canceled the passage for one made increasingly complex:

The population of Debra Dowa became (increasingly) /strikingly/ cosmopolitan as its reputation as a land of opportunity spread among the less successful classes of (Europe) /the outside world./ Indians and Armenians came first and continued to come yearly in increasing numbers.

This is canceled for the novel's reading:

Many of Amurath's (army) /soldiers/ settled round him in the new capital; in the first few years (they) were (joined) /reinforced/ by a (small migration) /trickle/ of detribalized natives, drawn from their traditional grounds by the glamour of city life; the main population, however, was /always/ cosmopolitan, and as the country's reputation as a land of opportunity spread through the less successful classes of the outside world

31. See my "Title, Theme, and Structure in *Vile Bodies," Southern Humanities Review* 11 (Winter, 1977):21–27.

Debra Dowa gradually (abandoned) /lost/ all (claims to /trace/) /evidence of/ national character. Indians and Armenians came first and continued to come in yearly increasing numbers. Goans, Jews and Greeks followed, and later a race of partially respectable (prospectors) /immigrants/ from the greater powers, mining engineers, prospectors, planters and contractors, on their world-wide pilgrimage in quest of cheap concessions. A few were (fortunate) /lucky/ and got out of the country with modest fortunes; most were disappointed and became permanent residents, hanging round the bars and bemoaning over their cups the futility of expecting justice in a land run by a pack of niggers.

Waugh took similar pains to establish a sense of physical movement in the service of scenic atmosphere. The opening pages of the novel, as the previous quotation indicates, were particularly important for giving the reader a sense of the movement and tone of the novel as a whole, however much the tone may—and does—change. When Ali leaves Mr. Youkoumian, for example, Waugh originally brings him back to the fort and into the guard room in three simple sentences: "Ali returned to the fort. Before going in he visited the guard room. He spoke rapidly in Sakuyu." The revision covers nearly a page of the printed text (pp. 24-25); it describes his progress through the rumor-filled town, first to the harbor, where he joins the crowd watching the campfires of the unidentified army in the hills, and then to the guard room, where the dialogue introduces and begins to characterize the laconic Major Joab.

While for the most part Waugh sought to fix his story more securely in time and space, he was very far from desiring circumstantial realism. In fact, he borrowed T. S. Eliot's technique of symbolic detail to imply without directly stating the author's attitude. The device is most notable in Waugh's treatment of the affair between Basil and Prudence Courtenay. Their second assignation originally ended: "And a short distance away the (legation) ponies shifted restlessly on the /dusty/ hillside; there was no grass /any where/." This was altered to "shifted restlessly among the (dry) stones of a dry water hole" before attaining its final form:

> And a short distance away the legation syce moodily flicked with his whip at a train of ants while the ponies shifted restlessly among the stones and shelving earth of a dry watercourse. [p. 154]

The bored cruelty in the desert scene emphasizes, among other things, both the hopelessness of Basil's task—he has been talking about his job—and the casualness with which he attempts to alter others' lives.

Waugh also worked carefully on the setting of the couple's first assignation, making the cigar that disintegrates in the cold water of the hip bath an objective correlative for his emotional responses and attempting to find the precise shade of meaning for each word and for the whole. Thus the cigar "end" is changed to "butt," the smell from "heavy" to "rank," and Prudence's position from standing "in the middle" to "isolated, waiting for him." Both versions lead to the nauseating imagery of sexual pollution of the climactic sentence, "In the bath water, the soggy stub of tobacco emanated a brown blot of juice" (p. 144).

This is obviously quite different from Waugh's Olympian view of the offstage couplings of Margot or the author's rather strained objectivity in portraying the sentimental toughness of Adam and Nina. One explanation for the change might be Waugh's conversion, for this was the first novel he wrote as a Roman Catholic. Certainly his attitude is implicitly moral, and he is for the first time taking his characters seriously enough to condemn them. Moreover, the increased complexity of his characters opened new technical possibilities at the same time that it imposed new difficulties. The new possibilities can be demonstrated by similar passages from *Vile Bodies* and *Black Mischief*. The first two use the viewpoint of a young woman in an airplane; the third is the author's view:

> Nina looked down and saw inclined at an odd angle a horizon of straggling red suburb; arterial roads dotted with little cars; factories, some of them working, others empty and decaying; a disused canal; some distant hills sown with bungalows; wireless masts and overhead power cables; men and women were indiscernible except as tiny spots; they were marrying and shopping and making money and having children. The scene lurched and tilted again as the aeroplane struck a current of air.
>
> "I think I'm going to be sick," said Nina.
>
> "Poor little girl," said Ginger. "That's what the paper bags are for."
> [p. 197]

. . . .

> Prudence crouched in the cockpit, clutching her beret to her head. The air shrieked past her ears while the landscape rolled away below in a leisurely fashion; the straggling city, half shrouded in smoke, disappeared behind them; open pasture dotted with cattle and little clusters of huts; presently the green lowlands and jungle country. She knew without particular regret that she was leaving Debra Dowa for good . . . .
>
> The aeroplane dipped suddenly, recalling her to the affairs of the moment. The pilot shouted back to her something which was lost on the

wind. They were the extremity of one of the arms of the V. A goggled face from the machine in front looked back and down at them as they dropped below him, but her pilot signalled him on. Green undergrowth swam up towards them; the machine tilted a little and circled about, looking for a place to land.

"Hold tight and don't worry," was borne back to her on the wind. An open space appeared among the trees and bush. They circled again and dropped precisely into place, lurched for a moment as though about to overturn, righted themselves and stopped dead within a few feet of danger. [pp. 217–19]

. . . .

Rain broke late that afternoon with torrential tropic force. The smouldering warehouses of the city sizzled and steamed and the fire ended in thin black mud. Great pools collected in the streets; water eddied in the gutters, clogging the few drains with its burden of refuse. The tin roofs rang with the falling drops. Sodden rioters waded down the lanes to shelter; troops left their posts and returned to barracks huddled under cover in a stench of wet cloth. The surviving decorations from the pageant of birth control clung limply round the posts or, grown suddenly too heavy, snapped their strings and splashed into the mud below. Darkness descended upon a subdued city. [p. 219]

The first passage is merely panoramic; no relationship between viewer and scene exists, and Nina's airsickness, though it may serve as a commentary on modern civilization, is externally imposed. Both scene and response are essentially static. In the second passage, however, the reader is placed in the context of Prudence's sensory and emotional responses, so that she cannot be observed merely as a puppet but to some extent demands empathy. Waugh has moved from caricature toward something like impressionism. In the third passage, he speaks in the full confidence of the authorial voice, more remote from actors and readers than in the confidential asides of *Decline and Fall* and entirely unlike the overly knowing tour guide of *Vile Bodies.* Furthermore, here and throughout *Black Mischief*, especially in the opening and concluding passages, he has moved beyond the necessity that he seems to feel in the first two novels to give the scene a human central focus. This is probably the result of his new ability to create a firm context of space and time.

There were, of course, new challenges in creating more complex characters, for Waugh could no longer rely solely upon stock figures or idiosyncrasies of speech like Miss Runcible's "too sick-making." Not that he abandoned these devices: Youkoumian, for example, is a variation of the tricky slave–Sancho

Panza figure endemic in comedy, and his "what's the use in having bustups" is as characteristic a phrase as Agatha's. But Waugh had to make the response to him more complex and his impudence absolute. Early in the novel, barely saved from hanging, he comes home, a "weary little figure dragging down the lanes" to his shop. There he encounters his wife, tightly bound, but rolls into bed without releasing her, causing a radical shift in attitude toward him. In revising the passage, Waugh underscored his lack of empathy by adding to his dialogue, "Would you believe it? The noose was actually around my neck," and, "You're always thinking of yourself. What about me?" Later he sells Basil the seat reserved for his wife, driving up the price by evoking the picture of her in the stock car with "the General's mules, *very* savage *stinking* animals. All day they will stamp at her. 'Orrible, unhealthy place. Very like she die or is kicked." Waugh added the words I have italicized and the sentence "She is good wife, work 'ard, very loving" to emphasize still further Youkoumian's business sense and render even more ironic Basil's view that "you seem to me a good chap" (p. 102). And the brief glimpse of Mme. Youkoumian among the mules is revised from "a few feet away mad [?] hoofs stamped restlessly on the straw braying & whinnying" to "a few feet from her in the darkness came occasional brays and whinnies and a continuous fretful stamping of the straw" to emphasize her impressions. Also reworked is the startling detail about the "little jar of preserved cherries which her husband had given her to compensate for the change of accommodation." Surprising because one never expected Youkoumian to recognize her feelings in any way, it makes him even more unsympathetic. Yet by this and other means Waugh raises Youkoumian from a mere monster to a perfection of type almost beyond judgment, the perfect survivor who is the only major character to remain and prosper in Azania at the novel's end. Grimes was also raised to an archetype, but Waugh never showed him indulging his ruling passion or any of its effects.

The most complex character in *Black Mischief*, of course, is Basil Seal, and Waugh took particular pains in creating him. Introduced at his club cashing a bad check (p. 70), he is obviously not going to be a conventional hero, but in the manuscript Waugh presented an internal view that did not survive to be printed. After the sentence about the old member eating hot muffins, he wrote: "He had meant to resign anyway, Basil reflected, as he folded the notes into his pocket-book. That cheque would save the trouble of writing a letter to the secretary." As Waugh developed Basil, he must have seen that the passage was at odds with his essentially childish, unreflective, unanticipating slavery to impulse. To establish the quality still further, he inserted Basil's theft and sale of his mother's emerald bracelet. Even then Basil originally sells it in Port Said for "a fair price," before Waugh decided that getting "a third" and finally "a fifth of its value" (p. 92) was more in character. Waugh also, however, took pains to keep Basil from becoming a mere film tough, cutting his "O.K. sister" and later postponing Seth's view of him as "the personification of all that glittering, intangible Western culture to which he aspired" to provide further objective evidence of Basil's social and intellectual eminence at Oxford before giving Seth's response. At the end of Chapter 3, Waugh took a good deal of trouble to adjust the tone of the sentence describing Basil's theft of his cabinmate's possessions and even what possessions these were. Finally, having discarded "Basil had packed" and "Basil had taken," Waugh simply wrote that the man "missed" his possessions, removing entirely the idea of Basil's will or purpose.

Two other related techniques emphasized in the manuscript revisions were less departures from than developments of methods used in *Vile Bodies.* Related to impressionistic methods in their goal of ease and rapidity of movement and their ability to˙ combine sensory impressions in new and striking ways outside normal syntactic and logical patterns, the cinematic intercutting from scene to scene in space at the beginning of Chapter 3 and from place to place in time at the end recall the opening pages of *Vile Bodies,* while the associational, fragmented monologue of Basil's mother develops from Agatha Runcible's delirium. Waugh used both devices more deftly in *Black Mischief,* and he appears from the manuscript to have consciously worked on them, inserting additional fragments into Lady Seal's lament and breaking off and canceling "Basil's plane to Marseilles" for "Croydon, Le Bourget, Lyons, Marseilles" and the rapid series of sensations that follow.

The other English characters, such as Lady Metroland, the Trumpingtons, and Lord Monomark, gave Waugh far less trouble, not simply because he was working over familiar material but because they were of secondary importance. The vitality that had animated them in *Decline and Fall* and *Vile Bodies* now resided in the Azanian natives.[32] Waugh's England is now

32. Waugh energetically repudiated Edmund Wilson's thesis in " 'Never Apologize, Never Explain': The Art of Evelyn Waugh" that "the savagery he is afraid of is somehow the same thing as the audacity that so delights him." Edmund Wilson, " 'Never Apologize, Never Explain': The Art of Evelyn Waugh," first published March 4, 1944; reprinted in *Classics and Commercials* (New York: Vintage Books, 1962), p. 146. Wilson's praise uses the same terms as the condemnation of the *Tablet* editor in 1932; it must have been particularly unwelcome to the Waugh of 1945, who regarded himself as an explicitly Catholic author. See his letter to A. D. Peters, January 16, 1946, *Letters*, p. 218, in which he rejoices at having alienated Wilson with *Brideshead Revisited.* For the background of the *Tablet* controversy, see Christopher Sykes, *Evelyn Waugh: A Biography* (Boston: Little, Brown, and Co., 1975), pp. 122-23.

full of aimless, incurious, complacent citizens who reject new experience in favor of their own dull and messy lives. As a social historian Waugh had already moved beyond the Bright Young People before he recorded their antics in *Vile Bodies,* and in *Black Mischief* he confronted, though obliquely, the same group and their elders grown older and, because poorer, much duller.

Perhaps because the contrast between England and Azania needed more careful planning, *Black Mischief* is a more solidly crafted work of fiction than its predecessors. The unity of *Decline and Fall* is largely external, and although *Vile Bodies* is constructed more carefully than most readers, including Waugh, have been able to recognize, it is thin in texture and sentimental, more because than in spite of its stiff upper lip, in tone. In the first novel Waugh created an atmosphere; in the second he formalized an argot. In *Black Mischief* he created a solid fictional world and made a serious if oblique commentary on the dry rot in modern civilization. As his short fiction reveals, this theme, at most a counterpoint in *Black Mischief,* continued to attract him, and by the time he began his next novel in earnest, it had become a major theme.

Adjusting the Tone:
A Handful of Dust

By the time Waugh wrote his fourth novel, he had learned to embody rather than to state his criticism of modern England, which in *A Handful of Dust* is everywhere clear and nowhere stated. Vehicle for the criticism is Tony Last, owner of Hetton Abbey, preposterously reedified in Victorian Gothic, who clings to attenuated social values irrelevant to the grimy and sordid modern world to which his wife, Brenda, wishes to escape. She begins an affair with the colorless John Beaver, and after their only child and heir dies in a hunting accident, she demands a divorce settlement that will force Tony to sell Hetton. With uncharacteristic spirit he refuses and joins an expedition to discover a lost city in South America, which he dimly confuses with Hetton as refuge and goal. Rescued from and imprisoned in the bush by Mr. Todd, who requires him to read aloud in endless cycle the novels of Dickens, he is presumed dead. At the end of the novel Brenda has married Tony's best friend, and a cadet branch of the Lasts had taken over the hopeless task of trying to preserve the factitious glories of Hetton.

Waugh's trip to British Guiana and Brazil from December, 1932, to April, 1933, recorded in *Ninety-two Days,* has for obvious reasons been regarded as the inspiration for *A Handful of Dust.* Waugh's developing image of Boa Vista as a refuge from the discomforts of bush travel anticipated Tony Last's vision of the Victorian Gothic City in which he can find refuge from the betrayals of contemporary London, and Mr. Christie, the religious eccentric who conversed daily with the Trinity and the Blessed Virgin, is even more clearly the model for the far less fanatical but more obsessive Mr. Todd of the novel, to whom was transferred Waugh's newly regained pleasure in reading.[1] Mechanical mice and emerald-green drawers as trade goods fused into the "mechanical green line rats" of *A Handful of Dust,*[2] while the rumors of plant poisons, the observable fact of the Indians' passive resistance to coercion, and details about diet and landscape anticipate Tony's

1. Evelyn Waugh, *Ninety-two Days* (New York: Farrar and Rinehart, 1934), p. 181.
2. Evelyn Waugh, *A Handful of Dust* (London: Chapman and Hall, 1964), p. 231. This is the new uniform edition of the novel, the last supervised by Waugh. It also contains the "Alternative Ending" used for the serial version.

journey. In fact, Waugh wrote "The Man Who Liked Dickens" while stranded in Boa Vista: "The idea came quite naturally from the experience of visiting a lonely settler and reflecting how easily he could hold me prisoner." That does not, however, explain why "after the short story was written and published, the idea kept working in my mind. I wanted to discover how the prisoner got there, and eventually the thing grew into a study of other sorts of savage at home and the civilized man's plight among them."[3] In fact, Waugh's interest in the theme of the dull, decent man betrayed by bleak modern circumstances had been obvious even before he finished *Black Mischief,* and it could be argued that the trip was catalyst rather than cause for the major themes of *A Handful of Dust.*

Even before Waugh completed Chapter 3 of *Black Mischief,* in which he used England to frame the action in Azania, he was making it the center of a smaller picture. "The Patriotic Honeymoon," retitled "Love in the Slump" for *Mr. Loveday's Little Outing,* deals with the marriage of Tom Watch and Angela Trench-Troubridge as "completely typical of all that was most unremarkable in modern social conditions."[4] The two marry out of a sense of desperation on her side and bewildered acquiescence to "one of the few bright fragments remaining from his glamorous [undergraduate] past" (p. 170) on his. They are separated by accident; Tom discovers hunting on his host's new mare and Angela satisfactory sex with the same Etonian-Oxonian friend of Tom's who gives them a cottage near his estate in Devon, which "would be such a good place for her to go sometimes when she wanted a change" (p. 183). As students of *A Handful of Dust* will realize, the story is almost a negative image of the novel: Tom, the Beaverish Londoner with neither qualities nor prospects, is cuckolded by a lively country squire, a counter-Tony, in a cottage, as opposed to a flat in London, both "very suitable for base love."

The themes of the faithless wife and of the mild man whose betrayal he cannot even recognize are repeated in a story commissioned for the *John Bull* series on "The Seven Deadly Sins of Today." Waugh chose the one sin to which he can never have felt the slightest temptation: tolerance. In

3. Evelyn Waugh, "Fan-Fare," *Life* 20 (April 8, 1946): 51. For more immediate inspiration, see Waugh's comment to Lady Mary Lygon after writing 18,500 words: "About adultery so far. I am so afraid Periwinkle [Lord Brownlow] will think it is about him — it isn't but bits of it are like." *The Letters of Evelyn Waugh,* ed. Mark Amory (New Haven and New York: Ticknor & Fields, 1980), p. 84.

4. Evelyn Waugh, "Love in the Slump," *Mr. Loveday's Little Outing and Other Sad Stories* (London: Chapman and Hall, 1936), p. 167. Subsequently this story, "Incident in Azania," and "Out of Depth" disappeared from the canon in Waugh's later collections, *Work Suspended and Other Stories Written Before the Second World War* (London: Chapman and Hall, 1949), and *Tactical Exercise* (Boston: Little, Brown and Co., 1954).

the introduction to the series Waugh asserted, "It is better to be narrow-minded than to have no mind, to hold limited and rigid principles than none at all." The danger, he continued, was "to put up with what is wasteful and harmful with the excuse that there is 'good in everything'—which in most cases means the inability to distinguish betwen good and bad."[5] Set in Africa, where everyone else has pronounced opinions on every subject, the story presents the monologue of "a jaunty, tragic little figure, cheated out of his patrimony by his partner, battened on by an obviously worthless son, deserted by his wife, an irrepressible, bewildered figure striding off under his topee, cheerfully butting his way into a whole continent of rapacious and ruthless jolly good fellows." Reacting against Victorian ideas of marriage, he lets his wife pursue her own interests and activities and is mildly surprised because "after she'd been going out with this fellow for some time she suddenly fell in love with him and went off with him."[6]

"Bella Fleace Gave a Party," completed before Waugh left for British Guiana, deals with the decay of a once lively country house and the failure, through senile oversight, of Bella to maintain her sense of superiority. In contrast, "Period Piece," dated 1934 in *Tactical Exercise,* shows the betrayed husband losing his wife to his parasitical heir but acquiescing in her return and rejoicing when she bears him a son. Both in his actions and in the tone of Lady Amelia, the story's narrator, one hears "the organ voice of England, the hunting-cry of the *ancien régime.* "[7] Privilege is asserted, the outsiders kept outside.[8] Though "Period Piece" was almost certainly written after "The Man Who Liked Dickens" and perhaps after *A Handful of Dust,* its resolution in the birth of a new heir mirrors the ending to the serial version, "A Flat in London," in which Brenda, subdued and carrying the heir of Hetton, is regarded as unlikely to escape it again.

Ordinarily Waugh did not seem to take his short fiction very seriously, but he was enthusiastic about "The Man Who Liked Dickens" from the time it was written, telling Peters that it was "first-rate" and should command a large fee on the American market.[9] Technically it is superior to his other short pieces. The middle, a flashback that recounts the origin and dissolution of the Anderson expedition, is weakened by rather obvious at-

5. *John Bull,* April 2, 1932, p. 7.

6. Evelyn Waugh, "Too Much Tolerance," *John Bull,* May 21, 1932, p. 24.

7. Evelyn Waugh, *Vile Bodies* (London: Chapman and Hall, 1965), p. 101.

8. The same social truth is enunciated in "Winner Takes All," written in July, 1935, in which the elder son consistently receives the benefit of the younger's efforts. Waugh obviously remembered his father's label of Alec as "the heir of Underhill." See Alec Waugh, *My Brother Evelyn and Other Portraits* (New York: Farrar, Straus & Giroux, 1967), p. 164.

9. Letter to A. D. Peters, February 15, 1933.

tempts at humor, but in the scenes at the house of Mr. McMaster (Todd in the novel) that enclose the flashback the major themes are implied through dialogue and setting rather than overtly stated, as they had been in "Love in the Slump," by a knowing, superior narrator. The story shares with its predecessors the theme of the casually faithless wife. In this case, like Virginia Crouchback in *Sword of Honour,* whose conversational style she anticipates, Mrs. Henty falls in love with a captain of the Coldstream Guards. Henty is less dim than the central male figures of the other short stories; his impotence is the result more of circumstance than of character. The theme of confinement runs through several stories from this period: the dim wife of "Period Piece" has the walled "Garden of Her Thoughts" where nothing grows; the flirt of "On Guard" is rendered a harmless and lonely spinster when her dog bites off her adorable nose; the central character in "Out of Depth" is thrust forward in time to a shattered London whose denizens have degenerated into barbarism.

This story is especially important in the gestation of *A Handful of Dust* because it introduces the major theme of that novel, which Waugh described as "a study of other sorts of savage at home and the civilized man's helpless plight among them."[10] The central figure, Rip Van Winkle, lives in an "orderly succession of characterless, steam-heated apartments, . . . cabin trunks and promenade decks, ... casinos and bars and supper restaurants."[11] Displaced, he is submerged in delirium, more fully rendered than Henty's in "The Man Who Liked Dickens," from which he emerges only after perceiving "a shape in chaos" at a Roman Catholic mass. This overtly religious theme is at most implied in *A Handful of Dust,* but the story presents London as a waste inhabited by "other sorts of savage" and moves a step further toward the portrait of contemporary London as essentially sordid and dull present in Waugh's fiction from *Black Mischief.*

Waugh's retrospective accounts of the composition of the novel make it seem as though he worked carefully backward from "The Man Who Liked Dickens" with the central theme clearly in mind. In the long view Waugh was probably truthful but certainly misleading, for late in December, 1933, when Waugh had settled in Fez for two months, he was not at all sure that he would use the story as the end of the book, and by the time he finished "Book I," he still was "uncertain what form the next half will take."[12]

10. Waugh, "Fan-Fare," p. 58.
11. *Mr. Loveday's Little Outing,* p. 136.
12. Letter to Peters, ca. February 10, 1934. However, he thought the novel "faultless of its kind. Very difficult to write because for the first time I am trying to deal with normal people instead of eccentrics. Comic English character parts too easy when one gets to be thirty." *Letters,* p. 84. To Lady Mary Lygon he called it "My good taste book." *Letters,* pp. 85, 86.

As with *Black Mischief,* lack of a goal did not delay him. The first two chapters had already been typed and sent to Peters by January 24, 1934; three more followed a week later; and the first four chapters of Part 2 (later called "Hard Cheese on Tony") a week after that, on February 6. Waugh's original pagination of the manuscript gives evidence that he composed the novel in these stages. Despite the major struggle with the events and tone of the passages following John Andrew's death, Waugh wrote to Peters about February 10 that he had just sent the concluding chapters of Book 1 to McLachlan, taking the novel certainly to the end of "Hard Cheese on Tony" and perhaps through the next part, what is now "English Gothic — II."

Almost from the beginning Waugh hoped for serialization. Though he did not know exactly where he was going, he was reasonably sure that magazine editors would not be willing to follow him, and he asked Peters to negotiate for the sale of Book 1 as a self-contained work. Anticipating objections that too many issues were left unresolved, he reluctantly offered to "write another 5,000 words giving it a complete form,"[13] but only if serial publication both in England and in America depended upon his additional effort.

Two weeks later he was back in England, announcing his intention to remain at Chagford until he finished the novel, now titled "A Handful of Ashes" or "A Handful of Dust"—he used both in one letter—asking for Peters's copy of the typescript to work over for volume form, and indicating where—after Tony refuses the terms for divorce—the serial ending would fit and what—a reconciliation—would happen in it. He said nothing about his plans for the conclusion of the novel, but he must have had them clearly thought out, for the manuscript of the last three parts is very clean, with just enough revision to indicate that it was not recopied. Waugh's remark that the novel was written to lead into the short story is obviously true of this section, for he used the typescript of "The Man Who Liked Dickens" for major portions of the manuscript of what, until 1944, was "À Côté du Chez Todd."[14] So confident of direction was he by this time that, if his numbering of the manuscript pages is any indication, he was able to pause after the death of Dr. Messinger, then pick up the thread of his narrative and carry through the end of "À Côté" in a sustained effort. With the brief "English Gothic—III," the novel was finished, probably in March, for by mid-April he had corrected proofs of the first half. Negotiations about the serial continued: Waugh planned to cut the manuscript himself, but apparently let the *Harper's Bazaar* editors do so. He sent a list of titles, of which he preferred "Fourth Decade," but agreed to any title the editors chose; and he kept promising and

13. *Ibid.*
14. Waugh discovered the error and corrected it for the Little, Brown edition. Letter to Peters, January 7, 1943.

failing to deliver "the happy ending" until early May. He had so far lost interest in the serial that he went to Spitzbergen before proofs of the last three episodes were ready, leaving W. N. Roughead of Peters's firm to correct them.[15]

This account of the novel's composition helps explain not only the reason for the critics' uneasiness about what they regard as the novel's lack of unity in structure and tone but also the increasingly elaborate means that Waugh devised to solve those problems. He was as much aware as, for example, Richard Wasson that the novel breaks in half at the end of "English Gothic— II," not just in tone but in style and to some extent in narrative method. As in *Black Mischief,* Waugh arrived at a solution in working through the novel, but this time the unifying device had less to do with plot than with more obvious structural features like those found in *Decline and Fall:* the major divisions of the novel and recurrent or slightly variant chapter titles.

When he began the novel, Waugh apparently had no elaborate plans for its external form. The title page carries only "Novel (as yet unnamed)," the author's name, and, in capitals, "Chapters One & Two." Since the opening page of text is an inserted revision, one cannot be sure that the "Beaver" or "beaver's way" were his original choices of title, but Chapter 2 is headed "A Happy Family." If Waugh had originally planned nothing more than a series of chapters consecutively numbered, he abandoned this idea after five chapters, beginning Part 2 with the sixth. Seven chapters later (his numbering or renumbering is confused; two chapters are numbered 5), he at first labeled the new part 4, then changed it to 3 (it became "English Gothic II"), which may indicate that he had considered introducing a new division earlier in the manuscript or, by this time, the typescript. The scheme is further complicated by the "V Two" at the head of what is now Chapter 3 of the section (Chapters 1 and 2 of the novel are thus numbered in manuscript). He had begun a new pagination sequence, and perhaps he had sent the previous segment to the typist and had a lapse of memory. Perhaps he had some vision of another method of construction.

Thereafter, matters became a bit simpler. "Book Two" is headed, in capitals, "In Search of a City. Chapter One"—the first title used since the second chapter. The next chapter heading, however, introduces and then cancels one principle of division and inserts still another: first *"Sixth Sequence —In Search of a City* follow on fro" [sic] is broken off and canceled; under it Waugh wrote in capitals "Sixteen." The first makes sense if one recalls

15. For a discussion of the serial see my *"Harper's Bazaar* and *A Handful of Dust,"* *Philological Quarterly* 48 (October, 1969): 508–16; and my " 'A Flat in London' and 'By Special Request': Some Variant Readings," *Papers of the Bibliographical Society of America* 69 (1975): 565–68.

the earlier "V" and canceled "Part Four" and if one assumes that this simply continues "In Search of a City" as Part 6. The second accords with Waugh's numbering of chapters in the manuscript; it strongly implies that he had either lost patience with his part-division or, if he planned to retain it, that he would number chapters consecutively. Whichever the case, he continued the practice for three more chapters: the rest of "In Search of a City" and "À Côté du Chez Todd." The final chapter has a title, "English Gothic III," but neither a chapter number nor a part designation.[16]

Judging from the titles of the last two sections, Waugh had begun working out the structure used in printed form. Like a number of his contemporaries, he reflected in his very lack of continuity in plot the disorder he found in the modern world. Instead, modern and especially modernist writers have substituted aesthetic patterns—regular and sometimes almost mathematical patterns that they impose upon inchoate material both to achieve a degree of artistic control and to emphasize the artificial nature of that control. Waugh, for example, once said that the artist in the modern world could only "create little independent systems of order of his own."[17] At any rate, *A Handful of Dust* is in final form symmetrical, and that symmetry is emphasized in the chapter titles:

16. The following chart gives Waugh's chapter headings and numbers. Bracketed material gives the corresponding chapter numbers and titles and page numbers of the corresponding divisions in the novel.
ONE (Beaver's Way) [I Du Côté de Chez Beaver]
TWO (II Happy Family) [II English Gothic—I]
THREE [English Gothic—I, section II, p. 44]
Part Two One [II Hard Cheese on Tony]
Two [Hard Cheese on Tony, section II, p. 88]
(Two) /Three/ [Hard Cheese on Tony, section III, p. 95]
(Three) /Four/ [Hard Cheese on Tony, section IV, p. 107]
(Four) /Five/ [Hard Cheese on Tony, section V, p. 112]
Five [Hard Cheese on Tony, section VI, p. 126]
FIVE [midpage, p. 136]
Six [Hard Cheese on Tony, section VII, p. 139]
Part (Four) /Three/ [IV English Gothic—II]
  One [I]
  Two [II]
V Two [English Gothic—II, section III, p. 166]
Book Two In Search of a City Chapter One [V, In Search of a City, I]
(Sixth Sequence. In Search of a City follow on from) SIXTEEN
  [V In Search of a City, II, p. 193]
SEVENTEEN [In Search of a City, section III, p. 204]
EIGHTEEN [In Search of a City, section IV, p. 220]
À CÔTÉ DE CHEZ TODD [VI Du Côté de Chez Todd]
English Gothic III [VI English Gothic III]
17. Waugh, "Fan-Fare," p. 60.

1   Du Côté de Chez Beaver

2   English Gothic—I

3   Hard Cheese on Tony

4   English Gothic—II

5   In Search of a City

6   Du Côté de Chez Todd

7   English Gothic—III

The first and sixth chapters reflect two strongholds of barbarism, the one in London, the other in Brazil, and Waugh clearly asks the reader to compare their essential heartlessness, materialism, and lack of meaningful values. In the second, fourth, and seventh chapters the meaning of the words "English Gothic" changes as the novel progresses. At first, the words seem merely to describe the architecture of Hetton, Tony's country house, but as the chapter develops, they expand to encompass his whole way of life and that of his class. The second use of the words, in Chapter 4, describes English divorce procedure of the period, in which absurd chivalry and ritual make adultery—the only grounds for divorce—respectable, formalized, and dull. In their third use, the words again refer to Hetton, now inhabited by Tony's cousins, who look back to the glorious days of Hetton under Tony. Two of the three remaining chapters, 3 and 5, show the loss of continuity and direction occasioned by the death of Tony's heir and by the death of his guide. The other, chapter 6, is like "English Gothic—III" in that it breaks the pattern: it shows Tony's final imprisonment before shifting to the successors' vision of life. Yet this inversion offers no hope, for the final chapter demonstrates that, unlike characters in tragedy, these people have learned nothing, that delusions as well as property are handed on, and that the process of social entropy continues. The structure thus emphasizes Waugh's satiric message.

As usual, some of Waugh's most effective local touches as well as his structural pattern were second thoughts. In a series of revisions one can, for instance, see him breathing life into the unforgettable Reverend Mr. Tendril. Since Tony goes to church as part of his Sunday pattern, a vicar is needed, but at first mention in the manuscript he had neither a distinct character nor a name, only scruples to explain why there is no longer a fire in the fireplace that Tony's great-grandfather built into the family pew. Waugh excised the line for two reasons: it posited a character attentive to points of conscience about ritual if not religion, and it contradicted the sentence later inserted about Tony's plans to revive the practice. As Waugh developed the religious theme, he increasingly stressed the irrelevance of religion in Tony's life, and these alterations, especially the subtle contrast between inward spiritual zeal and outward, personal ritual ending in physical warmth, provide a suitable overture. The theme is further supported in the revision of Tony's physical response to church from inhaling "the familiar, slightly moldy" to "the agreeable, slightly musty atmosphere" to emphasize pleasant associations and to eliminate the implication of progressive decay in favor of an arrested condition.

Tendril first appears climbing, "with some effort, into the pulpit." Waugh originally made one motive for his appointment the notion that he would not live long, but he must have seen that the idea of progression, even into death, was unsuited to the major theme implied by Tony's fate. He also changed the vicar's sponsor from Tony's father's solicitor to his dentist; as Graham Greene's *The Complaisant Lover* shows, the English seem to find dentists inherently comic. By this time Waugh had formed the conceit, perhaps in anticipation of Tony's exile, upon which the vicar's character—the name Tendril is an insertion—is finally based: the sermons written when he was a chaplain in India and delivered, unchanged, to an uncomprehending and indifferent rural audience who respond only to the sonority of his voice. Thereafter Waugh revised to extend the conceit to its most absurd limits. Thus "our Queen" became "our Gracious Queen Empress"; later, in the unforgettable Christmas sermon, "heathen" is canceled for the extended and Kiplingesque "subjugated, though no doubt grateful, heathen"; and the tiger becomes "ravening" instead of the inserted and canceled "ferocious," "exotic" is inserted before "camel," and Waugh doubles the compound by adding the final two elements to make the delightfully inapt "we have for companions the ravening tiger and the exotic camel, the furtive jackal and the ponderous elephant" (p. 70).

The last revisions are primarily for local effect, though they heighten the fantasy and create a positive character for the way of life that Brenda and her London friends would thoughtlessly destroy. Other revisions indicate that Waugh realized that, because the plot line was relatively weak, he had to make the most of foreshadowing and of parallel incidents and characters. Though he systematically changed John to Beaver in the opening pages to distance the reader from the character, he must have decided by Chapter 5 ("English Gothic — I") to exploit the possibilities of confusing his name with that of Tony's son, for from this point on the boy is referred to as John Andrew, and earlier in the manuscript the middle name has been inserted. The distinction, of course, assumes major importance more than seventy pages later, when, told of her son's death, Brenda thinks that Beaver has died and, on learning the truth, says "John, . . . John Andrew, . . . I . . . oh thank God" (p. 136).

One would think that this speech, one of the most excruciating in modern literature, would destroy all sympathy for Brenda, but Waugh created her so carefully that later in the novel, losing Beaver and casually ignored by her friends, she arouses some pity. Since she is the most complex or at least the most enigmatic figure in the novel, Waugh's gradual outlining, filling in, and retouching of her character are important to an understanding of his purpose and of his increasing range as an artist. At times the motive for the change is fairly simple, as when Waugh replaced "half-drowned," which survived into the serial, with "underwater" in Mrs. Beaver's description of Brenda's "very fair, underwater look" because she is considerably less appealing as Ophelia than as naiad and because the latter accords better with the later view of her as "the /imprisoned/ princess (in the tower) of fairy (books) / story /" in whose escapades with Beaver, whom everyone had thought pure frog, the onlookers find, in the manuscript, "(roma)/ enchantment/" as Waugh both avoided varied meaning of "romance," used just above, and achieved more exact connotation.

Elsewhere, however, Waugh took pains to make Brenda less appealing. At the beginning of "Hard Cheese on Tony," when Tony makes a surprise visit to London, Brenda first remarks to Beaver, "If I'd known I could have made arrangements and given him a jolly." At the very least this must have seemed an odd remark to make to her lover, and Waugh took the opportunity to increase the sense of her casual and callous manipuation of Tony by changing the sentence to, "He's got to be taught not to make surprise visits" (p. 77).

For the most part, however, Waugh avoided even the implication of judgment, striving for the greatest precision in describing her behavior. Brenda's first evening with Beaver is central to Waugh's presentation of her, for he must establish in speech and events the quality of the relationship and define the attraction that Brenda cannot explain even to herself. He must, in other words, be explicit without being sordid or banal. Thus, as Brenda's sister Marjorie leaves the couple, she regards Brenda in a canceled reading as "walking out for the first time" and then as "timid and expectant at the beginning of an adventure" (p. 53). The first phrase is slangy and vulgar; when Beaver says, a page later, "You talk to me as if I was (eighteen) /an undergraduate / having his first walk out" (p. 54), Waugh was tempted to have Brenda remark that it is "rather sordid [?]" but decided to trust the reader to provide the label.

Waugh's handling of the sexual maneuvering is even more careful. Beaver's first attempt to kiss Brenda takes place, in an insertion, at a traffic jam by the Marble Arch. Brenda accompanies her rejection by "shaking her head /several times /"; then, in first draft, "she put her hand in his," and in revision "she put out her hand to his." There is a subtle but important difference between the two gestures: the first is submissive; the second implies at least equality and perhaps superiority. The struggle for advantage is made more explicit in the second taxi ride. Aware that she wants him to kiss her, Beaver "decided it was time (he asserted himself) /he took the lead. So he sat at a distance from her and/ commented on an old house that was being demolished to make way for a block of flats" (p. 55). But she takes the lead with unexpected abruptness, telling him to "shut up" and "come here"; after the kiss, "she rubbed against his cheek in the way she had" —the first of the devastating echoed phrases that reverberate throughout the novel (pp. 20, 55). Her sense of superiority is extended into the party by means of Waugh's change of the sentence's subject from "poor John" in "How my poor young man must be hating this" (p. 57).

Her confidence is undermined, however, the next morning when, expecting and in first draft receiving a telephone call from him, she is frustrated by Waugh's insertions designed to keep her in suspense and thereby sharpen her interest. It is clearly rather perverse, for she is fully aware of Beaver's shortcomings, finds his main attraction his need "to be taught a whole lot of things" (p. 59), and tells him that nobody likes him "except me. You must get that clear. . . . it's very odd that *I* should" (p. 88).[18] To emphasize the poverty of his mind, Waugh inserted the text of his letter thanking Brenda for her Christmas present in place of a summary description, showing Brenda even more clearly her folly and his lack of concern for her. The relationship is renewed, as it began, through a series of casual accidents. Thereafter, the course of the relationship determined, Beaver scarcely appears until "In Search of a City," when he gradually drifts from Brenda's grasp, passive and indifferent as always.

Waugh's greatest challenge in portraying Brenda came after her initial response to John Andrew's death. Like Jock, the reader has heard what she said, and like him the reader cannot finally hold it against her. After delivering the line, "she burst into tears," and Waugh originally ended the scene there. As he did so often, he realized that the material could be exploited to greater effect, and he added the ironic contrast between Brenda "turning around in the chair and pressing her forehead against its gilt back" and the pedomancer delivering to Souki Foucauld-Esterhazy the prediction she had given Brenda. Both the physical symptoms of anguish and the scene that offsets it complicate the reader's attitude toward Brenda. It is altered still more by Waugh's description of her at Hetton, moving slowly and expressionlessly through the rooms and up the stairs to gaze "out (at) /across/

---

18. The new uniform edition reads "good" instead of "odd," which is the reading of the manuscript and of all other texts I have consulted.

the (illegible; ends "less") /troubled/ landscape" (p. 141). With a sense of the novel's rhythm, Waugh inserted the participles of "the sunlight through the stained glass windows (casting [?] spectrums of light all) glowing and sparkling all about her" (p. 141) to recall more vividly her descending the same stairs to Beaver through "countless points and patches of coloured light" more than a hundred pages earlier, perhaps to indicate without specifying the effect the intervening experience has had upon her.

In creating Brenda, Waugh took pains to establish various and contradictory responses, but for the most part he revised to strengthen a single reaction. Tony, for example, is by no means complex, and Waugh is careful not to make him too obviously "the betrayed romantic."[19] On the other hand, while Brenda's dissatisfaction must be comprehensible, the reader must not share entirely the London circle's opinion that "he's rather a stick" (p. 11). To arouse some sympathy for Tony, Waugh expanded the description of him penitent and forlorn after his drunken night with Jock at the beginning of "Hard Cheese on Tony." At first, after sitting before the fire, he simply goes upstairs. In the revision, his inability to read and his preparations for bed emphasize his solitude, and to arouse still more sympathy, Waugh inserted the adjective in the final sentence of the chapter: "That night he went into Brenda's empty room to sleep." A few pages later, when Tony goes to her occupied room in search as much of companionship as sex, Waugh made two drafts of the scene's beginning, and in the second, after Brenda has used weariness to reject his unspoken advance, Waugh first wrote: "He crossed to the bed and kissed her goodnight. She lay quite still, with closed eyes." On second thought, he struck the "goodnight," making Tony's gesture not a conclusion but another overture and emphasizing still more excruciatingly his rejection.

Many of Waugh's local revisions sought to strengthen the reader's aversion or distaste. That is most obviously true in his treatment of commercial vice. In introducing Polly Cockpurse, retired lady of pleasure, aristocrat by marriage, and leader of the set for whom Brenda abandons Hetton and Tony, Waugh wrote in the manuscript version, "/She enjoyed herself hugely and did very little harm to anyone else./ But men, except the very young and the very old for whom she had (great) /the/ glamour /of the reputation she was trying to shed,/ mostly found her a bore."[20]

19. Preface to the new uniform edition.

20. The serial, "A Flat in London," was published in five installments in vol. 68 of *Harper's Bazaar* between June and October, 1934. Parenthetical references indicate first the installment number and then the page number, followed by the book page number. The passage quoted is from 1.138.

In this version, which survived into the serial, Polly is made first into a jolly old rake and then into a harmless bore. The novel, by omitting the passage, emphasizes her influence. This influence, Waugh makes clear, is pernicious precisely because she lacks values and is indifferent to anything but coterie gossip, and these qualities make her acceptable on "all but the highest peaks of every social mountain" (p. 47).

A similar modification of tone in the novel can be seen in Waugh's recasting of the introduction of the "Sixty-four Club." In both novel and serial the history of the club is eventful:

> Times out of number, magistrates have struck it off, cancelled its license, condemned it premises; the staff and until her death, the proprietress, have been constantly in and out of prison; there have been questions in the House and committees of enquiry, but whatever Home Secretaries and Commissioners of Police have risen into eminence and retired discredited, the doors of the Sixty-four have always been open from nine in the evening until four at night, and inside there has been an unimpeded flow of dubious, alcoholic preparations. [3.96; p. 81]

At this point, the texts of serial and novel diverge:

> Mrs. Weybridge, founder and martyr of its fortunes, is dead, but she has left /behind her/ a vast and (attractive) /handsome/ progeny to carry on her work; /while/ some married into the aristocracy and limited their interest in the concern, others /grew up/ to take their places, and it was a younger son, still (dressed to) /wearing/ the short black coat in which during the day he practiced as a barrister, who admitted /Tony and/ Jock to the ramshackle building. [3.96]
> A kindly young lady admitted Tony and Jock to the ramshackle building. [p. 81]

In the novel, the club remains picturesque, but it is no longer quite as domestic and cozy as in the serial version. A house, as the saying goes, is not a home, and in darkening the description of the Sixty-four by cutting this passage and adding the information that the patrons are frequently robbed, the novel emphasizes the pathos of Tony's attempt to enjoy himself apart from Brenda and the essential sordidness of still another aspect of life in London.

Waugh took even greater pains in describing the inhabitants of what became in the novel the "Old Hundredth." In the first scene in which it figures, he inserted several passages to convey more fully, in dialogue he had borrowed from Hemingway because he liked the way Hemingway's drunk people talked, the confused bonhomie of Jock and Tony. In the process he

made them even more annoying to Brenda, capping their persecution with
Jock's plan to ring her doorbell on the way home. Their second visit follows
Tony's interviews with his lawyer about the evidence of infidelity he is to
provide. Waugh wrote two versions of these scenes, adding the echo of "the
habit of loving and trusting Brenda," the fact that, in discussing the partner
in adultery, "no hint of naughtiness lightened" the solicitor's gloom, and the
fact that the wife of a client "of very high scruples" (changed to "very rigid
morality and a certain diffidence") wore a red wig to help him provide
evidence. The scene at the Old Hundredth, sordid at best, is further en-
gloomed by the cold, by the inserted "Babs sniffed into a little ball of
handkerchief," and by the addition of the four lines of dialogue (pp. 151–52)
that clearly imply that Winnie will accompany her mother and Tony to the
seaside.

By this time in his career Waugh must have been aware of his tendency to
cut off a scene too early, but he still had to struggle against it. Thus at the end
of Tony's lecture on proper language, John Andrew originally replies to a
question about falling off his pony with a simple affirmative. Then to show
the futility of the lecture, Waugh added the boy's unforgettable "/It wasn't
Thunderclap's fault. I just opened my bloody legs and/ cut an arser" (p. 28).
More often, instead of changing direction, Waugh developed further the logic
of a scene, allowing characters to reveal themselves more fully. Brenda's
"Goodness . . . . People do think that young men are easily come by" (p. 60),
her speculation about whether a girl she plans to provide for Tony's distraction should be "like me, or quite different" (p. 95), her observation that
Tony is "much odder than you'd think" (p. 105), and her complacent remark
after leaving Tony that "everything is going quite smoothly now" (p. 145) are
added in manuscript. More extended is the passage describing her alone in her
flat, isolated from the social life of London. The manuscript shows that
Waugh first thought of breaking off the scene at "that was mean" (p. 206)
with the signal to the typist "[White line]" and that the decision to expand
was virtually immediate.

Waugh also knew when development had been a mistake. For example,
when Mrs. Rattery comments that she "doesn't notice houses much" (p. 113),
she originally goes on to ask Jock:

"What does Mr. Last do?"
"Nothing much."
"He's not bad."

Neither her curiosity nor her approval accords with the way in which her
character develops, and Tony's lack of purpose has been abundantly demonstrated. Waugh canceled the passage as, after John Andrew's death, he did
Tony's and Mrs. Rattery's dialogue on religion:

After a pause Tony said, "I suppose it *is* all nonsense."
"What."
"Well, all that (Mr.) Tendril talked about."
"Yes, I should think so. I never thought about it."
"It was so embarrassing coming from him."

The passage replacing it, including Tony's "the last thing one wants to talk about at a time like this is religion" and Mrs. Rattery's "Some like it," is a less obvious way of emphasizing Tony's lack of spirituality.

It is not surprising that Waugh made this false first step, for the aftermath of John Andrew's death caused him as much effort as anything else thus far in his career. He worked over other passages, including the scenes at the seaside hotel and the opening paragraph, but in those he was not reduced to doodling in the margins, repeating page numbers, and enclosing them in elaborate boxes. It is a painful sequence, and the manuscript shows that it must have been almost physically painful for him to write. When he began it, Waugh had no clear idea of what he wanted to happen or how to manage the tone. In a canceled draft corresponding to pages 122 to 124, he described the preparations and departure of Jock and Mrs. Rattery in her airplane. The movement is clear and direct; the dialogue extremely matter-of-fact— Tony even says, "It was delightful having you," to the departing Mrs. Rattery. In the revision, exceptionally clean for this part of the manuscript, Waugh leads up to their departure but, in another canceled passage closer to the final version (pp. 124–25), has Mrs. Rattery perceive the disturbance underlying Tony's outward calm and insist on staying with him. However, the dialogue is looser and less precise than Waugh desired, as a comparison of cancel and final drafts shows. Mrs. Rattery has asked Tony not to consider her feelings:

"All right . . . you know the absurd thing is I'm not thinking it, I'm just saying it . . . I'm thinking of other things all the time."
"I know," said Mrs. Rattery. "You don't have to bother about me."
"I'm thinking this is going to be so much worse for Brenda. You see, she'd got nothing else, much, except John. I've got her, and the house . . . with Brenda John always came first . . . naturally . . . and she'll feel awful about having been away /from him/ so much lately, doing economics. That's going to hurt her terribly . . . . I know Brenda so well."

'I'll try . . . the absurd thing is that I'm not thinking it, just saying it . . . I keep thinking of other things all the time.'
'I know. You don't have to say anything.'
Presently Tony said, "It's going to be so much worse for Brenda. You see she'd got nothing else, much, except John. I've got her, and I love

the house . . . but with Brenda John always came first . . . naturally . . . And then you know she's seen so little of John lately. She's been in London such a lot. I'm afraid that's going to hurt her.'

'You can't ever tell what's going to hurt people.'

'But, you see, I know Brenda so well.'

In both passages the irony of his view of his relationship to Brenda is clear, but in the second the simpler rhythm of the three sentences ending the third paragraph is more suited to Tony's mental condition, and his view of her guilt feelings is speculation rather than assertion. Moreover, the interruption by Mrs. Rattery is useful both as foreshadowing and as rhythmical punctuation to lead to Tony's stronger claim to knowledge of his wife.

Less intense but no less important was the elaboration of Tony's vision of the City:

For some days now, Tony had thought less about the events of the immediate past. His thoughts were occupied with the City, the Shining, the Many Watered, the Bright Feathered, the Aromatic Jam. He had a clear picture of it in his mind. It was Gothic in character, all /vanes and/ pinnacles, (and) gargoyles, battlements, groining and tracery, /pavillions and terraces,/ a transfigured Hetton, /pennons and banners floating on the sweet breeze, everything luminous and translucent; a coral citadel/crowning a /green/ hill top /sown with daisies,/ among groves and streams; a tapestry landscape filled with [MS, peopled by] heraldic and fabulous animals and symmetrical, disproportionate blossom.

Because it replaces a "whole Gothic world . . . come to grief" (p. 177), the more fanciful and elaborate the vision the better, and the increased complexity of rhythm, as well as the heaped-up detail, serves Waugh's purpose admirably.

The same thing is true of Tony's final delirious vision at the climax of "In Search of a City." After the mock council meeting Waugh initially wrote:

"The City is served," (sai) /announced/ Ambrose. (delete paragraph symbol) The ramparts were clearly visible between the trees. Tony climbed out of the hammock and made towards them. He was stronger when the fever was on him and he walked quickly though unsteadily. He pushed through the thorn bushes towards the City.

The corresponding passage (pp. 233–34) adds details about Tony's painful progress through the bush towards the City's walls. Then, in a virtuoso passage of description Waugh leads toward the climax that after the fact seems inevitable:

At last he came into the open. The (doors) /gates/ were before him and trumpets were sounding along the walls, saluting his arrival; from bastion to bastion the message ran to the four points of the compass; (the way into the fortress) petals of almond and apple blossom were in the air; they carpeted the (road as in springtime) /way, as, after a summer storm,/ they lay in the (walks [?] of) /orchards at/ Hetton. Gilded cupolas and spires of alabaster shone in the sunlight.

Ambrose announced, "The City is served."

This passage, which apotheosizes Tony's absurd vision of Hetton trans-figured, is followed by the typescript, much amended, of "The Man Who Liked Dickens." By juxtaposing hallucination and the drab reality of Todd's house in the savanna immured by forest, Waugh emphasized the emptiness of Tony's ideal and presented not a sentimental Ruskin Gothic estate but a real feudal community, based on real patriarchal authority—the Indians are in many cases Todd's offspring (p. 241)—and on force—he has the only gun (p. 235). To paraphrase *Helena,* this small society is based on power without grace; the spirit informing it comes from limited and sentimental under-standing of what Waugh regarded as the limited and sentimental Dickens.[21] Ironically, therefore, Tony has found the reality behind the delusive object of his quest: having sought the form without awareness of spiritual content, an embroidered Camelot rather than the Grail, he is left bound in undiffer-entiated time, like Ovid's Sybil reduced to a voice, without hope of rescue or redemption.[22]

Waugh noted in 1946 that *A Handful of Dust,* his favorite book until he wrote *Brideshead,* "dealt entirely with behavior. It was humanist and con-tained all I had to say about humanism."[23] Waugh apparently meant by this term specifically secular, anthropocentric philosophies. Thus in quite a different way from *Black Mischief,* this novel illustrates the assertion in "Converted to Rome" that "civilization . . . has not in itself the power of survival. It came into being through Christianity, and without it has not significance or power to command allegiance."[24] Todd's clearing holds living death, but no more so than contemporary London or, despite its traditional decencies, the destroyed and artificially rebuilt Hetton Abbey. Even more artfully than in his previous work Waugh used art to embody rather than to

21. See Richard Wasson, *"A Handful of Dust:* Critique of Victorianism," *Modern Fiction Studies* 7 (1961–62): 327–37.

22. See my "Title and Theme in *A Handful of Dust,* " *Evelyn Waugh Newsletter* 6 (Autumn, 1972):1.

23. Waugh, "Fan-Fare," p. 60.

24. *Daily Express,* October 20, 1930, p. 10.

state theme, and for this reason *A Handful of Dust* remains, despite Waugh's preferences, not only his greatest achievement but, as Frank Kermode has called it, "one of the most distinguished novels of the century."[25]

25. Frank Kermode, *Puzzles and Epiphanies* (New York: Chilmark Press, 1962), p. 171.

5 Wit – and Structural Alterations
Scoop

During the two years between the publication of *A Handful of Dust* and the writing of the opening chapters of *Scoop*, Waugh's political and religious convictions were becoming, if not firmer, more strongly articulated. In *Edmund Campion*, written during the fall and winter of 1934, he blended narrative and apologetics, and he consolidated his position as Catholic spokesman in letters, articles, and reviews for the *Tablet*. All of these were written solely for personal satisfaction and out of gratitude: royalties for the biography went to Campion Hall at Oxford; work for the *Tablet*, donated to his friend Douglas Woodruff, gave Waugh a voice in the official paper of the Catholic Diocese of Westminister, a paper that under the previous editor had attacked both *Black Mischief* and *A Handful of Dust* as irreligious.[1]

Also becoming more pronounced, though tied to no party or program, were Waugh's views on international politics and England's place in them. On his first trip to Africa in 1930, Waugh wrote sympathetically of the English settlers in the highlands of Kenya and disparagingly of the East Indian immigrants and concluded that "it is just worth considering the possibility that there may be something valuable behind the indefensible and inexplicable assumption of superiority by the Anglo-Saxon race."[2] In 1933, writing on the centenary of the abolitionist William Wilberforce, Waugh questioned the ability of freed slaves to function in a civilized way, calling their descendants in the British Empire "a shiftless and dissolute lot," attacking the Liberian regime's "rigid racial bar between the immigrant and aboriginal negroes" and the "system of forced labour more onerous than the slavery from which they were themselves freed," and criticizing Wilberforce as being "inflated by the true nineteenth century arrogance of thinking a little local uplift could reverse the development of centuries." Waugh concluded that

1. See the account by Christopher Sykes, *Evelyn Waugh: A Biography* (Boston: Little, Brown and Co., 1975), pp. 122–23, 140.
2. Evelyn Waugh, *Remote People* (London: Duckworth, 1931), p. 191.

"British power and British sentiment were strong enough to upset" an ancient system, "but British intelligence was not up to anticipating the problem it created."[3]

By 1935, as Abyssinian-Italian relations deteriorated, Waugh had become a spokesman not merely for Western civilization—in view of his statement about Catholicism as the basis of Western culture, not a surprising development—but for progress. Months before he decided to become a war correspondent, he had lost the largely aesthetic interest "in the border lands of conflicting cultures and states of development, where ideas, uprooted from their traditions, become wildly changed in transplantion."[4] Instead he maintained that "it is one of the facts of history that it is impossible for two peoples of widely different cultures to live side by side. Sooner or later one must absorb the other. It is not necessarily the higher culture which survives. It is the more virile. Early history is full of the records of advanced and fine cultures being absorbed by barbarians." Abyssinia was in Waugh's view barbarous by any test or standard, not merely inhabited by picturesque survivors from a happier age who chose not to accept the gadgetry and industrialization of Europe but "capriciously and violently governed" with insufficient power "to cope with its own lawless elements." Furthermore, the Abyssinians were themselves imperialists, holding and exploiting a number of subject races by force—an argument that probably has more weight in the 1980s than it did in 1935. Consequently, Waugh supported Italian ambitions and concluded that the conquest of Abyssinia, "an object which any patriotic European can applaud, will be of service to the world."[5]

By the time he finished *Waugh in Abyssinia* in early October, 1936, Waugh had brushed aside not only "the peevish whinny of the nonconformist conscience"[6] from the modern Wilberforces but his own doubts about Italy's chances of success against guerrillas and lack of adequate sanitation— "they are the race who have inhabited and created the slums of the world"[7]—and about Italian use of poison gas as "intolerable, . . . an action which all friends of Italy must deplore."[8] In the book the use of gas, mentioned only in a footnote, was excused as necessary "to sterilise the bush along the line of ad-

3. Evelyn Waugh, "Was He Right to Free the Slaves?" *Daily Express,* July 15, 1933, p. 8.

4. Evelyn Waugh, *Ninety-two Days* (New York: Farrar and Rinehart, 1934), p. 6.

5. Evelyn Waugh "We Can Applaud Italy," *Evening Standard,* February 13, 1935, p. 7.

6. Evelyn Waugh, *Waugh in Abyssinia* (London: Longmans, Green and Co., 1936), p. 215.

7. See Evelyn Waugh, *The Diaries of Evelyn Waugh,* ed. Michael Davie (Boston: Little, Brown and Co., 1977), p. 402 (August 31, 1936).

8. Evelyn Waugh, "A 'Times' Correspondent," *Tablet,* January 23, 1937, p. 128.

vance,"[9] and the concluding pages glow with praise of "the eagles of ancient Rome" bringing "the inestimable gifts of fine workmanship and clear judg-ment—the true determining qualities of the human spirit by which alone, under God, man grows and flourishes."[10]

Certainty about international politics did not carry over into Waugh's career as an imaginative writer. After he finished *Campion*, he planned for a short while to write the life of Mary Tudor[11] instead of another novel. By late April, 1935, he was thinking of working in Hollywood on his way to the South Seas. And even after his first trip to Abyssinia in 1935 he seems to have had no plan to use his experience in fiction. Though he knew that Abyssinia would "make a funny novel" in October, he was conscious of reaching a climacteric when he visited Bethlehem at Christmas:

> I was of an age then—thirty-two—when, after I had struck lucky with three or four light novels, it did not appear entirely absurd, at any rate to myself, to look about for a suitable "life's work." . . . So elated was I by the beauties about me that I there and then began vaguely planning a series of books—semi-historic, semi-poetic fiction, I did not quite know what—about the long, intricate relations between England and the Holy Places.[12]

However irresolute Waugh may have been in late 1935, by the time he returned from his tour of conquered Abyssinia in September, 1936, it was, in Mrs. Stitch's term, "foregonners" that he would recast his experience in fictional form. The external pattern of *Scoop* is identical to that of *Decline and Fall*. William Boot, happily immured at the family estate, Boot Magna, is mistaken for another Boot and sent as unwilling and even more incompetent war correspondent to Ishmaelia, site of the latest ideological war. By a series of coincidences and with the aid of a mysterious financier and a beautiful adventuress, he gets the only genuine scoop, while his more cynical but no more competent colleagues are pursuing rumor clear across the horizon and out of the novel. Bewildered by his sudden fame but cannier than before, he escapes to Boot Magna and resumes, only marginally disturbed by memories of the girl, the placid, traditional, and more than slightly absurd life he loves while the outer world continues to seethe.

Neither precedent from the first trip to Abyssinia and the visit to British Guiana nor the pattern of Waugh's career gave any warning of the form that

9. Waugh, *Waugh in Abyssinia*, p. 239 n. 1.
10. *Ibid.*, p. 253.
11. Letter to A. D. Peters, February 4, 1935.
12. *Letters*, p. 100; *The Holy Places* (London: Queen Anne Press, 1952), p. 2.

Scoop would take or the difficulties that it would cause him. Characters, settings, and incidents from wartime Abyssinia figure largely and obviously in the novel: the Press Secretary, the Press Association and its idiosyncratic members, the truck journey, the pension at which William Boot stays, the nightclubs, even Rickett, the unsuccessful commercial adventurer who is transposed into the mercurial and omnicompetent Baldwin. *Scoop* ignores the real issues of the war, however—perhaps because *Waugh in Abyssinia* purged Waugh of his political opinions, more likely because he did not want to repeat the setting of *Black Mischief*—and the ruling caste of Liberia is transposed to a kind of Black Ruritania. The result is lighthearted farce in which Waugh made unexpected technical advances. But good farce does not come easily, and the process of composition dragged out over the course of sixteen months between October 15, 1936, and February 20, 1938.

The immediate impulses for the novel were practical as well as artistic. As in the case of *Decline and Fall*, Waugh needed to write a novel "so as to get spliced."[13] The sight of Lady Diana Cooper "with face expressionless in mud mask"[14] just after his return from his first trip to the war inspired his opening gambit in ridiculing the methods of contemporary journalism. The economic motive, however, created many obstacles to the pursuit of the literary. Buying, furnishing, and redecorating Piers Court; marrying and honeymooning with Laura Herbert; and settling in to receive, with considerable satisfaction, a series of callers with double-barreled names took not only a great deal of time but a considerable amount of money; anticipated revenue from the novel was less tempting than projects that could produce ready cash: a series of articles for *Nash's Pall Mall Magazine* and of book reviews for *Night and Day*, a film treatment for Sir Alexander Korda once called *Lovelies over London*, and negotations for the revision of Henri Bernstein's play *Le Venin*. Charity work may have paid better in the long run: a week before beginning *Scoop*, Waugh was reading P. G. Wodehouse's *Laughing Gas* in bed, preparing to review it, unpaid, for the *Tablet*, and though he had read Wodehouse for years, Waugh's close study of his methods in preparing the review was to have considerable influence on Waugh's novel.

He began *Scoop* on October 15, and at first he moved with his old facility, finishing the second chapter on October 29 and the third by December 14. But Korda and the Christmas season intervened, and Waugh apparently added nothing to the manuscript between December 2 and December 28, and during January, 1937, he was constantly on the move. On February 4,

13. Letter to Peters, October, 1936.
14. Waugh, *Diaries,* p. 391 (July 7, 1936).

however, he retreated to Chagford, where he corrected proofs, wrote articles, questioned Peters about negotiations for the sale of the incomplete manuscript as a serial, and finished the first half of Chapter 4, probably to the point at which William Boot finally leaves Croydon Airport. The rest of the chapter and all of its successor, which takes William to the verge of landing in Ishmaelia, went to Peters early in April. But Waugh was beginning to be uneasy about the book: it had, in his view, "good material but shaky structure."[15] After his wedding and part of the honeymoon, however, he added to the manuscript, probably through the first half of Book 2.

By full summer he had faced the fact that serial rights could not be sold, and he revised the first chapter for independent publication.[16] Though the revision did not immediately find a market, it may have forced Waugh to look more closely at the novel as a whole, for during the first week in July he wrote to Peters that he was entirely rewriting the book, now titled *Scoop*, to be ready for the Christmas trade. This resolution produced little result, for in late September he informed Peters that because neither serialization nor publication before Christmas seemed possible he had temporarily abandoned the book. Two months later, however, he expressed both in his diary and in a letter to Peters his satisfaction with the new shape the novel was taking, and, though subject to many distractions, he pushed on. Roughead had pages 101 to 251 of the typescript—probably all of Book 2— by January 17, 1938; a month later Waugh promised to deliver "three short chapters"—probably Book 3—by the twentieth; and on February 22, Roughead sent the final pages, 252 to 314, to Waugh's American publisher, Little Brown.

What Waugh did in composing and revising the novel is not as clear as the chronological account makes it sound. For one thing, this is the earliest Waugh manuscript at the University of Texas that was not bound but was placed in a box designed to resemble a bound volume—a practice he followed only when the manuscript was exceptionally chaotic. It is possible to reconstruct from the physical evidence of the manuscript an outline of the novel as Waugh conceived and wrote it, to speculate about why he found it unsatisfactory, and in the process to learn a good deal about Waugh's working definition of "structure."

A summary of the basic events of the original version of the novel would not reveal marked differences from the published version, but in structure—

---

15. *Ibid.*, p. 420 (the entry is dated February 4, but was obviously written near Easter).

16. Evelyn Waugh, "Mrs. Stitch Fails for the First Time," *Town and Country* 92 (November, 1937):56, 108, 110, 137.

the disposition of the events—the two differ considerably. Mrs. Stitch begins both, but originally she made only one brief appearance in the first five chapters[17] after her conversation with Lord Copper. The history of Ishmaelia and the account of its recent troubles that now begin Book 2 came in manuscript immediately after William's departure from England. The cause of the upheaval there is a dispute over brandy butter at a Jackson Christmas dinner, and the information is the product of William's reading of "press cuttings, pamphlets and Chatham house (booklets) /reports/ which were put into his hands by Mr. Salter at his final leave-taking." The takeoff, passage through customs, and encounter on the train—here the initial one—with the mysterious polyglot financier are then given in flashback. Book 2 begins with what is now the second section of Chapter 1, the journalists' arrival in Jacksonburg, and proceeds as in the book version until approximately section 10 (p. 135). This is followed by William's meeting with an old school friend, Bannister, now vice-consul; by Corker's lament that the journalists are not being accorded proper respect, William's move from the hideously crowded Hotel Liberty to the Pension Dressler, and his meeting with the lovely Kätchen; by Shumble's false scoop; and finally by William's real scoop. Originally the press secretary was Bonham Carter Jackson, and even when he became Dr. Benito, he viewed William's decision to let all the other reporters leave without him with friendly understanding rather than the bland discouragement and attempted bribery with which he responded in the final version. The climax of Book 2 is impossible to reconstruct because the manuscipt has been so completely rewritten—even the paper is totally different from that of the preceding pages—that no trace of hesitation survives, but it is clear from Waugh's preparations that the massive Swede, Erik Olafsen, and the dapper man who calls himself Baldwin had major roles in it. The final chapters, titled in manuscript "Harvest Moon" and then "Harvest Thanksgiving," survive in what is obviously a second or later manuscript draft. The concluding pages lack any mention of Mrs. Stitch, Corker, or Pigge in Waugh's series of paragraphs settling the characters' futures; Kätchen's letter is introduced not as the last in this series but separately, after William goes upstairs. He contemplates answering it, and the manuscript concludes with "Outside the owls (swooped) hunted among the stubble."

To give better shape to his material, Waugh made two kinds of major alteration, both of them apparently in the typescript stage: what he termed

---

17. Evelyn Waugh, *Scoop* (Boston: Little, Brown and Co., 1938), p. 65. This edition is cited because Waugh used it in collating the manuscript with the printed version. Hereafter it is cited parenthetically in the text.

"insertions made in revision"[18] and reorderings and revisions. Neither is part of the basic manuscript, the first set being laid in a separate foolscap folio, and most of the second not surviving in manuscript stage at all.

Waugh reordered material on three basic principles: chronology, logic, and dramatic effectiveness. Both of the flashbacks in the first version were removed, and William's progress from Croydon to the Blue Train and his meeting with Bannister were presented in direct scene. In the process Waugh added or augmented — the evidence is not conclusive — William's first meeting with Baldwin at the airport to give the latter an obligation that he can repay and changed Baldwin's alarm at William's casual query about his destination to Baldwin's question about and laconic interest in William's. Both are more characteristic of Baldwin as finally envisioned. The second major alteration in Book 1 was the removal of the Ishmaelian history from the beginning of Chapter 4 and its connection with William to the beginning of Book 2, all of which is set in Ishmaelia. Perspective as well as logic dictated this change, for, in separating the material entirely from William, Waugh not only preserves his amateur standing (both mentions of his research were removed for the book version) but, in putting it entirely in the omniscient author's voice, creates an effective contrast between his authority and the bumbling inconscience of the journalists. For much the same purpose Waugh had already inserted into the manuscript Bannister's survey of local conditions later in Book 2 (pp. 140–41), including the preparation for the reporters' fruitless journey to the nonexistent town of Laku, put on the map because, when asked the name of a hill, a native replied "Laku"—Ishmaelian for "I don't know." And as the journalists leave, Waugh revised to broaden the visual perspective to have the sun break through clouds to spread not just across Jacksonburg but "the heavens" (p.179).

18. The "insertions made on revision" were:

    1.   Troutbeck and the telegram, pp. 26–28: "Curiosity and resentment . . . , After an early departure . . . ."

    2.   Mrs. Stitch in the Gentleman's lavatory, pp. 51–55: "William was left standing . . . Lord Copper was at his desk."

    3.   a)   Revised introduction of Corker, p. 84: "The newcomer was British . . . . steaming visibly."

            b)   The Frenchman's protest, p. 86: "The Frenchman leaned towards William . . . 'Hope I'm not butting in,' said the Englishman."

            c)   Corker buying curios, p. 90: "The winches were silent . . . —working for a paper."

    4.   Introduction of Pappenhacker, pp. 40–41: "See that man there . . . .go to Ishmaelia."

    5.   Mrs. Stitch and John Courtney Boot at the Duchess of Stayle's Ball, pp. 100–101: all of Section 5, Chapter 5, Book 1.

Authorial control of a different sort was needed for the reordering of incidents in the first third of Book 2. The original arrangement had several flaws, not least of which was aimlessness and repetition. Bannister had been introduced too soon, before the disorientation for which he provides relief had become comically and acutely painful. The same is true of William's move to the Pension Dressler and his meeting with Kätchen. By reordering, Waugh alternates discomfort and surcease, disappointment and relief. Corker's lament and lack of direction, followed by the issuing of hastily altered identity cards for prostitutes, is succeeded by the comfort of the familiar—recurrent in the novel—in the meeting with Bannister; Shumble's false scoop gives way to Bannister's precise and knowledgeable discourse that provides William with a real scoop, which, anticlimactically, is aborted, ending Chapter 1. Chapter 2 begins aimlessly but gives a brief glimpse of Kätchen and leads to William's well-motivated move to the Pension Dressler, a surrogate Boot Magna in its ramshackle arrangements and, in the root sense, familiarity. There he finds Kätchen, and both place and person help remove him from the world of the journalists. By the end of the chapter they are gone, and the affair has been consummated, so that Chapter 3 begins "in a new world."

The new disposition of materials allows a steady progression of interest and may have been the result of Waugh's growing understanding of his major themes as well as his plot. This is certainly true of the insertions placed at the end of the manuscript. Three of the four are structural in the neoformalist rather than the Aristotelian sense: they are clearly intended to establish thematic contrasts rather than to advance the action. Those concerning Mrs. Stitch are the easiest to explain. She reappears in the basic manuscript only twice after the first chapter, the second appearance hundreds of pages removed from the first. Waugh obviously realized that this was too long, and he inserted two major scenes in which she figures centrally. In the first he involves William Boot in her antics, when, mistaken in the *Beast* office for a reporter of local news, he is sent to discover what she and her little car are doing in a men's underground lavatory, the ironic first fruit of her efforts on behalf of John Courtney Boot. This incident also gave Waugh the occasion of rendering more portentous William's audience with Lord Copper. He postponed it and emphasized the contrast between the uproar of the outer office and the quiet in Lord Copper's, symbolized by special typewriters whose keys "made no more sound than the drumming of a bishop's finger tips on an upholstered prie-dieu" (changed from "plush armchair"). Then, to underline firmly the breakdown of "The Stitch Service"—the phrase that becomes the title of Book 1 was itself an addition to the manuscript—Waugh added a final scene to Book 1 in which Mrs. Stitch and John Courtney Boot speculate about what has happened and lament his failure to escape the American girl by going to Ishmaelia. And finally, though represented in no manuscript stage, her future is included in the series at the end of the novel, one more instance of aimless activity.

Two other sets of insertions, the creation of Pappenhacker and the augmentation of Corker, are clearly complementary. Originally used for the character now called Cohen, the name Pappenhacker was transferred to the young Jewish socialist of the *Daily Twopence.* Unlike the other journalists, he is intelligent—"the cleverest man in Fleet Street"—well educated, and unillusioned about his job. He also serves as foil to William, leaving Croydon with typewriter and small bag in contrast to the mountains of equipment William is burdened with. He is no less ridiculous than the others, however, with "great horn goggles and a receding, stubbly chin" (p. 41), treating waiters rudely because politeness helps to "bolster up the capitalist system," and playing with a toy train (pp. 115-16).

Corker is Pappenhacker's antithesis: cynical and credulous at once, ignorant, brash, and voluble. If insertions over-page and separate additions represent different periods of composition, Waugh twice went back to what are now pages 84 to 90 and added a total of sixty-two lines, or two and a half pages. The additions do not alter Corker's character, but they reveal it more thoroughly. First, to underscore the impression that he appears in answer to William's thoughts of home, as Baldwin does later, Waugh revised the flat, "And at that moment another voice," to read, "And suddenly, miasmically, in the fiery wilderness, there came an apparition," and continued, first in an over-page insertion and then in a revision of the typescript, to emphasize Corker's sweat-sodden appearance. Another over-page insertion describes the Captain's lady and is followed immediately in the book by the added exchange between William and the disapproving Frenchman. This is itself a revision of a longer passage giving unnecessary farcical detail. A bit later Waugh inserted over-page the bottle of "Edouard VIII" Scotch, made in Saigon; it is as ludicrous as the canceled passage, in which various functionaries shrug off Corker's presence at the captain's table, but the revision focuses on Corker. Finally Waugh added after first draft the passage in which Corker describes his collection of Oriental souvenirs.

He was not finished with Corker, however, who becomes more and more vivid as the novel progresses because of his utterances, the most memorable of which are revisions. To an offer to find him a good mission boy as servant, he first responded, "That's very decent of you," far removed from the Corkerish "Sounds like hell to me" of the revision. Waugh also changed his plaint about the journalists' situation to make it more economical and less purposeful. On several other occasions Corker's speeches are revised to embody clichés reflective of his professional myopia about language.

The fourth addition is local rather than structural and, though longer than most insertions in the manuscript, typifies those that Waugh made to exploit material more effectively, to adjust tone, and to move delicately along the line between genuinely amusing and stereotyped material drawn from the English farcical tradition. This addition comes at the end of Book 1, Chapter 2, section 1. The first draft does not contain the final sentence on page 26 describing Troutbeck's mixed reaction to the telegram's arrival and the character of the servants' meal, and it ends with the text of Salter's telegram. In the added material (p. 27 and first phrase on p. 28), Uncle Theodore's shady past and desire to go to London—both elements in the novel's resolution—are further emphasized, as is "the elaborate household machinery" of Boot Magna and William's reluctance to leave it.

Throughout the process of composition and revision Waugh steadily elaborated to achieve greater complexity and variety. Thus he changed from seven to ten the number of servants at Boot Magna, broke off the introduction of William's Uncle Bernard to insert Aunt Anne, and made the arrival of the newspaper the occasion of even more comic anxiety by inserting details about its usual fate (p. 24). This process of elaboration was sometimes due to his decision to dramatize, to make summary seem more dramatic, or to specify. For instance, Kätchen observes that moving the bag of stones to her room "will be difficult." The revision to, "It is up a ladder," is obviously more effective (p. 161). While Salter's terrified and laborious progress through the alien countryside is kept in flashback, Waugh realized in the process of writing that the detailed summary of the ordeal (pp. 289-90) would be much funnier than the original, simple cut from station to front door. On the same principle—the more awful the better—he deleted William's consciousness of his circumstances in the Liberty Hotel and moved directly to oppressive details that graphically reveal those circumstances (p. 129).

Three other revisions show Waugh's care for the smallest details of thematic reinforcement and contrast. William must get Ishmaelian visas from each of the rival consulates, and Waugh established a basic contrast between that of the Communists, in a basement beneath the office of a shady doctor in Maida Vale, and that of the Nazis in South Kensington, far more elegant. Originally Waugh had both consuls charge fifty pounds for the visa, but in the detail of the not-yet-delivered rubber stamp to the Nazi consul he discovered opportunity for comic inconguity. When it arrives C.O.D., the charge is four and eightpence, and the revision of the fee to five shillings, with the consul returning and "jingling four pennies in his breeches pocket" (p. 70), undercuts his pretensions. The second instance concerns the animals in the yard of the Pension Dressler. Both the three-legged dog and the milch-goat are to be important, the first to signal William and Kätchen's sexual encounter by his "cries of protest" and the second to begin the counteroffensive against Benito's forces by downing his chief aide. At first Waugh wrote, "The three-legged dog flew out of his barrel, barking; the milch-goat shot at him like a cork from a popgun." Then, avoiding duplication, he changed the dog's action to "barked furiously from," establishing the contrast between motionless noise and soundless velocity. A third example comes in William's "Lush Places," at the very end of the novel, where a phrase about pheasants originally followed that about "maternal rodents." Waugh deleted it, perhaps to preserve the contrast with the column about the great crested grebe at the beginning of the novel and — this conjecture is based on the supposition that he was working with both manuscript and typescript — to prepare for the contrast between winged predator and earth-bound prey in the unforgettable final sentence of the revised novel: "Outside the owls hunted maternal rodents and their furry broods" (p. 321).

Though the final sentence and indeed the last three pages introduce a note that moves the novel away from mere farce, it is obviously farcical. The descent of *Scoop* from P. G. Wodehouse, obvious enough from internal evidence, is rendered inescapable by Waugh's diary entry, six days before he began the novel, that he had been reading Wodehouse in bed and by his subsequent review of *Laughing Gas*. His observations in that review, as well as the manuscript and text of *Scoop* itself, show that, though he transcended his master, he was an observant and dexterous pupil. As his review showed, he was not uncritical; two "very unworthy jokes" are quoted and sadly compared to those of "a wireless comedian," but the "superb dialogue and narrative grace" gain his approval. Citing, "'What ho,' I said reverently," as "a classic sentence of this style," he goes on to analyze the speech of a character whose soul has been translated into another body:

> "Funny you should say that. Because myself, in a nutshell, is precisely what I'm bally well not." The operative words are "nutshell" and "precisely."[19]

Waugh applied even more exacting standards to his own work. Though not beyond mere burlesque, as in Salter's "How are your boots, root?" (p. 35), he concentrated on more elaborate contortions of language that blur the distinction between sense and nonsense. Salter's analysis of Ishmaelian politics in terms of Black, White, and Red, over which Waugh understandably had to take pains, is worthy of a Woosterish "Oh, ah" as well as William's

---

19. Evelyn Waugh, "An English Humourist," *Tablet* 168 (October 17, 1936):533.

"Up to a point," which continues another joke. Earlier the art of fiddling an expense account is exemplified by Sir Jocelyn Hitchcock's entry of three hundred pounds for camels in Shanghai. At first William's response was, "Perhaps camels are very expensive in Shanghai. Anyway I don't want camels." Waugh may have thought this too ingenuous, and he changed it to, "But I don't think I shall know what to do with a camel" (p. 42), which has the additional advantages of implying a crumbling in William's resistance to becoming a correspondent and representing in its structure the laborious movement of his mind. Improved comic timing in the Wodehouse manner was probably the motive for revising William's initial rejection of the offer from, "I mean, how will it look in *Lush Places* when I start writing about sandstorms and lions. Pretty unlush," to, picking up after sandstorms, "lions and whatever they have in [Ishmaelia].[20] Not *lush, I mean*" (pp. 39-40).

Both character and style were obviously influenced by Wodehouse. One characteristic device is the "take," in which the character absorbs information in slow motion. Working on the passage involving Lord Copper's demand that William be produced to show him how to draw a cow, Waugh demonstrated that he had profited from his reading:

FIRST DRAFT	FINAL DRAFT
"Well, have him come back."	"Well, have him come back.
"He is on his way back now. It was Boot who brought off the (big scoop) /great story/ in Ishmaelia. (He was your own choice, Lord Copper.)"	What's he doing there? Who sent him?"
"Ah, yes . . . ."	"He is on his way back now. It was Boot who brought off the great story in Ishmaelia. When we scooped Hitchcock," he added, for Lord Copper was frowning in menacing way. Slowly the noble face lightened. "Ah, yes . . . . [p. 261]

Lord Emsworth could not react with more glacial slowness. Later Waugh encapsulated the poverty of Copper's mind in the inserted cliché, "The banquet must go on," and used it as a refrain for the rest of the scene.

Politics as well as the press felt the Wodehousian influence. Originally the prime minster, ordered by Copper to give Boot the knighthood that miscarries to John Courtney Boot, deals directly with his principal private

20. In manuscript the space is left blank; Waugh had not yet decided on the country's name.

secretary. In revision Waugh moved the scene several steps nearer absurdity and rendered the mistake inevitable by sending the competent assistants on vacation and leaving details to the prime minister's "third and fourth secretaries, unreliable young men related to his wife" (p. 264) who address him as uncle.

All farce, including Wodehouse's, needs a victim, and in *Scoop* the role is lugubriously filled by Mr. Salter, foreign editor of the *Beast*, whose major sufferings stem from his desire to have a quiet job and his ignorance and fear of the countryside. Waugh added the passage in which Salter calls the Foreign Contacts adviser to learn the route to Boot Magna, carrying the ridiculous a bit further. The augmentation of his odyssey through the fields, already discussed, illustrated Waugh's sense that detail was important, but he also knew when to cut back. On Salter's return to London he is surveyed by his superior. In garbled first drafts the manuscript reads:

> The Managing Editor of the Beast was not easily moved to pity but (the ravaged figure which hobbled into his room) /Mr. Salter's appearance/ caused him at the sight of Mr. Salter next afternoon caused him to lower his cup and say in a shocked voice "I say old man you look terrrible."

This must have seemed overly explicit and perhaps too reminiscent of the *Boy's Own Paper* brand of humor. The final draft reads: "The Managing Editor of the *Beast* was not easily moved to pity. 'I say, Salter' he said, almost reverently, 'you look terrible'" (p. 308). Waugh had no objection to broad farce, however, for in the scene in which the two men toss a coin to determine who will tell Lord Copper the bad news, Waugh decided that having it roll under the desk would be both funnier than having a winner and more effective as a way of introducing Uncle Theodore. Oddly enough, the broadest joke in the novel, the names *Beast* and *Brute* for the rival newspapers, occurred to him very late in the process of composition and were substituted for *Voice* and *Excess*; it was probably the alliteration of "Boot of the *Beast*" as much as satiric intent that dictated the change.

Waugh was not content to remain within the narrow if delightful limits even of Wodehousian farce, partly because of his (largely implied) judgments but mostly because his imaginative love of language made him restive. Wodehouse and the English farcical tradition could account for the inserted detail at the end of the Communist consul's speech about his turning on the radio again when he learns that William wants a visa rather than an interview, but something more was required to enable Waugh to discern that he need not give the text of Sir Jocelyn Hitchcock's cable, included in manuscript, about the imaginary interview with Smiles at Laku and to use the moving of the pin on the map instead of an imagined journey to symbolize at a single brilliant stroke the journalists' lack of contact with reality (p. 145). Moreover, Waugh's interest in words, always strong, was developing into a concern for metaphor and analogy and leading him to the creation of more complex emotional states. This process operates in two passages in the manuscript. One deals with Kätchen and her pseudo-husband in William's collapsible boat just before they disappear. Waugh's first and final versions read:

FIRST DRAFT	FINAL DRAFT
The two figures sat opposite one another, knees touching, expectant /as though in an Amusement Park/ like holiday makers, lovers for the day's outing, who had (waited) /stood/ in the queue, paid their sixpence, and now waited for the attendant to launch them upon the ornamental waters, to drift a few minutes among grottoes & transparencies[?]	The two figures sat opposite one another, knees touching, expectant, as though embarking upon the ornamental waters of a fair-ground; lovers for the day's outing, who had stood close in a queue, (taken their tickets) and now waited (to launch) half-reluctant to launch into the closer intimacy of (the dim) /the/ grottoes and transparencies. [p. 234]

The second version, especially after the deletion of the tickets, emphasizes the relationship of the pair rather than the outer world, and the shift of ornamental waters to the beginning creates more quickly the atmosphere of fantasy and remoteness picked up in "half-reluctant" and "intimacy," an atmosphere wholly absent from first draft. Moreover, the second version, on the evidence of the manuscript written immediately after the first, draws the reader closer to Kätchen and the nameless German and makes them, for an instant, more real than figures of farce can be.

The same process is observable in the passage describing William's emotional response to Kätchen. Waugh began with the image of William as previously "celibate and heart-whole"; after manuscript he added "landbound," but even in manuscript he developed, in a second draft, a metaphor: ". . . Now, for the first time, he was scalded and (consumed) /submerged/ in (the fiery seas? that) strange, deep waters." Those versed in psychology might find significant Waugh's association of submersion, heat, and strong emotion here and in "the hot spring of anarchy rose from deep furnaces."[21] Here Waugh detected the mixed metaphor before publication (the second he

21. Evelyn Waugh, *Brideshead Revisited* (Boston: Little, Brown and Co., 1946), p. 44. Waugh deleted the mixed metaphor in the Chapman and Hall revised edition of 1960.

overlooked for fifteen years), and in the process of removing it he developed and strengthened the conceit:

> Now for the first time he was far from shore, submerged among deep waters, below wind and tide, where huge trees raised their spongy flowers and monstrous things without fur or feather, wing or foot, passed silently, in submarine twilight. A lush place. [p. 181]

For the Waugh who had developed through *A Handful of Dust*, this is a remarkable, in fact, an unaccountable, passage. He had used symbolic detail to force the reader to judge the affair of Basil and Prudence in *Black Mischief*, but nowhere before had he given this developed or complex a view, however indirect, of a character's mental state. Paul Pennyfeather's sexual initiation is presented by a rustle of silk and the laconic, "There was no mistake," but his feelings at the time or later are pointedly not developed. The world William has entered is both attractive and repellent, soft and subtly threatening, with imagery at the same time phallic and embryonic.

Not surprisingly, the characters began developing new complexity in their dialogue and in authorial analysis. Waugh's treatment of Kätchen is a good example. Neither above the law, like Margot Beste-Chetwynde, nor subject to nemesis like Prudence Courteney, nor as ignorant of her past and future as Chastity, she is at once innocent and rapacious. Waugh revised several passages to emphasize these disparate qualities. When Kätchen sells her husband's mineral specimens to William, at first she makes this arrangement: "You shall buy them for twenty pounds and then, when my husband comes back and is angry, you will sell them to him again." On reflection this must have seemed too simple, for Waugh revised it to read: "You shall buy them and then, when my husband comes back and says they are worth more than twenty pounds, you will pay him the difference" (p. 166). The calm and unmalicious assumption that leaves William open for further exploitation on demand is to become characteristic of Kätchen. At the same time she verges on the pathetic, coming on the scene dripping wet to buy medicine and coughing out the end of a laugh. There was always the danger that she might become pathetic beyond the limits of the dominant tone. In manuscript she very nearly did. Telling William about having, at sixteen, worked in a dance hall in England, she adds:

> "I don't know. It was by the sea. I met my husband there("), he was drunk that evening and next day he was sorry. He was the first man I knew who was ever sorry."

Immediately thereafter she answers William's, "How long must you wait for him?" with, "I don't know. I might go with you now and then when he comes back I will go with him." The first passage emphasizes too strongly Kätchen's role as waif; the second veers too far toward callousness. Sometime between the manuscript and final drafts Waugh brought the tone of both under control. The first now continues: "I met my husband there; he was so pleased to find someone who would talk German with him. How he talked . . . ", and to the second, after, "I don't know," Waugh inserted the passage (pp. 203–204) in which Kätchen makes a false nose from the champagne bottle's foil, says "I have been serious too much, too often," and continues, hopefully, with the possibility of going now with William and later with her husband. By this means her relationship with her husband is made more personal than sexual, and both her essential fidelity and the external strains on it are made clearer, while her playfulness emphasizes her essential innocence and softens the abruptness of her offer.

Waugh faced similar problems in portraying William, moving him in revision further and further away from journalistic competence toward farcical amateurism and at the same time giving him a psychological depth new to his fiction. The first process, fairly simple, consisted of deleting references to William's research on Ishmaelia, strengthening the role of Corker as journalistic mentor, and altering the style of William's cables. His first, about the false scoop, read in manuscript, in capitals:

> Report completely groundless Saturdays arrival well known Swiss Resident Giraud employed railway Russia diplomatically unrepresented here.

Not very noteworthy, but far less likely to cause editorial qualms than the book's version, also in capitals:

> All rot about Bolshevik he is only ticket collector ass called Shumble thought his beard false but its perfectly all right really will cable again if there is any news very wet here yours William Boot

And Waugh cut "Stop" from a later cable to preserve William's total innocence of journalistic protocol and sustain the rambling breathlessness of his style (p. 173).

The process of giving William what is in effect a subconscious with an active store of images is more complex. He is the first Waugh character, excluding the delirious, who experiences any but a conscious, waking state. Early in the novel Waugh describes his desire "to go up in an airplane," a desire that one need not be a psychologist to interpret, and makes it clear that it is deeply internalized. Nannie Bloggs's knowledge of and promise to abet it was an almost immediate afterthought, designed to emphasize William's infantile state and to add the farcical touch of her belief that the Irish Sweepstakes is "a Popish trick," but this daylight knowledge is subordinated to the fact that the desire still haunted his dreams and returned to him, more vividly, in the minute of transition between sleep and wakefulness, on occasions of physical exhaustion and inner content, hacking home in the twilight after a good day's hunt, fuddled with port on the not infrequent birthdays of the Boot household. [p. 62]

Later Waugh inserted a different dream, "about his private school—now, he noted without surprise, peopled by Negroes and governed by his grandmother" (pp. 80–81). This was probably added as much to underscore the subtle similarities of the Boot and Jackson families as to add depth to William's psyche, but it is the first fictional dream in Waugh's novels, and there is no doubt that psychological as well as stylistic considerations dictated the change of William's attitude toward Kätchen's rebuff from, "His anger softened and ceased, and he fell asleep," to, "His anger softened and turned to shame, then to a light melancholy; soon he fell asleep" (p. 189). The emotional range covered in a single sentence took earlier characters a whole book to span. And the uncertainty and delicacy of feeling in William's leading up to the question, "Is he really your husband?" (p. 191), is far beyond the scope of any previous character except, perhaps, Tony Last.

Even this exception points toward an essential contrast between the two. Tony has a vestigial internal life, but, as his concept of Hetton shows, it is formalized, static, tending toward allegory rather than symbol. William's, though not highly complex, is not overdetermined. His store of images— based on the concept "lush places" or "the green places of my heart" (p. 237), on the sea metaphor, and on the "region of light and void and silence" that he hopes to reach in flight—is introduced sparingly but at significant moments in the story. On board ship, confronted with the unappetizing and undoubtedly poisonous fish served for dinner, William invokes the image of the trout at home and of associated "colours of distant Canaan, of deserted Eden" just before Corker's entrance. Waugh took the trouble to insert the image of "the barbed fly, unnaturally brilliant (above them /over them/) /over head/" perhaps to prefigure the predatory owls at the end, and to delete any mention of human activity or even presence. The Edenic motif is repeated and in revision made more emphatic when, returned to Boot Magna, William looks out the window at the moonlit park:

> On such a night as this, not (a month) /four weeks/ back, the tin roofs of Jacksonburg had (been [illegible] white with moonlight) /lain open to the [illegible] sky/; a three-legged dog had awoken, started from his barrel in Frau Dressler's (yard) /garden/, and all over town, in yards and refuse heaps, the pariahs had taken up his cries of protest. [p. 275]

Waugh may have used "garden" to void repeating "yard," but the connotations are obvious, and "lain open to the sky" is unquestionably sexual. These overtones have been strengthened because they have to carry over forty-six pages to the penultimate paragraph: "Before getting into bed he drew the curtain and threw open the window. Moonlight streamed into the room" (p. 321). Unlike Paul Pennyfeather, the passage implies, William cannot entirely erase the memory of his love affair; unlike Tony Last, he can see out of his enclosure.

So, of course, could Evelyn Waugh, and from the chosen confines of Piers Court, where he had settled in as one of the "New Rustics" or "New Countrymen,"[22] he regarded with alarm as well as amusement the literary and political worlds. Journalism had sunk so low as to be unfit for an Englishman, let alone a gentleman;[23] literary values were becoming distorted by the mutual self-praise of the Auden group;[24] the leftist attack on "escapism" was really an attack on imaginative writing;[25] "the present neurotic state of the general mind"[26] gave him little hope for the future.

In these circumstances, Waugh's praise of P. G. Wodehouse and emulation of him in *Scoop* were the result of literary nostalgia, just as his creation of Boot Magna reflected his social nostalgia for, as he put it in *Vile Bodies*, "great, healing draughts from the well of Edwardian certainty." Wodehouse's novels appealed to Waugh because the characters were "happily segregated from any contact with reality" by the Master's use of "a carefully selected range of emotions and attitudes."[26] Boot Magna was attractive because it lay beyond the rule of Lord Copper and his bumbling political underlings. Moreover, Boot Magna is the first of Waugh's country houses to be full and lively, its inhabitants self-satisfied in the full sense of the term. In creating the Boots and for that matter the Jacksons, another large and jolly family, Waugh may have remembered the Dedjasmach Matafara—the only Abyssinian he seems to have liked—whose courtesy gave Waugh "a glimpse of the age-old, traditional order that still survived, gracious and sturdy, out of sight beyond the brass bands and bunting, the topees and humane humbug of Tafari's regime; of an order doomed to destruction."[27]

22. See Waugh's essay, "The New Rustics," *Harper's Bazaar* (London) 20 (July, 1939): 20–21, 72, and his review "The New Countryman," *Spectator* 161 (July 8, 1938): 54–55.

23. Evelyn Waugh, "An Old Liberal Says his Say," *Night and Day* 1 (September 23, 1937), 24. It also contains an attack on the English Liberal conscience.

24. See Evelyn Waugh, "First Things First," *Spectator* 160 (May 20, 1938), 930; and Evelyn Waugh, "Present Discontents," *Tablet* 172 (December 3, 1938), 743–44. The latter, a review of Cyril Connolly's *Enemies of Promise,* is particularly important.

25. Evelyn Waugh, "A Victorian Escapist," *Spectator* 160 (May 6, 1938): 813–14.

26. See not only Waugh's "An English Humourist" but also his "An Angelic Doctor: The Work of Mr. P. G. Wodehouse," *Tablet* 173 (June 17, 1939): 786–87.

27. Waugh, *Waugh in Abyssinia,* p. 202.

Waugh's own aesthetic and thematic resolutions in *Scoop* were unstable. The final pages indicate that the aimless careening of the outside world will continue and probably prevail, and there is a moralistic tone quite unlike the placid acceptance at the end of *Decline and Fall*. In reviews for the secular as well as the Catholic press Waugh began to emphasize the importance of Christianity for the artist because "a writer's material must be the individual soul."[28] Moreover, Waugh obviously had a sense that it was time for a change. His collected novels had been mentioned in *Night and Day* as the work of "an author we can read for amusement and not for exercise, somebody who isn't standard and isn't an ornament to any home."[29] Like John Plant, his novelist-narrator in *Work Suspended*, he may have felt that "I have got as good as I ever can be at this particular sort of writing. I need new worlds to conquer." Plant's editor is soothed by the admission that the work in progress merely has "some new technical experiments. I don't suppose the average reader will notice them at all."[30] Most of Waugh's readers probably noticed nothing new in *Scoop*, but Waugh was contemplating more radical departures from his early method that were not to be fully realized until six years after *Scoop* was published.

28. Evelyn Waugh, "Art from Anarchy," *Night and Day* 1 (September 16, 1937): 24-25.
29. *Night and Day,* 1 (December 16, 1937): 26.
30. Evelyn Waugh, *Work Suspended* (London: Chapman and Hall, 1942), pp. 43,44.

6

Divine Purpose
and Pagan World:
Brideshead Revisited

In 1944, Waugh could call his new book a "Magnum Opus" without blushing, but it is clear that as early as the late 1930s he had begun regarding himself as a serious spokesman for quality in fiction and that the war interrupted, perhaps redirected, but did not abate his ambtion. In 1945 he hoped to please "those who have the leisure to read a book word by word for the interest of the writer's use of language."[1] Soon after he published *Scoop* he suggested that "one of the tests of literary style is that one cannot read it to oneself any faster than one could read aloud; another is that you cannot immediately turn from it and pick up a piece of writing by someone else; a decent interval must elapse; one needs a diver's 'decompression chamber.' "[2]

The same week he repudiated Cyril Connolly's injunction to judge style by "isolated passages, as a wine taster judges a vintage." The analogy is false, Waugh argued, "for wine is a homogeneous substance," but "writing is an art which exists in a time sequence; each sentence and each page is dependent on its predecessors and successors; a sentence which he admires may owe its significance to another fifty pages distant. I beg Mr. Connolly to believe that even quite popular writers take great trouble sometimes in this matter." Thus, Waugh argued more generally, "architectural" would be a better term than "creative" for distinguishing the real writer from "a clever and cultured man who can write" because the former has "an added energy and breadth of vision which enables him to conceive and complete a structure."[3]

These dicta could obviously be applied to Waugh's earlier novels or inferred from his earlier criticism, but their significance rests in the fact that he

1. Quoted on front flap of dustjacket, Evelyn Waugh, *Brideshead Revisited,* 3d ed. (London: Chapman and Hall Ltd., 1945). This is the earliest dustjacket I have seen. The material is reprinted in Harold C. Gardiner, "Follow-up on Waugh," *America* 74 (February 16, 1946): 536.

2. Evelyn Waugh, "Mr. Belloc in the North," *Spectator* 161 (December 2, 1938): 964.

3. Evelyn Waugh, "Present Discontents," *Tablet* 172 (December 3, 1938): 743.

states them explicitly at this point in his career. Whether or not they were new, they were, like his membership on the board of directors of Chapman and Hall and his purchase, improvement, and peopling of Piers Court, evidence of his assumption of the role of solid citizen and aspirant to stature as a serious novelist. Not until the publication of *Brideshead Revisited* did he receive the attention, if not the praise, accorded to major writers.

Work Suspended was clearly an attempt to write a major work, and in this fragment Waugh introduced what were for him major technical innovations. The most obvious difference between this work and his previous fiction was the use of a first-person narrator, John Plant, mystery novelist and connoisseur of domestic architecture whose aesthetic principles and circle of friends closely resemble Waugh's.[4] The choice of point of view is ironic in light of Waugh's remark early in his career, reported by W. Somerset Maugham, "that to write novels in the first person was a contemptible practice."[5] Maugham went on to argue that "if the proper study of mankind is man it is evidently more sensible to occupy yourself with the coherent, substantial, and significant creatures of fiction than with the irrational and shadowy figures of real life" and that since "as we grow older we feel ourselves less and less like God I should not be surprised to learn that with advancing years the novelist grows less and less inclined to describe more than his own experience has given him."[6] The distinction between characters in fiction and people in life resembles John Plant's principle that "there is no place in literature for a live man, solid and active," the

---

4. Of course, Waugh had used first-person narration in his travel books, and it could be argued that John Plant is a slightly older and more ruminative version of the "Evelyn Waugh" of *Labels* or *Remote People.* For an excellent description of the innovative features of the fragment, see Frederick J. Stopp, *Evelyn Waugh: Portrait of an Artist* (Boston: Little, Brown and Co., 1958), pp. 101–107. Christopher Sykes discusses the auto-biographical aspect of the fragment and confesses, characteristically, that he was told how the story was to proceed, but forgot. Christopher Sykes, *Evelyn Waugh: A Biography* (Boston: Little, Brown and Co., 1975), pp. 223–27.

5. W. Somerset Maugham, *Cakes and Ale,* the Collected Edition (London: William Heinemann, 1934), pp. 187–88. The source of Maugham's paraphrase of Waugh's remark in the *Evening Standard* I cannot trace. It is not "The Claim of Youth" or "Matter-of-Fact Mothers of the New Age" or *"Tess* as a 'Modern' Sees It."

6. *Ibid.,* pp. 188–89. This novel is not in Waugh's library at the Humanities Research Center, but he reviewed it for the *Graphic,* October 11, 1930, p. 74. He also reviewed Maugham's *Christmas Holiday* in "The Technician," *Spectator* 162 (February 17, 1939): 274, and praised Maugham in much the same terms as John Plant praises his father, the Academician.

alternatives being to maintain "a kind of Dickensian menagerie" and to take "the whole man and reduce him to a manageable abstraction."[7]

Nevertheless, Waugh was trying to create a character with a social background, an intellectual milieu, an ability to develop and change, and the capacity to summarize and judge his own experience—tasks Waugh had not before attempted. Plant is living and narrating a far different kind of novel from those he had previously written—they "had nothing of myself" in them (p. 45)—and one of his fears of owning a home is that he will provide "a sitting shot to the world" (p. 49) and lose the privacy on which he places enormous value. In this respect *Work Suspended* prefigures *The Ordeal of Gilbert Pinfold* as a confession of the relationship between the writer's work and his life, but in more obvious respects the fragment can be seen as a preparation for *Brideshead Revisited*, not only in point of view but also in style and pace. In both books the pace is slow because the style is figurative, ornate, allusive, and analytical; the central character is less concerned with action than with understanding what has happened.

By late February, 1940, Waugh had decided that his military duties would prevent him from finishing the novel, even though he knew that, "so far as it went, this was my best work."[8] When he published the fragment in 1942, he announced that, "even if I were again to have the leisure and will to finish it, the work would be vain, for the world in which and for which it was designed, has ceased to exist." This premonition did not prevent him, in mid-1941, from turning to the immediate and very remote past in *Put Out More Flags*. Returning from the Mediterranean by an extremely circuitous route, he wrote the novel in a single month with great pleasure: "The characters about whom I had written in the previous decade came to life for me. I was anxious to know how they had been doing since I last heard of them, and I followed them with no preconceived plan, not knowing where I should find them from one page to the next."[9]

7. Evelyn Waugh, *Work Suspended* (London: Chapman and Hall, 1942), pp. 82–83. The story was revised, largely to account for its existence as a fragment, for inclusion in *Work Suspended and Other Stories* (London: Chapman and Hall, 1949) and in *Tactical Exercise* (Boston: Little, Brown and Co., 1954). See my "Textual Problems in the Novels of Evelyn Waugh," *Papers of the Bibliographical Society of America* 62 (1968): 259–63.

8. Evelyn Waugh, Dedicatory Letter to Alexander Woollcott (in *Work Suspended*). Waugh announced to Peters his decision to abandon the novel in a letter received February 23, 1940, *The Letters of Evelyn Waugh,* ed. Mark Amory (New Haven and New York: Ticknor & Fields, 1980), p. 137.

9. Evelyn Waugh, Preface, *Put Out More Flags* (London: Chapman and Hall, 1967), [p. 7].

Although *Put Out More Flags* has obvious links with Waugh's novels of the preceding decade, it differs from them in a number of instructive ways. Basil Seal returns, very little altered except by age, from *Black Mischief* and for that matter from *Work Suspended:* impulsive, irresponsible, and irrepressible. But Peter Pastmaster discovers in himself unexpected dynastic longings, and Alastair Trumpington, like T.E. Lawrence, goes into the ranks as a form of penance. On the whole the characters have far more interior life than their predecessors had: Margot Beste-Chetwynde in *Decline and Fall* was inscrutable, beyond judgment or even comprehension. Angela Lyne, her counterpart in *Put Out More Flags* insofar as she is rich, fashionable, and independent, is vulnerable, a victim rather than a controller of events, capable of sliding into alcoholic despair and then, with an effort of will and the aid of Basil, recovering. In Ambrose Silk, the absurd and touching aesthete who is a real artist, Waugh created a character entirely new in his fiction. Like Otto Silenus, Silk can generalize on the follies of his contemporaries while himself remaining ridiculous; unlike Silenus, he is more than a flat figure. Nevertheless, the novel is essentially a conclusion rather than a beginning: Waugh laid the "race of ghosts,"[10] and they were never again to figure prominently in his work.[11]

Even before *Put Out More Flags* was published in the spring of 1942, "the new spirit" of the "Churchillian renaissance" that it celebrated was considerably deflated for Waugh by personal as well as global defeats. He knew that his commando unit had been a failure, though for his article, "Commando Raid on Bardia," he concealed the worst lapses of that particular operation.[12] Between and in fact during various postings, special training courses, and far from irksome army duties Waugh found time to read a great many books on a wide variety of subjects, as the marginalia in his library testify; do himself well with wine; wreck at least two cars; carry on skirmishes with his landlady at Westbridge House;[13] and, in the fall, "meditate starting a novel."[14] The book was mentioned no further, and in the

10. Evelyn Waugh, "Dedicatory Letter to Randolph Churchill," *Put Out More Flags* (London: Chapman and Hall, 1948), [p. 11].

11. The obvious exception is Evelyn Waugh, *Basil Seal Rides Again* (Boston: Little, Brown and Co., 1963) which carries Basil and his circle into advanced middle age.

12. Evelyn Waugh, "Commando Raid on Bardia," *Life* 11 (November 17, 1941): 63ff. See Evelyn Waugh, *The Diaries* of *Evelyn Waugh,* ed. Michael Davie (Boston: Little, Brown and Co., 1977), pp. 495-96.

13. See the unpublished "Westbridge House Treaty" at the Humanities Research Center.

14. Waugh, *Diaries,* p. 529 (October, 1942).

ensuing year Waugh and the army became increasingly aware of their mutual grievances.[15] Waugh conceived the pleasant alternative of practicing his vocation:

> I dislike the army. (and) I want to get to work again. I do not want any more experiences in life. I have quite enough (stored away) bottled & carefully laid in the cellar, some still ripening, most ready for drinking, a little beginning to lose its body. . . . I have succeeded . . . in dissociating myself very largely with [*sic*] the rest of the world. I am not impatient of its manifest follies and don't want to influence opinions or events or expose humbug or anything of that kind. I don't want to be of service to anyone or anything. I simply want to do my work as an artist.[16]

The emphasis upon stored experience is new for Waugh. In earlier novels like *Decline and Fall, Work Suspended,* and *Put Out More Flags* he had drawn from experience even and sometimes especially for the most bizarre characters like Captain Grimes and Ambrose Silk,[17] and for other novels like *Black Mischief* and *Scoop* he had drawn upon impressions of the social scene still vivid to his contemporaries and still relevant to their social and political concerns. *Work Suspended* he abandoned because the society it depicted had ceased to exist, and while in *Put Out More Flags* he was consciously chronicling "that odd, dead period known as 'the Great Bore War,'"[18] he was not ready to become a historical novelist.

While earlier experiences could be distilled into "comedy and sometimes tragedy from the knockabout farce of people's outward behavior,"[19] the wartime experiences would have to mature for six years before they could be used in the war trilogy. From the pleasant vantage of hindsight it seems obvious that the nature of the experience now ripening or beginning to go off affected the kind of book he wanted to write and perhaps the way in which he would write it.

Even if one knew nothing of Waugh's intentions, it is obvious that *Brideshead Revisited*, subtitled *The Sacred and Profane Memories of Captain*

15. For an account of Waugh's disaffection with the army, see Sykes, *Evelyn Waugh,* pp. 218–43.

16. Waugh, *Diaries,* p. 548 (August 29, 1943).

17. See *Ibid.,* p. 213; and Evelyn Waugh, *A Little Learning* (Boston: Little, Brown and Co., 1964), pp. 227–28 for Grimes; for Silk, see my "Evelyn Waugh and Brian Howard," *Evelyn Waugh Newsletter* 4 (Autumn, 1970):5–6.

18. Waugh, *Put Out More Flags* (1948), p. [11].

19. Evelyn Waugh, "Fan-Fare," *Life* 20 (April 8, 1946):56.

Charles Ryder, represented a radical departure in tone, form, and theme from his earlier novels. Looking back from the bleak years of World War II, Ryder remembers an Oxford more realistic if not less bizarre than that of *Decline and Fall* and contrasts to its glamour the solid beauties of Brideshead Castle, seat of the Roman Catholic Flyte family. Drawn into it by his love for Sebastian, the charming and beautiful younger son, he is first involved with and then estranged from the family as he watches Sebastian collapse into alcoholism in an attempt to escape from his mother's frilly if real piety and from adult responsibility. Ryder turns to architectural painting as an outlet for his unrecognized spiritual longings, but ten years later he again feels arid, unsatisfied by his art and by his marriage. An affair with Sebastian's sister Julia seems to promise renewal as well as possession of Brideshead, but the last-minute repentance of her father leads to her return and Ryder's conversion to Catholicism. In the Epilogue Brideshead has been despoiled by its military occupants, but Ryder, recognizing his failure in secular terms, takes comfort in his newfound faith as the novel ends.

The manner of writing Waugh was to use in *Brideshead Revisited* he had considered publicly as early as 1938. In 1943, while preparing his review of Robert Graves and Alan Hodge's *The Reader over Your Shoulder,*[20] he was given added reason to think about the relationship between language and action and about the contrast between what he valued and what he could perceive all around him. Characteristically Waugh praised the book by asserting that in a healthy age of rigorous education it would not be necessary but in "the century of the common man," who is urged to "write as he speaks" and to "speak as he pleases," it is invaluable as "a call for order." Less interested in functional prose than in art,[21] Waugh moved beyond the book's immediate concerns to the plight of literary artists in the bleak new world:

> Society is changing in a way which makes it increasingly difficult for them to live at their ease. A few potential artists will doubtless be found to submit to the new restraints and, as State functionaries, busy themselves in Public-Relations offices and Ministries of Rest and Culture, popularizing the ideas of tomorrow and the undertakings which, in peace, replace the Giant Salvage Drives of today. For the more vigorous, however, the choice lies in the two extremes of anarchic bohemianism and ascetic seclusion. Each provides a refuge from the State. The Bohemians will have a valuable function in teasing, it may be hoped to madness, the new

---

20. Evelyn Waugh, "The Writing of English," *Tablet* 182 (July 3, 1943):8-9.
21. He had, however, been "reducing the verbosity of the proposed reorganization of the Special Service Brigade" in March. See Waugh, *Diaries,* p. 533 (March 29, 1943).

bourgeoisie, but I believe it will be left to the ascetics to produce the works of art in which, if at all, English culture will survive.

In the past Waugh had done his share of teasing anyone within reach of his barbs—the gentlefolk who are the prey of Basil Seal in *Put Out More Flags* were the most recent examples—but he had obviously begun to see himself as one of the ascetics, in language if not in personal habits.

Going still further—and here, looking back from *Brideshead*, one finds further evidence that he had already begun to think of writing a new kind of book—Waugh turned to the value of the aristocracy to the artist:

> By its patronage it offered him rewards more coveted than the mere cash value of its purchases; in its security it invited him to share its own personal freedom of thought and movement; it provided the leisured reader whom alone it is worth addressing; it curbed the vanity of the publicist and drew a sharp line between fame and notoriety; by its caprices it encouraged experiment; its scepticism exposed the humbug. These and countless other benefits are now forgotten or denied. Its particular service to literature was that it maintained the delicate and unstable balance between the spoken and the written word. Only a continuous tradition of gentle speech, with all its implications—the avoidance of boredom and vulgarity, the exchange of complicated ideas, the observance of subtle nuances of word and phrase—can preserve the written tongue from death, and lifelong habitude to such speech alone schools a man to write his own tongue.

The lower classes and Americans, he concluded, were in particularly desperate plight, as every bookstore testified. Yet, he concluded, even the literate could learn from the book "to consider questions too long disregarded," himself included, for, having read it, "I have been haunted by this pest to a condition approaching persecution mania; I have taken about three times as long to write this review as is normal, and still dread submitting it to print."

This contact with the world of precise language was in sharp contrast to other aspects of Waugh's life. Disillusioned with the army, comparatively deprived of the luxuries of good wine, good food, and stimulating conversation, Waugh, like Ludovic and other writers in *Unconditional Surrender,* "averting themselves sickly from privations of war and apprehensions of the social consequences of the peace," turned "from the drab alleys of the thirties into the odorous gardens of a recent past transformed and illuminated by disordered memory and imagination."[22] Prospects were grim enough to

22. Evelyn Waugh, *Unconditional Surrender* (London: Chapman and Hall, 1961), p. 243.

depress the Waugh who believed in Western Christian civilization—he observed that Germany stood for Europe against the world and thanked God that Japan was not an ally—[23] and to elate the Waugh who delighted in spreading alarm and despondency in auditors all the way from Lord Beveridge to his army servant, who, informed that Park West was what postwar accommodations would be like, asserted that surely there would be gardens, only to receive the pitiless reply, "No Hall no gardens."[24]

Waugh's recent past was grim; in his fiction he made it even worse. Like Charles Ryder he was stationed at Pollock, an unfinished housing development in Glasgow, with a subaltern who, like Hooper, said, when tasked for preparing his own kit, "Well you know how it is. If you get on the wrong side of [the men] they take it out of you in other ways."[25] Waugh suffered from what he considered the persecutions of a supposed inferior commanding officer, and in the manuscript of *Brideshead Revisited*, General Haydon threatened to replace C. R. M. F. Cruttwell in Waugh's private hall of infamy, for his name was used first for the character who became Hooper and then, until final revision of proof, the elder Ryder's butler. Unlike Ryder, however, Waugh spent "most of my available leisure drinking vintage port" in the Western Club.[26]   Against the professional disappointments and personal deprivations of the present Waugh could set a heightened and superficially glamorized but not fundamentally sentimentalized version of his past. The roman à clef elements in the novel were obvious to the inner circle who read the private edition of 1944 and subsequently to everyone familiar with Waugh's life. The Lygon family home of Madresfield is the obvious model in spirit if not style for Brideshead.[27] Its owner, Lord Beauchamp, was estranged from his family and country for sexual irregularities quite different from Lord Marchmain's. The manuscript gives evidence, by occasionally using 'Alastair' instead of 'Sebastian,' that elements of Alastair Graham, the 'Hamish' of *A Little Learning*, went into the character of Sebastian Flyte, and Waugh's homosexual period at Oxford is hinted at with delicate broadness. Despite annoyed denials by all directly concerned and by some outsiders, elements of Harold Acton as well as of Brian Howard were incorporated in the character

23. Waugh, *Diaries*, p. 558 (February 13, 1944).

24. See Lord Pakenham (now Earl of Longford), *Born to Believe* (London: Catholic Book Club, n.d.), pp. 134–35, and Waugh, *Diaries*, p. 535 (April 16, 1943). Davie adds punctuation.

25. Waugh, *Diaries*, p. 518 (early March, 1942).

26. *Ibid*, p. 522 (May 26, 1942).

27. See Lady Dorothy Lygon, "Madresfield and Brideshead," *Evelyn Waugh and His World ed. David Pryce-Jones* (Boston: Little, Brown and Co., 1973), pp. 49–52.

of Anthony Blanche.[28] Even Sebastian's drunken driving was based solidly on Matthew Ponsonby's escapade of 1925.[29]

All of this experience was, of course, available to Waugh in late 1943, and all of it was used in the novel. Apparently he moved from recollection at least to preliminary planning when, having on September 23 obtained indefinite leave pending posting, he went to Buxton House a month later "to stay and start writing." This plan was interrupted by the parachute training course that resulted fifteen years later in an incident of *Unconditional Surrender* and more immediately in a cracked fibula, bearing out his prophecy that he would not prove to be a man of action.

In the meantime two widely different incidents helped establish his attitude toward his material, one of them providing a major incident in the novel. In late September, despite his abjuration of all but aesthetic aims, he attempted to expose the humbug in Marie Stopes's assertion that, statistically, Catholic education preceded a life of crime more frequently than did other forms of schooling. This seemed to Waugh the kind of sociometric, socialist nonsense that would pervade and deaden the postwar world, and he rejoiced in the combat.[30] About the same time he began visiting his old friend Hubert Duggan, "pathetically ill" (Diaries, October 4, 1943), who talked of his abandoned faith but rejected repentance because he thought it disloyal to his woman companion (October 12). Impatient of such scruples but on the surface more tactful than usual, Waugh found a priest to give Duggan absolution and, over the objection of Duggan's sister, Extreme Unction in an episode recreated in the final chapter of *Brideshead Revisited.* Thus Waugh concluded his diary entry on the episode: ". . . we spent the day waiting for a spark of gratitude for the love of God and saw the spark" (October 13).

Characteristically, Waugh's next sentence records dinner with Peter Fitzwilliam, who was influential enough, despite severe rationing, to get Waugh not only a decent meal in "a fashionable restaurant" but also a box of cigars. Except during Lent, and then not always beyond the requirements of canon law, Waugh was far from ascetic, and though he was surprisingly tolerant of and even more amused by the vagaries—some technically defined

---

28. See Waugh, *A Little Learning,* p. 196, for his disclaimer of fundamental resemblances between Acton and Blanche.

29. See *Times* [London] April 16, 1925, p. 9f.

30. Evelyn Waugh, "Religion in State Schools," *New Statesman and Nation* 26 (October 20, 1943): 217; (October 16, 1943): 251. See my *Modern British Short Novels* (Glenview, Ill.: Scott, Foresman and Co., 1972), pp. 287–88, for a discussion of the theme in *Love Among the Ruins.*

as capital sins—of nonbelievers, he was a very practical Catholic who rejoiced in conversions and reconciliations, lamented defections, and employed a kind of hectoring zeal in reforming friends like Alfred Duggan from drunkenness to sober authorship, in helping convert wavering friends like Frank Pakenham (subsequently Lord Longford), and in denouncing the obduracy of friends like John Betjeman.[31] Perhaps, as some have asserted, he did not have a complex or subtle or even first-rate mind, but he knew a good deal about the theology of the Roman Catholic church.

Donat O'Donnell (Conor Cruise O'Brien) and others have promulgated and perpetuated the theory that Waugh regarded the church as a preserve of the aristocracy, a sort of spiritual White's Club where only the right sort were admitted.[32] It is true that Waugh tended to write almost exclusively about the church rather than about Christ and about discipline rather than about love, but anyone with a historical sense who was reared in the Church of England had a predilection for ecclesiological controversy, and any Catholic who attained the use of reason before the Second Vatican Council—Graham Greene is a notable example—tended to define the practice of faith as exclusive rather than expansive. In fact, though the theme is more clearly if not more artistically rendered in *Helena,* Waugh was attracted by the *idea* of a universal Church whose mission was to save not the righteous but sinners and in whose theology it is possible to have good come of apparent evil.

It seems clear that Waugh intended *Brideshead* to reflect these doctrines. Writing after the fact to warn his readers that the novel was "*not* meant to be funny," Waugh outlined his theme, "at once romantic and eschatological," as "the workings of the divine purpose in a pagan world." He expected to displease "those who look back on that pagan world with unalloyed affection, and . . .those who see it as transitory, insignificant and, already, hopefully passed," but he hoped to please those interested in writing and "those who look to the future with black forebodings, and need more solid comfort than rosy memories." While he could not see that "anything but disaster lies ahead," he could offer the hope that "the human spirit, redeemed, can survive all disasters."[33]

31. See Sykes, *Evelyn Waugh* on Duggan, pp. 290–92; see Pakenham, *Born to Believe,* pp. 115–16; see Waugh's letters to Betjeman, now in Victoria University, Victoria, B.C., *Letters,* pp. 242–43, 244–47.

32. Conor Cruise O'Brien, *Maria Cross: Imaginative Patterns in a Group of Modern Catholic Writers* (London: Burns and Oates, 1963), pp. 109–23. Waugh responded to the original version in "The Pieties of Evelyn Waugh," *Bell* 14 (July 1947):77, pointing out that money and title had not saved Rex Mottram or Lady Celia Ryder from criticism.

33. See "Warning," dustjacket of British edition of *Brideshead,* and Gardiner, "Follow-up on Waugh," p. 536.

In concrete and immediate terms, the repentance and death of Hubert Duggan provided an obvious link between the secular, hedonistic world of Waugh's youth on which he looked with nostalgia and the enforced asceticism of the present—the first a preparation for the second—and between the physical deprivations and psychological disappointments and apprehensions of the present and the promise of a future in which all would in the providence of God be well.

The Duggan incident was obviously the catalyst for *Brideshead Revisited;* the end of the diary entry of October 15, "I have done all in my power in that matter," is followed immediately by the entry at Pixton Park, "where I came on Friday 22nd and intend to stay and start writing."[34] No evidence survives to indicate that he did start, but by late January he was able to assert in applying for leave that he had "formed the plan of a new novel which will take approximately three months to write."[35] This estimate carries conviction for two reasons. First, Waugh was, except on certain kinds of official forms which in his ethics seemed not to count, not only veracious but brutally honest. Second, nowhere in the manuscript, his diary, or his letters to A. D. Peters does he reveal any hesitation about the incidents of the novel or their order. To be sure, he took four and a half months rather than three to finish it, but allowing for official interruptions on what Waugh considered the most frivolous pretexts, he was very near the mark.

As his diary entry of January 31, 1944, indicates, Waugh planned "an ambitious novel," a phrase that seems to indicate a clear conception of treatment as well as subject. Six weeks later he was able to plan "the work of the next five weeks."[36] Even a major interruption failed to daunt him. Ordered on April 1 to report to London, he was undiscouraged because, having finished Book 2 (Book 1 of the first edition), "I have come to a suitable halting stage, . . . and a week or two away from it may do no harm."[37]

As these passages indicate, Waugh kept in his diary, in correspondence with Peters, and in the manuscript itself an account of the process of composition far more circumstantial than that for any other novel. His motive is not hard to determine. Ephemera excepted—three letters to the editor, the review of Graves and Hodge, and a sketch for the *Book-of-the-Month Club News*—he had done no professional writing since he had composed *Put Out More Flags* in considerable leisure and without anxiety. Neither of these pleasant

---

34. Waugh, *Diaries*, p. 553 (October 25, 1943). And see *Letters*, p. 206: "I wrote the book about that scene."

35. *Ibid.*, p. 557, n. 1 (January 24, 1944).

36. *Ibid.*, p. 560 (March 13, 1944).

37. *Ibid.*, p. 561 (April 1, 1944).

117

conditions existed during the composition of *Brideshead.* His leave was indefinite, increasingly uncertain, and subject to interruption. Perhaps more important, he was becoming more and more conscious that his new novel represented a climacteric in his career.

The day before he began writing he went to Chagford feeling "full of literary power which only this evening gives place to qualms of impotence." Once under way he worked slowly but steadily, rewriting some passages two or three times, noting two weeks into the process that "every day I seem to go over what I did the day before and make it shorter. I am getting spinsterish about style"—the influence of Graves and Hodge may have persisted—and having occasional bursts like the "3,000 words in three hours" on the following day.[38] In fact, he was writing it "with a zest that was quite strange to me."[39] Writing to Peters on February 8 to learn his typist's new address, Waugh made the ironic prediction that the novel, perhaps because it was "*very* good," would have a small public including fewer than a half-dozen Americans and asked about handmade paper, typefaces, and other typographical details for an edition suited to the quality of his work and perhaps to his new conception of his role as a writer. He was certainly aware of a change: having just sent off Chapter 1 of Book 2 (Book 1, Chapter 4 of the first edition) and satisfactorily begun another, he observed—providing a variation from the dichotomy of bohemian and ascetic in the Graves-Hodge review and anticipating his remark in "Fan-Fare"—that "English writers, at forty, either set about prophesying or acquiring a style. Thank God I think I am trying to acquire a style." Halfway through the penultimate chapter and eager to complete the whole, Waugh was "in alternate despondency and exultation about the book. . . . I think perhaps it is the first of my novels rather than the last."[40]

Waugh's last major diary entry on the novel reveals rather ostentatiously his self-satisfaction at being an artist rather than a man of action. During the hours when his contemporaries were engaged in the major action of the European war, he was bringing his novel to a satisfactory conclusion:

> 6 June. This morning at breakfast the waiter told me the second front had opened. I sat down early to work and wrote a fine passage of Lord Marchmain's death agonies. Carolyn came to tell me the popular front was open. I sent for the priest to give Lord Marchmain the last sacraments. I

38. *Ibid.,* p. 558 (February 13, 14, 1944). In "Marxism: The Opiate of the People," *Tablet* 183 (April 11, 1944): 200–201, Waugh judged Harold Laski's language shoddy and his thinking muddled.

39. Evelyn Waugh, *Brideshead Revisited* (London: Chapman and Hall, 1960), p. 9.
40. Waugh, *Diaries,* p. 566 (May 21, 1944).

worked through till 4 oclock & finished the last chapter—the last dialogue poor—took it to the post, walked home by the upper road. There only remains now the epilogue which is easy meat. My only fear is lest the invasion upsets my typist at St. Leonards, or the posts to him with my manuscript.[41]

Despite some revision, the Epilogue was in fact "easy meat," and on Corpus Christi—June 8 in the liturgical calendar then in use—he met his deadline for completing the novel.

The process of writing and revising the novel was, of course, far more complex than this account indicates. As Waugh noted, he rewrote some passages several times, and not all of the abortive drafts survive. What he saved and bound in the manuscript volume now in the Humanities Research Center differs so widely from the published text that a variorum format would require many appendices or foldouts, since even facing page texts would be inadequate to depict variant states of some half-dozen lengthy passages. Waugh's progress can be traced most readily in outline form (bracketed numbers are those of the 1945 Little, Brown edition).[42]

Prologue	February 1–3:	Writes.
Chapter 1	February 8:	Finishes, after rescription, reordering.
Chapter 2	February 12:	Rewrites.
	February 15:	Finishes.
Chapter 3 [3–4]	February 20:	Rewrites opening.
	February 23:	Finishes rewriting.
	February 26:	Finishes.
	(To this point:	corrected typescript April 2.)
Book 2,		
Chapter 1	March13:	Cancels opening.
Book 1,		
Chapter 5	March 14:	Rewrites opening.
	March 16:	Rewrites booking into cells.
	March 21:	Sends chapter to typist.
Chapter 2 [5]	March 22:	Rewrites and stitches.
	March 23:	Rewrites pp. 94–95 [p. 159]. Finishes rewriting [of first part of Chapter 2?]
	March 24:	Sends off about 8,000 words [to ca. p. 168].
Chapter 3 [6]	March 27:	Sends off 7,100 words.

41. *Ibid.,* pp. 567–68 (June 6, 1944).

42. Evelyn Waugh, *Brideshead Revisited* (Boston: Little, Brown and Co., 1945). I cite this edition in most references to the text of the novel, though it is by no means the best text, because American readers have ready access to it and because the English editions are almost unavailable except in a few highly restricted research libraries.

Chapter 4 [7]	March 28:	Revises Anthony Blanche's report of Sebastian.
	March 29:	Sends off 8,500 words—the end of Book 2.
	(April 16:	Completes revision of Books 1 and 2, possibly including some of the "MS. Interpolations in Second draft.")
	(Ca. May 26:	Realizes that Book 2 must be rewritten.)
	(June 3:	Finishes rearrangement of Book 2.)
Book 3, Chapter 1 [Book 2, Chapter 1]	April 23:	Rewrites opening.
	May 4:	Picks up lovemaking on ocean liner.
	May 5–7:	Blocked.
	May 9:	Sends off Chapter 1.
Chapter 2	May 14:	Rewrites.
	June 6:	Cancels second draft.
Chapter 3		[4; MS is misnumbered, with two chapters numbered 2.]
	June 5–6:	Works on and finishes chapter.
	June 7:	Cuts a version of [p. 345]; writes Epilogue.
	(June 8–15:	Finishes last revisions and corrects typescript.)
	(June 20:	Delivers complete manuscript to Chapman and Hall.)

However sketchy, the chart indicates three major issues that were to concern Waugh off and on for the next fifteen years through ten authorized states of the text: how to divide the material, how much material to include, and how to arrange it. The first is on the surface the simplest: whether to have two books or three. The manuscript and the 1960 edition have three, though they divide differently. No other text, including carbon and proof, divides in this fashion. Three-book division makes sense in terms of mathematics and bulk: Prologue and Epilogue frame books of three, four, and three chapters of 84, 119, and 117 pages in the Little, Brown setting.[43] Book 1 of the manuscript records the idyllic, Arcadian life of Sebastian Flyte and Charles Ryder at Oxford, Brideshead, and Venice. Book 2 begins with a new year at Oxford and traces the decline of the Flyte family: Sebastian into drink, Julia into marriage outside the church, Lady Marchmain into death, and Marchmain House into the hands of developers. Book 3, which begins ten years thereafter, moves

43. The third chapter of Book 1 was first divided into Chapters 3 and 4 in typescript. Book 2 begins with Ryder's last year at Oxford. In the 1960 edition Book 1 ends with that year.

from spiritual desolation to love of Julia to or past the verge of faith in and love of God. As even this summary indicates, however, serious objections can be raised. Though the chapters and the pages devoted to each of the books are in proportion, the time sequence is not: the ten-year break between Books 2 and 3 is greater not only in time but in tone, action, and characterization than that between Books 1 and 2 (the 1960 edition remedies the flaw to some extent by beginning Book 2 with the return of Samgrass, Sebastian, and Ryder to Brideshead after a five-month gap).

It is obvious that Waugh was at least subliminally aware that his principle of division was logical rather than structural not only because he revised it but also because he tended to think of the third book as distinct from the first two, on April 1 regarding the end of Book 2 as "a suitable halting stage" and two days later thinking of publishing it as a complete unit. Sending Peters the first, very rough typescript, probably of the Prologue and Book 1, he observed that "my Magnum Opus is turning into a jeraboam" and continued with a mixture of artistic and practical considerations that would have delighted Henry James. He had completed 62,000 words:

> The original scheme of the book was three sections of which two are complete. The total length would be about 90,000 words. I now find that what I have written could be profitably enlarged and what I have to write could be an entire book. The leisure at my disposal is limited. Should I be well advised to expand what I have written to 70,000 words & publish it as Vol I, leaving the second for next year? . . .we could publish a single volume of 120,000 words incorporating the first volume which would have had the limited circulation of the time. Expansion would be an artistic benefit.

The manuscript he had sent Peters was, he added, "a first draft requiring much alteration even if there is no expansion."[44]

Peters successfully discouraged the plan by arguing that readers would be confused if the circular structure was not completed and therefore that Waugh's effect would be diminished, and less than two weeks later Waugh finished revising and expanding. He may have been wrong in predicting that Book 3 would make a volume in itself — in fact, his letter indicates that he may have realized that it would not — but his tentative figures were remarkably close to the final total: the prologue and the first eight chapters of the published novel run a bit more than 75,000 words, and the whole novel is very nearly 120,000 words long.

44. Letter to A. D. Peters, April 3, 1944, *The Letters of Evelyn Waugh,* ed. Mark Amory (New Haven and New York: Ticknor & Fields, 1980), pp. 182–83.

The questions of how long the book was to be and how it was to be divided could be answered finally, of course, only after Waugh had worked through to an understanding of the characters and of their relationships. In earlier novels neither characters nor relationships had been as complex as those he was in the process of creating, nor had the earlier characters lived in a world that had a real dimension in time. The old process of composition, in which Waugh could "set a few characters on the move, write 3,000 words a day and noted[d] with surprise what happened"[45] was no longer adequate. In evolving a new method, Waugh was forced to stretch his inventive and critical faculties to an extent and in a detail far greater than in any of the earlier books.

45. Evelyn Waugh, *Vile Bodies* (London: Chapman and Hall, 1965), p. 7.

7

Qualifying the Narrator In
Brideshead Revisited

Waugh's experiment with a first-person narrator in *Work Suspended* may have been undertaken to allow him to use not only his external experience but also his reflections upon it, and judging from the materials that went into *Brideshead*, he had a similar motive in making Charles Ryder the narrator of the novel. Yet while Waugh knew that the novelist's "raw material is compounded of all that he has seen and done,"[1] he was also aware that the material must be imagined or reinvented to become a harmonious whole. In earlier books he had recast his material to give variety and a certain degree of complexity to his characters, but in *Brideshead* he had to solve a new problem: establishing a causal relationship between the other characters and the narrator, who is in effect the sum of his experiences rather than a dispassionate commentator on action seen from the outside. Furthermore, Waugh insisted on the distinction that appeared in every version of the text beginning with carbon typescript: "I am not I; thou art not he or she; they are not they." Obviously Ryder is not Waugh; less obviously but no less certainly, Ryder the actor is not the same as Ryder the narrator, whose knowledge, perspective, and spiritual condition are much altered between 1923 and 1942. To be made convincing, the distinction had to be established not merely by direct characterization of the narrator but also by subtle correction of or support for the youthful Ryder's views. As a result Waugh was forced to struggle with the problem of how much and what kind of detail to include on a day-to-day, sentence-to-sentence basis; this struggle, which involves local revisions for the most part, can be distinguished from the longer and more complex revisions that will be discussed in the following chapter.

Although the general background and character of the narrator seem to have been clear in Waugh's mind, he did revise important details. In the first draft the narrator was named Peter Fenwick well into the second chapter, far enough that, though Waugh frequently inserted "Charles Ryder"

1. Evelyn Waugh, *A Little Learning* (Boston: Little, Brown and Co., 1964), p. 196.

before having the manuscript typed, he saw the need to indicate the name change in a note to the typist.[2] Elsewhere, in contrast to his usual practice, Waugh tended to remove details about Ryder's background. Originally he had Peter/Charles go into considerably more detail about his family and had Sebastian augment it, but, probably revising in typescript, he compressed the scene:

Manuscript

"Anyway I'll tell you about my family. There is only myself and my father. My mother was killed in the war."

"Oh . . . how very unusual."

"Yes, she was in the Red Cross in Serbia and was buried by a shell. You hear a lot about the fatherless younger generation—never about boys who lost their mothers. I suppose there aren't many. My father is a very shy and peculiar man. He lives in London (practically) all the year round and collects almost everything. We have a (large, stucco) house on Camden Hill full of his collections. I think he must be quite rich. My mother was, I know."

"You can look my family up in Debrett. /Thats what Hardcastle would do./"

"Well, for that matter, you can find me there."

"Yet (Peter) /Charles/," said Sebastian, surprisingly, "I know. (I found you) /I look everyone up. It's one of the healthy habits I learned from Nanny Hawkins. I found you—at last./ Issue of second son of (third) /second/ baronet—*very* obscure. And you've a madly middle-class cousin at your college /who'll be the fourth baronet/ (who used to know /my brother/ Brideshead). You can't stump me on the (Fenwick) /Ryder/ family."

"I told you about Jasper."

"(But) /And/ I remembered him. I don't believe I shall ever forget him."

Novel

"Perhaps I am rather curious about people's families—you see, it's not a thing I know about. There is only my father and myself. An aunt kept an eye on me for a time but my father drove her abroad. My mother was killed in the war."

---

2. Other anomalies in naming characters occur in manuscript because earlier chapters were at the typist's or the agent's office. Waugh forgot Mulcaster's name and instructed the typist to insert it in the blanks left in the manuscript of Book 2, Chapter 1. In Book 2, Chapter 2, Cordelia is called Bridget.

"Oh . . . how very unusual."

"She went to Serbia with the Red Cross. My father has been rather odd in the head ever since. He just lives alone in London with no friends, and footles about collecting things."

Sebastian said, "You don't know what you've been saved. There are lots of us. Look them up in Debrett."[3]

Ryder's brief editorial perhaps reminded Waugh too much of youthful indiscretions like "The War and the Younger Generation," and not only did the explicit definition of Ryder's place on the social and economic scales misdirect the reader's attention—for the glamour of Brideshead and the Flytes in contrast to the eccentricity of Ryder's home is what really matters—but Sebastian's curiosity must have seemed uncharacteristic as well as a weak way to set off Ryder's interest in families.[4]

Waugh took as much care with minor characters as with his narrator. Ryder's commanding officer, for example, appears only in Prologue and Epilogue and serves as one of the more significant minor irritants that alienate Ryder from the army. Still, perhaps because the Colonel's presence gives the reader early insight into Ryder's nature, Waugh worked hard on minor shades of meaning. At first mentioned as a replacement for the regiment's original colonel, Ryder's superior is described in four different ways as (1) "a fatuous, youngish professional soldier, surly by day, facetious by night" [cancel]; (2) "a different type of officer, a fatuous (ambitious) fellow" [cancel]; (3) "a coarse, youngish, very professional soldier, fatuous, highly professional soldier" [cancel]; and (4) "a younger and less lovable man" [insertion]. Since Waugh was going to present the Colonel scenically—and various insertions expanded these scenes—he deleted Ryder's harsh judgment to allow the reader to make it and to keep Ryder from seeming unduly captious. A few pages later, presenting a direct conflict between Ryder and the Colonel, Waugh changed a ditch to a fence as the boundary between Ryder's platoon and the offending carrier-platoon and deleted a phrase about "disputed territory" to affix firmly the responsibility for the rubbish uncovered and make definite Ryder's disclaimer of responsibility to his platoon

3. Evelyn Waugh, *Brideshead Revisited* (Boston: Little, Brown and Co.,1945), pp. 39–40. Hereafter references to this edition are given parenthetically in the text.
4. Waugh's interest in Ryder's family exfoliated in the manuscript and in the fragmentary "Charles Ryder's Schooldays," written in late 1945. Not until after he had corrected proof did Waugh reconsider the prominence given to the eccentricities of the elder Ryder. Furthermore, Waugh's reading of his own schoolboy diaries in preparing to write the fragment casts some doubt on the "Author's Note." Evelyn Waugh, *The Diaries of Evelyn Waugh,* ed. Michael Davie (Boston: Little, Brown and Co., 1977), p. 636.

sergeant. Thus Ryder is shown as victim of ignorance or oppression rather than as malcontent (p.11). A page later, to underscore the Colonel's professionalism, Waugh inserted the line that casts doubt on whether the Colonel actually says or conveys by other means the petulant, "I do not intend to have my professional reputation compromised by the slackness of a few temporary officers" (p.12, line 32–p.13, line 2), and in manuscript continues: "I know who these officers are. I shall say no more."

Earlier in the text Waugh had inserted the first of his thematic contrasts in character: the hyperprofessional Colonel and the hopelessly unsoldierly Haydon/Hooper, who, even more than Ryder, is the object of the Colonel's wrath because of his haircut and who becomes for Ryder the symbol of "Young England." Perhaps Waugh's imagination was spurred by the contrast, for to the insertion he added yet another (p. 8, line 32–p. 9, line 25)[5] to contrast Hooper's pragmatic fog of illusion with Ryder's own youthful romanticism, now vanished, a passage that helps prepare for Ryder's celebration of Brideshead and of the vanished but not vain past. Much later, into the passage characterizing Lady Marchmain's brothers, symbolically the last of "the Catholic squires of England" (p. 139), Waugh inserted this passage: "These men must die to make a world for Hooper; they were the aborigines, vermin by right of law, to be shot off at leisure so that things might be safe for the traveling salesman, with his polygonal pince-nez, his fat wet hand-shake, his grinning dentures."

Ryder's and probably Waugh's distaste for the modern world comes through all too clearly for some critics, but in other, more elaborate, and more pervasive revisions at all stages of composition Waugh paid close attention to Anthony Blanche and Viscount Mulcaster, nicknamed "Boy" after the manuscript was completed, the ill-sorted pair who serve to qualify or at least call into question Ryder's attitude toward Sebastian, the exemplum of aristocratic grace. Because the revisions are both major and local, it is simpler to discuss their progress through all stages of the text before returning to the growth and change of the text as a whole from one state to another. Blanche's overt homosexuality and malicious, brilliant gossip help establish Sebastian's careless behavior and Ryder's delight in joining it as carefree rather than immoral at the same time that they raise questions about the viability of Sebastian's insouciance in the serious, adult world to which Ryder feels sporadic, uneasy attraction. In contrast, Mulcaster is crudely and mindlessly heterosexual, a friend of Sebastian's, like Blanche, whom

5. The basic insertion is on the back of p. 4 of the manusript; the further insertion is on the front of page 3. Since Waugh rewrote these pages several times, physical priority is meaningless.

Ryder does not really like but accepts as part of his ambience. Mulcaster should have been sufficient corrective to the impression that Ryder and his creator loved lords indiscriminately, for he has position without grace in any sense. Yet hostile critics of *Brideshead* overlooked Mulcaster's and Blanche's importance for the novel's theme, perhaps because they were thought to be survivors from Waugh's early manner.[6] Though reminiscent of figures from the novels through *Scoop*, they are far more complex and far more interlinked with theme than such exotics as Alastair Digby-Vaine-Trumpington and Miles Malpractice.

Blanche is particularly important because he offers Ryder the first and most consistent criticism of the Flyte family, in particular stating the limitations of Sebastian's character and their deleterious effects upon Ryder's vocation as an artist. His eccentricity and his talent for vivid and malicious gossip cause us to examine our evaluation of the characters and make him perhaps the most memorable figure in the novel. Because Anthony is neither authoritative nor unreliable to a predictable degree, Waugh expended great pains to control more and more accurately the reader's response both to him and to Ryder's attitude toward him.

Blanche first appears midway through the first chapter of Book 1 as a belated guest of the luncheon party at which Ryder first meets Sebastian. The luncheon is preceded by a summary of Ryder's earlier life at Oxford, which contains little overt rebellion against the extensive and prosaic advice of his cousin Jasper, conformist and careerist. Blanche's function is to dominate the luncheon, to provide with his frenetic and factitious brilliance a sharp contrast not only to the prosaic virtues of Jasper and of Ryder's previous circle of friends but also to Sebastian's quiet and whimsical charm, and to render Sebastian's considerable eccentricities more acceptable. Furthermore, Blanche's appearance implies a darker or more sinister side to the way of life offered by Sebastian.

Waugh's first draft of the scene, as of many others in the manuscript, is a mere outline: Sebastian's dialogue of greeting is flat, the other guests have no dialogue or business but are merely listed, Ryder leaves with the other guests, and Blanche himself does not emerge very clearly:

> The party assembled. (I cannot recall their names.) There were three Etonian freshmen, mild, elegant, detached young men and [cancel draft continues in left column; revision in right]

6. See, for example, Edmund Wilson, "Splendours and Miseries of Evelyn Waugh," *Classics and Commercials* (New York: Vintage Books, 1962), p. 298. The essay was first published in 1946.

Anthony Blanche a daemonic	/in sharp contrast to them/
(notoriety) notability; who	Anthony Blanche /of whom
greeted Sebastian	at this time I knew nothing
	except that he was a byword (for)
	//of// iniquity from Cherwell
	Edge to Somerville, and
	that he held the table
	that day with unflagging
	energy./

it was he who stood on the balcony with a megaphone and recited *The Waste Land* to the sweatered and muffled throng on their way to the river. "How I have sup-p-p-prised them," he said swaying in the Venetian Gothic window, with his luxurious, self-taught stammer, "All b-b-boatmen are Grace Dddarlings to me." /It was for me the first of many such parties and its details are now merged with those of its successors I think/

In Waugh's revision, after first typescript, the scene was considerably expanded to include the recurring business with the plovers' eggs, a strong emphasis on Sebastian's beauty, and at the end of the scene Charles's and Sebastian's tranquil visit to the Botanical Gardens, which contrasts with Blanche's teasing and seals their friendship. Blanche himself is much more fully characterized in the passage (p. 32, line 16–p. 33, line 9), which presents his entrance, describes his manner and his reputation at Oxford, and moves to his recitation from the balcony. As an afterthought Waugh decided to present the recitation as scene rather than summary and added:

"'I, Tiresias, have foresuffered all,'" he (chan) called to them from the Venetian arches—"old man with wrinkled d-d-dugs"

"Enacted on this same d-divan or b-bed,
I who have sat by Thebes below the wall
And walked among the l-l-lowest of the dead."

And then, stepping lightly into the room, "How I have surprised them! All b-boatmen are Grace Darlings to me."

By presenting Blanche's dialogue before he is characterized, Waugh strengthened the impression that rumor and his appearance do not belie him, and the expansion of *The Waste Land* reading, in the insert to the revision, changes a mere gesture into an important thematic element. Identified with Tiresias (though the phrase about wrinkled dugs was deleted before publication), the bisexual Blanche becomes a prophetic through impious observer of Waugh's waste land, the secular world envisioned in Julia's self-reproaching monologue on "living in sin" 250 pages later. In this version, which except for small details was preserved through all editions before 1960, Blanche is exotic, rather fascinating and attractive to Ryder, and self-consciously eccentric, especially in the speculation about the cause of his stateliness as his being more at ease in robes.[7]

Blanche's next appearance, which occupies more than half of Book 1, Chapter 2, is far more significant to theme and characterization than the first. The chapter records Charles's encounters with his cousin Jasper, with Blanche, and with Sebastian. Jasper censures Charles for his disregard of conventional Oxford wisdom about dress, conduct, friends, and finances, while Sebastian exhibits an aimless charm and bland tolerance even of the malicious Blanche. Anthony, however, dominates the chapter. He invites Charles to dinner at Thame to give his warning about the harmful effects of Sebastian's charm on Charles's artistic sensibility. First Anthony is characterized in summary by Ryder; next he recounts his ducking by Boy Mulcaster and a group of hearties and his subsequent encounter with them in Sebastian's rooms; then he makes an extended comparison between Sebastian and Stefanie de Vincennes, his former lover who drained him emotionally and according to Anthony made him what he has become; next he places Sebastian in the context of his "*very sinister* family"; and finally he offers Charles his own kind of "appreciation and criticism and stimulus" (p. 57).

This general outline is preserved in all versions of the scene, but the details are so complex as to defy reasonable limitations on quotation or chronological summary. Logically, three categories are discernible: Anthony's past, re-

---

7. By 1959, Waugh must have decided that Blanche was too attractive. For the paragraph beginning "From the moment" he substituted a wholly new one, and in the succeeding paragraph he made three important cuts:

> He was tall, slim, rather swarthy, with large saucy eyes. The rest of us wore rough tweeds and brogues. He had on a smooth chocolate-brown suit with loud white stripes, suede shoes, a large bow-tie and he drew off yellow, wash-leather gloves as he came into the room; part Gallic, part Yankee, part, perhaps, Jew; wholly exotic.
>
> This, I did not need telling, was Anthony Blanche, the "aesthete" par excellence, a byeword of iniquity from Cherwell Edge to Somerville. He had been pointed out to me often in the streets, as he pranced along with his high peacock tread; I had heard his voice in the George challenging the conventions; and now meeting him, under the spell of Sebastian, I found myself enjoying him voraciously.[p. 41]

In the revisions Waugh emphasizes Blanche's singular, indeed odd, appearance, drawing implicitly on Cousin Jasper's earlier discussion of proper attire at Oxford. The national and ethnic labels, by typifing him, make him a more ordinary kind of eccentric, less exotic, inscrutable, and original, while the shift from lizard to peacock makes Blanche less sinister and more ludicrous than in the earlier text.

vealed in Charles's summary and in his monologue; gossipy characterization of the Flyte family; and Blanche's prediction and the subsequent proof of Sebastian's response to Charles's account of Anthony's stories.

The first category is most obviously important because it shapes our response to everything else, and Waugh expended most pains upon these passages. In the manuscript he wrote two overlapping versions of the summary characterization before canceling both in favor of a revised version very close to all those before 1960. In contrast to his general practice, these first drafts were considerably more detailed than their replacement, in which he cut and polished. For example, Anthony's parentage was given in much fuller detail: his mother is Russian, his father a French painter who in the first canceled version burned his canvases on his wife's departure and in the second added himself to the holocaust. Anthony's peripatetic way of life is made clear enough in the revised version, but the canceled drafts emphasize far more strongly the constant unsettling changes of locale and residence as his only concept of home, as well as the grossness and decadence of the aged whores and flabby men who give him presents. In revision change is made to seem rather exhilarating, in keeping with Charles's description of Anthony, in second draft, "like a Hogarthian page boy waxing in wickedness," and in the final, far more emphatic, "waxing in wickedness like a Hogarthian page-boy"; the only acquaintances are prominent homosexual artists and "fading beauties"; and Anthony is made to seem less a victim of his environment than innately and zestfully depraved and avid for experience.

Having formulated the introduction, Waugh left it almost untouched through successive revisions. In the 1960 edition, however, he added before "he had practiced black art in Cefalu" the phrase "by his own account" (p. 56), probably to remind us that Charles's knowledge comes largely from Anthony himself and to raise in our minds doubts of his veracity.

Anthony's story of his romance with Stefanie de Vincennes is barely accessible to the variorum format and represents vividly Waugh's changing conception of him.[8]

> "Of course those that have charm don't really need brains. Stefanie de Vincennes intoxicated* me four years ago; but I was besotted with her, crawling with love like lice.† You have heard of the species of spider among whom the male takes up permanent residence in the interior of his mate? I was like that; I lived in Stefanie de Vincennes, I saw through her eyes and breathed through her nostrils; my dear, I even used the same

8. The copy text for this passage is the 1944 special edition, published by Chapman and Hall (pp. 47–48), the last edition in which these variants appear. Waugh cut them in correcting proof. No attempt has been made to treat accidentals.

coloured varnish for my toe-nails. I used her words and lit my cigarette
in the same way and spoke with her tone on the telephone so that the duke
used to carry on long and intimate conversations with me, thinking that
I was her. It was largely that which put his mind on pistol and sabres in
such an old-fashioned manner. I learned to lie in bed exactly as she did,
with one hand under the pillow and the other palm upwards, the fingers
just curled round the fold of the sheet, as though drawing it away from
her face—and I assure you, Charles, until you have tried, it is a most
irksome posture to maintain for long. My dear, I could sleep in no other
position.‡ And yet that woman has not the wits of Mulcaster.§ Pure
charm. I was her lover for barely eighteen months, and for three months
of that time we did not see each other. You would not think such a
thing could have a lasting effect. //My step-father thought it an excellent
education for me. He thought it would make me grow out of what he calls
my 'English habits.' Poor man, he is very South American. Well, I have
kept my 'English habits,' but I think I lost something else. At seventeen
I might have been anything; an artist even; it is not impossible; it is in
the blood. At twenty-one I am what you see me. To have squandered
everything, so young, on a woman who, except that I was more present-
able, would as soon have had her chiropodist for her lover . . . . I never
heard anyone speak an ill word of Stefanie, except the Duke; everyone
loved her, whatever she did."**

———————————————————

*1960: really tickled

† Cancel draft in manuscript:

lice. I followed her completely, in taste, in judgment, in her tone of voice
/over the telephone/ and her (turns of phrase) /favourite words/, in (what
she did with her hands) /the way she ate fruit and smoked a cigarette, in
the way she lay asleep with one hand under the pillow and the other palm
upward with the fingers just curled about the fold of the sheet—and I
assure you, Peter, until you have tried you can have no idea what a difficult
pose that is to maintain. I loved her so much that I could sleep in no other
position.

  Corrected proofs, all published book versions: ago. My dear, I even
‡Serial: manner. And yet the woman had no wits.

  In manuscript the material from "You have heard" to "no other position"
is an insertion.

§Manuscript: Mulcastle.

//Corrected proofs and all published book versions:

  manner. My

  In manuscript, the sentence "you would not . . . lasting effect" is an
  insertion.

#1960: South American . . . . I never
**1960: Duke: and *she,* my dear, is positively cetinous.

Waugh's revision of this paragraph consistently and increasingly made Anthony's romance less affecting through the 1960 edition. For the final version Waugh cut Anthony's paragraph-long dialogue four pages later about Stefanie's producing cancerous boredom and killing what might have been the artist in Anthony (p.57; 1960, p. 67). Shorn of drama, flattened, and made tickling rather than intoxicating, the romance and Stefanie are made to seem banal. Perhaps Waugh wished to make the obsession less fatally attractive in order to render the analogy with Sebastian more fitting and less suggestive of sexuality and thus to accord with Anthony's characterization of Sebastian as "insipid" and "simple and charming." In the final version Sebastian is not presented as harmful to Charles's artistic career; Anthony is not the artist *manqué* but a potential audience and source of help. Furthermore, what in previous versions is Sebastian's casual denial that Anthony's story is true is changed in 1960 to equally casual corroboration. Being less affecting, it need not be an invention, and, as we shall see later, it gives Anthony an authority unsettling to Charles and the reader alike.

Waugh's handling of the gossipy characterization of the Flytes exhibits his tendency to expand in manuscript and to cut in the final version, as well as another kind of revision found in the manuscript: to rearrange material. The order as we now have it goes back to the revised manuscript: Anthony characterizes Sebastian's family, disparages Sebastian's conversation, and compares him explicitly to Stefanie. In the canceled first draft, however, Waugh had put the disparagement before the family; the reordering provides a more effective summary and conclusion to the main theme of Anthony's discourse.

The first versions of Anthony's discussion of the Flytes, canceled and rewritten in manuscript, contain most of the information but little of the flavor of the author's second, final thoughts. Speaking of Sebastian at Eton, Blanche is first made to remark flatly that only Sebastian was never beaten because, "Of course he was very religious and that meant he never quite did anything wrong." The revision conveys Anthony's malice, his characteristic rhythms of speech, and his genius for recalling or inventing *ad hominem* details:

> I can see him now, at the age of fifteen. He never had spots you know; all the other boys were spotty. Mulcaster was positively scrofulous. But not Sebastian. Or did he have one, rather a stubborn one at the back of his neck? I think, now, that he did. (He was cherub) /Narcissus/ with *one* pustule. He and I were both Catholics so we used to go to mass together. He used to spend *such* a time in the confessional, I used to wonder what he had to say,

because he never did anything wrong; /never quite;/ at least he never got punished. Perhaps he was just being charming through the grill.[9]

Waugh's revision of Anthony's discussion of Brideshead, Julia, Cordelia, and Lord and Lady Marchmain illustrates the same general principles. The first, canceled draft is roughly seven hundred words long; the second draft, model for all subsequent versions, is some three hundred words longer. The addition of extravagant and enlivening detail can be represented by the following passage, which uses as copy text the Little, Brown edition and marks additions by single parenthetical letters at each end of the inserted material and double letters for insertions within insertions. Of course, the passage as a whole is itself an insertion, replacing: "From the way people behave you would think he had beaten & robbed her and indulged in what my stepfather calls 'English habits'":

(*a*)   You would think that the old reprobate had tortured her, (illegible) stolen her patrimony, flung her out of doors, (*bb*) roasted, stuffed and eaten his children, (*bb*) and gone frolicking (off into all the high jinks) (*cc*) about wreathed in all the flowers (*cc*) of Sodom and Gomorrah; instead of what? Begetting four splendid children by her, (leaving) (*dd*) handing over to (*dd*) her Brideshead and Marchmain House in London and all the money she can possibly want to spend, while he sits with a snowy shirt-front at Larue's with a personable, middle aged lady of the theatre, in the most conventional Edwardian style. (*a*)

(*b*)   And she meanwhile keeps (((her)) /a/ little coterie) (*ee*) a small gang (*ee*) of enslaved and emaciated prisoners (*ff*) for her exclusive enjoyment. (*ff*) *She sucks their blood.* You can see the tooth-marks all over Adrian Porson's shoulders when he is bathing. And he, my dear, was the greatest, the *only,* poet of our time. He's bled dry; there's nothing left of him. There are five or six others of all ages and sexes, like wraiths following her round. They never escape once she's had her teeth into them. (*b*) It is (black art) witchcraft. There's no other explanation.

Both the detail and the rhythm of the inserted passages not only give a more vivid portrait of the Marchmains but further dramatize Anthony. The series within a series of (*bb*) is especially notable for introducing a complicating rhythm into the verb-object pattern first established. Furthermore, in view of Anthony's predilictions, "high jinks" is less suitable than wreaths of flowers to describe homosexual adventures. For that matter, the canceled "English

9. See p. 51 of the Little, Brown edition for the final version, slightly altered.

habits" reflects a certain odium upon Anthony that, as Waugh concieves him, he would probably reject or ignore.

Waugh's few deletions in the passage about the Flytes mostly affect Julia. The one exception, deleting "like a toad in the coal" of Brideshead from the proof copy, probably reflects Waugh's recognition that he had used a very similar phrase, added to the manuscript, in Lord Marchmain's dying monologue (p. 333) and wished to avoid the echo. The changes affecting Julia seem largely calculated to make her look less ridiculous in anticipation of her role as Charles's lover. In the manuscript but deleted from printed texts is Anthony's description of her "sister-act" with Lady Marchmain in Venice, which in tone is out of keeping with Julia's actual dialogue. Removed from the 1960 edition are sentences labeling her as "Renaissance tragedy" and as "a fiend—a passionless, acquisitive, intriguing, ruthless *killer*" (p. 54; see 1960, p. 64). Cordelia is dismissed as "abominable," and later, in revising for fair typescript, Waugh echoed the passage by inserting the memory of her governess's suicide to contrast the actual Cordelia with the monster whom Blanche posited.

More immediately important to the chapter—none of the Flytes save Sebastian appears until late in the next chapter—is "Boy" Mulcaster—nicknamed only in "Ms interpolations in second draft." Waugh put into Anthony's dialogue three widely variant if not contradictory descriptions of him ranging from clod to degenerate to mere cad. In the first draft Blanche focuses upon Mulcaster's plebian and grotesque appearance:

> (He is a peer like pig.) /If you see (a man li) //someone like// a butcher's boy only much grubbier—no one would let him handle meat—with clothes that are a kind of negative photograph—I mean (where he goes in) they (go out) //flap on his little concavities// and where he bulges, they cling—that is Mulcaster/

In revising the manuscript to the version present in all editions before 1960, Waugh converted Mulcaster from a bumpkin lord of Restoration comedy to a symptom of all that is wrong with the English aristocracy:

> (If you happen to see) Seen at a distance—at some considerable distance—you might think him rather personable: (a nice meaty [?]) /lanky, old-fashioned/ young man you might think; (give him a red coat and all the vague [?] maidens in Hyde Park would make a set at him) But look at him closer and his face all falls to pieces (in one great gape & [illegible] aspiring young maiden [?]) in an idiot gape. People are rather free with the word "degenerate." They have even used it of me. If you want to know what a real degenerate is, look at Boy Mulcaster.[10]

10. See Little, Brown edition, pp. 48–49, for the printed version.

Thematically this characterization not only establishes Mulcaster as the antithesis of Blanche and of Sebastian but prepares for later scenes involving Mulcaster and begins preparing the reader for the revulsion he should feel at Ryder's becoming his brother-in-law: for in Book 2 (3 of Little, Brown, 1960), Celia Mulcaster Ryder will become the antithesis of Julia Flyte Mottram, who very nearly becomes Ryder's second wife. In the final, 1960 version, Waugh is less interested in later effects than in the dynamics of this one chapter. The wholly revised passage reads:

> Of course you've met Boy? He's always popping in out (*sic*) of dear Sebastian's rooms. He's everything we dagos expect of an English lord. A great *parti* I can assure you. All the young ladies in London are after him. He's very hoity-toity with them, I'm told. My dear, he's scared stiff. A great oaf—that's Mulcaster—and what's more, my dear, a *cad* (pp.58–59).

This version reinforces Mulcaster's link to Sebastian, already established in Anthony's account of meeting his tormentors in Sebastian's rooms. The motive for the change is made clear only at the chapter's end, when Charles is testing Anthony's veracity by questioning Sebastian. All versions have Anthony predict that Sebastian will turn the conversation to his toy bear and Sebastian's doing so; the 1960 version adds, "And then Boy Mulcaster came into the room" (p. 71). This line, together with Sebastian's casual testimony about the de Vincennes affair, tends to make Anthony even more credible, to create further suspicions about the superficiality of Sebastian's charm, and to link him so strongly to the doltish Mulcaster that it is no surprise when the two and Charles go to a London dance together in Chapter 5.

Blanche disappears after this chapter for three years and 145 pages, but Waugh stresses his importance in Charles's *vale* to him as the increasingly dismal autumn term begins Book 2, Chapter 1 (Little, Brown, 1960, Chapter 5). Waugh's attempts to refine this passage were limited to the manuscript and first typescript stage, but they show him dramatizing with increasing effectiveness Blanche's importance. All of the material from page 107, line 24, to page 108, line 18 was inserted to replace an abortive summary of the deflating effect of Blanche's departure. The order differed slightly from the present version: the first sentence of the paragraph beginning "The Charity matinee" originally followed the second sentence, but Waugh apparently shifted it because it made a better topic sentence. The various stages of insertion, indicated by single, double, and triple virgules, show Waugh adding details to the extended metaphor and making the forsaken amateurs entirely feminine and passive material on which Blanche had worked:

> Without him they forgot their cues and garbled their lines; they needed him to ring the curtain up at the right moment; they needed him to direct

the limelights; they needed his whisper in the wings, /and his imperious eye on the leader of the band;/ without him there were no (advanced bookings /or advertisement/) /photographers from the weekly press/, no prearranged goodwill and expectation of pleasure. //The Charity matinee was over, I felt; the impresario had buttoned his astrakhan coat and taken his fee and the disconsolate ladies of the company were without a leader. No stronger bond held them together than common service; now the gold lace and velvet were packed away and returned to the costumier and the drab uniform of the day put on in its stead. For a few happy hours of[11] rehearsal, for a few ecstatic minutes of performance, they had played splendid parts, their own great ancestors, the famous paintings they were thought to resemble; now it was over and in the bleak light of day they must go back to their homes; to the /// husband who came to London too often, to the/// (husband) /lover/ who lost at cards, and to the child who grew too fast.//

Blanche reappears with Mulcaster at a raucous party for the Blackbirds on the eve of the General Strike, and Waugh uses him to give Charles information about Sebastian's further decline in the year since Charles last heard of him. In both manuscript versions, the second very close to all printed versions (except the serial, where it does not appear at all),[12] Anthony conveys the same basic information: Sebastian lived with him in Marseilles, became more alcoholic and less responsible, was introduced to but rejected drugs, went to Africa, and took up with a nine-toed German former Legionnaire. The deleted version is characteristically shorter, flatter in style, and less attentive to chronology and climax than its successor. Furthermore, Mulcaster imparts information about Sebastian. This is deleted in the second manuscript draft, perhaps to avoid having Mulcaster pass judgment, but not until the carbon typescript is Mulcaster shown playing with the fire alarm and announcing, as Blanche had predicted 150 pages earlier, that he had dunked Blanche in Mercury fountain. In these revisions Mulcaster is made more consistently useless and cloddish. Another addition to the revised manuscript is Anthony's dialogue about Lady Marchmain (see Little, Brown, 1945, p. 205, lines 6–9), which prepares for her request that Charles visit Sebastian.

In writing Blanche's fourth and final appearance, at Ryder's exhibition of paintings, Waugh canceled a draft that is very close to page 269, except that Blanche's dialogue is less staccato and idiosyncratic, but after the characters

11. The rest of the paragraph and to the end of the first paragraph on p. 109 of the Little, Brown edition are in typescript that has been pasted in the manuscript. One long sentence, beginning after "expectation of pleasure," was deleted and replaced by the inserted material.

12. See my "The Serial Version of *Brideshead Revisited,*" *Twentieth Century Literature* 15 (1969):35–43, for an extended discussion of the serial's text.

move to the Blue Grotto so that Blanche can summarize his views on Ryder's career, Waugh inserted the description of the garish club—changing "blue" to the more vivid "cobalt"—and of its seedy denizens (page 271, lines 3-9) and then canceled a much shorter draft (p. 271, line 16-p. 272, line 28) and replaced it with the current text. In the process Blanche's style is raised to the level of extravagant fantasy characteristic of him, as in:

CANCEL DRAFT

I went to your first exhibition and I thought it charming—an interior of Marchmain House in particular, quite delicious, very English, very correct. "My friend Charles wished to paint like a gentleman,' I said, 'and he has done it. What will he do next?' My dear, I bought your book of provincial architecture and what did I find? Charm again. (Before, at least, it was the English) It is the English tea party; it is the chit-chat of the rectory garden. I said to myself: 'Well these things are not for me.' The shade of the cedar, cucumber sandwiches, the silver cream jug (the tennis rackets.) /English maidens dressed in what ever English maidens put on to play tennis— this is Charles's taste./ My taste is for something a little more spicy, my dear. /To be frank I despaired./

REVISED DRAFT

"I went to your first exhibition," said Anthony; "I found it— charming. There was an interior of Marchmain House, very English, very correct, but quite delicious. 'Charles has done something,' I said; 'not all he will do, not all he can do, but something.'

"Even then, my dear, I wondered a little. It seemed to me that there was something a little *gentlemanly* about your painting. You must remember I am not English; I cannot understand this keen zest to be well-bred. English snobbery is more macabre to me even than English morals. However, I said, 'Charles has done something delicious. What will he do next?'

"The next thing I saw was your very handsome volume— *Village and Provincial Architecture,* was it called? Quite a tome, my dear, and what did I find? Charm again. "Not quite my cup of tea,' I thought; 'this is too English.' I have the fancy for rather spicy things, you know, not for the shade of the cedar tree, the cucumber sandwich, the silver cream-jug, the English girl

> dressed in whatever English girls
> do wear for tennis—not that, not
> Jane Austen, *not* M-m-miss
> M-m-mitford. Then, to be frank,
> dear Charles, I despaired of you.
> 'I am a degenerate old d-d-dago,'
> I said, 'and Charles (is a clean
> old maid.)—/I speak only of your
> art, my dear—is a dean's daughter
> in flowered muslin.'/
> [pp. 271–72]

Particularly noteworthy in revision are the sharp contrast between the hackneyed pedantry of "tome" and the stereotyped colloquialism "cup of tea," the reviving and expansion of the deliberately vague reference to tennis in contrast to the specific images that precede it, and, most important of all, the change of focus from Ryder to Blanche himself by the use of first person and by the striking and absurd contrast that concludes the paragraph. Less striking but no less important is the passage added in revision (p. 271, lines 17–24) contrasting the sordid present scene, which fades as Blanche talks, with Ryder's sharp memory of Oxford, "looking out over Christ Church Meadow through a window of Ruskin-Gothic." The contrast embodies an obvious judgment of Blanche's aestheticism that has degenerated into modernist sensationalism; it may also contain, far less explicitly, a judgment of the aesthetic movement as sponsored by Ruskin.

Limited to this choice, Ryder and his creator would choose Ruskin-Gothic, and in fact Ryder does not bother to dispute Blanche's judgment of his paintings, but leaves him to go to Brideshead, which embodies the central aesthetic standard of the novel. The ancestral estate of the Flyte family, Brideshead is as much a structure in Ryder's imagination as a real edifice. After the manuscript stage Waugh reinforced the theme in various insertions and revisions, but in the initial stages of composition he concentrated on the passage in the Prologue in which Ryder realizes where he is and receives the beginnings of imaginative renewal from hearing the name and viewing the prospect before him. Because the setting must capture the reader's imagination as well as Ryder's, Waugh introduced detail and modulated verbal rhythms to make the strongest possible impression. In a first draft he outlined both content and structure of the transition to the physical scene:

> He told me and, as he said the name, it was as though someone had switched off a wireless which had been bawling,—for how many years?—in my head (leaving?) bringing on the instant an immense (and [illegible]) tranquility, quite empty at first but filling, slowly, as (the) /my/ ears grew

used to it, with a multitude of sweet and natural and long forgotten sounds. It was a conjuror's name of such ancient power over me that the phantasy of the past four years vanished before it /and left me solitary in the world of real things./

This established the contrast between sordid present and beauteous past, but the response was too swift, the thematic contrast too simple to satisfy Waugh. In writing the second version, on the same page as the first, he replaced the rhetorical question with the more descriptive and rhythmically more effective adverbial compound; he elaborated and made more precise the process by which first silence and then tranquility replace the mental noise, and in a victory over sentimental nostalgia he recognized the reality of present as well as past:

> He told me and, on the instant, it was as though someone had switched off the wireless, and a voice that had been bawling in my ears, incessantly, (unendurable) /fatuously/, for days beyond number, had been suddenly (stilled) /cut short/; an immense (still) silence followed, empty at first, but gradually, as my outraged sense (recovered) regained authority, full of a multitude of sweet and natural and long-forgotten sounds—for he had spoken a name most familiar and most dear to me, /and/ most unexpected. It was a conjuror's name of such ancient power (over me) that, at its mere sound, the (phantasies) /phantoms/ of (four) /those haunted/ last years began to take flight.
>
> Outside the hut I stood bemused between two realities and two dreams. [Page 15 varies slightly.]

The physical scene went through three drafts. In the first, continuous with the canceled passage quoted above, Waugh merely sketched the rhythmic, almost cinematic progression from foreground to wider prospect:

> I (left) /went (out of) from/ the hut and found about me the familiar foreground, ([illegible] now an impalpable mirage) of corrugated iron and the familiar smell & clatter /and chatter/ of the cookhouse and washhouse; and beyond it, beyond the mirage, a broad lake, (and) beyond that another, and, around the lakes, green glades and towering /grey/ woodland, (just) /faintly/ dusted with green now in the first breaking of the (leaves) /buds/. The house could not be seen from (where I stoo) our lines but I knew /well/ where it lay, ahead, out of sight, (behind) /below/ the soft green curve of the opposing (hill) rise.

In a canceled revision at the bottom of the manuscript page, continuous with the end of the second quotation above, Waugh began to elaborate on the setting, still moving from the particular—the stream and the lakes—to the general before returning to more specific details:

Evelyn Waugh, Writer

> Outside the hut I stood awed and bemused between two realities and two dreams. We were camped in parkland on the gentle slope of a valley; (all round) /on all sides/ rose the clatter and chatter & broken song of the battalion, the reek & smoke of the cookhouses, the haphazard litter of corrugated iron and ash paths. /All this I knew./ Below, down the valley, (flowed) the gentle Bride flowed to join the Avon; the stream was dammed here in three broad lakes which mirrored the morning clouds /and the great trees at their margin/; (and) it was an ([illegible] place of [illegible]) sequestered place, enclosed & embraced by its surrounding hills; an exquisite manmade landscape of green glades and towering grey woodland, faintly dusted with green.

Here he broke off, perhaps conscious of the illogic of the progression, and composed the passage that leads the eye from sky to ground, along the hillside cluttered by the encampment to the frame of the two slopes before filling in the landscape in far more specific detail to indicate the continued process of growth as well as static beauty, a work of art as well as a landscape (p. 15, line 25–p. 16, line 22).

In the final book of the novel, Brideshead and Lady Julia Flyte become inextricably associated in Charles Ryder's mind. In both he finds refuge from the horrible, fashionable world represented at two different extremes by his wife and by Anthony Blanche. In Julia he finds continuous "new wealth and delicacy" (p. 277); in Brideshead, which through marriage to Julia he stands to inherit, [13] he discovers "such a prospect perhaps as a high pinnacle afforded after the hungry days in the desert and the jackal-haunted nights. Need I reproach myself if sometimes I was rapt in the vision?" (p. 322). The question is not rhetorical, for, while Charles need not reproach himself, he must abandon the vision, reject the kingdoms of the earth, and attain a higher kind of love to reach the understanding he displays in the Epilogue.

In local and immediate terms, however, Waugh had to establish the validity of Ryder's attraction to Julia not only as symbol but as woman. One crucial passage describes their meeting aboard ship after ten years of separation. As on so many other occasions, the first draft was merely functional:

> I walked through some of the halls of the great ship and in the corner of one of them, sitting idly without a book or anything to employ her, I found Julia.

13. In one local revision Waugh deleted a summary of the visit of Beryl, the new Lady Brideshead, to the Castle and Lord Marchmain's refusal to see the couple in favor of direct presentation of the visit (pp. 322–23), probably to give the reader a view other than Lord Marchmain's jaundiced one and to make more plausible his determination to leave the Castle outside the direct male line.

140

"My maid's complaining so bitterly about my cabin," she said, "I can't think why. It's [*sic*] seems a lap to me. She's (been in a bad temper) /made my life a misery/ ever since we left England. I couldn't bear another minute of her so I'm hiding till she's finished unpacking."

"I heard Celia telephoning to you"

"Yes, what luck finding you on board. Everyone else looks very madly grim."

"Celia seems to have found friends."

"She always was a friendly girl. I never see her now. I can't think why. I never see anyone I like. Is she as pretty as ever? I always admired her looks"

"Yes, she hasn't changed."

"You have Charles. So thin & manly. Not a bit like that soft friend Sebastian used to have about."

"Was I soft?"

"I used to think so. Perhaps I was harder myself then."

She had changed, too. She (was rounder and more womanly) /had lost her spidery look; (and)/ her figure (and grace of movement) now matched her quattrocento head; her eyes seemed to see more; she no longer had the air of picking her way, delicately & intently, as in the old days she seemed to do; ([illegible]) it was symbolic of the change that (I) /she/ should (find her) /be found/ thus, sitting quietly, unoccupied, waiting for a cross servant to leave her in peace. Her welcome was (frank and un [illegible] as in) /candid. How often, meeting old/ friends after a long separation one finds a barrier of formality, a grudging (lack [illegible]) /hint/ that an earlier intimacy must not be allowed to

As in the description of Brideshead, Waugh broke off in midsentence and began a second draft that with minor revision covered more than three pages of the published text (p. 236, line 26–p. 240, line 2). First he described fully the ship's decor, with blotting paper the dominant color image, and had Ryder reflect on the setting as symbol:

Here I am, I thought, back from the jungle, back from the ruins. Here, where wealth is no longer gorgeous and power has no dignity. *Quomodo sedet sola civitas* (for I had heard that great lament, which Cordelia once quoted to me in the drawing-room of Marchmain House, sung by a half-caste choir in Guatemala, nearly a year ago). [p. 237; Waugh's parentheses]

Then the horrors of America are echoed when, in a brief dialogue with the steward, Ryder cannot get an uniced whiskey and soda. Only then is Julia introduced as a relief from the sterile modernity represented by the decor and by Celia Ryder. The description by negation at the beginning and the editorializing at the end of the first draft were replaced by the more subtle "She opened the empty hands on her lap with a little eloquent gesture" and the dialogue about her maid. In a canceled second draft Waugh introduced a version of the contrast between her manner now and that of ten years earlier. In a revision in second draft Waugh decided to emphasize more strongly the contrast between her looks as girl and those as woman, and he wrote two elaborate versions of the analogy with Italian painting, the second a refinement of the first:

> She had grown up to the quattro centro head which before /she/ had borne a little oddly, had lost the spidery look of fashion and though she was dressed with contemporary elegance it was not of Scaparelli I thought but of Leonardo; of one of his attendant angels, half-heathen creature of the Renaissance, (with) /whose/ head, still full of lingering celestial memories, (at ease neither with /her/ august companions and sacred duties nor with the sharp, dim-lit rocks and fallen humanity about her) turns from her sacred duties and glances at the sharp, dim-lit rocks and fallen humanity about her, and is happy with neither; such was her beauty and into such terms was it my trick to translate my thoughts; "Leonardo," I thought, sitting beside her, /but all the/ while /(in the woods)/ deep (below) /beneath/ this trivial acquaintance, other senses were silently doing their work, making another image; certainly I did not think of Mona Lisa; of that smug old smiler, whose many deaths and sea-bathing and haggling at the bazaars and confusing progeny—all that famous catalogue of experience applauded in Brasenose—had been 'but as the sound of lyres and flutes'; not of her, for Julia /in spite of her beauty—because of it perhaps —/ was plainly /(sad)/ despondent . . . .

In the fourth and final manuscript draft, after minor revisions, this had become "they [the years] had (saddened her) been more than 'the sound of lyres and flutes' and had saddened her," and Ryder explicitly denies that her beauty is "connected in any way with painting or the arts or with anything except herself,—" though he later added the overt negation of the comparison with La Giaconda (p. 239). This limits the range of reference to the matter at hand,[14] and in another, structural revision, Waugh moved the characterization of the intimacy of Charles and Julia from after to before the dialogue that illustrates it.

---

14. The revision also eliminates the paraphrase of Pater, which is an elaborate and not very funny inside joke. Aside from the fact that Pater was a fellow of Brasenose College, see the pub-crawling hearties from BNC—Brasenose College—mentioned on p. 109.

The references to Tenebrae and to the Renaissance were probably introduced as echoes of the earlier sequence in which Charles is completing his first major painting. Cordelia alludes to the service, and Charles, impatient with "convent chatter," thinks as "a man of the Renaissance . . . of Browning's Renaissance" (pp. 220, 222). Here the convent chatter is stilled, but Charles is attuned to the beauty of the real Renaissance rather than the vainglorious nineteenth-century version. Still later, in the episode on the liner after the consummation of Ryder's and Julia's love, Waugh inserted the description of the stars sweeping the sky as, "I had seen them sweep above the towers and gables of Oxford" (p. 261). This is echoed in the passage inserted after the manuscript stage about the final youthful carouse of Sebastian and Ryder in which Charles "reeled back to my rooms under a starry heaven which swam dizzily above the towers" (p. 145). The echo not only provides a subtle link between Ryder's love for the brother and the sister but also reinforces the idea that a return to reality—immediately with the end of the storm, more remotely with Julia's recovery of her faith—threatens the lovers.

One other significant alteration in the original manuscript of this sequence expanded the role of Charles's and Julia's casual shipboard acquaintance. At first the acquaintance merely compliments them on their bravery in passing the heavy swinging doors of the lounge (pp. 252-53), but in an over-page insertion he confronts them again, invites them to a party, and thereafter falls, breaks a collarbone, and disappears into the ship's hospital. Because he thinks the two a married couple, he serves to bring them psychologically closer; and his tale about a romantic shipboard encounter contrasts with their view of the developing relationship. Alone before they meet him, they seem still more isolated after he is removed from the scene. This passage and others like it indicate that when Waugh wrote of "drama and suspense" he was not thinking in melodramatic terms, for it postpones but subtly modifies the perception of the love affair. And, of course, he sets off and complements the odd little man who crashes Celia's party and is taken away by police when the ship reaches England. This character provides an atmosphere of daring and seediness combined in which Charles and Julia unknowingly function.

Most of the revisions in characterization discussed in this chapter serve as implicit correctives to Ryder's judgment of his experience as it occurs rather than the way he judges it retrospectively. Because of the point of view, of course, the same thing could be said of everything in the novel, with the possible exception of the Epilogue; however, a logical distinction can be made between these passages and those in which detail is altered or augmented to create more fully the texture of the world that Ryder perceives, and Waugh, aware of the problem, sought to address it at all stages of writing the manuscript.

8

Clarifying and Enriching *Brideshead*

At the same time that Waugh faced new problems in managing the first-person narrator of *Brideshead,* he was aware that he had not resisted a long-standing "temptation in writing to make everything happen in one day, in one hour on one page and so lose its drama and suspense." To combat this temptation, which from the evidence of the manuscript he felt more frequently than at any other stage of his career, he repeatedly canceled as many as six closely written pages within a day or two of writing them and forced himself to recast the material, "rewriting and stitching until I am cramped."[1] Other extended passages were reshaped or augmented in revision of typescript. At both stages the manuscript reveals the ways in which he dealt with the complexities of "the time sequence and the transitions"[2] created by his choice of focus and angle of narration, and some, especially major transitions from one chronological sequence, one mood, or one dominant character to a successor, reveal more clearly than anywhere else in Waugh's manuscripts the author in the process of transmuting inchoate thoughts into polished language.

These revisions might profitably be discussed not in the order in which they occurred but in increasing order of complexity. Some were, speaking very relatively, straighforward and simple. For example, Waugh's chief motive in revising the beginning of Book 3, Chapter 2 (Little, Brown, 1945, Bk. 2, Chap. 2), seems to have been a desire to give greater balance to the account of the private view of Ryder's paintings. In first draft, canceled on June 4, all the incidents save the appearance of Anthony Blanche occur before luncheon and are climaxed by the appearance of royalty. The revised passage, almost identical to that of the printed text (pp. 264–69),[3] distributes

1. Evelyn Waugh, *The Diaries of Evelyn Waugh,* ed. Michael Davie (Boston: Little, Brown and Co., 1977), p. 561 (March 22, 1944). Davie reads "stretching" instead of "stitching," but the context makes this unlikely.

2. *Ibid.,* p. 228 (February 1, 1944).

3. The major exception is the description of Mr. Samgrass as a contributor to the *Evening Standard's* "Londoner's Diary" rather than as "one of Lord Copper's middle-aged young men on the *Daily Beast.* " See the discussion of the page proofs.

the incidents more evenly. The morning is still climaxed by the royal visit, but to the afternoon are shifted the major accolades: commendation from a previously condescending critic, visits from representatives of the major collections, various encomiums that Ryder contrasts with comments at his previous exhibition, and, climactically, Ryder's discovery that, having learned before the earlier exhibition of his wife's infidelity, he can no longer be embarrassed by her. Only then, in sharp contrast to Ryder's public and personal triumphs, is the censurious Blanche introduced.

Book 2, Chapter 2 (Little, Brown, 1945, Bk. 1, Chap. 5), the account of the Christmas party at Brideshead after Sebastian's grand tour with Mr. Samgrass, is the passage that Waugh "rewrote and stitched until I am cramped." Furthermore, he rearranged the material to greater advantage:

CANCELED PASSAGE	REVISION
Arrival	Arrival
Samgrass's story	Samgrass's story
Julia and Ryder on Sebastian and Samgrass	Visit to Nanny; Ryder on Paris, art school
Cocktails and dinner	Cocktails and dinner
Ryder on Paris to Sebastian	Sebastian's plans for the morrow
Sebastian's story	Sebastian's story
Sebastian's plans for the morrow	Reactions to Sebastian by others in direct scene
Reactions to Sebastian in retrospective scene	Ryder painting in garden room as usual; talk with Julia
Walk to village with Julia	

The scenes in the nursery and in the garden room recall similar episodes in the rest of the novel, and the first, in providing occasion for Ryder's account of his life, allows Waugh to separate it from Sebastian's considerably more important revelations, which, by being the sole subject of conversation, become more dramatic in the revision.

In first draft Waugh again succumbed to the temptation to summarize rather than portray, but he conquered it in revision. Lady Marchmain's preliminary account of Sebastian was expanded by giving the text of her letter (p. 150). Later Waugh developed the preparations for Sebastian's joining the hunt from three very brief paragraphs to fifteen lines (p. 155, line 32–p. 156, lines 13, 22–24) and moved the order for whiskey from before to after the discussion to underline the family's satisfaction with Sebastian and, by introducing a double shift in mood, to show the precariousness of their optimism. To put Sebastian's tour in perspective, Waugh made his plans to get drunk anticipate his story, introduced in revision the scene of Sebastian's return

(p. 167, lines 4–11), and presented dinner scenically to show the effect of those plans on the rest of his family.

As was his custom, Waugh also introduced subtle touches to emphasize his themes. In first draft, in response to Julia's question about his disappointment at not reaching a destination, Sebastian replies simply, "Me? Oh, I don't think I was there that day, was I Sammy?" In revision Waugh emphasized Sebastian's isolation with the lines that precede this reply: "'Me?' said Sebastian from the shadows beyond the lamplight, /beyond the warmth of the burning logs,/ beyond the family circle and the photographs spread out on the card-table" (p. 149, lines 18–20). Furthermore, the hiatus between "Me?" and its repetition and the echo of Samgrass's "You were ill" gives the answer overtones far beyond its denotative content. Later the analogy of Samgrass as poker player was developed from an even earlier version than that cut, and the aura of guilt "like stale cigar smoke" (pp. 150–51) was introduced in second draft. The extended simile comparing the subject of Sebastian and fire in a ship's hold (p. 163, lines 18–23) appears only in third, final draft.

More extensive and more obvious is the addition of Rex Mottram's Christmas gift to Julia, "a small tortoise with Julia's initials set in diamonds in the living shell" (p. 164, line 22–p. 165, line 2). Conciously introduced as an objective correlative of Sebastian's decline—it is "one of those needle-hooks of experience which catch the attention when larger matters are at stake, and remain in the mind when they are forgotten so that years later it is a bit of gilding, or a certain smell, or the tone of a clock's striking which recalls one to a tragedy"—it also characterizes and indeed symbolizes Mottram here and in Julia's attention to it while Mottram is being mocked.

Waugh's revision of the beginning of Book 3 (Little, Brown, 1945, Bk. 2) was the most complex and laborious of any sequence in the manuscript. In practical terms he had finished Book 2 on the Wednesday before Holy Week (March 29), and he did not resume writing, as opposed to correcting and revising, for almost a month. When he did, he knew what he needed—a major transition bridging the ten-year gap in the characters' lives and a major shift from Ryder's mood of confidence at the end of Book 2—but he had to struggle to achieve it. Six drafts of the opening paragraphs survive.[4] Though they vary in details of expression, all begin, "My theme is memory," compare the memories to the pigeons in Saint Mark's Square, and develop the analogy at considerable length. Then the figure changes to that of the real self lost in a crowd of abstractions and shadows that are imposed on the person and from

4. Three canceled drafts are on the verso of sheets turned over and revised (MS pp. 125, 126, 129). Another, much longer, is on the front of MS pp. 124–25, 128–29.

which he can rarely escape. The many and essentially minor corrections can be illustrated by drafts of the opening sentences:

My theme is memory, the winged past which soared about me, that grey morning in wartime when I returned to Brideshead; they had never been far off [and so on, in an unbroken sentence for several lines]. [p. 125]

My theme is memory, the winged (past) /host/ which soared about me that grey morning (in wartime, when I) /of my/ return(ed) to Brideshead. (126 verso)

My theme is memory, that winged host which soared about me one grey morning of war time, [p. 129v ends and second draft, p. 124r continues]

My theme is memory, the host of winged somethings that soared about me that bleak morning in wartime, like the pigeons [etc.] (p. 124r first draft)

My theme is memory, that winged host that soared about me one grey morning of wartime. [MS, p. 126; Little, Brown, 1945, p. 225]

Not until the final manuscript draft, however, did Waugh introduce the analogy between the sudden eruption of a sedentary race into grandeur and collapse and the "rare, classic periods" which the human spirit enjoys (p. 225, lines 14–25). He may have wished to reinforce the parallel, strongly implied in the Prologue and Epilogue, between the individual's spiritual state and the social context. Here and in the Prologue, especially in the imagined archeological report (p. 7), he emphasized discontinuity and detachment from the vanished, failed races, while in the passage on building (p. 226) and in the Epilogue he emphasized organic growth and spiritual continuity, a shift that accords with the movement of the novel. More locally, this final draft of the manuscript, in an insertion within an insertion, identifies "these hours of afflatus in the human spirit" with "the springs of art." As revised, the passage accords with one reference (expanded in second draft) to Ryder's increasingly rare perception of a vital creative impulse (p. 226, lines 12–15) and a second, which appears for the first time in second draft, to the "fading light" of the inspiration he had felt while painting Marchmain House (p. 227, lines 16–21).

In the first canceled draft, after the reunion of Charles and Celia Ryder, Waugh named Celia's elder child Jenny, but in an over-page insertion he changed it to "JohnJohn," probably as a result of his decision on the following page to make the boy emulate his uncle, the arrested adolescent John (not until typed second draft "Boy") Mulcaster. Then, after describing a mechanical sexual encounter between Charles and Celia, Waugh altered the end of the hotel sequence considerably in second draft:

FIRST DRAFT	SECOND DRAFT
As I was shaving my wife, from the bath, said, "I'm not (frightened)/worrying/ anymore, Charles."	As I was shaving, my wife from the bath said: "Just like old times. I'm not worrying any more, Charles."
"Good."	"Good."
"I've been so afraid that two years might have made a difference. Now I know we can start again exactly where we left off."	"I was so terribly afraid that two years might have made a difference. Now I know we can start again exactly where we left off."
So we started that day exactly as we had left off two years before.	/I paused in my shaving
	"When?" I asked. "What? When (did we leave) //we left// off what?"
	"When you went away, of course."
	"You are not thinking of something else, (some) //a// little time before?"
	"Oh, Charles, that's old history. That was nothing, (I [illegible] That's) //It was never anything. It's// all over and forgotten."
	"I just wanted to know," I said. "We're back as we were the day I went abroad, is that it?"/
	So we started that day exactly where we left off two years before. (but in a dull, nervous city where they paid people to be light hearted)
	/with my wife in tears./ [p. 234]

Ryder's attitude toward his wife—Alec Waugh maintains that his tone exactly reproduced Evelyn's[5]—and his motive for it makes the conflict sharper and more comprehensible and raises the end of the sequence from anticlimax.

5. Alec Waugh, *My Brother Evelyn and Other Literary Portraits* (New York: Farrar, Straus and Giroux, 1967), p. 166.

Distinct from revisions in process are Waugh's "Ms. interpolations in second draft," bound with the manuscript and numbered 198 to 218. While the pagination indicates very little about the order of composition, pages 198 to 201 and 206 contain revisions to Book 1, and though the sequence is not numerical—the insertions of the Eliot quotation (p. 33, lines 10–16) and the characterization of Mulcaster (p. 48, line 29–p. 49, lines 4–7) are probably third rather than second thoughts—they and the additions to Book 2, pages 207 to 208 almost certainly and pages 209 to 212 possibly[6] were made between April 2, when Waugh "completed the corrections of the first batch of typescript," and April 16, when he "completed the revision, with many changes, of the first two books of the novel." Additions to Book 3 were probably completed by mid-June, for on the eighth Waugh completed the "last revision"[7] to the manuscript itself, during the next week he corrected typescript, and by June 20 he had delivered the completed typescript to Chapman and Hall, while another copy was at Oxford being checked for errors in theology.[8]

In general, the interpolations extend the process of augmenting detail, improving transitions, and clarifying themes observable in Waugh's day-to-day revisions of first draft. The reconsiderations of Anthony Blanche and other revisions of the first two chapters of Book 1 have already been discussed, and those of Book 2, Chapter 1, the most complex, deserve separate consideration. Others are relatively simple, however. The addition to Cara's account of Lord Marchmain's madness, for instance, originally focused entirely on him and his hatred of his wife, but in revision he hates "all the illusions of boyhood—innocence, God, hope," and Sebastian "is in love with his childhood" (p. 103, lines 3-20). This passage is important for predicting not only the immediate fate of Sebastian but also, in light of his submission to the church, that of Lord Marchmain. Moreover, it reinforces and restates, in terms that other insertions pick up, the central theme of the illusions of love as reflecting the only true reality. Earlier, insertion E on page 199, like the beginning of Book 2, reflects Waugh's awareness that he was making a major transition, generalizing from a single sequence of events and intensifying our perception of that experience as he expanded the description of "The langour of Youth" that begins Chapter 4 of the final version. Later he made even more sweeping changes; for the moment he was content

6. Possibly because these pages contain added detail about Ryder and Mottram's meal, and on May 7, Waugh wrote in his diary that he wished that he could give as much detail of the "two coitions" as he had of the meals.

7. The last long revision in manuscript was p. 345, line 27–p.349, line 15. The last insertion of more than a few words corresponds to p. 351, lines 18-20.

8. Letter to A. D. Peters, June 20, 1944.

to recast and to sharpen focus. Thus he changed, "How unique and essential to Youth, more than its energy or generous affections or any of its familiar attributes, is its langour!" to the briefer and more emphatic, "The langour of Youth—how unique and quintessential it is!" with the series of traditional attributes relegated to another sentence. The final sentence of the first draft lists physical attributes of repose; the revision focuses on "the mind sequestered and self-regarding, the sun standing still in the heavens and the earth throbbing to one's own pulse," giving the attribute a link with the cosmos and thus a more suitable link to the concept of Limbo, the epitome of natural blessedness, and finally with Heaven. This passage more obviously foreshadows the theme of ascension from love of creatures to love of God.

Insertion G, which augments the description of Ryder's sketch of the fountain (p. 81, lines 18–28), has less obvious thematic importance—and here too Waugh later felt obliged to develop the idea—but in commenting on the success and fate of Ryder's drawing Waugh emphasizes the source of his inspiration and links his art with the clear if simple responses of Nannie Hawkins in implied contrast to those of Anthony Blanche.

Waugh's interpolations in Book 2, Chapter 2 fall into two rather indistinct categories. The first, represented by the canceled and revised insertion B (p. 209), is the overtly thematic transition between Brideshead and Paris. Originally Waugh had used Cordelia's letter to Ryder as the vehicle of transition and had moved directly to it:

> "I shall never go back," I said to myself /but I shall always be there/. I have left my youth behind.
>
> I returned to Paris and about three weeks later got a letter from Brideshead....

In the first revision Waugh picked up the image of "the low door in the wall" that he had introduced in insertion H (MS, p. 200; p. 31, line 11) and made the reference to Sebastian overt:

> I returned to Paris, to the friends I had made there and the habits (of life) I had formed feeling that the door in the wall had closed behind me and (that) /all/ the world /it hid,/ of imagination & first love was to be forgotten. But that was not how things turned out. I was to experience, as Sebastian had done before me, the pain of finding the image & secret thing become reality and part of a drab universe.
>
> Within three weeks of setting up again in the Isle [*sic*] de Paris I had a letter from Cordelia, in a neat convent hand.

During the revision to the final text (MS, p. 210; p. 169, line 14–p. 170, line

2), Waugh definitely exiled Ryder from "the world of imagination and first love." First he added to the image of the closed door the clause "which opened on the enchanted garden"; then he canceled it and dispelled the enchantment itself by changing the end of the sentence to "...open it now and I should find no enchanted garden." Then, drawing upon his recurrent image—see the "Lush Places" of *Scoop*—for the region of the psyche in which imagination and libido cohabit, he had Ryder "come to the surface, into the light of common day and the fresh sea-air, after long captivity in the sunless places and waving forests of the ocean bed."[9] He reinforced this image with the analogy of the "Young Magician's Compendium," an association with his own youth.[10] Ryder associates both sea-world and magic with illusion, and he abjures both, as he loses imaginative as well as physical vision of Brideshead, to "live in a world of three dimensions—with the aid of my five senses." Then, in another anticipation of the link between youthful, Arcadian love and the mature love of God, parallel to the link between Brideshead and Heaven (p. 79), the mature Ryder insists that the merely three-dimensional world does not exist.

The other five interpolations to this chapter result from Waugh's hunger "for food and wine, for the splendours of the recent past, and for rhetorical and ornamental language."[11] Insertion A, page 209, substituted for the manuscript's compound-complex sentence that moves Ryder from the drawing room to Sebastian's room the much longer passage (p. 153, line 25–p. 154, line 6) that uses the pretext of Ryder's bath to contrast the ornate bathroom with its "deep, copper, mahogany-framed bath, that was filled by pulling a brass lever heavy as a piece of marine engineering" and other amenities with "the colourless [revised proof: "uniform"] clinical little chambers, glittering with chromium plate and looking-glass, which pass for luxury in the modern world." Insertions C to F (pp. 209–11) were all interpolated into the description of Ryder's lavish meal with Mottram, in all senses the graceless representative of what passes for luxury. The eulogy to the burgundy (p. 175, lines 10–23); Rex's pseudo-expertise about cognac (p. 177, line 19–p. 178, line 8), though Waugh later grew ashamed of the excess of the former and pared it;[12] and the change to pressed duck from the manuscript's "saddle of hare"[13] to allow the "music of the press" to punctuate

9. This may be another echo of Eliot, here of the concluding lines of "The Love Song of J. Alfred Prufrock."

10. Evelyn Waugh, *A Little Learning* (Boston: Little, Brown and Co., 1964), p. 61.

11. Evelyn Waugh, Preface, *Brideshead Revisited* (London: Chapman and Hall, 1960), p. 9.

12. *Ibid.*, pp. 9–10.

13. External evidence for the date of this revision is provided by Peters's letter to Waugh in May about the anomalous retention of "hare" in typescript—p. 176, line 34, has the

the meal luxuriously (p. 174, lines 13–22) and to contrast Ryder's final glass of wine with Rex's first cigarette were obviously important to Waugh's vision of the past. When he lamented restrictions on describing sexual congress, for example, he wished that he could "give as much detail as I have to the meals, to the two coitions" (May 9)—an association of which the psychoanalysts may make what they will.

Of the revisions to the final chapter of Book 2, only insertion H, page 212, has major significance. Insertion G, page 211, polishes the description of the drawing room at Marchmain House and the account of Ryder's access of inspiration (p. 218, lines 6–27), and K adds the logical conclusion of the Tangier sequence by showing rather than merely summarizing Sebastian's deference to Kurt's wishes and the pointed contrast in his attitude toward his old friend, Ryder, and his new. The final sentence, "There was nothing [added to proof: "more"] I could do for Sebastian," needs to be definitive because at this point Sebastian disappears from Ryder's life (p. 216, lines 7–31). Insertion H, however, like the revisions to Book 2, Chapter 1 discussed below, represented Waugh's awareness of a troublesome vagueness about Lady Marchmain's character. He confessed to Peters in a letter of May 19 that "Lady Marchmain is an enigma" but that "I hoped the last conversation with Cordelia gave the theological clue" that her mother

was saintly but she wasn't a saint. . . . when [people] want to hate [God] and his saints they have to find someone like themselves and pretend it's God and hate that. They put up idols to hate instead of worship. I suppose you think that's all bosh."[14]

Only two interpolations to Book 3 were introduced. The first, which may have been one of the "interpolations" mentioned in Waugh's diary for June 5, seems to be rhythmic in purpose, for the extended and frenetic dialogue of Rex Mottram and his cronies—modeled, perhaps, on Eliot's Sweeney

---

proper "duck"—and Waugh's reply that "duck into hare shall stop" (before May 20; Waugh's reply to the Peters letter, which is not in the files, was received May 20). See *The Letters of Evelyn Waugh*, ed. Mark Amory (New Haven and New York: Ticknor & Fields, 1980), p. 185.

14. The sentence about idols does not appear elsewhere. In the interpolation Ryder answers, "It's bosh to me, I'm afraid," but in carbon typescript the line reads, "A much older woman than you said something rather like it to me once." The printed text, however, reads, "I heard almost the same thing once before—from someone very different." This revision is almost unprecedented for Waugh because it becomes less specific. The ambiguity, which could cover Blanche as well as Cara, was probably deliberate. But the original absence of reference to anyone at all indicates that the revisions on p. 206 were probably made some time after those on pp. 211–12, for Lady Marchmain is not in manuscript characterized as "a good and simple woman who has been loved in the wrong way."

poems—and the contrasting scene of Julia and Ryder in the moonlight (pp. 293-95) echo and extend the contrast at the end of the preceding chapter (pp. 275-76), which emphasizes the lovers' isolation from the world and their fear of the future. In the second Waugh deals with his awareness that his push to finish the last chapter had made "the last dialogue poor" (diary entry for June 6). Rhetorically weaker than the revision it certainly is. In first draft, as was his habit, Waugh moved directly into the scene, from "Julia remained with her father until he died, late in the afternoon, an hour before Brideshead & Cordelia arrived from London" to "Julia said: 'So I can't marry you Charles . . . .' The interpolation ends the death scene with the rhythmically hesitant, "Julia remained in the Chinese drawing-room until, at five o'clock that evening, her father died, proving both sides right in the dispute, priest and doctor," and begins the next scene with the preparatory, "Thus I come to the broken sentences which were the last words spoken between Julia and me, the last memories" (p. 339). The interpolation also disposes physically of the characters—Cara taken away, Brideshead and Cordelia arrived, and Julia and Ryder meeting "in the shadow, in the corner of the stair"—and extends Ryder's knowledge of the coming breach between them from "this morning" to "all this year." Emphasis as well as coherence is improved. The first draft is rhetorically ineffective because Julia moves from theology to a personal plea that sounds as though she is open to persuasion:

"Try to understand. It would hurt me less if I thought you understood a little."
"What are you going to do?"
She gave the sad little shrug that expressed so much of her. "Just go on, alone. I don't believe in sudden in conversions [*sic*]; I've always been bad. I expect I shall be bad again. There's only one thing I know I can never do—what I nearly did—to set up a /sort of/ rival goodness; /that's the only unforgivable sin;/ that's what I should have done with you, and (I realised) /I thanked God/ this morning (that) /to find/ I wasn't (quite as bad as) /quite bad enough for/ that.

/"I should say my heart was breaking but/ I don't think I believe in broken hearts. I'm being punished now, but I don't say there may not be compensations later. I don't think I shall mourn for you all my life or you me. I love you now more than I did this morning; more than I have all this year; not more than I did at first, perhaps not so much. These things come and go. We shall both be lonely. Oh my darling, if only you understood the reason of it, I could part more easily. This isn't an emotional whim of mine—all my emotional whims are yours; you must know

that—it's something quite else, in the conditions on which we're given
life. Try to understand."

"I don't want to make it /any/ easier for you," I said; "(but I do
understand) I want your heart to break. But I do understand." [End of
Chapter]

After a canceled draft that preserves many elements of the first draft and
introduces the final metaphor, the interpolation focuses entirely on Julia's
spiritual state, and, in reasoning about the causes for her ability to receive
God's grace, she accepts not only the grace but her past and the consequences
of her decision. Ryder's response, she implies, is his own spiritual problem.
Then, climactically, the interpolation echoes from the end of the previous
chapter the image of the snowbound trapper and the avalanche that sweeps
away the cosy human comfort isolated from the outside world:

It may be because of Mummy, Nanny, Cordelia, Sebastian—perhaps
Bridey and Mrs. Muspratt—keeping my name in their prayers; or it may
be a private bargain between me and God, that if I give up this one
thing I want so much, however bad I am, He won't quite despair of me
in the end.

"Now we shall both be alone, and I shall have no way of making you
understand."

"I don't want to make it easier for you," I said; "I hope your heart
may break; but I do understand."

The avalanche was down, the hillside swept bare behind it; the last
echoes died on the white slopes; the new mound glittered and lay still
in the silent valley. [pp. 340–41]

Logically if not chronologically, Book 2, Chapter 1, which depicts
Sebastian's deterioration, culminates Waugh's revision of the manuscript
and first typescript, for it caused him by far the most difficulty over the
longest period. He began the first draft of the new book on March 13, and
though as usual he had a clear idea of where he was going, he was dissatisfied with the embodiment, and he broke off before reaching the end
of the page (MS, p. 65) and drafted a new beginning on the following day.
Despite uncertainty about his leave, insomnia, and drugs to relieve it, he
sent to the typist the long first chapter of Book 2 on March 21, having
written what he considered thirteen thousand viable words in a week.

Even those thoroughly familiar with the published version, however, will
find it difficult to match text with manuscript, for the chapter underwent
two stages of revision to attain final form. An outline of the manuscript,

with references to the published text in parentheses, gives some idea of the original and of the complexity of revision.

First Sunday of term (p. 104 beginning of Chapter–p. 105, line 19, ending "worse")

Missing Jasper (p. 106, lines 7–16 variant)

First Sunday of term to Aloysius in purdah; lectures from Oxford officials (p. 105, line 19–p. 106, line 3 and variant p. 106, lines 16–19)

Jasper on shaking friends; Blanche's set; pubcrawling (p. 107, line 18–p. 109, line 5, with considerable variation and revision)

Spending leisure together (not in text), Ryder and history school, art school (revised March 15, p. 106, lines 20–32), new style of dress (p. 107, lines 4–9), drawings that survive (p. 106, line 32–p. 107, line 3)

Ryder busy (great variation, p. 107, lines 9–11), Sebastian as Polynesian (variant, p. 127, lines 17–27)

Transition to two stories: Lady Marchmain and Sebastian, Rex and Julia (not in text)

Meeting with Lady Marchmain (major variation, p. 110, lines 27–33)

Lady Marchmain on wealth and on pious legend (p. 126, line 29–p. 127, line 12)

Sebastian's dislike of her proselytizing (p. 126, lines 6–8)

Characterization of Lady Marchamin (not in text)

Introduction of Mr. Samgrass (p. 109, lines 23–27)

Papers of Lady Marchmain's brothers (variant, p. 109, lines 13–22)

Mr. Samgrass's talents and predilictions (p. 109, line 28–p. 110, line 22)

Anticipation of Ryder's and Sebastian's gratitude to Samgrass; contrast of Samgrass and Rex; contrast of gratitude to Samgrass and to Rex (not in text)

Rex with Julia (p. 111, line 6–p. 112, line 5) inserted over page

Party, Old Hundredth, arrest (revision, March 16), aftermath (variant, p. 112, line 6–p. 123, line 33)

Transition to and summary of New Year's Party at Brideshead (not in text but roughly parallel to though far shorter than p. 123, lines 1–27)

Easter Party (p. 129, line 25–p. 135, line 26)

"Little talks" with Lady Marchmain (p. 126, lines 9–13)

Description of weather (p. 135, lines 26–30)

Description of room (p. 126, lines 14–27 with major variation)

Description of weather (not in text)

Lady Marchmain on Sebastian to end of chapter (p. 135, lines 31–p. 148)

Those who prefer a simpler account of the chapter's progression in manuscript will be content to know that Waugh there established his transitions by what are almost topic sentences, as in:

In this,—for me,—more tranquil period two stories (emerge)/spring/ in which I play no part but that of observer; one is /of/ the courtship of Julia and Rex Mottram, the other /of the/ estrangement of Sebastian & Lady Marchmain and the growth in her mind of the (belief) /conviction/ that he was a dipsomaniac. Both stories developed independently, side by side, and I, noting them, would first be occupied with one, then by the other; in the telling, however, it is convenient to treat each separately as a whole.

Furthermore, Waugh presented in summary Sebastian's coming deterioration and emphasized the disastrous Easter party at Brideshead almost to the exclusion of the New Year's party, pointedly ignored chronology in the first scenes of Ryder's acquaintance with Lady Marchmain, and put just before Ryder's crucial interview with her about Sebastian's problem the description of her room that helps characterize her.

In correcting typescript, probably in April, Waugh introduced several revisions, primarily local rather than structural. Insertion A, page 207, polished Ryder's resolve to live within his means (p. 106, lines 12-16), and C adds Lady Marchmain's lament about the extended family's probable reaction to Sebastian's arrest (p. 122, line 32-p. 123, line 2), thus fulfilling Sebastian's and Julia's predictions about her. Insertion E, page 208, made more complex and personal the first draft's ascription of a pathological cause for Sebastian's alcholism:

FIRST DRAFT

First of Sebastian and Lady Marchmain: there is a fine distinction between the man who drinks freely and heavily and the habitual drunkard; I do not know precisely when Sebastian changed from one to the other; at the age of twenty he was often drunk, as was I and most of our friends; at twenty two he had become, and remained, a medical case. [Then a variant of the lines quoted below: "Julia used to say . . . the over-mastering hate or love of any two people."] The word served its purpose in giving a modern colour to the old theological hypothesis of determinism but I /was/ never happy in its application to my friend; I prefer the metaphor of the Polynesian. There was his religion as he half understood and half accepted it, there was his family & there was myself all intruders in his impossible solitude, but there was nothing irremediably destructive in /any/ one of us. I believe quite simply that (Lady Marchmain) /his mother/ drove him mad.

INSERTION E

It was during this term that I began to realize that Sebastian was a drunkard in quite a different sense to myself. I got drunk often, but through an excess of high spirits, in the love of the moment, and the wish to prolong and enhance it; Sebastain drank to escape. As we together grew older and more serious I drank less, he more. I found that sometimes after I had gone back to my college, he sat up late and alone, soaking. A succession of disasters came on him so swiftly and with such unexpected violence that it is hard to say when exactly I recognized that my friend was in deep trouble. I knew it well enough in the Easter vacation.

Julia used to say, "Poor Sebastian. It's something chemical in him."

That was the cant phrase of the time, derived from heaven knows what misconception of popular science. (to explain the [illegible]) "There's something chemical between them" was used to explain the over-mastering hate or love of any two people. It was the old concept of determinism in a new form. I do not believe there was anything chemical in my friend; I believe quite simply that his mother drove him mad.

In second draft Waugh developed the distinction between Ryder's and Sebastian's drinking habits that Cara mentioned in the previous chapter (p. 103) and to which Ryder alludes in the next (p. 163). Moreover, the transition from casual excess in London to premeditated drunkenness at Brideshead prepares for a new stage in Sebastian's decline.

While this passage was ultimately made less dramatic—"his mother drove him mad" was removed before clear typescript—Waugh became dissatisfied with the way in which Lady Marchmain was introduced to the reader and in revision that involved some structural changes he tried to present her more clearly. The manuscript draft reveals most of the flaws possible in subjective, retrospective narrative:

I do not remember when I first met her for it was not her way to make a conspicuous entry into anyone's life. Every other member of his family I met at a clearly defined time and each made a sharp impression on me. In the case of Lady Marchmain I can only say that by Easter I knew her quite well. She came once or twice to Oxford in the autumn & spring; I stayed at Brideshead when she was there at a New Year party; I was often at their London house both in term & vacation but it surprises me at this distance that after all Sebastian's avowed resolution to keep us apart, we should have eventually come together without my remembering where or how. I suppose it was in his rooms in Meadow Buildings in the early part of the Michelmas [sic] Term. /(I had sharp curiosity about her) I cannot say as storetellers [sic] do, "I came on her unawares by firelight" or "she stood framed in the door way," nor can I (record) //recall// what she first said to me or the steps by which we came to know one another. I remember certain conversations vividly./

I remember her saying, either at New Year or at Easter, "We must make a Catholic of Charles" and my thinking this natural and charming, and at one or /the/ other of these parties /—I think the former—/ when she and I found ourselves alone together, she talked to me seriously, I then thought dishonestly but, I now believe, with perfect sincerity, on the subject of (money) /her wealth/. [Then as p. 126, line 29–p. 127, line 12. Then after "of religion" to p. 126, lines 6–8]. From time to time she and I had (sever) /many/ 'little talks'; she had great delicacy in that kind of intercourse, and though I am easily made shy I never knew her, however intimate or personal the subject, to give me the sense of trespass I should quickly have resented in anyone else. I found her neither saint nor witch but an accomplished (and wholly) feminine, and wholly human woman and, surprisingly for she was the most important person in the lives of the two people I most loved, one who made no very definite impression on me. I suppose it was, as Julia would have put it, /the lack/ "something chemical" between us.

I do not even remember clearly how she looked. I have the impression of someone unnaturally fragile, with huge (luminous), /limpid/ eyes and a ready, intelligent smile. She wore the clothes of an uncouth decade with (singularity &) /singular/ grace; I saw her as the majority saw her— the (lovely) /exquisite, impeccable/, ethereal (Lady) /Marie-Louise/ Marchmain, and yet . . . and yet I firmly believe it was she who drove Sebastian mad.

The wonder is not that Waugh revised the passage but that he waited until typescript. Then he took the opportunity to introduce another warning of Sebastian's flight from the pressures of his family and of the world outside Oxonian Arcadia (now at p. 127, line 28) and presented his mother's entrance through impressions rather than lapses of memory:

INSERTION B

As my intimacy with his family grew I became part of the world from which he (was in flight) sought to escape; I became one of those bonds which held him (captive). That was how Sebastian came to see me, and so too, did his mother.

It was not Lady Marchmain's way to make a conspicuous entry into anyone's life. I met her first during that autumn term when she spent a week in Oxford in order to correct with Mr. Samgrass's help the book /about her brothers which/ she was having printed for private circulation.

During that week we saw her constantly and when she realized how close Sebastian & I were to one another, she set about making me her friend.

(In) The many letters which after her death were printed (to supplement) /in/ The Times /to supplement/ her obituary, all mentioned in that, or some similar phrase, her 'genius for friendship.' It was there that her fame lay, in her many, unique multiform human relationships. She had an aptitude for them which (long ago) a life-time's refinement had (brought to) almost perfected. It was a rare experience for a boy of my years to find himself (delicately) courted [*sic*] a woman of her beauty & wit & taste & gentleness, and yet she never quite succeeded with me, though I was willing enough to be won. She never got to the heart of me as she did so easily with so many others, but (one) it was impossible to be ill at ease or out of temper with her.

She wanted to change me, make me into the friend she wanted for Sebastian, make me into (the) /a/ bond between her and him. It was there that all failed, partly by reason of something hard in myself, but more because Sebastian was moving so steadily away from her & from all human contacts of the kind she understood.

Lady Marchmain enjoyed 'little talks' with her guests.

Waugh must also have realized that he had violated another principle of exposition in first draft by waiting until the crucial scene to describe the setting. In revising, he put here the two pages of typescript that describe Lady Marchmain's room which in manuscript preceded her lament over Sebastian's alcoholism (Little, Brown, 1945, p. 135, lines 31ff.). The interpolation concluded with the chronologically anomalous anticipation, "In this room Lady Marchmain & I had many talks for it was assumed that I would spend most of the next two vacations at Brideshead." Only then is Mr. Samgrass introduced.

Waugh's perception of the anomaly apparently led him to realize six weeks later that mere patchwork was not enough, but for the moment he was content with one fairly simple insertion. In the middle of the manuscript's summary of the New Year party (which itself had been an overpage insertion) he added insertion D, a summary description of Lady Marchmain as source of the harmony and vitality of the party and of her being a "greater poet," in her way, than Sir Adrian Porson. This not only reinforced somewhat heavily Ryder's impression of Lady Marchmain's benevolent tyranny but also gave a bit more body to the still sketchy New Year's party. Then the story moved through a two-paragraph bridge to the Easter party.

The second set of "MS interpolations" to the chapter (pp. 213–18) differs physically from the rest, being a montage of typescript and manuscript. Waugh realized after May 30 that "long passages must be rewritten in Book II"; a week later he asked Peters to return the typescript so that he could "make substantial changes";[15] and on June 3 he "finished the rearrangement of Book II" and turned back to Book 3, Chapter 4. In fact, he rearranged only one chapter. He did not record his reasons, but he did have leisure enforced by a visit to Pixton to see his new daughter, Harriet Mary, and he had thought carefully enough to make the rearrangement, which orders the chapter as we now have it, in one working day. In doing so, he distributed incidents more evenly between autumnal Oxford and the two visits to Brideshead, indicated without overenforcing the narrator's attitude toward Lady Marchmain before presenting her scenically, and discriminated more clearly among the various stages of Sebastian's decline. Dramatically more effective and far more circumstantial than its precedessors, the final arrangement moves directly from Sebastian's sullenness (p. 109, line 5) to Lady Marchmain's arrival in Oxford and introduces Mr. Samgrass as a "foil to her own charm." Then, rather than anticipate Ryder's visits to Brideshead, Waugh moved without overt transition to Rex Mottram (p. 111, line 1) and, after an expanded version of the party that precedes the visit to the Old Hundredth (p. 112, line 5-p. 113, line 15),[16] to Sebastian's disaster in London. Then, realizing that he had succumbed to the temptation to make everything happen at once, Waugh expanded the New Year's party from a few paragraphs to five pages (pp. 124-28). First, to give Mr. Samgrass more than an offstage presence, Waugh developed his role as undesired patron at Oxford and had him summarize the guest list at the New Year's party—the first mention of Celia Mulcaster is made in this insertion. Only then, with Ryder established at Brideshead as Lady Marchmain's guest, did Waugh have his narrator attempt to describe her:

> The atmosphere of the house was completely changed by Lady Marchmain's presence. I have yet to describe her, and still I hold back from doing so because there was always a failure in correspondence between us, a hardness in me, a preeminent loyalty to Sebastian, whom I took to be her foe, which made me impervious to her charm. She had beauty of a rare and delicate kind; she seemed older than her age; her hair once as dark as Julia's, was now nearly white; she had a nun's transparency of complexion (,) and great grace (of movement) /in all she did & said/; she had wit & humour & gentleness. All this was open to the world and that was as (far) /much/ as I (saw her) knew of her. It was an

15. Letter to Peters, received May 31, 1944.

16. This passage includes Mrs. Champion, Rex's mistress, to reinforce her introduction two pages earlier and to indicate by her quarrel with Rex his growing interest in Julia.

> unusual experience for a boy of my years to find himself courted, as I was by Lady Marchmain during that and the succeeding vacation, but she never got to the heart of me, nor I to hers.

Even this came to displease Waugh, and, probably since Lady Marchmain is immediately characterized through her surroundings, he deleted this passage from later versions. Thereafter he interpolated the description of her room and the fragments of her dialogue about wealth, poetry, and religion, making Sebastian's sour comment about her "little talks" precede rather than follow them to place them in the context of Ryder's most important relationship to the family. Then, after the description of the "little talks," the passage on Sebastian as Polynesian and on Ryder as hand-picked friend are placed to show his mother's effect on his condition. Later the climactic evidence of the condition is presented in the Easter-party sequence.

By the time Waugh had finished the "ms. interpolations in second draft," the novel had begun to assume the shape in which readers of 1945 saw it. Waugh, however, managed to introduce still further revisions into a typescript that in final form can now be only reconstructed. Waugh's revised typescript was typed into fair copies for his English and American publishers, and further copies were probably made from those. The carbon copy now at the University of Texas, in a folder with Harold Matson's name printed on the cover, has a pencil note "(from Edmund Wilson)" on the title page, and the copy may have belonged to or been delivered by Wilson. That copy is uncorrected by any hand and was probably never seen by Waugh, but it represents a more advanced state of the text than the bound manuscript.

The most important changes between manuscript and carbon typescript were in structure: what had been Chapter 3 of Book 1 became two chapters, breaking at the revised and obviously transitional passage on "The languour of Youth" (p. 79), and the manuscript's three books had become two. Other revisions in the text are also structural. Waugh changed the book Lady Marchmain reads aloud from *The Napoleon of Notting Hill* to *The Wisdom of Father Brown* and revised Cordelia's dialogue about the family's religious life to include the quotation about the "twitch upon the thread" (p. 220) by which the sinner is recalled to God to foreshadow later action and to give the title of Book 2. Moreover, Waugh added to the description of the skull in Ryder's rooms "the motto *'Et in Arcadia ego'*" (p. 42) both to strengthen and to reinforce the pastoral theme and to echo in the text the new title of Book 1.

Less obvious were passages inserted to strengthen characterization. The question of Mulcaster's first name was resolved—originally he had none;

then it was "John" in Book 3 of the manuscript before becoming "Boy" on page 200 in the "Ms. interpolations"—and Waugh further underlined Mulcaster's subadolescent nature by adding the lines in which he finds it "witty to give the fire alarm" and fulfills Blanche's prophecy (p. 50) that Mulcaster and his cronies will talk thus about dunking him (pp. 204, 205). His puerility is further emphasized by the lines in which Waugh augmented his approval of his sister's second husband, Robin, who in carbon Ryder terms "a pimply, half-baked youth" (p. 295, lines 17–19; p. 296, lines 8-9). In doing so, Waugh emphasized the depths to which Ryder had sunk in accepting Mulcaster as companion and his sister as wife. Another revision removes from Ryder's first association with Brideshead and its central feature, the fountain, the imputation of aesthetic fraud. In the "Ms. interpolations" Ryder's drawing "by judicious omissions and some dishonest, stylish, secondhand tricks" is "a very passable echo of Piranesi." To make the work contrast more sharply with Ryder's later barrenness, Waugh removed "dishonest" and "secondhand," and the emphasis on physical luxury was further augmented in the description of the lavish dinner with Rex by the passages on caviar (p. 173, lines 7–13) and soup (p. 173, lines 33–34).

Other revisions altered subtly the presentation of the Flyte family. Most obvious was the increase in rank. For most of the manuscript Lord Marchmain was an earl, Lord Brideshead a baron, and Sebastian the Honourable Sebastian Flyte or Mr. Flyte, but by the last chapter the eldest had become a Marquis, the next an Earl, and the last, as a younger son, "Lord Sebastian." The fair typescript also removed anomalies. Lord Brideshead's dialogue was given minor touches to make it more formal and precise, his fiancee's name was changed from Blessington-Andrews to the more obviously comic Muspratt (p. 284), and his recreations became not yearly fishing in Norway and one Caribbean cruise, which at least took him outside England and showed some volition, but dutiful and joyless hunting (p. 280). Lady Marchmain, originally named Marie Louise, became Teresa by fair typescript (p. 148). Waugh deleted Ryder's melodramatic "his mother drove him mad" (p. 120) and changed Sebastian's portentous, "Now you've seen the whole family except mother," to the description of his father as "rather a poppet" (p. 100), an echo of Julia's phrase about the elder Ryder.[17] Lady Marchmain's significance is more marked but more ambiguous because of

17. Waugh was also conscious of unwanted echoes. Ryder originally says, "I understand," of Sebastian's vomiting into his room, but the words were to attain far stronger meaning not only in Ryder's line to Cordelia, ". . . you knew I would not understand" about Sebastian's holiness (pp. 310, 311), but also in his final scene with Julia. Waugh seems to have been unwilling to risk the reader's linking the phrases and cut the first "I understand."

two other revisions. When Ryder leaves her room, he moves from "the intimate, feminine modern world" to "the great, masculine atmosphere of a better age" (p. 138) rather than the manuscript's "former age," and the introduction to Cordelia's analysis of her mother is expanded from, "I didn't love her," to, "I don't believe I ever really loved her. Not as she wanted or deserved," to make her seem human and vulnerable as well as manipulative and inflexible.

Julia received most attention in the carbon typescript. For one thing, Waugh had to decide whether her hair was to be dark, as in the first half of the manuscript, or golden, as in the lushly romantic scenes aboard ship. He curbed his usual preference—at least in fiction—and chose dark. He also made her looks in the 1920's, including "the blank stare and gape of the period, and the clownish dabs of rouge high on the cheekbones," not the result of her action—"try as she might" in the manuscript—but of the impersonal act of the times and of fashion that "could not reduce her to type" (p. 179). This is the first of several revisions to the chapter that introduces her fully (Ms, Book 2, Chapter 3; typescript, Book 1, Chapter 7); others change her status and ambitions to include the remote possibility of a royal marriage made still more remote by her family scandal and her religion (p. 181); another cancels, after describing her ideal husband, her meeting with Rex Mottram in favor of her meeting with Ryder and the repeated image of her rejection of him by taking "the cigarette from my lips" (p. 183), and still another adds between dashes a detail of social history about lunching at the Ritz (p. 183, line 33–p. 184, line 2).[18] A chapter later Waugh decided to end the scene in which Julia asks Ryder to find Sebastian not with the mere summary of their casual conversation but with, "All this talk was nothing; we had said all we had to say in the first two minutes; I stayed for ten" (p. 209), to prepare for the time, already anticipated, in which they will have something to say to each other. The passage about Julia's stillborn child was toned down, from, "I believe the nurse christened her; they do I believe" (p. 144)—which presents a rather facile fulfillment of Julia's wish to raise the child a Catholic—to the bare "I never saw her" (p. 259), which accords with the subsequent "/Nameless and/ dead, like the baby they wrapped up and took away before I had seen her" (p. 288). More complex is the passage that precedes Julia's lashing out at Charles:[19]

18. The change of the counter revolutionary Dadaist to a Futurist (p. 201) gives the aesthetic and political sympathies greater accord.

19. Manuscript p. 167. The whole passage is a revision.

INSERTED IN MANUSCRIPT	TYPESCRIPT
On the steps Julia idly snapped off a /small/ branch from one of the trees that stood there in tubs, & stripped /it/, as she walked, with little (nervous) /petulant/ (twiches) /tugs/ of (her) /the / fingers, that were not like her way. She began peeling the bark, scratching it with her nails.	We walked round the house; under the limes Julia paused and idly snapped off one of the long shoots, last year's growth that fringed their boles, and stripped it as she walked, making a switch, as children do, but with petulant movements that were not a child's, snatching nervously at the leaves and crumpling them between her fingers; she began peeling the bark, scratching it with her nails. [p. 291]

The rather plebian association of 'tubs" has been removed, and the increased kinetic imagery anticipates the explosion that releases and temporarily dispels her tension. Even more important is the symbolic use of "last year's growth," which parallels the change in the couple's perception of their love, as the object first of Julia's nervous destruction and then as the instrument with which she attacks Ryder. Coming after the couple's retrospective account of their separation and before Ryder's perception that she has regained "the magical sadness" that she displayed on the liner, the revision and its context intensify Julia's dissatisfaction with human love.

Waugh continued to make minor adjustments in the novel's final scenes in the typescript, which I have not seen, used as copy text for Chapman and Hall's page proofs of the novel. Since most of the dozen or so variants between carbon typescript and uncorrected page proof[20] occur in the final twenty-two pages of proof, Waugh's corrections in the last batch of typescript—Peters refers to Waugh's "revised typescript"[21]—were probably not transferred to the copy sent to America because Waugh did not intend the American edition to be set from that copy.

Many of these final revisions were slight: "oil" to "chrism" for the substance used in Extreme Unction (p. 338, proof 291), "advert" to "revert" (p. 326, proof 286), and so on. One seemingly minor change corrected an

20. I am citing a reproduction of the uncorrected page proofs now at the Berg Collection of the New York Public Library.
21. Peters to F. B. Walker of Chapman and Hall, February 26, 1945.

error that made the *Town and Country* serial version even more like a novelette.[22] At Lord Marchmain's deathbed, Charles longs for a sign because Julia is, in manuscript, "praying for one." Carbon typescript and serial read "praying for me"—not a grossly negligent reading of Waugh's handwriting, but an unfortunate limitation of the spiritual to the merely romantic. The proof and all subsequent texts read "for a sign" to remove any doubts.

More substantial revisions removed the doctor who lives in the house during Marchmain's last illness (pp. 323, 331), added the detail about Cordelia's daily attendance at mass to the signs of conflict over the question of bringing a priest to a dying man, and removed the words I have emphasized in the following sentence: ". . . the threat[23] that I had felt hanging over Julia and me ever since that evening *at dusk* by the fountain, *when she had, I thought, wept away the illusions of childhood,* had been averted, perhaps dispelled, for ever" (p. 327, proof 287). This makes Ryder, who is beginning to have doubts about his agnosticism, seem too assured, and it does not accord with his earlier speculation that the weary Julia may be murmuring a prayer from childhood (p. 293).

After these corrections, made by June 20,[24] Waugh had no opportunity to change the text for five months. On the following day he left London, which was under attack by V-1 buzz bombs, for the comparative safety of active duty in Scotland, where he promptly began to languish. Within the week he was rescued—or so he thought at the time—by Randolph Churchill, who asked Waugh "to go with him to Croatia in the belief that I should be able to heal the Great Schism between the Catholic and Orthodox churches —something with which he has just become acquainted and finds a hindrance to his war policy."[25] After a farewell to his family, he left for Yugoslavia on July 4.

---

22. See my "The Serial Version of *Brideshead Revisited,*" *Twentieth Century Literature* 15 (1969):35–43. I had not seen any manuscript materials, including Waugh's indignant letters to Peters, when I wrote it. Waugh did not cut it and did not approve the truncated version, to put it as briefly and mildly as possible. The serial was probably set not from manuscript but from an uncorrected typescript of the same family as the carbon at Texas.

23. "Thread," clearly an error, appears only in the Little, Brown edition. In proof and in all other texts it is "threat."

24. See Waugh's letter to Peters, June 20, 1944.

25. Waugh, *Diaries,* pp. 568–69.

9

Brideshead
in Type

As Churchill soon discovered, not only was Waugh unable to heal the Great Schism, he was not even interested in healing the breach that developed between the two comrades in arms.[1] In fact, Waugh's major interest in Croatia soon became the conditions of the Catholic church under Partisan rule; non-Catholic Yugoslavians he found almost as tedious as he did Churchill. Meanwhile, *Brideshead* was reaching its first readers free from authorial interference. Page proofs were ready before the end of October, and by this time the editors at Chapman and Hall had grown apprehensive about the description—preserved from manuscript through early page proof—of Mr. Samgrass as having "lately been roped in among some thousand others to write the Londoner's Diary in the *Evening Standard.*" They substituted "the gossip page" for "Londoner's Diary" and *Evening Bulletin* for *Evening Standard,* querying the possibility of libel and adding that they had consulted Peters.[2] This reading was used in the special edition of 1944, circulated among Waugh's friends.[3] Otherwise this edition, which Waugh could not see through the press, seems to have been set from an editorially

1. For the ludicrous history of Waugh and Churchill in the British Military Mission, see not only the diaries for late 1944 (Evelyn Waugh, *The Diaries of Evelyn Waugh,* ed. Michael Davie [Boston: Little, Brown and Co.,1977]) but also Earl of Birkenhead, "Fiery Particles," in *Evelyn Waugh and His World,* ed. David Pryce-Jones (Boston: Little, Brown and Co., 1973).

2. "F." of Chapman and Hall to A. D. Peters, November 1, 1944. For the variants see p. 233 of Waugh's corrected proof copy, cited below, and the pages with amended readings in Peters's files.

3. The privately issued edition is dated 1945 on the title page but 1944 on the spine of the box in which the paper-covered volume is enclosed. A printed label on the front paper cover notes: "This edition was issued privately for the author's friends; no copies are for sale. Messrs. Chapman & Hall urgently request that until they announce the publication of the ordinary edition in the early part of 1945, copies will not be lent outside the circle for which they are intended, and no reference will appear to the book in the Press." A printed slip, laid in, reads: "Captain Evelyn Waugh greatly regrets that his absence abroad renders him unable to inscribe this book as he would have wished. / Christmas 1944."

corrected set of page proofs. While rare and extremely valuable, it has a minor place in the history of the text.

The corrected proofs, now at Loyola College, in Baltimore, are quite another matter.[4] Before Waugh received page proof, he announced his intention to "revise the first half" of the novel and predicted that "the changes may be extensive,"[5] though he did not think the changes crucial enough that publication should be delayed if his corrections did not arrive in time. After weeks of rain, a scheme to write a mystery story frustrated by the boisterous presence of Randolph Churchill, and his gloomiest birthday since 1933, Waugh finally received proofs on November 20, 1944. In the ensuing week he revised sometimes, to escape Randolph, in his cold bedroom. They were finished on Sunday, the twenty-sixth, while Churchill was attending a film.[6]

As Waugh later told Peters, "The corrections are extensive and very important."[7] At the very beginning he included the subtitles in the table of contents—never printed in American editions—which emphasize parallel actions and characters, as in "Sebastian at home," "Sebastian abroad"; "Lord Marchmain abroad," "Lord Marchmain at home." He not only dealt with the publisher's libel query, reaching back to *Scoop* and making Samgrass "One of Lord Copper's middle-aged young men on the *Daily Beast*" (p. 265, proof 233) but thought it better to name a butler Hayter rather than Haydon, the name of the general who had forced him out of the commandos, and changed, from Runciman to Irwin, the name of the politician called "a mediocre fellow" in Lord Marchmain's rambling monologue (p. 331). Concern for his audience also dictated revisions away from stilted diction: "habitues" to "company" (p. 108), "*crise* of nerves" (addressed to a policeman) to "a matter of nerves" (p. 119), "ubiquitous" to "every-

4. Peters wrote to Alfred McIntyre, of Little, Brown, that he was sending (editorially?) corrected proofs from which type could be safely set. (August 22, 1944). He forgot to tell McIntyre of Waugh's announcement that he planned to revise heavily.

5. Letter to Peters, September 30, 1944. *The Letters of Evelyn Waugh*, ed. Mark Amory (New Haven and New York: Ticknor & Fields, 1980), pp. 188-89.

6. The page proofs, with Waugh's holograph note describing the way in which they reached him and were returned, he gave to Loyola College, Baltimore, when he received an honorary doctorate from the college in 1947. See Gene D. Phillips, S.J., "The Page Proofs of *Brideshead Revisited,*" *Evelyn Waugh Newsletter* 5 (Autumn, 1971):7-8. See the brief diary entries (Waugh, *Diaries*, pp. 592-93), on the correction of the proofs.

7. Letter to Peters, January 7, 1945. In *The Letters of Evelyn Waugh*, ed. Mark Amory (New Haven and New York: Ticknor & Fields, 1980), p. 206, Waugh informed Mgr. Ronald Knox that he had "cut out of the published edition any turns of phrase which were hard to read aloud . . . ." And to Tom Dreiberg Waugh wrote that he had revised "an immodest scene between C. Ryder & Celia in New York" and had dealt with the problem of Charles's father, "who took more than his due space." *Letters*, p. 210.

where" (p. 225), "nebulous" to "cloudy" (p. 326). He would, however, choose formal words to improve precision—"mutual" to "reciprocal esteem" for more than two people (p. 252), "consummation" to "apotheosis of adult grandeur" (p. 316), "thought" to "reflected" (p. 138)—or, as in the change from "made a mess of it" to "made a *bêtise*" to accord better with a character's style. Furthermore, he was sensitive to echoes: Samgrass's long talk became "a little talk" (p. 160) to continue the private reference to Lady Marchmain's style of discourse; Celia is made to say "disreputable" rather than "*louche*" (p. 262) of Ryder's gambling because eight pages later Blanche will more characteristically use the Gallicism of the bar to which he takes Ryder; and a watercolor becomes a woodcut (p. 265) as a symbol of minor work because earlier Waugh had implicitly rejected the distinction between water and oil painting as amateur and professional (p. 147).

Apparently minor revisions sometimes had major implications. For example, in the opening paragraphs of Book 2 over which he had worked so hard, Waugh had come by proof stage to this version:

> I *had* always loved building, holding it to be not only the highest achievement of man but one in which, at the moment of consummation, things *are* most clearly taken out of his hands and perfected, without his intention by other means, and I regarded men as something much less than the buildings they *make* and inhabit, as mere lodgers and short-term sublessees of small importance in the long, fruitful life of their homes. [Proof 198; italics added]

This passage is crucial to our understanding not only of the novel's architectural symbolism but also of Ryder's character and of the very complex relationship between present and past. In the final pages of the novel Ryder accepts his past as leading to his present conversion, but he explicitly does not mourn the fact of its passing. As Waugh examined the lines just quoted, he apparently felt that his intention could be rendered more exactly, for he changed "had" to "have" to indicate that Ryder's predilection continues, "are" to "were" (then writing and canceling "stet.") to indicate that the inspiration is definitely in the past, and "make" and "inhabit" to past tense to reinforce instead of contradict, by position if not grammatical relationship, the past tense of "regarded." All of this indicates—too subtly for some critics—that Ryder still loves building but no longer finds mankind inferior.

Like the buildings that Ryder loves most, Brideshead Castle continued to change in successive revisions, and in revising proof Waugh gave it even greater importance. In all previous versions Ryder comes upon the house in this fashion:

> In the early afternoon we came to our destination: lodge gates, a lime avenue, more gates, a turn in the drive into open park land and, at last, half a mile ahead of us, inevitable but unexpectedly splendid, prone in the sunlight, grey and gold against a screen of boscage, shone the dome and columns of an old house.
>
> "Well?" said Sebastian stopping the car.
>
> I studied the prospect with soaring delight. Nothing was lacking from the simple, massive plan and the exuberant enrichment. You could ask no more.
>
> "Well?"
>
> "There's nothing to say," I said. "It's completely perfect."
> [proof 32]

This came to seem unsatisfactory not only, perhaps, because of the unintentional humor of saying that there is nothing to say but also because of the repetition and exclamation. In revising, Waugh picked up the image of "an enclosed and enchanted garden" from a few pages earlier and used it to create an impression rather than to describe directly:

> We drove on and in the early afternoon came to our destination: wrought-iron gates and twin, classical lodges on a village green, an avenue, more gates, open parkland, a turn in the drive; and suddenly a new and secret landscape opened before us. We were at the head of a valley and below us, half a mile distant, prone in the sunlight, grey and gold amid a screen of boscage, shone the dome and columns of an old house.
>
> "Well?" said Sebastian, stopping the car. Beyond the dome lay receding steps of water and round it, guarding and hiding it, stood the soft hills.
>
> "Well?"
>
> "What a place to live in!" I said. [pp.34-35]

This serves the purpose exactly. The opening phrases use less regular rhythm and fit detail together less homogeneously than the proof version to establish by sentence structure the surprise that Ryder feels, and by dividing the proof's first sentence in two, Waugh is able to rise more surely from one climax, the "new and secret landscape," to the second and greater, skillfully delayed by the modifying phrases, of the view of the house. Throughout the revised passage Waugh shows his concern for precision—"at last" and "inevitable but unexpectedly splendid" are inaccurate—and for supporting detail that replaces the negatives of the third and fifth paragraphs of the proof with positive description of the harmonizing landscape.

Waugh was concerned not merely with static picture but with description that would serve his major theme. Ryder emphasized the fact that "more even than the work of great architects, I loved buildings that grew silently with the centuries, catching and keeping the best of each generation" (p. 226). In proof, however, Brideshead is the result of a static plan:

PROOF	NOVEL
The plan of Brideshead, as of many contemporary houses, was a central block with two flanking pavilions joined to it by a colonnade. One of these pavilions was the chapel.	The last architect to work at Brideshead had sought to unify its growth with a colonnade and flanking pavilions. One of these was the chapel. [p. 38]

The later version not only makes the house a fit object of Ryder's love but emphasizes the fact, important in the plot and in the theme and made increasingly clear in subsequent revision, that the chapel uses but alters the fabric of the house and is a result of both architectural and spiritual conversion and growth.

Later, in reconsidering Chapter 4, Waugh must have decided that he had not exploited fully enough the house as symbol and inspiration. After the first paragraph the proof has a brief summary transition from Sebastian and Ryder playing in the nursery, then playing "with the treasures of the house" before moving to Ryder's drawing of the fountain. Waugh expanded this to include a conversation illustrating "those languid days at Brideshead," a description of the young men playing in the nursery, and an overt statement that "it was an aesthetic education to live within those walls" (pp. 79–81, line 11). Then, after the scene in which Ryder completes the drawing, Waugh inserted the three paragraphs that outline the history of Ryder's taste, emphasize his "conversion to the baroque," and establish the fountain as, aesthetically, "a life-giving spring" (p. 31, line 29–p. 32, line 10).

The meaning of Ryder's experience is further amplified in the passage inserted in the retrospective account of the first summer at Oxford, which characterizes it as "a brief spell of what I had never known, a happy childhood, and though its toys were silk shirts and liqueurs and cigars and its naughtiness high in the catalogue of grave sins, there was something of nursery freshness about us that (made for joy of a quality I never knew before and have ((never)) /not/ known since) fell little short of the joy of innocence" (p. 45, proof 41). This reinforces the contrast not only between Jasper and Ryder but also between Sebastian and Blanche, whose invitation to less innocent pastimes follows.

While the Arcadian motifs were strengthened, some of the humor must have seemed too crude. In proof the small room at Brideshead that Charles decorates with some of his first paintings is described as being designed "for a softer use; perhaps as a tea-room or as the study where a literary guest might polish an ode." Perhaps the wit made the room seem too quaint for the scene of Charles's work, however amateurish, for the novel speculates on its use "as a tea-room or study" (p. 82). Similarly, the romantic aura with which Waugh seeks to invest Lord Marchmain's Venetian palazzo is dispelled by the comic geyser installed in the serial version:

"I have a room the size of this and a very decent dressing-room."
"And a bath?"
"I have a bath*room*. It is not always a success. We have only been here a fortnight and Plender has not yet got the hang of the geyser. Cara is more adventurous. I prefer to take my bath at the Excelsior after tennis."

The sentence substituted in the novel for these last two paragraphs, "Cara has taken possession of the other sizable room" (p. 98), throws the emphasis where it is needed—onto the fact of Lord Marchmain's mistress and the youthful Ryder's awe. Nanny Hawkins does not presume to judge the actions of the Flyte family, but the proof's version of her reaction to the news of Julia's coming divorce from Rex and marriage to Ryder—"'Yes, dear, that'll be a nice change'"—is flippant and seems to condone adultery, and Nanny is nothing if not pious. The tone and implication are adjusted by the novel's "'Well my dear, I hope it's all for the best'" (p. 301).

Other revisions also modify characterization by small touches. Beryl Muspratt, for example, is changed from "a year or two younger" than Bridey to "a year or two older" and finally to the equivocal "just about" his age (p. 284, proof 249), and what had been his "sexual stupour" over her becomes the more general and for Bridey more believable "amorous stupour" (p. 298, proof 261). Bridey's concern about the possible viciousness of Kurt's relationship with Sebastian is at first resolved with Ryder's denial, supported by, "For one thing, I happen to know the man has syphilis," to the gentler and far more consoling, "I'm sure not. It's simply a case of two waifs coming together" (p. 217, proof 191),[8] and on the same page Waugh expunged the vulgar mention of "two hundred pounds the set" for the paintings Ryder is to do of Marchmain House.

This new delicacy is observable in two other passages. The page proof and all earlier states of the scene at the Old Hundredth included Sebastian's overt plans to lose his virginity. The dialogue picks up from the banter of Mulcaster and Effie:

8. In the 1960 edition this unaccountably becomes "I'm not sure" (p. 241). The corrected copy from which the final edition was set has the original and contextually inescapable reading.

Sebastian leaned back and said to me: "You know, Charles, I've never slept with a woman."

"I know you haven't," I said. "Neither have I."

"Shall we? To-night?"

"Why?"

"Well, one has to some time."

"But these are all so frightfully ugly."

"I don't see that that matters. I'm going to ask that pair to join us." [Proof 103]

Perhaps to preserve the impression of Sebastian's pregenital narcissism and to expunge the overt intention to commit grave sin, Waugh removed the passage and replaced it with Effie's failure to recognize Mulcaster (p. 116, lines 2–8). At any rate, since Sebastian readily accepts the invitation to "a little party," the implication is clear enough.

Later, in the scenes in which Ryder rejoins his wife after a two-year separation, Waugh worked hard to establish the exact tone of their relationship. At first, on the natural assumption that Ryder's sexual appetite has been stimulated by abstinence, Waugh expressed himself more and more directly. This first draft is entirely reticent: "We lay /far apart/ in our twin beds; it was three o'clock. . . ." The second, interlined in the manuscript, is more explicit: "(At) First we lay together; then I left her for my own bed a yard or two distant." Next Waugh established a link with the previous dialogue in a passage inserted from the bottom of the manuscript page:

She talked in this way, with an effort to appear at ease, while she undressed (and put away)

"Shall I do my face now?" she asked.

"Not yet."

Then she knew what was wanted & did not speak until later when we lay apart, in our twin beds, a yard or two distant.

This provided a structure for the little scene, but Waugh decided that Celia could be made even more unappealing by the use of added detail about her sexual invitation:

She talked in this way while she undressed, with an effort to appear at ease; then she sat at the dressing table (and) ran a comb through her hair and with her /bare/ back (to me) towards me, looking at herself in the glass, said, "shall I put my face to bed?"

It was a familiar /phrase/, one that I did not like; she meant should she remove her make up, cover herself with grease and put her hair in a net.

"No," I said, "not at once."

Then she knew what was wanted and did not speak until later, when we (lay apart in our twin beds) parted and lay in our twin beds, a yard or two distant, smoking. I looked at my watch; it was four o'clock.

Between manuscript and final typescript Waugh changed the final paragraph to make Celia even more mechanical and calculating:

Then she knew what was wanted; she had neat, hygienic ways for that, too, but there was [1960: were both] relief and triumph in her smile of welcome . . . .

In correcting proof, Waugh replaced this passage with Celia's praise of her own lack of curiosity and with Ryder's indifference both to her question and to whether or not she turns out the light. Gene D. Phillips argues that this underscores "the fact that Charles's relation with his wife had completely deteriorated by the time Charles takes up with Julia."[9] He thinks that a single line replaces the sexual encounter and that it takes place aboard ship, but his argument is otherwise plausible. Furthermore, Ryder's abstinence would give further edge to "that fierce appetite" in which he possesses Julia (p. 261). On the other hand, as pointed out earlier, Waugh's diary records the lament that he could not show "two coitions—with [Charles's] wife and Julia" in the same amount of detail that he gave the meals. Also, a revision in manuscript of the transition from Ryder's shutting the window to his wife's monologue seems to imply something between the lines:

| I shut it and returned to bed. At length my wife's voice grew drowsy. | I shut it and turned back towards my wife. At length began [sic] talking again, more drowsily. [p. 233] |

In the narrative conventions of the mid-forties, a good deal of sexual activity had to be implied between lines in novels and shots in movies, and if Waugh had not changed his mind about "the two coitions," he may have felt that the reader would catch the implication. Whatever the case, Waugh restored the original passage to the 1960 edition.

If Waugh desired to make Celia unattractive even physically, he was still attempting to make Julia more appealing to the narrator and to the reader. The later and more general analysis of Julia's social position was in proof

9. Phillips, "The Page Proofs of *Brideshead Revisited,*" p. 8. But see *Letters,* p. 196. In a letter to his wife dated 9 January 1945, Waugh noted that "All the passages, including the coarse phrases with the tarts, which upset d'Arcy have been cut for the public version."

somewhat melodramatic; it makes of her religion a blight and an inescapable martyrdom.

PROOF

The young princes looking for native brides could not hope for finer descent or a more gracious presence. But for that, and for the second and much blacker taint—her religion.

There indeed Julia felt wronged, as though scarred by a birthmark. She accepted it as inescapable, now; she believed what she was taught; she must be faithful, she supposed, as the martyrs had been; but why was the palm thus thrust into her hand? It was none of her seeking. As it had been explained to her, the thing was a dead loss.

NOVEL

One subject eclipsed all others in importance for the ladies along the wall; whom would the young princes marry? They could not hope for purer lineage or a more gracious presence than Julia's; but there was this faint shadow on her that unfitted her for the highest honours; there was also her religion.

Nothing could have been further from Julia's ambitions than a royal marriage. She knew, or thought she knew, what she wanted and it was not that. But wherever she turned, it seemed, her religion stood as a barrier between her and her natural goal.

As it seemed to her, the thing was a dead loss. [p. 181]

The revision makes her religion an obstacle, but one based on fact, not on speculation, and the passage that follows both versions—"Protestant girls of her acquaintance, schooled in happy ignorance, could marry eldest sons, live at peace with their world, and get to heaven before her"—can shift more easily to a partly comic adolescent response to religion.

After dealing with Ryder's reunion with Celia, Waugh reconsidered the impression Julia produces. Originally the passage read:

She seemed to say, I see it in every eye. Wherever I go, I bring delight. You, Charles at this moment are enraptured at being near me. I give hope of ineffable things to those who seek. But where is my reward?

On reflection, this must have seemed a bit complacent in the consciousness of power and mystery, and Waugh replaced it with lines more colloquial in diction and humanly plaintive in tone:

She seemed to say, "Look at me. I have done my share. I am beautiful. It is something quite out of the ordinary, this beauty of mine. I am made for delight. But what do *I* get out of it? Where is *my* reward?" [p. 239]

The most obvious if not the most important revisions of proof involved Ryder's war with his father, and they may have been foremost in Waugh's mind when he told Peters that he would revise the first half. All the way into proof a good deal more detail about Ryder's Aunt Phillipa is given, and the skirmishes between father and son involved not merely the lunch with Jorkins and the retaliatory dinner with the Orme-Herricks as focus but the elder Ryder's escalation with the Angus Farthing dinner party, which involves "three hours of drawing-room entertainment," including imitations by a Miss Pomfrey. Ryder counters by asking her to lunch, only to be out-flanked by his father, who not only absents himself but convinces his son that she is a professional entertainer and must be paid (proofs 65–67). Waugh obviously came to feel that, himself amused by the comic malice of the elder Ryder, he had extended the sequence beyond its formal purpose—to emphasize Ryder's rootlessness and to establish the basis for the contrast with the visit to Venice and Lord Marchmain at the end of Chapter 4. More to the point was a passage inserted to replace part of the material excised: Sebastian's airy letter, which recalls Anthony Blanche's indictment of his shallow charm and temporarily estranges Ryder from his friend (p.72–73).

Like some of Shakespeare's memorable passages—Jaques's "Seven ages of man," which gives Orlando time to get off, get Adam, and get back on, is but one example—many of Waugh's inspired touches seem to have been at least partly dictated by necessity: in this case, that of causing the least possible disturbance to the pagination. He had asked for galley proof and received page proof, a significant stage farther along in the printing process in which extensive revisions were a serious matter. His note for the compositor on the corrected proofs gives evidence of his purpose: "The passages omitted between pages 58 and 67 [Ryder and his father] and 73 [brief paragraphs about Brideshead] are designed to be filled by the manuscript insertions at pages 66 and 72, 73." These are the extensive revisions in Chapters 3 and 4; the deletions total ninety-nine lines of type, while the inserted passages of Sebastian's letter, the dialogue about Brideshead, and the history of Ryder's aesthetic theories come to ninety-eight lines. Elsewhere Waugh seems to have worked very carefully; almost every insertion was balanced by a comparable deletion.[10] A close examination of major revisions bears out this theory. The introductory description of Brideshead Castle has twelve lines in both versions (p. 32); (proof page numbers are cited in this paragraph) and the twelve lines on Ryder's adolescence (p. 41) are offset by twelve lines and three fragments deleted from Blanche's reminiscence about his love

10. F.B. Walker, of Chapman and Hall, may have obscured Waugh's efforts by calling for new proofs. See his letter to Peters, January 1, 1945.

affair (pp. 47–48). The extended banter of Effie and Mulcaster (p.103) adds six lines and a fragment to replace the six lines containing Sebastian's decision tc sleep with a woman, and the eight lines substituted for Celia and Ryder's sexual encounter (p. 202) are offset by six lines of the original and two lines (pp. 197, 200) saved by the printer.

At the end of major divisions, of course, Waugh had less worry about replacing deleted material. He was uncharacteristically moderate on such occasions, however. The ends of Book 1 and the Epilogue are briefly but significantly revised. At the end of Book 1, Cordelia rejects Ryder's suggestion that she will fall in love with, "Oh, I pray not," and Ryder replies, "Now you've thoroughly shocked me." This emphasizes Cordelia's importance unduly, and since she has not previously shocked him, the line is misleading. Therefore, Waugh gave Cordelia a final, casual sentence that appropriately if perhaps unconsciously caps the theme of gluttony glorified: "Oh, I pray not. I say, do you think I could have another of those scumptious meringues?" (p. 222). The changes at the end of the novel were even simpler. Proof ended thus:

> I quickened my pace and reached the hut which served us for our ante-room.
> "You're looking unusually cheerful today," said the second-in-command; "have you had a good morning?"
> "Yes, thank you," I said; "a very good morning."

Since Ryder has reflected in the previous paragraph that all has not been in vain and has stepped briskly, the implication is clear enough that Waugh cut the question and response about "a good morning."

Revisions in proof had clarified focus and satisfied censors, internal or external, but Waugh remained uneasy about the novel. After it was published, he kept returning to it, revising, deleting, and adding in ways that would least disturb the printer. Chapman and Hall issued a "revised edition" in 1945 that has about a dozen variants from the first edition, and on August 8, 1946, Waugh insisted to Peters that the Albatross edition be set "from the latest i.e. this month's revised C & H edition," the fourth edition. By the first uniform edition (1949),[11] Waugh had introduced a dozen more new readings.

Considered as a group, the most significant changes reveal Waugh's focus on a few major themes. For example, he altered the basic plan of Brideshead Castle. The nurseries where Nanny Hawkins presides were in early editions

11. Evelyn Waugh, *Brideshead Revisited,* new uniform ed. (London: Chapman and Hall, 1949), p. 33.

"high in the dome in the centre of the main block" (p. 35). The revised version sounds more practical as well as more feasible: "The dome was false, designed to be seen from below like the cupola of Chambord. Its drum was merely an additional story full of segmental rooms."[12] Later Waugh changed "formal" to "sculptured" rocks and "tricky" to "coffered" ceilings (pp. 72,73) and made the transition from Nanny's attitude toward the fountain to Ryder's aesthetic growth more accurate, canceling, "I was myself in almost the same position as Nanny Hawkins," and inserting, "For me the beauty was new-found."[13] Near the end of the novel, perhaps remembering that he had first described the chapel as being "gutted, elaborately refurnished and redecorated," Waugh changed Lord Marchmain's memory from the fact that he "pulled down the pavilion that stood there; rebuilt with the old stones" to "in the shade of the pavilion; rebuilt with the old stones behind the old walls."[14]

The beginning of Book 2 also received Waugh's attention. In comparing human life to historical process, he had been perhaps too dramatic in outlining the progress of a race that might "commit all manner of crimes, perhaps, follow the wildest chimeras, go down in the end in agony, but leave behind a record of new heights scaled and new rewards won" (p. 225). This covered extremes, certainly, but sorted rather ill with the label "rare classic periods," and in revising, Waugh shifted the emphasis away from violence and failure to positive achievement, in which the race can "bring to birth and nurture a teeming brood of genius, droop soon with the weight of its grandeur, fall, but leave behind a record of new rewards won" (rev. ed. p. 197).

Even more important thematically is the later passage that summarizes Ryder's movement from love of Sebastian to love of Julia and prepares for the further movement to the love of God. Waugh used Ryder's speculation that "all our loves are merely hints and symbols" and in early editions continued with a rather conventional pair of metaphors: "a hill of many invisible crests; doors that open as in a dream to reveal only a further stretch of carpet and another door" (p. 303). The new reading is more vivid and thematically more appropriate because it reveals the weariness of the worldly journey without, like its predecessor, denying the existence of a goal and the commonality of experience: ". . . vagabond-language

12. Nanny's remark that Julia "was up with me nearly all the morning telling me about London" was deleted, probably to make room for the added words.

13. Waugh, *Brideshead Revisited,* 3d ed. (London: Chapman and Hall, 1945), p. 73. The pagination of all English editions, from proof copy through the first uniform edition, is almost identical. None of the emendations after page proof was made by Little, Brown.

14. First edition and revised edition, p. 293.

scrawled on gate-posts and paving-stones along the weary road that others have tramped before us" (3d ed., p. 265).

The most significant of Waugh's brief alterations comes at the climax of the novel in which Lord Marchmain has been anointed, the spectators wait for a sign, and Ryder feels a growing desire to see one. The two versions read:

All over the world people were on their knees before innumerable crosses, and here the drama was being played again by two men—by one man, rather, and he nearer death than life; the universal drama in which there is only one actor. [Little, Brown, 1945, p. 338]

I prayed more simply: "God forgive him his sins" and "Please God, make him accept your forgiveness."
So small a thing to ask. [3d ed., p. 296]

The first version is melodramatic in language and beside the point of the scene. The second focuses on Ryder's state of mind and establishes more firmly his movement from doubt in the previous line, "O God, if there is a God, forgive him his sins, if there is such a thing as sin," to implied faith and sincere petition. The last line of the revision is rather insistently repetitious, especially isolated as a one-sentence paragraph, but typography seems to have necessitated something to replace the excised verbiage.

In June, 1959, Chapman and Hall asked Waugh to "produce a revised version for resetting."[15] Mechanical restrictions were removed, and he was able to reconsider the novel not merely in itself but in the perspective of his career.[16] The text for the revised edition Waugh provided in a marked copy of the first uniform edition[17] that incorporated all previous revisions. As his correspondence with Peters indicates, he was conscious that he had reached his peak and perhaps declined from it; aside from the conclusion of the trilogy and his autobiography, he looked forward to little except worthy hack work. *Brideshead* was the first volume in the final uniform edition of his novels, and the Preface established the pattern for the series: an account of the circumstances of composition, the book's reception, the author's subsequent attitude toward it, and any major textual changes introduced. Now conscious of the "glaring defects" of the novel's form, he traced them to his reaction

15. Letter to Peters, June 9, 1959.
16. Paul A. Doyle reports that in 1950 Waugh was planning "a complete rewriting of *Brideshead."* *"Brideshead* Rewritten," *Catholic Book Reporter* 2 (April–May 1962): 9. See Waugh's letter to Graham Greene, March 27, 1950, *Letters*, p. 322, in which he announces his intention to rewrite it.
17. This copy is now at the University of Texas. It is the second impression, dated 1952 on the verso of the title page.

against "a bleak period of present privation and threatening disaster" and movement toward "a kind of gluttony, for food and wine, for the splendours of the recent past, and for rhetorical and ornamental language," all of which were now "distasteful" but, unfortunately, "an essential part of the book."[18] Form in the broad, external sense was the major concern in Waugh's return to the manuscript's three-book structure. The fifth chapter, which ends with Sebastian and Ryder going down from Oxford, was placed at the end of Book 1 to preserve the unity of that section; the new title of Book 2, "Brideshead Deserted," comes midway between and gives added point to the "Brideshead Revisited" of Prologue and Epilogue and underlines the resemblances among the lives of the Flyte family. The subtitles of each chapter, introduced only in the table of contents in revised proof, are placed at the head of each chapter to underline parallel actions more clearly still.

Since in the ensuing paragraphs of the Preface he discusses expression rather than construction, he seems to mean by form what others would call style, and in most of the revisions he "modified grosser passages" by trimming them. That involves phrases all the way through paragraphs. For example, the paragraph describing Ryder's first sight of the grounds of Brideshead in the Prologue begins with the heightened double compound, "Outside the hut I stood *awed and* bemused *between two realities and two dreams,*"[19] and ends with, "From where I stood the house was hidden by a green spur, but I knew well how and where it lay, couched among the lime trees like a hind in the bracken. *Which was the mirage, which the palpable earth?*" (1960, pp. 16, 25). The italicized words (my emphasis) removed, the passage became more precise without losing the heightened pictorial effect. And though here and elsewhere Waugh retained romantic figures of speech, he unscrambled some ("the spring of anarchy" is made to come from depths, not furnaces [p. 44/p. 54]) and removed others, like the "Dresden figures of pastoral gaiety" and the ensuing sentence (p. 62/p. 73), and the comparison of autumnal Oxford and a foreign village (p. 104/p. 118). The analogy between Ryder's worry and a "sea-mist in a dip of the sand-dunes" (pp. 325—26/p. 358) and its reinforcing "cloudy" were also removed, perhaps to emphasize more strongly the recurrent figure of the impending avalanche that follows. The

18. Elsewhere Waugh spoke of "the mood of sentimental delusion" in which at least parts of the book were written. Evelyn Waugh, *A Little Learning* (Boston: Little, Brown and Co., 1964), p. 191. To Graham Greene he wrote that "the only excuse he could offer for *Brideshead Revisited* was 'spam, blackouts and Nissen huts.' " Graham Greene, Introduction, *The Heart of the Matter* (London: William Heinemann and The Bodley Head, 1971), p. vii. *Letters*, p. 322.

19. Little, Brown, 1945, p. 15; 1960, p. 24. Further paired references in the next paragraphs given parenthetically in this order, the page citations separated by a virgule.

extended comparison of fire in a ship's hold to the topic of Sebastian's drinking was retained, but ornamental details—smoke which "curled up the ladders, crept between decks" and "hung in wreaths on the flats"—were pared, as were details about the "moon-landscape" of Lord Brideshead's mental world (p. 163/p. 185). And though the other courses of Ryder's meal with Rex survive, the praise of the Burgundy is shortened by a half-dozen lines (p. 175/pp. 196–97).

Waugh exercised a proportional ruthlessness in dealing with longer atmospheric passages that had gone through many drafts to reach the state of the first uniform edition. In the passage on "the languour of Youth" that begins Chapter 4, he removed the five lines detailing the qualities that are *not* lost and the cosmic sympathy of sun and earth with the human body (p. 79/p. 91). Surgery would have to supply the metaphor to describe Waugh's treatment of the beginning of Book 2 (Book 3 in manuscript and 1960). In the second paragraph he removed details about pigeonlike memories ("singly in pairs" and "pecking a broken biscuit from between my lips"), excised the passage distinguishing Ryder's love of buildings from his contempt for their inhabitants (p. 226/p. 251), leaving "I became an architectural painter" in emphatic, terminal position, and amputated paragraphs three and four, two dozen lines, in which he had so laboriously drawn the parallel between history and the human soul (pp. 226–27/p. 251).

Waugh distinguished mere excess from shifts in method: the monologues of Julia on sin and Lord Marchmain on health belong, he said in the Preface, "to a different way of writing from, say, the early scenes between Charles and his father. I would not now introduce them into a novel which elsewhere aims at verisimilitude." He did not expunge them entirely, he said, because like other "grosser passages" "they were essentially of the mood of writing." In Julia's monologue, for example, he retained the conceit of living with a personified sin, but he cut the sentence of quotidian activities that begin with waking and end with a sleeping pill (p. 287/p. 316), and he also deleted the first, second, and fourth sentences of the paragraph describing the waste land in which Julia wanders (p. 288/p. 317). Lord Marchmain's soliloquy is less heavily revised, but Waugh did remove the simile of Aladdin's treasury, which perhaps gave too much prominence to the figure, used earlier (p. 319/p. 350), that was introduced in revised proof, since he was moving from fantasy to spiritual reality. He also deleted the dying man's delusion of being trapped in a tunnel (p. 333/p. 366) and his melodramatic confession, "I committed a crime in the name of freedom" (p. 334/p. 366).

Waugh's revisions and insertions, though less extensive than his deletions, are no less interesting. His denigration of Mr. Samgrass's "literary manners" as being the result of "a concealed typewriter" (in manuscript "fountain pen") becomes the even more mechanical and from Waugh's point of view more damning "dictaphone" (p. 110/p. 124). Ryder's and Julia's unnamed acquaintance on the liner is made to break his thigh rather than his collar bone (p. 235/p. 282), probably because Mr. Krumm's arm injury does not prevent him from reappearing after the storm, and Waugh needed definitely to dispose of the witness to and partial occasion of the couple's growing intimacy.

In the Venetian sequence Waugh further cut back the low comedy and the hot wash as he had done in proof, and he added to the description of Lord Marchmain, lest the reader miss the point, "the hint of deep boredom which I knew so well in my own father" (p. 99/p. 112). He also added the conversation about painting to emphasize the youthful Ryder's interest in the subject and virtually complete ignorance of it, including that there were not one, not two, but three Bellinis.

Perhaps because he had already developed Ryder's aesthetic history at some length, Waugh was more attentive in this revision to his religious history. The accounts differ markedly:

The view implicit in my education was that the basic narrative of Christianity had long been exposed as a myth, and that opinion was now divided as to whether its ethical teaching was of present value, a division in which the main weight went against it; religion was a hobby which some people professed and others did not; at the best it was slightly ornamental, at the worst it was the province of "complexes" and "inhibitions"—catchwords of the decade—and of the intolerance, hypocrisy, and sheer stupidity attributed to it for centuries. No one had ever suggested to me that these quaint observances expressed a coherent philosophic system and intransigeant historical claims; nor, had they done so, would I have been much interested. [pp. 85-86]

The masters who taught me Divinity told me that biblical texts were highly untrustworthy. They never suggested I should try to pray. My father did not go to church except on family occasions and then with derision. My mother, I think, was devout. It once seemed odd to me that she should have thought it her duty to leave my father and me and go off with an ambulance, to Serbia, to die of exhaustion in the snow in Bosnia. But later I recognized some such spirit in myself. Later, too, I have come to accept claims which then, in 1923, I never troubled to examine, and to accept the supernatural as the real. I was aware of no such needs that summer at Brideshead. [1960, p. 98]

The first account focuses on reason and alternative systems to theology; the revision emphasizes the statements of faith in Scripture and the overt act of prayer and gives Ryder's mother a larger part in his heritage and his destiny.[20] Also, of course, in making Ryder indifferent rather than actively hostile to or condescending toward religion, Waugh makes more plausible his movement into faith.

Critics have not regarded Waugh's revisions for the 1960 edition with much favor. The revisions involving Ryder's sex life attracted inevitable but in view of their length disproportionate attention. The overt sexual reunion with Celia is striking, and it illustrates vividly the conflict between Ryder's physical desires and aesthetic aspirations soon to be resolved in Julia and also gives an implied motivation for the fact, which Waugh did not describe and Ryder feebly traces to "physical attraction. Ambition . . . . Loneliness . . ." (p. 252/p. 284), that he married her at all.

The meaning not the fact of the sexual act is at issue in Waugh's alteration of the passage in which Ryder consummates his love for Julia:

So at sunset I took formal possession of her as her lover. It was no time for the sweets of luxury; they would come, in their season, with the swallow and the lime flowers. Now on the rough water, as I was made free of her narrow loins and, it seemed now, assuaging that fierce appetite, cast a burden which I had borne all my life, toiled under, not knowing its nature—now, while the waves still broke and thundered on the prow, the act of possession was a symbol, a rite of ancient origin and solemn meaning. [p. 261]	It was no time for the sweets of luxury; they would come, in their season, with the swallow and the lime flowers. Now on the rough water there was a formality to be observed, no more. It was as though a deed of conveyance of her narrow loins had been drawn and sealed. I was making my first entry as the freeholder of a property I would enjoy and develop at leisure. [1960, p. 288]

Bernard Bergonzi thinks that Waugh wisely removed the implication in the first version that Ryder "is becoming carnally incorporated into the magic circle of Brideshead, a kind of earthly beatitude"—which would accord with Ryder's earlier feeling that at Brideshead he "believed myself very near heaven"—but thinks it unfortunate (and therefore unconscious?) that "Julia

20. Excellent discussions of these and other revisions can be found in "Yet Another Visit to Brideshead," *TLS*, September 16, 1960, p. 194; in Bernard Bergonzi, "Evelyn Waugh's Gentleman," *Critical Quarterly* 5 (Spring 1963):28–30; and in Doyle, *"Brideshead* Rewritten."

could never be just a woman he was in love with. She inevitably stood for much more—for Brideshead Castle and all its treasure, both material and spiritual." The *TLS* reviewer argues that the revision contains a "horrible double meaning [that] can hardly be unintentional. Suddenly it seems as if all the time it has been the house, the property, that he loved." and goes on to find "the real grossness of the novel . . . not in any details of style but in its apparent identification of grace with property and its relegation of humanity to a bad third place."[21] Bergonzi concludes that on examination the revisions "have the possibly unwelcome effect of drawing attention to the weak points in the narrative" and that "It is . . . questionable whether the novel has gained very much from these changes."

The *TLS* reviewer is correct, I think, in assuming that Waugh intended the effects he perceives. The evidence is found in textual history. In preparing the 1945 revised edition, Waugh anticipated the revision of this passage by changing the description of the light "drawing out all the hidden sweetness of color and scent" (p. 279) to its "spreading out all the stacked merchandise of colour and scent" (p. 245). In both the atmosphere is associated with "the head and golden shoulders of the woman beside me." In the surrounding passages Ryder has just asked, "Isn't this peace?" and is assured that it is not, which seems to indicate that merely physical values—"the world of three dimensions" perceived by the five senses that, he learns, does not exist (p.169)—are insufficient. Moreover, in revising proof, Waugh removed references to "the black gowned Hoopers" of the Reformation, which would have limited the scope of Ryder's newly discovered charity at the end of the novel.

Perhaps these changes were not enough to clarify Waugh's theme. The obvious difficulty with the novel before 1960 is that of distinguishing the Ryder who experiences from the Ryder who narrates.[22] The latter accepts the primacy of spiritual values, confesses his failings to the affectionately despised Hooper—"I'm homeless, childless, middle-aged, loveless" (p. 300)—and is resigned to the physical devastation of Brideshead. It is not clear, however, that Ryder as narrator is distinct from the actor in condemning Rex and Celia

21. The manuscript reads: 'So /at sunset/ I became her lover and by a formal act took possession of what was already my own, and more even than in the assuaging of that (keen) /fierce/ appetite (the movement was immortal for me as the symbol and ceremony of love) /the casting, rather/ of a /great/ burden which, it seemed, I had borne all my life, toiling under, not recognizing its (purpose) /nature/—The movement was immortal for me in the symbol and ceremony of love.'

22. For an extended discussion of this issue see William J. Cook, *Masks, Modes, and Morals: The Art of Evelyn Waugh* (Rutherford, N.J.: Fairleigh Dickinson University Press, 1971), pp. 193–235.

not for their moral failings, which are plentiful, but for fraudulent taste in brandy, jewelry, and personal publicity—in short, for aesthetic shortcomings.[23] Still greater is the problem of Ryder's character in the Prologue. He is already Catholic—though Waugh removed from the manuscript the sole implication of the fact—but he is presented as barren and alienated. Only after he has seen Brideshead and remembered the past is he consoled and reconciled to his lot at the end of the Epilogue.

Throughout the long and intricate textual history of *Brideshead* it is clear that, whichever text one reads, the novel is in texture Waugh's richest and most complex work and, except for the *Sword of Honour* trilogy, his most ambitious in scope. His many revisions over fifteen years reveal, perhaps, his desire to justify the conception of himself as writer embodied in the novel, and his later repudiation of the novel's stylistic excesses indicates either great artistic humility or a commitment to the sparer style and clearer linear method of the trilogy. Whichever the case, his sentiments do him credit as a critic of his own work.

The effects of his self-criticism are difficult to judge. As he said of Ronald Knox's translation of the Bible, "It is extremely difficult to read . . . without being distracted by echoes."[24] We have, that is, double rather than binocular vision: neither 1945 nor 1960 text, let alone the intermediate stages, can be seen as a whole because our view is cluttered with details. We can, of course, judge the novel by various standards, including those established by the other novels in the canon, but, whatever our final judgment, we can appreciate in studying the process the struggle of a conscious and dedicated artist to realize his intention.

23. In "The Pieties of Evelyn Waugh," *Bell* 14 (July 1947): 77, *Letters*, p. 255, Waugh argued that he criticized the worldliness of those with money and rank in the persons of Mottram and Lady Celia, but this does not deal with my distinction between morals and aesthetics.
24. "A Literary Opinion," *Month*, n.s. 2 (July, 1949): 42.

10

Thinking about Death and Art: *The Loved One*

Waugh's postwar career shows a marked division between what he intended as his vocation and what happened as a result of circumstance. On the day of Germany's surrender to the Allies he was as complacent at beginning his novel on Saint Helena as thirteen months earlier, on D Day, he had been at completing *Brideshead:*

> It is pleasant to end the war in plain clothes, writing.... I regard the greatest danger I went through that of becoming one of Churchill's young men, of getting a medal and standing for Parliament; if things had gone, as then seemed right, in the first two years, that is what I should be now. I thank God to find myself still a writer and at work on something as "uncontemporary" as I am.[1]

In something of the same mood he asserted that he did not regret his self-imposed exile at Piers Court, for in his youth and "in the preposterous years of the Second World War I collected enough experience to last several life-times of novel writing. If you hear a novelist say he needs to collect copy, be sure he is no good."[2] To replace physical adventure as a source of excitement, he announced, he had discovered "the English language . . . the most lavish and delicate which mankind has ever known," and he warned his readers that "in my future books there will be two things to make them unpopular: a preoccupation with style and the attempt to represent man more fully, which, to me, means only one thing, man in his relation to God."[3]

Waugh, however, proved unable to keep the resolution that "my own travelling days are over" because "there is no room for tourists in a world of 'displaced persons,'"[4] and his movements about the postwar world in-

---

1. Evelyn Waugh, *The Diaries of Evelyn Waugh,* ed. Michael Davie (Boston: Little, Brown and Co., 1977), p. 627 (May 6, 1945).
2. "Fan-Fare," *Life* 20 (April 8, 1946): 54.
3. *Ibid.*, p. 56.
4. Preface, *When the Going Was Good* (Boston: Little, Brown and Co., 1947), p. xi.

spired his two longest works of the postwar 1940s, both of which are secular in context and tone. It is somewhat artificial to divorce this aspect of his work from his pronouncements on the need to portray man in a supernatural context, but the split between sacred and profane does exist, and separate discussion of the two helps solve some awkward chronological problems.

It is obvious from his diaries and from his journalism that even while he was renouncing the modern world Waugh remained quite aware of it. His "sense of guilt" about what he viewed as the British betrayal of Yugoslavia to the Communists had been somewhat allayed by his agitation at the Foreign Office, in Parliament,[5] and in the press.[6] More immediately vexing was the course of political and social events in an England governed by Labour. The government seemed determined to destroy the very idea of the English gentleman, upon which British society, education, and foreign relations had so long depended. The austerity regulations of the Atlee regime confined Englishmen to their own island and subjected them, and especially him, for whom civilization was measured in part by liberal drinking laws and large quantities of good food, wine, and cigars, to the rigors of a new iron age. In the 1930s he had often predicted such an age, but for a future sometimes vague and often remote. It was more difficult to contemplate with equanimity the decline of the West when the boiler did not work, there were few servants, and only the plainest food was available.

Not that Waugh was physically starved—at least, a man sixty-seven inches tall with a thirty-nine inch waist seems in no immediate danger of inanition.[7] His imagination, however, was on very short rations. Whatever the reason—perhaps the "sense of guilt" about Yugoslavia, perhaps an inability to deal at such short distance in time with the complexities of the material—he was not ready to use his war experience as the basis for fiction. Nor was he impelled to write, even derisively, about contemporary England. Instead, he sought inspiration in the past, first in the fictionalized biography of Saint Helena, begun several weeks before the publication of *Brideshead* on May 28, 1945, dropped, resumed early in 1946, dropped again, and finally completed in 1950. In October, 1945, he turned to the less remote past in a novel, "Charles Ryder's Schooldays," where he tried to resurrect

5. "Church and State in Liberated Croatia," dated May 17, 1945, R 5927/1059/92, Foreign Office Archives.

6. See the letters signed "A British Soldier Lately in Yugoslavia," *Times,* May 23, 1945, p. 5; and June 5, 1945, p. 5. See also my "Two Suppositious Letters by Evelyn Waugh," *Evelyn Waugh Newsletter* 9 (Spring, 1975):3–5. In view of Waugh's diary entry of May 28, 1945, the identification can be regarded as certain.

7. As Waugh would no doubt comment "What honourable reason is there for keeping thin?" Evelyn Waugh, *Wine in Peace and War* (London: Saccone & Speed, 1947), p. 19.

the narrator of *Brideshead* in a third-person narrative based on his own diaries and set late in the World War I. He carried this project through twenty pages before abandoning it. Until late 1946 his other projects were largely fiddling: making selections from his prewar travel books for *When the Going Was Good,* reissuing *Edmund Campion,* writing *Wine in Peace and War* for Saccone and Speed to replenish his cellar, doing literary journalism of various sorts that others could have done as well.

His chief preoccupation with the present seemed to be finding ways to escape England, temporarily or even permanently. He went to Nuremberg for the war-crimes trials in April, 1946; two months later he went to Spain for the Francisco de Vitoria celebrations. In February, 1947, he and his wife, Laura, traveled to Hollywood for discussions about the possibility of filming *Brideshead,* an eventuality he hoped to avoid. In August he went to Scandinavia to gather material for the *Daily Telegraph.* He was ready to go to Baltimore to accept an honorary degree from Loyola College but was prevented by currency restrictions.[8] He fretted and, soon after his return from America, fumed in the *Times* that authors "may not even spend the royalties on our translations in the countries where they are earned."[9] The only people not confined to England, he thought, were "the politician, the journalist, and the commercial traveler,"[10] a trinity to whom he added in another context criminals and members of UNESCO.[11] Except for criminals, with whom he had some sympathy, public figures and tradesmen, whom he detested, were the only ones allowed to move freely. Yet, as he ruefully confessed in *Vogue,* he was becoming by virtue of his fame and his willingness to travel himself a public figure, an interviewee— a neologism he would probably have hated less than the process it names—to escape England.[12] Perhaps to make permanent the escape, perhaps in reaction against his public life, he began thinking of selling Piers Court and buying a castle in Ireland, a fancy he entertained for almost a year between October, 1946, and September, 1947, and pursued on several trips to Ireland.

---

8. Evelyn Waugh, "A Visit to America," *Times* [London] November 6, 1947, p. 5. Reprinted in *The Letters of Evelyn Waugh,* ed. Mark Amory (New Haven and New York. Ticknor & Fields, 1980), p. 249.

9. Evelyn Waugh, "Foreign Travel for Young Writers," *Times* [London] April 17, 1947, p. 5.

10. Evelyn Waugh, "The Scandinavian Capitals: Contrasted Post-War Moods," *Daily Telegraph and Morning Post,* November 11, 1947, p. 4.

11. Evelyn Waugh, "Honeymoon Travel," *The Book for Brides* (London: Forbes Publications, 1948), p. 52.

12. Evelyn Waugh, "Let My Pulse Alone," *Vogue,* 112 (July 1948): 68–69.

The seemingly aimless travel stimulated Waugh to begin and, more important, to finish his first creative work of any length since mid-1944. *Scott-King's Modern Europe* ranks well down in the Waugh canon, but it does represent his first fictional attempt to deal with the bewildering and unlovely modern world. In many ways Waugh was using old forms for new material: Scott-King resembles the innocents, Paul Pennyfeather of *Decline and Fall* and William Boot of *Scoop,* not only in his inability to deal with the confusion of experience but also on his solution, taking refuge in a hallowed but crumbling institution. He cannot use his experience; indeed, he cannot even confront it; and like Paul Pennyfeather he must undergo a pseudo-death in loss of identity to prepare for a death to the outside world that results from a refusal to meet or even to countenance the world's terms.

While Waugh was writing *Scott-King,* he found two seemingly diverse occupations for his mind: reading Henry James and planning a trip to Hollywood. The beginning of the journey was not auspicious, for Waugh was still recuperating from an operation for piles. Once in Hollywood, however, he did not repine because he had expected nothing. The "story conference" introduced him to "a world that is at once haphazard and banal," in which no one can "follow a plain story" and to a miasma of moral confusion in which divorce can happen if it is not mentioned, as in *The Best Years of Our Lives,* but a story suspiciously like *Brideshead* is "condemned as likely to undermine the conception of Christian marriage." The only significance of Hollywood, Waugh concluded, was in its threat to artists, at a time when "the European climate is becoming inclement. . . . [Artists] are notoriously comfort-loving people. The allurements of the modest luxury of Hollywood are strong. Will they be seduced there to their own extinction?"[13]

Waugh wrote these words within a month of his return from America, but he was far less excited by the plight of the artist than by Forest Lawn, where he had spent "long periods of delight penetrating the arcana of that lustrous trade."[14] Both Waugh's diary entry and his letter to his agent, Peters, show that "the work of the morticians" at Forest Lawn—"the *only* thing in California that is not a copy of something else"—provided the strongest initial impulse for *The Loved One.* During his many visits to the memorial park he formed an acquaintance with "the chief embalmer"

13. "Hollywood Is a Term of Disparagement," *New Directions in Prose and Poetry* 10 (1948):34–41. The article was originally published in the *Daily Telegraph and Morning Post* in two parts: "Why Hollywood is a Term of Disparagement," April 30, 1947, p. 4; and "What Hollywood Touches It Banalizes," May 1, 1947, p. 4.

14. Evelyn Waugh, Preface, *The Loved One,* new uniform ed. (London: Chapman and Hall, 1965), p. [7]. Later citations are given parenthetically in the text.

and perhaps met Dr. Hubert Eaton, the original of Wilbur Kenworthy, the Dreamer. How far he was admitted into the mysteries of the trade cannot be determined exactly, but he did write to Peters that he had "seen dozens of loved ones half painted before the bereaved family saw them."[15] Like Dennis Barlow, Waugh returned to England with "the artist's load, a great, shapeless chunk of experience." Unlike Dennis, he brought mementos as well, including copies of the *Art Guide to Forest Lawn* and Ray E. Slocum's *Embalming Techniques.*[16] The first doubtless reminded him of the experiences that aroused his initial excitement. The second provided not only technical details about the treatment of corpses but also, in passages no ironist could improve, an impetus for his satiric thrusts at the very basis of the undertaker's theory. Among the details Waugh borrowed were those about methods of trimming cards to shape the corpse's lips, of closing the inner corner of the eye, of shampooing, and of shaving to avoid razor burns (pp. 8–12). He did not mark but almost certainly read Chapter 45, "Hanging—Crushed Chests," which contains details about facial discoloration and distortion parallel to those describing Francis Hinsley in the novel. Other passages that clearly amused Waugh dealt with nail varnish made especially for the dead (p. 18); an injunction not to skimp on embalming fluid (p. 51); a caution against techniques that would ruin the cosmetic brush, "to say nothing of the work itself" (p. 18); an instance in which "nature has come to the embalmer's aid" (p. 6). There is an anticipation of Aimee's belief in the artistic nature of her craft and of the authorial comment on the harshness of tone of her painting of Sir Francis's face in this passage: ". . . the world's greatest artists have never been able to paint their masterpieces so that they will look well in any but a subdued light" (p. 22). Perhaps the most striking passage, from Waugh's Christian point of view, is a defense of cosmetics for the corpse that points out the loss of "an indefinable something" if the "dark cast about the eyes" is bleached out (p. 16).

Waugh returned to England eager to get to work on *The Loved One.* In 1964 he wrote, "it was some time before the book took shape,"[17] but in fact he began writing on May 21. Once he began, however, the writing did not go forward rapidly. Impatient to give form to his material, he resolved to try a new method of work, or, rather, resume the method of his youth: push ahead to a conclusion and then revise a typescript at leisure and with

15. Letter to A. D. Peters, March 6, 1947. *Letters,* p. 247.

16. Ray E. Slocum, *Embalming Techniques* (Boston: Dodge Chemical Company, 1937). Both books are in Waugh's library at the University of Texas—Austin. References to Slocum are given parenthetically in the text.

17. Waugh, Preface, *The Loved One* (1965 ed.).

a sense of the form of the whole novel, instead of going laboriously over material just written. Shortly thereafter, unable to resist the impulse to put things into shape, he revised heavily what he had "hastily jotted down." There were interruptions, but he had finished a first draft and begun revision by July 6.

By September 16 the manuscript was complete enough to be offered to Cyril Connolly for *Horizon.* The decision to publish in a magazine was not in itself unusual; since *Vile Bodies,* Waugh had published all or parts of his novels in magazines before book publication. In fact, *Scott-King's Modern Europe* appeared in *Cornhill Magazine* as he was writing *The Loved One.* At least two features were unique, however; Waugh asked no payment from *Horizon* (though he was given an expensive architectural book), and he was aiming at a particular audience rather than, as in otherwise similar circumstances, publishing where and as advantageously as he could. He wrote to Connolly, "I anticipated ructions, . . . and one reason for my seeking publication in *Horizon* was the confidence that its readers were tough stuff."[18] Another reason, perhaps, was the nature of the magazine, defined in the opening pages of the novel itself as resolutely highbrow and avant garde, as far from the Book-of-the-Month Club readership of *Brideshead* as he could get. If that was his motive, he was successful, for he wrote to Randolph Churchill early in 1948 that *The Loved One* was "re-establishing my popularity in highbrow cirles here" and concluded the letter with, "Give my love to any friends you see in USA. There will be none after the publication of *The Loved One.*"[19]

The readers of 1948 needed to be "tough stuff." Despite Waugh's insistence to Peters on September 14, 1947, that "the tale should not be read as a satire on morticians but as a study of the Anglo-American cultural impasse with the mortuary as a jolly setting," he was fully aware of the outrageous possibilities of his material and took considerable relish in exploiting them. To do so, he used the point of view of Dennis Barlow, a young English poet who has fallen from grace with his movie studio and taken a job at a pet's mortuary. After his host, Sir Francis Hinsley, hangs himself out of despondency at losing his studio job, Dennis goes to Whispering Glades Cemetery to make arrangements for the funeral. He is fascinated by what he finds and by Aimee Thanatogenos, a mortuary cosmetician with an appealing air of decadence. Dennis and the chief embalmer, Mr. Joyboy, use their respective arts to court her. She chooses Dennis, but Joyboy

18. Quoted in Cyril Connolly, Introduction, *Horizon* 17 (February 1948):76.
19. Randolph Churchill, "Evelyn Waugh: Letters (and Post-cards) to Randolph Churchill," *Encounter* 31 (July, 1968):6.

reveals that Dennis works at the Happier Hunting Ground, which Aimee thinks a sacrilegious parody of Whispering Glades, and that his poems to her are plagiarized. When Dennis refuses to release her from their engagement, she commits suicide in Joyboy's workroom. Dennis cremates her at the pet's mortuary and with funds derived from blackmailing Joyboy and the English colony, prepares to return to England to write the poem inspired by Whispering Glades.

Waugh encountered two major problems in exploiting the material he brought back from the New World: making details about the mortuary suitable to the formal pattern of his book and making them disconcerting but not simply offensive to his readers. Waugh seldom shrank from causing offense either in social discourse or in his art, but he liked to do so with panache. Accordingly he opened his assault on the reader's sensibilities very mildly with Sir Francis Hinsley's analogy of the English exiles and the "dog's head severed from its body, which the Russians are keeping alive for some obscene Muscovite purpose [this phrase was added in revision of typescript] by pumping blood into it from a bottle. It dribbles at the tongue when it smells a cat" (p. 17). This prepares for the scenes in which Dennis collects the Sealyham and places it in the Happier Hunting Ground's refrigerator, "already occupied by two or three other small cadavers. Next to a Siamese cat stood a tin of fruit juice and a plate of sandwiches. Dennis took the supper into the reception room and, as he ate it, resumed his interrupted reading" (p. 22). This is nauseating only to the exceptionally squeamish or to those nonvegetarians who have never taken the trouble to think about the contents of their own refrigerators, but its real function is not only to reveal Dennis's desensitization but also to induce the reader to share it.

The chief shocks, of course, are produced by the body of Sir Francis Hinsley, and Waugh took great pains to arrange them in ascending order. In manuscript Sir Ambrose reveals at the Cricket Club that Sir Francis "hanged himself from the veranda roof," but revised typescript and all published versions refer only to the "unexpected death" and hint delicately at some irregularity about it. The ensuing section, which focuses on Dennis, went through several versions. In manuscript, Waugh could not resist vivid detail:

> Dennis Barlow was entirely free of guilt as he drove to Whispering Glades. He felt grief for his lost friend and (shock) /some horror/from /his memory of/the final spectacle of him, (swaying inert from the rafter with inky face, starting eyes and swollen, protruding tongue like a half-eaten sausage); [this cancel with red pencil] he felt uncertainty for his own

immediate future. But predominantly, it must be admitted, he felt ex-
hilerated [*sic*]& curious at his first visit to that famous necropolis.

Waugh was not squeamish, but he had more effective uses for the image
of Sir Francis's face, and in two subsequent versions it as well as Dennis's
grief were expunged, and, in a manuscript insertion into typescript, Waugh
decided to put the death into a larger context and to dismiss the physical
fact insouciantly:

> Dennis was a young man of sensibility rather than of sentiment. He
> had lived his twenty-eight years at arm's length from violence, but he
> came of a generation which enjoys a vicarious intimacy with death. Never,
> it so happened, had he seen a human corpse until that morning when,
> returning tired from night duty, he found his host strung to the rafters.
> The spectacle had been (disconcerting; but it did not) /rude and moment-
> arily unnerving/; perhaps it had left a scar somewhere out of sight in
> his subconscious mind. But his reason accepted the event as part of (an)
> /the/ established order. Others (before him) in gentler ages had had their
> lives changed by such a revelation; to Dennis it was the kind of thing (that
> had /was/) to be expected in the world he knew (/in the world of brutal,
> preposterous happenings/) and, as he drove to Whispering Glades, his
> conscious mind was /pleasantly/ exhilarated and full of (pleasant) curiosity.
> [p. 34]

The use of "conscious" anticipates a later, increasingly vivid passage in
which the physical horror of Sir Francis's death is revealed. In first draft,
" a picture arose in Dennis [*sic*] mind of the /indigo-marbled/ face he had
last seen hanging by the braces." Almost immediately Waugh decided that
this was inadequate, resurrected the sausage from the canceled opening
paragraph, and inserted a few lines below this version:

> As he said this there came vividly into Dennis's mind that [*sic*] the image
> that lurked there, seldom out of sight for long; the sack of body hanging
> dead still and the face above it with eyes (horribly staring) wide & red
> and (protruding) /forced as though from behind/ horribly from their
> sockets, the cheeks mottled in indigo like the marbled endpapers of an
> old book and the tongue swollen and protruding like a half (eaten) end
> of black sausage.

With minor revisions this became the final version; it allowed Waugh to
make consistent the professional detachment of Dennis's interview with
Aimee about makeup for the corpse. Originally, in part of a long canceled
draft of Dennis's conversations with the Mortuary Hostess and with Aimee,
Waugh had him respond to her question about facial disfigurement with
"It was (black) inky with eyes & tongue popping out." In revision he merely

replies, "Hideously," making somewhat surprising but not wholly incongruous Aimee's ensuing, "That is quite usual" (p. 47).

Waugh continued to have innocent fun with this scene through the final, English edition. In manuscript he had canceled a draft of Aimee's formulaic farewell to insert her question about dentures, the information that they frequently disappear at the morgue, and, in a passage that does not survive in print, the process by which Joyboy (still Boyes at this point) uses cardboard to remedy the deficiency. This prosthesis may have been suggested by the earlier discussion of Sir Francis's monocle. From manuscript through American edition Waugh allowed Dennis to be persuaded that "the eye being closed" was grounds for leaving off the monocle. To his copy of *Horizon,* however, Waugh added another macabre detail: Dennis insists on the monocle since "I like the idea of the eye being closed" (p. 48) and later notes that "the gold rim of the monocle framed a delicately tinted eyelid" (p. 62).

This passage, however, comes after a scene in which a wholly different view of the body is presented. An insertion in manuscript, the description of the embalming rooms (pp. 54-60) is not pure Slocum, for other thematic and structural purposes are also served, but Slocum's professional, in fact, technological, attitude informs it and helps lull the readers' sensibilities so that they will be vulnerable to Waugh's later attack. He begins by describing Sir Francis's body neutrally as "white and slightly translucent, like weathered marble" and then shows Joyboy giving it "a little poulterer's pinch" before commenting on his art:

> The head will have to incline slightly to (sha) put the (jugular) /cartoid/ suture in the shadow. The head [all printed versions: skull] drained very nicely. Practically no massage was needed. I removed the tongue and filled the mouth with cotton wool to support the cheeks which showed a tendency to sag. The superficial bruising round the throat should (yield to) quite disappear I think under cosmetic treatment.

The final sentence had apparently disappeared by the final typescript, but the remaining details were enough to evoke the suggestion from Little, Brown that the three previous sentences be omitted. Rather surprisingly—for he accepted four of the six other suggestions only for the American edition[20]—

20. The letter from Little, Brown was written ca. January 15, 1948. The suggestions were: (1) change the name of the Garden of Allah Hotel to a fictitious one; see "Tents of Kedar," p. 31, Little, Brown ed.; (2) cut the details about the skull and tongue; (3) change "a mean kind of cemetery" to "a more ordinary kind of cemetery"; *Horizon* and Chapman and Hall have "a low-down kind of cemetery": Little, Brown, "a cemetery"; (4) change "good style Jews" to "newly rich people" (not adopted); (5) omit the detail about Dennis's crushing the goat's skull and perhaps the last three sentences, Little, Brown, p. 104; not adopted); (6) omit the detail about breaking up Aimee's skull and pelvis (see Little, Brown, p. 163); (7) a mild suggestion that the references to Rotarians and Knights of Pythias be omitted.

Waugh removed details about the tongue even from the English edition, retaining only, "The skull drained nicely," perhaps on the grounds that excessive clinical detail, though in character for Joyboy, would unduly disturb the reader. And to Peters, who thought it certainly unwise to publish the novel in America and probably unwise to publish it at all, he admitted that he did not wish "to antagonize future customers" even by breaking his promise in "Fan-Fare" to write theological novels in the future.[21] Later in the same scene he devoted considerable care to Boyes-Joyboy's decision, on carefully explained artistic grounds, to embalm the baby. The manuscript describes him bending over a tiny white body and concludes the scene, after his instructions to Aimee about Sir Francis, with:

> I must go back to baby. They need great patience you know. (A little) /An ounce/ too much pressure with the formaldehyde pump and (you break a capillary) /they distend/.

Even more than in the case of Sir Francis's tongue, this detail must have seemed unduly graphic, for it did not survive for Little, Brown to complain about. It is more likely that Waugh's sense of tone and timing prevailed, for the final version preserves the aura of professional detachment while closing the scene more definitely and deftly:

> Mr. Joyboy lingered a moment, then turned away. 'Back to baby,' he said. [p. 60]

Considerations of finality and understatement certainly dictated Waugh's revision of the scene in which Dennis views the finished product of Aimee's and Joyboy's arts. At first Waugh depended upon direct statement of Dennis's malaise:

> The face was entirely horrible, painted and smirking like some obscene old catamite. (all its intelligence gone.) It was entirely unlike Sir Francis, unlike anything human. It was too much—the flowers, the choir, the smile.
> ... 'It is too much,' said Dennis, at which Aimee in accordance with the etiquette of the place, gently left him alone to his leave-taking. (He [several words illegible]) The leaded (pains) [sic] /window/ frame was screwed in its place; (conditioned) air came like the music; the temperature was rather lower than is usual in American living-rooms. Dennis had never fainted but he (now) sat down on one of the gilt chairs overwhelmed. Presently the black, empty mood passed & he regained command of himself

21. See Peters to Waugh, September 13, 1947; Waugh to Peters, September 14, 1947, *Letters*, p. 259.

enough to leave the room. Aimee Kraft was waiting in the anti-room [*sic*]

'I am glad you were pleased. (Mr. Boyes personnally [*sic*] did the work')

'Pleased?' it did not seem a word to connect with his experience.

'If there is anything you could suggest. I was not sure for instance about the flower in the hand. Is it characteristic? Would anything be more suitable,—a pen or piece of paper?'

'The smile', Dennis continued to utter.

'Yes. Mr. Boyes put it there personally.'

(Then he?) Its, its not characteristic'

'Not of the Loved One in life, perhaps, Mr. Barlow, surrounded by care and sorrow. But now in his Fuller Happiness. Could we not say that it is characteristic of eternity?'

'Anyway I suppose it is too late now to make a change?'

'Oh yes Mr. Barlow. He has firmed.'

'I see. Well thats that, isn't it?'

'Are you feeling quite well Mr. Barlow? You're very pale.'

'I'll go outside for a little. I haven't been to see the (Church) church yet.'

Then the scene trails off into his attempt at developing a closer acquaintance with Aimee. In a second draft, "catamite" is canceled, replaced by allusion to devil-masks and, perhaps an echo of Sir Francis's allusion to *Where the Rainbow Ends,* a Christmas party. With revisions this became:

the face was entirely horrible; as ageless as a tortoise and as inhuman, a painted and smirking obscene travesty by comparison with which the devil-mask Dennis had found in the noose was a festive adornment, a thing an uncle might don at a Christmas party.

Aimee stood beside her handiwork—the painter at the private view—and heard Dennis draw his breath in sudden emotion.

'Is it what you hoped?' she asked.

'More'—and then—'Is he quite hard?'

'Firm.'

'May I touch him?'

'Please not. It leaves a mark.'

'Very well.'

Then in accordance with the etiquete of the place, she left him to his reflections. [Pp. 62–63]

The description, with its moral, emotional context, is intended to shock the reader into an awareness of what he had accepted in the previous scene and to return to or to formulate a clearer response to the meaning of death. Waugh anticipates, in different terms, Joseph Heller's formulation in *Catch-22* of Snowden's secret: "The spirit gone, man is garbage." The religious man and the humanist can agree that making a fetish of the corpse is a radical dislocation of value. Moreover, in the context of the novel, this scene by implication purges Dennis's imagination of the vision that had haunted it and leaves it free to attend to the burgeoning inspiration of Whispering Glades.

The rest of the novel is less macabre. Of course, the Little, Brown editors were right to link Dennis's crushing the goat's skull and Amiee's skull and pelvis, for Waugh clearly designed the second to echo the first. But with the Slumber Room scene he had made his point about the cult of the cadaver, and most of the manuscript justifies his comment that the novel was not a satire on Forest Lawn.

Waugh's plan on May 21 to push ahead without pausing to revise seems to have stemmed less from impatience to exploit material than from the need to discover how and as a result of what relationships the action would come about. Judging from the manuscript, he was never in serious doubt about the outcome or the order of incidents, but he was considerably less certain, as the revisions of physical detail show, about the precise shadings of character, including the names, or the ways in which characters would work together in embodying major themes.

The most obvious instance of uncertain pupose is Waugh's changing conception of Sir Ambrose Abercrombie. At first he seems like a sketch for Trimmer of *Sword of Honour,* aged and successful, to be sure, but no less fraudulent. Christopher Sykes records the rumor that he was based on Sir C. Aubrey Smith, and Waugh's first draft may have been dictated by the impulse to caricature rather than by the needs of the work as a whole. As first presented, Sir Ambrose wears corsets under his daily costume and is given a full and thoroughly discreditable history. His past association with Sir Francis—in the final version limited to the fact that he "came almost nightly to Sir Francis for refreshment" and contrasted to his current disparagement of Sir Francis as a "Lloyd George creation"—continues in manuscript in the series "to swim in his pool, court the executives' wives who resorted there and to ask advice. He never tired of canvassing opinions about his own future. He need not have been anxious. All went well." The manuscript continues with a cancel and revision of the process by which he achieved wealth and knighthood.

Two pages later Waugh provided Sir Ambrose with a more distant and less reputable past: Cockney origins as "Our Syd"; next "an irresistible figure then in Cunard uniform, the young purser with the profile; cuff-links and cigarette-cases came to him from the wives of the mighty"; then panic and desertion at the outbreak of the first World War; "escape, a new name, women, the West, the movies, women, scenes from which he escaped scared and dishevelled"; then stardom in silent movies; then, with talkies, "the triumph of his false, his fruity, his entirely captivating English accent." Later still, showing the effect of Sir Francis's death on the members of the Cricket Club, Waugh allowed Sir Ambrose to dominate the scene, opening and closing it with his monologue.

This development of Abercrombie obviously came to seem excessive to Waugh. For one thing, the biographical information contrasted with the authorial comment—the last of at least three formulations—that "he lived existentially. He thought of himself as he was at that moment, brooded fondly on each several excellence and rejoiced" (p. 7). More important, the emphasis on Abercrombie's successful roguery may have seemed a distortion of his function in the opening pages of the novel as well as in the conclusion.

It was important for Waugh to establish the contrast between the two knights sharply—but not too sharply. The manuscript lacks Hinsley's comparison of his exile to that of the children in the Christmas play, but the analogy of the dog's severed head and the English exiles is present in cruder form, and Sir Ambrose's fear of being cut off from his sources of life is an explicit motive for his counsel to Dennis to return to England. To emphasize this fear, Waugh deleted the account of successful fraud in favor of the comparatively mild if futile ambition to be termed a "wonderful man for his age" (in an insertion to first draft) or a "grand old boy" (p. 3). The insecurity of his position and that of all the English is further emphasized in Waugh's revision in first typescript of the scene at the Cricket Club. Instead of beginning with Sir Ambrose, he shows the uneasiness of the whole expatriate community at the "words of ill-omen": "His contract wasn't renewed," and in concluding the scene shifted away from the purely social considerations of the original:

I think we may have to put our hands into our pockets for the funeral but it will be money well spent if it puts the British Colony back where it ought to be. I called Washington asking the ambassador to come but it doesn't seem that he can manage it. He is instructing the Los Angeles consul —not quite the same thing.	'This is an occasion when we've all got to show the flag (a bit). We may (all) have to put our hands in our pockets—I don't suppose old Frank has left much—but it will be money well spent if it puts the (English) /British/ colony right in the eyes of the industry. I called Washington and asked them to send the Ambassador to the funeral but it doesn't seem they can

> manage it. I'll try again. It would
> make a lot of difference. In any
> case I don't think the studios will
> keep away if they know *we* are
> solid . . . '
>
> As he spoke the sun sank below
> the /bushy/ western (wooded) hill-
> side. The sky was still bright but
> a shadow crept over the tough and
> ragged grass of the cricket field,
> bringing with it a sharp chill.
> [p. 33]

In the final version Sir Ambrose's fatuous chatter trails off into an atmosphere that seems to portend doom for all their hopes.

Sir Ambrose, of course, does not seem conscious of the threat; unlike
Sir Francis, he never had any past or any talent to betray, and despite
everything he is as obviously a survivor as Sir Francis is a victim. These
qualities may have recalled him to Waugh's attention some time after the
first draft of the final chapter. In manuscript Joyboy announces Aimee's
death, departs, leaving Dennis alone with unspecified thoughts, and returns
to make practical arrangements for disposing of her body. Subsequently—
probably after the first typescript—Waugh conceived the happy idea of
reintroducing Sir Ambrose to voice his disapproval of Dennis's becoming a
nonsectarian pastor, counsel his return to England, haggle over the price,
pay up cheerfully, and tie off a plot strand that the original ending had left
loose. Having exacted tribute from Joyboy and Abercrombie, Whispering
Glades and Hollywood, Dennis has triumphed over both institutions en-
thralled by death. Furthermore, Abercrombie's dialogue, redolent of cheerful
fraud, contrasts effectively with Joyboy's hysterics before and glum acquiescence after the knight's appearance and further helps detach Dennis
from any emotion aroused by Aimee's cremation.

The reader's response to this event, of course, is conditioned by the development of the relationship of Dennis—and of Joyboy—to Aimee throughout the novel, and Waugh revised heavily at almost every stage to exploit
his materials more fully. Even the characters' names were altered to fit the
satiric occasion: Andrew to Dennis (derived from Dionysius), Boyes
(in manuscript Elmer) to Joyboy by what is now page 80; Aimee Kraft
to Aimee Sprott by the scene at the Lake Isle of Innisfree to Aimee Thanatogenos (on the typescript page) just in time for Mr. Slump to cap his advice
of suicide with, "Well, for Christ's sake, with a name like that?" The shift
to Joyboy was inspired, and Peters was obviously right in convincing Waugh

that simple repetition of the name was funnier than a series of derisory travesties of it.[22] Aimee—the loved one, or beloved—was clearly part of Waugh's original inspiration, but the three changes in surname represent a deepening conception of her character. As Kraft she is simply labeled a practitioner of cosmetology; as Sprott she is the butt of sarcasm about America's polyglot and monosyllabic surnames that amused Waugh right through the revision of *Unconditional Surrender* to *Sword of Honour.* But as Aimee Thanatogenos—the loved one born out of death—she acquired a significance that even by the end of the manuscript draft Waugh had not fully realized.

Waugh must have realized that her name needed to be unusual because he had taken considerable pains to characterize her as sharply different from other American girls in all but the most superficial ways. At first he relied on simple contrast with the "other girls, indistinguishable one from the other, neat, friendly, hygenic" [*sic*], with exquisite teeth and hands & slim legs and curled hair," characterizing her only as "dressed as a hospital nurse" with "the air of a nun, of a postulant about whose vocation the novice mistress had doubts" and "pale, with black hair and green eyes." Perhaps in reaction, and remembering his life-long predilection for the "Pre-Raphaelite, the wistful and difficult,"[23] he expanded the description in second draft with an extended allusion:

> The cosmetician, who succeeded the hostess, was something different. She dressed in the same way, she entered the room in the same way, she seated herself at the table and produced a similar Eversharp pen, but she had something altogether lacking in her predecessor. Dennis was onto it at once. Decadent. That was what clumsily & inadequately expressed it. Sole eve of a bustling, hygenic (continent) Eden, this girl was decadent. Not perhaps with the rich overtones of Toulouse Lautrec; rather Pre-Raphaelite. She was like a Rossetti water colour in the mahogany pannelled dining room of a Gateshead magnate, not one of those voluptuous denizens of the Kings Road tricked out in renaissance costume but rather a product of his (submission to) Ruskin /period or of earlier/ something [*sic*] time with the shrinking virginal sisterly submission of Ecce Ancilli Domini. It was an aura rather than a visual likeness. The girl was of transparent delicacy, with a clearer skin than is usual in those steam heated, sun-rayed climes. Her eyes were greenish, her eyebrows unplucked, her lips, if (painted) /coloured/ at all /were pale/, not choked in all their sensitive pores by the thick crimson grease of her sisters, and gave promise of

22. Peters to Waugh, September 13, 1947.
23. Waugh, *Diaries,* p. 745 (October 30, 1955).

exquisite tactile communication. It must not be thought that she was
a drooping beauty of the Grosvenor Gallery; she was unmistakably an
American girl, even before she spoke, but she was decadent. She spoke
and it was prosaically in substance and broad [?] in utterance.

'(Your Loved one ([illegible]) is now at the Police Mortuary and is
expected here this afternoon; he is an elderly gentleman. Is that right?'

'Perfectly')

This wandered from the purpose, and in revising the first typescript Waugh
cut back and, after some reordering, produced a description much like that
of the published version except that the detail about "her eyes greenish &
remote with a hint of lunacy" was buried in mid-sentence rather than put,
as in all published versions, in climactic final position.

This among other revisions is probably what Waugh meant when he wrote
Peters about the third draft, "I have been sweating away at it and it is
now more elegant but not less gruesome."[24] Larger considerations of structure seem to have dictated Waugh's insertion, some time after the first
typescript, of what becomes in all printed texts the initial appearance of
Mr. Joyboy and the embalming rooms. Besides developing the theme of
physical horror, the long scene establishes firmly the attractions, in their
peculiar context, of the third member of the triangle to render more formidable the obstacles Dennis must overcome to win Aimee. Formerly the
relationship between Joyboy and Aimee was introduced only after Dennis
had met her three times (the third on the Lake Isle), and her interest in
him had begun to burgeon. More important still is the presentation in this
scene of Joyboy not simply as man but as artist. Throughout the novel
Dennis's plagiarized poems contend with the smiles on Joyboy's corpses for
Aimee's favor, and in the interpolated scene this motif is firmly established
in juxtaposition to Dennis's unwritten elegy to Sir Francis at the end of
the scene immediately preceding and more fully in the Lake Isle scene some
ten pages later.

As the rivalry progresses, of course, Dennis begins to prevail not only
because, as he observes, "I am younger,very much better looking, and I
wear my own teeth" (p.110), but also because his supposed art moves
Aimee more deeply. To cancel this advantage, Joyboy must destroy Aimee's
view of his rival. In the original manuscript he had one obvious weapon:
the revelation that the poems were not written by Dennis. As Waugh
prepared for him to use it, however, he seems to have been struck by the
potential of another weapon, latent since Dennis's conversation with Aimee

24. Letter to Peters, September 14, 1947, *Letters,* p. 259.

on the Lake Isle, in which she expressed pious horror at the blasphemous practices of the Happier Hunting Ground. The sequence of Waugh's decision to use this device cannot be determined, but judging from the manuscript evidence he may have worked backward. If so, he first returned to the scene in which Aimee visits the Joyboy home and on the back of the manuscript page added the four paragraphs in which the parrot Sambo is introduced and, if that is the right word, characterized. Then, though this is still more conjectural, Waugh went still further back in his manuscript to the passage describing the highlights of Dennis's life as pet's mortician. Originally Waugh had paired "the (splendid) /ritualistic/, non-sectarian funeral of a (cockatoo) /barbary goat/ over whose grave a squad of Marine buglers (played) (/blew/) /sounded/ the Last Post and the cremation of a (/nanny/ goat) /cockatoo/ with the rites of (the) /a/ Sister of Pythias." The two interchangeable beasts were replaced before the final version with "the ritualistic, almost orgiastic cremation of a non-sectarian chimpanzee and the burial of a canary over whose grave a squad of Marine buglers had sounded Taps" (p. 24). In the first place, Waugh needed bird and goat later; in the second, the contrast between sizes was greater and, as revised, the placement of "non-sectarian" far funnier. The goat he used in place of a Great Dane in the scene about tail wagging—goats "do when they go to the can" (pp. 54–55)—that presages Dennis's arrangement for Aimee's annual memorial card to Joyboy (p. 128). The cockatoo became, in ornithological metamorphosis, Sambo the parrot.

Thereafter, the movement to Aimee's death was fairly simple, though Waugh took considerable pains to embellish and to polish various adornments, consistently elevating diction, creating more formal tone, and eliminating the obvious. In first draft Mr. Slump's terminal advice to Aimee was to "order yourself a nice big bottle of poison and drink it to my health." Too close to Aimee's choice of death, this was modified in a subsequent draft to "take the elevator to the top floor. Find a nice window and jump out." Perhaps equally obvious, or at any rate faulty in tone, were the two drafts of Aimee's death scene:

> She lay down on the bench in Mr. Joyboys work shop and took a swig. Half an hour later the night watchman making his final round before (work?) going off duty noticed the body and covered it (with a) /the/ sheet /which lay near it on the ground/; (momentarily disconcerted /grateful/ that he should have ((neglected)) this simple act of tidiness on his previous round) he was getting old and (work shy) /slothful/. This was his first visit to the upper floors. He was grateful that he had not shirked it altogether, by his neglect of this act of tidiness betrayed his delinquency.

She sat on the bench, pricked her arm, pressed. Then she put down the syringe, (raised her legs lay back, lifting her legs) lifted her feet and lay back, drawing the sheet over herself & waiting for the poison to take effect. It did so swiftly with a sudden convulsion of all her limbs which nearly threw her from the bench; a second more violent spasm & then she relaxed & lay supine, almost as though laid out by an expert hand. Half an hour later the night-watchman making his final round before going off duty observed the disordered body and covered it again with its sheet. He was getting old and slack in his ways. This was his first visit to the upper floor. He felt very grateful that he had not shirked it entirely & betrayed his delinquency by neglecting this necessary act of tidiness.

The second is more detailed, but though both end with a dying fall, they introduce an unnecessary character and lack the point, vigor, and anticipatory quality of the sentence, "It was quite without design that she chose Mr. Joyboy's workroom for the injection" (p. 116), which in all published versions concludes the scene.

Moreover, this scene contains kinesthetic qualities that ill-suited Waugh's various attempts to minimize, in one direction, the sense of her physical and mental suffering in favor of her choice of "a higher destiny" and to increase, in another, both Dennis's and the reader's sense of detachment. To produce the second effect, Waugh heavily revised Dennis's dialogue with Aimee at the nutburger stand and his encounter with Joyboy at the Happier Hunting Ground. The second is simpler and easier to illustrate:

She's there, in my workshop, under a sheet."	"She's there, in my workshop, under a sheet."
This was grave news. "You're sure it's her?"	'That, certainly, is what your newspapers would call "factual." You're sure it's her?'
"Of course I'm sure. She was poisoned."	'Of course I'm sure. She was poisoned."
'This needs thinking about, Joyboy.' . . .	[Inserted after first typescript: "Ah! The nutburger?" 'Cyanide. Self-administered.'] 'This needs thinking about, Joyboy.' . . .
'She was my honey-baby.'	'She was my honey-baby.'
'What have you done (so far) about it?' . . .	'I must beg you not to introduce your private emotions [these private and rather peculiar terms

'I don't like this repetition of "gotta," Joyboy. If I help you it will be freely and from the highest motives. /As a non-sectarian preacher/ I am no more anxious for a scandal than you are. (It would do me no good) Tell me . . . .'

of endearment into what should be a serious discussion.] [Inserted after first typescript.] What have you done? . . .'

'I don't like this repetition of "gotta," Joyboy. Do you know what Queen Elizabeth said to her Archbishop—an essentially non-sectarian character, incidentally? "Little man, little man, 'must' is not a word to be used to princes." If I help you it will be freely and from the highest motives.[25] Tell me . . . .' [Pp. 120-22]

These revisions obviously help detach Dennis from the emotional effects of Aimee's death and, with the interpolated scene involving Sir Ambrose and unaltered passages like the divination of Joyboy's meaning from gulps and groans, permit the reader to regard Dennis' acceptance of her death as something more, or less, than simple callousness.

In fact, the process of putting Dennis on a plane remote from others' sufferings began somewhat earlier, as parallel texts show, in the revision of the nutburger scene, after the parrot's funeral:

'I don't wish to discuss it. The decent thing you can do to make up to me is to go out of my life quietly'

'But my dear girl, you seem to have forgotten that you're engaged to (me) /be/ married to me'

'I'd rather die. How dare you (come?) speak to me after the way you've behaved?'

'There's nothing you can say means anything now.'

'But, my dear girl, you seem to have forgotten that we're engaged to be married.[26] My theological studies are prospering. The day when I shall claim you is at hand.'

'I'd rather die.'

'Yes, I confess I overlooked that alternative. D'you know, this is

25. This sentence is in *Horizon* and in the Little, Brown edition but does not occur in any English edition.

26. Typescript as revised reads: "Unless I choose to release you, you're bound to marry me." [Paragraph] "I'd rather die."

'D' you know this is the first time that I've ever eaten a nutburger. I've often wondered what they were. They are revolting aren't they? Now let us get this clear. Do you deny that you are engaged to me?'

'A girl can change her mind, can't she?'

Well you know I don't honestly think she can. I mean that is what being engaged means doesn't it. You made up your mind and made a promise'

'Do you deny that you sent me a lot of poems you said were yours & were really by other people?'

'So you've cottoned onto that, have you? Yes, I do deny it'

'You deny sending me poems by other people?'

'I deny saying they were by me'

'(What) I can't stay here another minute. I don't want to eat anything'

'Well you (came here) chose the place. I never gave you a nutburger, did I.'

'As often as not you didn't pay at all.'

'But whoever paid, we had something better than nutburgers. (You should not cast my poverty in my face'

'Poverty.') You can't walk down the street crying like that. I've my car parked across the way. Let me drop you home.' They

the first time I've ever eaten a nutburger? I've often wondered what they were. It is not so much their nastiness but their total absence of taste that shocks one. But let us get this clear. Do you deny that you solemnly swore to marry me?'

'A girl can change her mind, can't she?'

'Well, you know, I don't honestly think she can. You made a solemn promise'

'Under false pretences.[27] All those poems you sent and pretended you'd written for me, that I thought so cultivated I even learned bits of them by heart — all by other people, some by people who passed on hundreds of years ago. I never felt so mortified as when I found out.'

'So that's the trouble, is it?'

'And that horrible Happier Hunting Ground. I'm going now. I don't want to eat anything.'

'Well, you chose the place. When I took you out I never gave you nutburgers, did I?'

'As often as not it was I took you out.'

'A frivolous point. You can't walk down the street crying like that. I've my car parked across the way. Let me drop you home.'

They stepped out into the neon-lighted boulevard. 'Now,

27. Corrected typescript reads: "Under false pretenses. Do you deny that . . .," and so on, as in the manuscript.

stepped out into the neon-lighted boulevard.	Aimee, 'said Dennis, 'let us not have a tiff.'
'Now Aimee,' said Dennis, 'Let us not have a quarrel.'	'Tiff? I loathe everything about you.' [Pp. 108–109]
'Quarrel. I've decided never to see you again.'	

The manuscript draft seems flat compared with its successor. Dennis insouciance is considerably increased by the insertion in first typescript of the prophetic "I confess I overlooked that alternative" after Aimee's "I'd rather die." The more carefully balanced digression upon the nutburger and the religious imagery used of the engagement further distance Dennis from Aimee, and his attempt to take high ground in "a frivolous point" is far better debating tactics than his quibble in first draft.

Later in the same scene Dennis attempts to explain the emotional situation in theological terms, and the two versions exhibit differences like those discussed earlier.

| 'In my rough European way I share your enthusiasm. Mr. Lollipop is the big noise at Whispering Glades. Apart from Dr. Kenworthy who's God almighty and quite out of reach, Mr. Hitiddlypush is the prophet and archangel and grand panjandrum. (You know about [?] psychoanalysts I'll bet [?]) Well you're in love with Whispering Glades—"half in love with easeful death" [texts identical until] and naturally you transfer your affections to its personification. I admit that by Joyboy standards I don't quite hit the mark. [Texts parallel until "what?"] You happen to be engaged to me & just so there shouldn't be any doubt about it you swore this thing on the most sacred oath of Whispering Glades. So you see the dilemma | 'In my rough British way I share your enthusiasm. I have been planning an opus on the subject, but I am afraid I can't say with Dowson, "If you ever come to read it, you will understand." You won't, my dear, not a word of it. All this is by the way. [The three preceding sentences are not in manuscript.] Now your Mr. Joyboy is the incarnate spirit of Whispering Glades—the one mediating logos between Dr. Kenworthy and common humanity. Well, we're obsessed by Whispering Glades, both of us—"half in love with easeful death," as I once told you—and to save further complications let me explain that I did not write that poem either—you're the nautch girl and vestal virgin of the place, and naturally I attach myself to you and you attach |

207

jam or impasse. You're all hotted up for the sacrifice of yourself on the altar of Whispering Glades. The high priest is all set for the operation. But you're already engaged elsewhere, Aimee. Mr. Joyboy is just as sacred as your oath. It all stands or falls together. If it isn't sacred to kiss me through the heart of the Burns or Bruce, it isn't sacred to go to bed with old Cheerible.

yourself to Joyboy. Psychologists will tell you that kind of thing happens every day.

'It may be that by the Dreamer's standards there are defects in my character. The parrot looked terrible in his casket. So what? You loved me and swore to love me eternally with the most sacred oath in the religion of Whispering Glades. So you see the dilemma, jam or impasse. Sanctity is indivisible. If it isn't sacred to kiss me through the heart of the Burns or Bruce, it isn't sacred to go to bed with old Joyboy.' [p. 112]

The second is far less casual and, to an interested amateur of theology, far more satisfactory an account and far more likely, because of its formality, to produce the intended effect of bewildering Aimee. Moreover, the revision directly involves Dennis in the theological-psychological pattern as both lover and poet, an involvement entirely absent from the first draft of the manuscript. The process by which Waugh came to an understanding of the full implications of his theme can only be conjectured, but judging from gross data it must have been something like this:

By what is now page 91 of the novel, Waugh was moving confidently through the scene involving Mr. Schultz and Dennis, and, again judging from the kind of paper—white and ruled, different from anything else in the manuscript—Waugh moved easily through the nutburger scene to its aftermath, Aimee's distress. Crude though it was, the first draft on the theology of Whispering Glades seems to have set off a whole chain of associations that led first to the elevation of Aimee's spiritual stature and ultimately, after the manuscript and the first typescript stages, to the discovery and development of the theme of poetry's drawing from and transcending death.

As the manuscript is bound, the last white ruled page is numbered 5 in red pencil. On that page first appears in clear text "Guru Brahmin" instead of "Aunt Lydia" as the advice columnist, a first move beyond the mundane, domestic level of consciousness. Continuous with the text of page 5 is a canceled passage on the back of what is now, in red pencil, 2a. Both sides of the page hold significant revelations of Waugh's growing clarity of intention. The cancellation, a first draft of the passage on pages 116 and 117, led Waugh past religion into mythology:

Ancestral longings were stirring in her. The impulse which had driven her (mother) father to the Four Square (Gospel) Temple and her mother to the bottle took in her a nobler form. The furies which had driven her grandparents from their native sanctuaries taking ship to the (Hesperides) west beyond (the) farthest ocean & still west to the garden of the Hesperides & found in the sweet song & the golden orchard the scaly black lengths of sleepless Ladon. A doom was being fulfilled in her. Women of her race going to sacrifice. The (/royal/ daughter of) royal victim on the altar of Aulis when the ships lay becalmed & the smoke rose straight it [*sic*] to the windless heaven and Agamemnon averted his eyes. The bold ([illegible]) mathematician torn by oyster shells.

Here, though the mythological allusions and the sense of doom and fulfillment are Greek, Aimee is not named Thanatogenos. But on the front of page 2*a* both her heritage and her name serve to distinguish her, for the first time since she was initially described, from her fellows. The final version, after being revised in many minor respects, reads:

. . . brain and body were scarcely distinguishable from the standard product, but the spirit — ah, the spirit was something apart; it had to be sought afar; not here in the musky orchards of the Hesperides, but in the mountain air of the dawn, in the eagle-haunted passes of Hellas. An umbilical cord of cafes and fruit shops, of ancestral shady businesses (fencing and pimping) [Waugh's parentheses] united Aimee, all unconscious, to the high places of her race. As she grew up the only language she knew expressed fewer and fewer of her ripening needs; the facts which littered her memory grew less substantial; the figure she saw in the looking-glass seemed less recognizably herself. Aimee withdrew herself into a lofty and hieratic habitation. [p. 106]

It would be an exaggeration to say that in these few strokes Waugh has given Aimee a soul, but he has, perhaps remembering Firbank's "If souls are rare, we've at least some healthy spirits" (*Vainglory*), given her one of the novel's few existences in any kind of spirit. And at the same time Waugh gave her a new surname, Thanatogenos, which accords perfectly and, to readers of the final text, inevitably with Aimee.

There, by the end of the manuscript and first typescript, the matter rested, with Aimee and Dennis released to death and England respectively, both escaping the death-in-life in which Joyboy and Abercrombie remain. But

Waugh was too careful an artist to be satisfied, and when in September he wrote to Peters that he had "been sweating away at it and it is now more elegant but not less gruesome" he may have been referring to broad thematic as well as local stylistic considerations. Certainly, by the time of publication he had realized that the manuscript version was thematically very loose. The most astonishing thing about it, in hindsight, is that nowhere after the pastiches of Sir Francis's funeral elegy is Dennis's vocation as poet—distinct from that of plagiarist—operative in any sense. In this version Dennis is even more *manqué* than Joyboy, who at least does his own corpses, and his attraction to Aimee, even allowing for her decadence, is virtually inexplicable. However, Aimee's new surname may have reminded Waugh of an earlier passage in the Lake Isle scene:

> 'And what do you think about when you come here alone in the evenings?'
> 'Just Death and Art,' said Aimee Thanatogenos simply.
> 'Half in love with easeful death.'
> 'What was that you said?'
> 'I was quoting a poem.
>
>
>
> "...For many a time
> I have been half in love with easful death,
> Call'd him soft names in many a mused rhyme,
> To take into the air my quiet breath;
> Now more than ever seems it rich to die,
> To cease upon the midnight with no pain ...." [pp. 77–78]
>
>

In effect picking up the idea of *"half* in love with easeful death" and associating Thanatogenos with that half, personal love, Waugh began thinking about Art. He had already altered the collected poems of Christina Rossetti to those of Tennyson and then to an anthology (p. 19), broadening the context in which the lines from "Tithonus," poetry made from unending decay in time, could be placed. He had also established a contrast between Dennis's life and his art, however, for the paragraph at the top of page 24 had, in manuscript, the additional sentence: "In his leisure hours he wrote poetry, at work he lived it—modern poetry, perhaps, but the genuine article." To indicate a new direction in Dennis's art, or perhaps to substitute a different attitude toward it, Waugh canceled this passage and inserted further on, probably in second or third typescript, the overture to what was to become the major theme:

> His interest was no longer purely technical nor purely satiric. Whispering Glades held him in thrall. In that zone of insecurity in the mind where none but the artist dare trespass, the tribes were mustering. Dennis, the frontier-man, could read the signs. [p. 65]

Thereafter, that Dennis is meditating on themes suggested by the cemetery if not actually composing is mentioned in no more than a half-dozen places (pp. 85, 116, 126, 128). On each occasion only an added sentence or two was needed to remind the reader of Dennis's active vocation.

The insertions were inspired, even if structure is the only consideration. Dennis's obsession with Whispering Glades blended with and helped motivate more comprehensibly his interest in Aimee, as evidenced by her puzzled complaint to the Guru Brahmin about Dennis's unhealthy interest in her work (p. 103) and his quasi-religious explanation, already quoted, during the nutburger stand debate (p. 112). The idea of Whispering Glades as inspiration also puts Dennis on an equal footing with Joyboy, since both exercise their talents on death; and it gives him, as the reference to the "zone of insecurity in the mind" indicates, an equal footing with Aimee in the world of the spirit.

Most important, the theme of inspiration gives Dennis a clear triumph over, as well as mere escape from, the death-in-life of southern California. The manuscript ended rather flatly, after the quotation from Poe—another plagiarism—with, "Then he picked up a novel which (Mr. Schultz) /Miss— //Poski// / had left on his desk and settled down to await the (fire's consuming action)/consummation/." The last alteration obviously plays on the *Liebestod* theme, but the sentence resolves only Dennis's role as lover, leaving him to be distracted by the art, or at least the writing, of another. After conceiving the idea of Dennis's inspiration, Waugh wrote at least two drafts before he was satisfied with the ending's cadence and emphasis.

HORIZON, UNITED STATES	ENGLISH EDITION
On this last evening in Los Angeles Dennis knew that he was singularly privileged. The strand was littered with bones and wreckage. He was adding his bit; something that had long irked him, his young heart. He was carrying back instead a great, shapeless chunk of experience, the artist's load; bearing it home to his ancient and comfortless shore; to work on it hard and long, for God knew how long—it was the moment of vision for which a	On this last evening in Los Angeles Dennis knew he was a favourite of Fortune. Others, better men than he had foundered (on this shore) /here/ and (been lost) /perished./ The /strand/ (beach) was littered with their bones, (and wreckage.) He was leaving it not only unravished but enriched. He (too) was adding his bit /to the wreckage,/ something that had long irked him, his young heart, and was carrying back instead the artist's load, a great, shapeless

lifetime is often too short. [pp. 163-64]	chunk of experience; bearing it home to his ancient and comfortless shore; to work on it hard and long, for God knew how long. For that moment of vision a lifetime is often too short. [p. 128]

Both versions contain the final line:

He picked up the novel which Miss Poski had left on his desk and settled down to await his loved one's final combustion.

The revision, made in a manuscript insertion to Waugh's copy of *Horizon,* emphasized more clearly Dennis's personal triumph. This is a new element not only in the novel but in any Waugh novel to date. Pennyfeather and his like had managed to escape the horrifying modern world, but they had simply retreated, unable to use in any except negative ways experience gained in that world. Even Basil Seal, in *Black Mischief,* returning to England from a cannibal feast in which his loved one was the main course, is subdued, and Basil anticipates most clearly the streak of caddishness in Dennis of which Cyril Connolly had complained, a charge to which Waugh admitted happily.[28] One might argue that Charles Ryder triumphs in *Brideshead Revisited,* since at the end he strides cheerfully from the chapel, but in the Prologue his religion does not enable him to escape acedia and in any case he has no clear future in the secular world nor any outlet for his artistic talent. Dennis does, and because of his dedication to his art, he not only escapes but promises to make something positive out of his experience.

Waugh explained in a letter to Connolly, part of which was used to preface the novella's appearance in *Horizon,* the ideas that informed *The Loved One:*

"1. Quite predominantly, overexcitement with the scene . . . 2. The Anglo-American impasse—never the twain shall meet. 3. There is no such thing as an 'American.' They are all exiles uprooted, transplanted, and doomed to sterility. The ancestral gods they have abjured get them in the end. 4. The European raiders who come for the spoils and if they are lucky make for home with them. 5. *Memento mori.'*[29]

28. Letter to Cyril Connolly, late 1947 or early 1948.
29. Connolly, Introduction, *Horizon,* p. 76. See *Letters,* pp. 265-66, for the complete text of Waugh's letter.

While these ideas provide a thematic structure for the novel, the emotional climate is dominated by at least three propositions strongly implied in the novel and reflected in Waugh's other work of the period: (1) A hearty relief at having escaped from Hollywood, a place without art or grace in any of the senses that Waugh would recognize; (2) The artist's fundamental responsi-. bility not to a system of morality but to his art; (3) The belief in art as a high calling, influenced perhaps by his reading of Henry James.

His desire to preserve the distinction between art and morals can be traced to the effect of *Brideshead* upon his public reputation. Even today readers are surprised to learn that he was converted to Roman Catholicism in 1930, not just before the composition of *Brideshead,* and until that novel appeared, many readers, including Catholics, were ignorant of his religious views. Those Catholics who did know were by no means unanimous in their enthusiasm for the moral implications of his work. After 1945, however, he became a Prominent Catholic Novelist, to be cherished, defended, recruited, admonished. Conor Cruise O'Brien, writing as "Donat O'Donnell," found *Brideshead* deficient in charity and Waugh's religion based more on romantic snobbism than on true righteousness.[30] A Mr. Cowles accused Waugh and Graham Greene of causing more harm to the Faith than its avowed enemies. Readers of "Fan-Fare" in *Life* and a summary of that article in *Time* took the occasion to point out what they considered to be defects in Waugh's orthodoxy, his practice of his faith, his example, or all three.

Against this background not only the seeming amorality of *The Loved One* but more explicit public statements become clearer. To Mr. Cowles's charge Waugh made a clear rejoinder: "The questions a Catholic writer shall ask himself are: First, when I write in *propria persona* am I correct in Faith and Morals? Second, do I always do my best to produce a workmanlike product that is fair for my hire? If he can answer these two questions confidently he need not bother about other criticism however kindly intended."[31] More daring in theory, perhaps because directed toward a secular audience, was his praise of Chaplin's *Monsieur Verdoux* as "a startling and mature work of art. I do not mean that I found an agreeable 'message.' There is a 'message' and, I think, a deplorable one." However, Waugh continued, "most men and women of genius have entertained preposterous

---

30. "The Pieties of Evelyn Waugh," *Bell* 13 (December 1946):38-49; reprinted several times, most recently under O'Brien's real name, in *Maria Cross: Imaginative Patterns in a Group of Modern Catholic Writers* (London: Burns and Oates, 1963), pp. 109-123.

31. "Mr. Waugh on the Catholic Novelist," *Duckett's Register,* March, 1948.

opinions," and these he was willing to ignore in view of the consummate artistry of the film.[32]

The third proposition, a belief in art, is harder to illustrate by explicit statement. While there is no doubt about Waugh's assent to this idea, it is by no means clear what, for him, that value precisely was. A survey of virtually the whole body of his work reveals only tangential statements, fluctuating if not contradictory. It would be foolish to ascribe to any single cause his belief in the mystery, the value, and, in the Jamesian phrase, "the madness of art," but his interest in James during this period is undeniable. In "Fan-Fare," Waugh praised James as the last of the "countless admirable writers, perhaps some of the best in the world," who succeeded as novelists by making their "characters pure abstractions" and leaving God out of their works.[33] Late in 1946, just before he went to America, he was reading James, including *The Portrait of a Lady,* rejoicing that he had saved these novels for his middle age. And he was reading James as he wrote *The Loved One.*[34] One can perhaps trace from Isabel Archer and other Jamesian heroines Aimee Thanatogenos's belief that "she held in her person a valuable concession to bestow; she had been scrupulous in choosing justly between rival claimants." Dennis Barlow sees himself as "the protagonist of a Jamesian problem, . . . American innocence and European experience. . . . The stories are all tragedies one way or another." More important, however, is the theme, discovered in the process of revision, of the artist's obligation, indeed compulsion, to respond to and render experience, whatever its nature. Morally speaking, Dennis is not so much reprehensible as nonexistent. Throughout the courtship Aimee is less important to him than the message from his muse about Whispering Glades, and while he expresses himself more brutally than a Jamesian artist would, his choice of art over love is one that James might find difficult to condemn.

The Loved One marked a new stage in Waugh's art and a new confidence in dealing with the hitherto unpromising postwar experience. The composition of the novel also accompanied and perhaps in some sense occasioned a major turning point in Waugh's life. Two weeks before he offered the book to Connolly and just after his return from Scandinavia, he decided not to move to Ireland but to stay in England and accept his position in English life as an English writer.[35]

32. "The Man Hollywood Hates," *Evening Standard,* November 3, 1947, p. 6.
33. "Fan-Fare," p. 56.
34. Waugh, *Diaries,* pp. 663 (November 17, 1946), 680 (June 2, 1947).
35. *Ibid.,* p. 690 (October 28, 1947).

11

Defiant Assertion
of the Supernatural:
Helena

Waugh's prediction in "Fan-Fare" that his future work would be concerned with style and with man's relationship to God was not immediately fulfilled, as the previous chapter demonstrated, but it was by no means based on whim. *Brideshead* met both of these criteria, and even before finishing it Waugh speculated that it would be "the first of my novels rather than the last."[1] As Catholic rather than artist, his loyalties were intensified by reports that the Communists were persecuting the church in Croatia, and as Catholic and artist he meditated early in 1945 on the relationship between faith and art:

> I had never before realized how specially Epiphany is the feast of artists — twelve days late, after St Joseph and the angels and the shepherds and even the ox and the ass, the exotic caravan arrived with its black pages and ostrich plumes, brought there by book learning and speculation; they have had a long journey across the desert, the splendid gifts are travel-worn and not nearly as splendid as they looked when they were being packed up at Babylon; they have made the most disastrous mistakes — they even asked the way of Herod and provoked the Massacre of the Innocents — but they get to Bethlehem in the end and their gifts are accepted, prophetic gifts that find a way into the language of the Church in a number of places. It is a very complete allegory.[2]

Though perhaps complete, the allegory was not to be embodied in fiction for another five years. More immediate and more personal was Waugh's response to Cyril Connolly's *The Unquiet Grave,* which reached him in Dubrovnik on January 8. Reflecting on the reasons for his interest, Waugh concluded that it lay not in his long and pleasant acquaintance with Connolly or in his own isolation but in the fact that

1. Evelyn Waugh, *The Diaries of Evelyn Waugh,* ed. Michael Davie (Boston: Little, Brown and Co., 1977), p. 566 (May 21, 1944).
2. *Ibid.,* p. 606 (January 6, 1945).

Cyril is the most typical man of my generation. There but for the grace of God, literally ... [Waugh's ellipsis]. He has the authentic lack of scholarship of my generation ... the authentic love of leisure & liberty and good living, the authentic romantic snobbery, the authentic wasteland despair, the authentic high gift of expression ... Quite clear in his heart that the ills he suffers from are theological, with the vocabulary of the nonsense-philosophy he learned, holding him back.[3]

Much of Waugh's nonfiction in the years after the war was devoted to making clear what he regarded as the sharp contrast between the jargon of modernist philosophies and the precision of Catholic theology. On Ash Wednesday in New Orleans, for example, he contrasted the crowd of "crapulous tourists" with the throngs receiving ashes at the Jesuit church:

... the old grim message was being repeated over each penitent: "Dust thou art and unto dust shalt thou return." One grows parched for that straight style of speech in the desert of modern euphemisms.[4]

In much the same mood as his Epiphany meditation, he went on to insist that "the Church does not exist in order to produce elegant preachers or imaginative writers or artist, or philosophers. It exists to produce saints."[5]

At his most intransigently orthodox, Waugh could argue that the Christian writer tended to be lazy because he knows that "five minutes after his death it will not matter to him in the least whether his books are a success or not."[6] He wrote to his brother that the reissue of their father's autobiography did not concern him because, if Alec was right, Arthur had ceased to exist, and if Evelyn was right, Arthur was beyond earthly vanity.[7] He was more often prepared to use theological concerns as a test of literary value. Novelists since James Joyce were condemned for "presumption and exorbitance" because "they try to represent the whole human mind and soul and yet omit the determining character—that of being God's creature with a defined purpose."[8] In contrast, J. F. Powers's stories were judged

3. Autograph note on half-title page of *The Unquiet Grave: A Word Cycle by Palinurus* (London: Horizon, 1944), in Waugh's library at the University of Texas—Austin. See the parallel passage in Waugh, *Diaries,* p. 618. Davie reads "teleological" where I would read "theological." See Cyril Connolly's response, "Apotheosis in Austin," *Sunday Times* (London), June 6, 1971.

4. Evelyn Waugh, "The American Epoch in the Catholic Church," *Life* 27 (September 19, 1949):143.

5. *Ibid.,* p. 149.

6. Quoted by John Pick in "London Letter," *Renascence* 9 (Autumn, 1956):16.

7. Letter to Alec Waugh, August 20, 1953.

8. "Fan-Fare," *Life* 20 (April 8, 1946):56.

effective in part because "Mr. Powers has a full philosophy with which to oppose the follies of his age and nation,"[9] and Antonia White was praised for "her superior vision of the nature of human life... [Man] is here to love and serve God, and any portrayal of him which neglects this primary function must be superficial." Therefore, the more that novelists try to explain human purpose in secular terms,

> the more they are betraying their duty. In this sense *No Orchids for Miss Blandish* is a better book than *Howards End*. You can show man bereft of God and therefore hopeless as Macbeth and Miss Blandish, but you must not flatter his pretensions to self-sufficiency.[10]

This is far different from his tolerant acceptance of what he termed the "deporable" message of Chaplin's *Monsieur Verdoux*. And though in 1949, when "a lot of Catholics were suspicious of [Graham Greene's] good faith . . . I officiously went round England and America reassuring them,"[11] in reviewing *The Heart of the Matter,* Waugh spent as much space on the book's dubious theological implications as he did on its technique.[12]

As Waugh observed, "In the last twenty-five years the artist's interest has moved from sociology to eschatology."[13] His own, with the glaring exceptions noted in the previous chapter, had certainly done so. Not long before he began *Helena,* he "recommended catacombs" as a response to modern Europe,[14] and the year before he finished that novel he expanded the idea: "I believe that we are returning to a stage when on the supernatural plane only heroic prayer can save us and, when on the natural plane, the cloister offers a saner and more civilized life than 'the world.' "[15]

In fact, Waugh chose to celebrate in *Helena* not monastic or, however much he admired Thomas Merton and the American Trappists, contemplative life, but, in a title he used elsewhere, "St. Helena, Empress."[16] In

9. Evelyn Waugh, "Pioneer! O Pioneer," *Month* n.s. 1 (March, 1949):216.

10. Evelyn Waugh, "An Admirable Novel," *Tablet* 195 (April 22, 1950):314.

11. Waugh, *Diaries,* p. 775 (January 4, 1961).

12. "Felix Culpa" *Commonweal* 48 (July 16, 1949):322–26.

13. *Ibid.,* p. 322.

14. Waugh, *Diaries,* p. 625 (April 18, 1945).

15. "Kicking Against the Goad," *Commonweal* 49 (March 11, 1949):534.

16. After the novel was published, in "Saint Helena," *Tablet* 189 (November 3, 1951): 324; and (November 17, 1951):364, Waugh objected to the implication that he depicted Helena as sainted because of her social position rather than the power of the Holy Spirit. Father Martin D'Arcy made the same objection in the *Tablet* on November 24, 1951, p. 384. Still later Waugh cited p. 145 of *Helena* (London: Chapman and Hall, 1950) to refute Frank Kermode's imputation to *Brideshead* of "the absurd and blasphemous opinion that divine grace is confined to the highest and lowest classes." Evelyn Waugh, "Evelyn Waugh Replies," *Encounter* 15 (December, 1960):83.

fact, Waugh suspected that "nowadays logical, rule-of-thumb Catholics are not a little too humble towards the mystics,"[17] and in *Helena* he celebrated not the kind of paradox for which Greene was famous but the "wider view" that "Right is homogeneous and indivisible, Wrong something foreign, eternally unassimilable, eternally at war with the Truth."[18] From the beginning he conceived *Helena* as cutting through mystagoguery with such questions as "When?" "Where?" and "How do you know?" Furthermore, she is so far removed from recommending catacombs that, in a passage Waugh inserted to expand the implications of a halfsentence, she wonders whether the wall that separates Roman from barbarian might someday be set "at the limits of the world and all men, civilized and barbarian, have a share in the City."[19] This attitude develops from and expands the hope of *Brideshead's* conclusion, but realizing the theme caused Waugh great pains.

Helena is unique among Waugh's novels in two respects: it presents a series of disjunct episodes from a long life, and it celebrates the central character's unshrinking and triumphant encounter with the external world. As he admitted in the Preface, he treated the story of Helena as legend, and the first episode presents her as the daughter of King Coel of the nursery rhyme, a horsy tomboy who hopes to see the City. Subsequent episodes deal with her marriage to Constantius; the thwarting and fulfillment of his passion to rule; her repudiation and retirement; her appearance at the court of her son Constantine; her faithful search for and qualified triumph in discovering the True Cross; and her return to the mists of legend.

Waugh began work on *Helena* on May 1, 1945. Less than a week later, assured that he had "done enough reading," he began the book, though "in a crabbed and halting way," in some complacency.[20] His attitude soon veered; almost immediately he returned to London to celebrate the publication of *Brideshead Revisited*, participate in the London season, engage in controversy over Tito's treatment of the church, read *Animal Farm* and reread *A Passage to India* with considerable enjoyment, and wait for the nuns renting Piers Court to vacate it. He returned to his home on September 10, and not long thereafter he reread his Lancing diaries "with unmixed shame" and, in a mood identical to that in which he began *Helena*, took up another task:

17. Waugh, "Felix Culpa?" p. 324. Waugh was aware of the distinction between contemplative and mystic, but there is an even greater distinction between these two classes and "rule-of-thumb Catholics."

18. Preface, *A Selection from the Occasional Sermons of the Right Reverend Monsignor Knox* (London: Dropmore Press, 1949), p. 9.

19. Evelyn Waugh, *Helena* (London: Chapman and Hall, 1950), pp. 48–49. Hereafter this edition is cited parenthetically in the text.

20. Waugh, *Diaries*, pp. 626, 627.

> News from the outside world more horrible daily—chaos & tyranny & famine and sheer wickedness throughout two thirds of Europe and all Asia, but my life seems more placid & happy than ever. I have begun a novel of school life in 1919—as untopical a theme as could be found.[21]

The school story made little headway, for Waugh took time to make public his strictures on *The Unquiet Grave*; to write and deliver a lecture to Catholic students at London University, Cambridge, and Oxford; to read *Ulysses* and "a preposterous commentary"; to gather excerpts from his travel books for *When the Going Was Good;* and to work on his garden at Piers Court. Furthermore, the anticipated returns from the American edition of *Brideshead* made work less urgent. After discussing happy financial details, Waugh told Peters on October 11 that he was "busy on two novels for publication in 1955." "Charles Ryder's Schooldays" soon languished, but Waugh had not abandoned Saint Helena. In the Christmas issue of *Tablet* he published "Saint Helena Meets Constantius: A Legend Re-Told."[22] Parallel to the text of the novel through the first paragraph of page 31 of the English edition[23] and almost identical to the first fifteen pages of manuscript (the last eleven lines of the story, which round it off, are not in the manuscript), the fragment may represent most of what he had written. He "began the New Year without previous resolutions by resuming work on Helena,"[24] reaching the fall of Palmyra (p. 69) by January 11, inserting the motifs of Longinus and the sapper sergeant on the twelfth, revising the account of the trip to Dalmatia on the fourteenth, and revising the opening of Book 2 on February 16. He had finished the first book about January 16 and sent it to the typist. A small press, he thought, might like to publish "The Quest of the Empress Dowager" in a small, very luxurious format, with a larger edition to follow "in five or six years' time." The Americans, he predicted, "will think it awful."[25] Meanwhile, he consulted sources, including the "Itinerary of Bordeau [*sic*]" and the Jewish encyclopedia, and he visited a Professor Marmonstein, "a Jewish authority on the 4th century, venerable, guttural, vague. He tried to convince me that a legend of a sword fallen from heaven at (Constantine's) /a peasant's/ feet & being used for his decapitation was identical with the story of the Empress digging up a bit of wood out of

---

21. *Ibid.,* p. 636 (October 2, 1945).

22. *Tablet* 186 (December 22, 1945):299–302.

23. To the end of paragraph 4, p. 31, of the United States edition: *Helena* (Boston: Little, Brown and Co., 1950).

24. Waugh, *Diaries,* p. 640 (undated).

25. Letter to A. D. Peters, January 16, 1946, *The Letters of Evelyn Waugh,* ed. Mark Amory (New Haven and New York: Ticknor & Fields, 1980), p. 219.

the ground & taking it to Rome."[26] The interview may have helped Waugh several years later, when he drafted the scene in which savants propound elaborate theories of the construction of the Cross, but the various kinds of research were to have no immediate result, for on the same day as the interview Waugh learned that he might be able to take a holiday in Spain; two days later he was invited to go to the Nuremburg trials; other distractions offered themselves. The decision in mid-May of the Golden Cockrell Press not to publish the life of Helena must have discouraged Waugh still more, since he made no further references to the book until February, 1948. With trips to Spain, Germany, Scandinavia, and the United States behind him and *Scott-King's Modern Europe, Wine in Peace and War, The Loved One,* and various articles and letters completed and published, Waugh informed Peters that he would complete the novel by Palm Sunday,[27] only to record in his diary several days later the rueful confession that "my Lenten resolution to start work on Helena has not come to much" and the subsequent decision to work when his hangover departed.[28]

Presumably it did, but more than a year later Waugh had still made little progress on the book. He confessed to Peters on July 20, 1949, that at least he was working on nothing else, took comfort in the theory that "great sloth at the middle climacteric may be healthy," and rejoiced that he at least would not "collapse through overwork." He noted on his forty-fifth birthday the end of "an unproductive and unhealthy year. The start pray God of a better."[29] In fact, he had finished editing Thomas Merton's *The Seven Storey Mountain* and writing "The American Epoch in the Catholic Church" and "Compassion."[30] By mid-December he had finished the second of three proposed books of *Helena* and revised the first. The third, "Jerusalem," he hoped to finish by Easter; it was to be as long as the first.[31] One prediction was accurate: he sent the complete typescript to Peters about March 15; the second was not, for the third part was only half the length of Book 1. The published text is divided into twelve chapters, not three books, and Waugh continued introducing these and other alterations through page proof.

26. Waugh, *Diaries,* p. 642 (February 21, 1946). Davie reads Marmostein, and my transcription varies from his in other minor details.

27. Letter to Peters, February 13, 1948.

28. Waugh, *Diaries,* p. 696 (March 1, 1948).

29. *Ibid.,* p. 703 (October 28, 1948).

30. Evelyn Waugh, "Compassion," *Month* n.s. 2 (August, 1949):79–98. This version contains material not in "The Major Intervenes," *Atlantic* 184 (July, 1949):34–41.

31. Letter to Peters, December 14, 1949.

Well into the manuscript Waugh planned to construct the novel, as the title "The Three Quests of the Dowager Empress" indicates, on Helena's desire to reach the City presented to her imagination: first Troy, then Rome, finally Jerusalem. Book 2 began with what is now Chapter 5, and Book 3 with what is now Chapter 10. In the manuscript only the beginning of Chapter 12 corresponds, in unrevised state, to its counterpart in the book, though in revision Waugh renumbered from Chapter 9 on to suit his new method.

Given Waugh's habit of breaking his novels into several large divisions — *Vile Bodies* and *The Loved One* are the only exceptions — and the care with which he inserted motifs to support the three-part structure — his decision to rely on consecutively numbered chapters requires some examination. He may have decided that, despite Helena's name and despite the links of Troy, by way of Rome, and Britain, many of them inserted in manuscript, the Trojan element was not as strong as he had first supposed. At the very least, it is not separable from the quest for Rome, which is introduced as early and as strongly as Troy. More important, Waugh may have felt that the three-book division failed to emphasize the fact that Helena's progression is essentially indivisible, that the impulses that drew her to the fact as well as the idea of Troy were the same as those that led her to discover and proclaim the fact and idea of the Cross.

Waugh's reconsideration of structure extended in two cases to chapter divisions. Originally the account of Helena's life at Nish extended past the end of what is now Chapter 3 (p. 65) through the report of Palmyra's fall and the birth of Constantine. This ends the chapter on a note of completion if not triumph, which in view of the growing estrangement between Helena and Constantius Waugh may have thought unsuitable. At any rate, in the final version the chapter ends, like most of the other early chapters, in anticlimax, with Helena winter-bound and waiting, vaguely discontent and homesick, for the birth. This has two effects: it keeps the personal life of Helena and Constantius in the foreground of the chapter, and it places within the context of empire, conquest, and betrayal the death of Longinus and the advent of Constantine. A more obvious shift of emphasis was made in revising what is now Chapter 10. The first manuscript version focuses exclusively on Bishop Macarius, with Helena's progress and arrival relegated to the following chapter. In revision after a typescript version, Macarius's hopes and fears about the Holy Places occupy most of the chapter, but Helena's slow and lavish journey to Jerusalem is traced at the beginning, putting subsequent material in the context of her impending and alarming benefactions, which threaten still further to disrupt the Bishop's see.

A less obvious and more pervasive concern for structure is evident in Waugh's insertion or reinforcement of various motifs. The most obvious of these he commented on with some satisfaction in his diary for January 12, 1946:

> Yesterday I had to mention the fall of Palmyra. Longinus was executed there. I brought this [*sic*] as decoration and made Helena have heard of him. Today I rewrote a paragraph of the first chapter making the tutor mention him. Then, because Mr. Hodges, my nurse's father, was a fabulous figure to me, I gave Helena two fables: first of the nursery, the exemplary soldier; secondly, of the schoolroom, the stupendous pundit. Then I introduced to the Longinus paragraph the fact that Helena felt his death as a bereavement, the final end of her education. Then I introduced into the passage about Tertricus's betrayal the sense [?] that Helena thought the grave of her nurse's father dishonoured. So the book prospers.[32]

The insertions are of course important in the usual sense of structure, since the theme of betayal is central to what is now Chapter 3 and the death of Longinus in the first scene of Chapter 4 further emphasizes the effects of ruthless imperial politics, but it also enforces thematic unity, establishing, in E. M. Forster's terms, rhythm as well as pattern in the novel.

Most of Waugh's revisions reinforced rather than created such motifs, and many were used to support the three-part structure, which, though abandoned, still provides an underlying framework for the novel. Helena's casual claim of kinship with Priam (p. 3), Coel's reference to "Brutus, great-grandson of Aeneas" (p. 2), and Constantine's response to the death of Hector (p. 88) were introduced at various stages of revision in order to reflect more clearly Helena's desire to visit the real Troy. The Roman theme was reinforced and given its only connection with sublime poetry by Waugh's insertion of the reference to Virgil's concept of a City without walls, open to all, to foreshadow the Mystical Body of the Church that Helena later joins. Helena responds to both cities, of course, as she later responds to Jerusalem: she wants to see for herself and to examine physical evidence. In the conversation with her tutor Waugh originally had her introduce the prospect of finding Priam's crown or Paris's carved bed. In revising, he put these details in Marcias's speech which denigrated them as spurious products for the tourist trade, prefiguring the series of false relics that runs throughout the novel. One of these is Constantines's preposterously elaborate labarum, the sign in which he conquered and which he insists was fashioned on the battlefield. Waugh inserted the passage (pp. 201–203), probably in typescript, to prefigure by contrast the "solid chunk of wood" of the True Cross and to foreshadow Constantine's hunger for relics, which leads him to use the

---

32. Waugh, *Diaries,* pp. 640–41.

Palladium—"a part of Troy," Helena observes with approval—in his monument along with Noah's adze and other "really important stuff" (p. 262). And though Waugh reduced Coel's indictment of Rome from a long list of details to the Blimpish *"Awful* place" (p. 33), he resurrected the detail about the senators' mechanical toys from Persian harems for Constantius's description (p. 76), and Constantine's distaste for Rome, at first developed at some length, is reduced, in an echo of his grandfather, to, "It's all falling down too, and the drains are shocking" (p. 195). Such echoes, most prominent of which is Helena's amused "Stabularia" when her son makes one of the Holy Nails into a snaffle, are one way of giving unity to a chronicle spanning two continents and four generations.

Of course, the characters themselves had to be sharply defined before they could be placed in useful dramatic or thematic juxtaposition, and much of Waugh's effort in the manuscript went into refining his conception of them. Constantius, for obvious reasons, was the first to require Waugh's second thoughts. He must seem lovable to Helena, so that she can retain the reader's sympathy, yet able to betray love in search of power without the reader's detecting inconsistency. Waugh evoked the balance of response by direct and indirect means. First, he puts Constantius in a male context that includes only Marcias, the eunuch tutor who lives in a wholly mental world and against whom Constantius seems desirable, even at a distance, as man of action as opposed to speculation. Constantius is also set off by the District Commander, a bluff regimental soldier suspicious of politics who scores off him, making him seem fallible and human. However, Constantius's energy, lack of complacency, and interest in the real situation make him even more attractive than the older man. Finally Waugh contrasts him with Coel, immersed in legend and family pride, who teases his future son-in-law about Roman military disasters with the compensatory wit of the defeated. The triad of mystery, fact, and legend is important throughout the novel, at the end of which Helena triumphantly fuses all three. At this point, however, Constantius is made to appear to Helena as the embodiment of the City, Rome, and as a mystery man who is also a man of action.

These basic contrasts seem to have been part of Waugh's original design. Except for changing Constantius's response to rumors about the Divine Valerian from cautious and roundabout confirmation to the blunt "Yes" (p. 10), he did little even in revision to alter the character. In direct presentation, however, Waugh strove to make him less unsympathetic. For example, his self-analysis (p. 21) ended in all versions with the idea that he wants "the World," but early drafts made his motive the desire "to live out his days in a world free from the prevailing discord, intelligently planned; and no plan seemed quite to fit the case which did not give himself the supremacy." In the novel his sole object is power, a less naïve or evasive attitude that is easier to respect. Waugh also changed the characterization of self-love from "generous, reckless emotion" to a "hot and reckless emotion that had glowed /so dangerously/ in the hearts" of his predecessors and then to "master-passion" and "sickness" and canceled the label of Constantius as "a young man on the make." In the final draft his simplicity may be monstrous, preparing the reader for his betrayal of Helena's love, but it is impressive.

Even so, Constantius remains an unpromising lover, a problem that Waugh neatly sidestepped by presenting him as first a projection of and then a complement to Helena's fantasy life. This he went to some pains to develop. On May 30, 1945, he wrote to John Betjeman, recalling his plan to write Penelope Chetwode Betjeman's life as Helena's and describing his heroine as "16, sexy, full of horse fantasies," and asking her husband to have her "write to me fully about adolescent sex reveries connected with riding." Though lacking experience, Waugh reported that he has already made her "always the horse and the consummation when the rider subdues her," requires confirmation or correction, and asked, ". . . is riding enough or must she be driven? Are spurs important or only leather-work."[33] Mrs. Betjeman may subsequently have confirmed Waugh's conjectures; in any event, they were incorporated into a tentative first draft and then, with the usual attention to economy and emphasis, into the final version (pp. 22-24). To this Waugh added in revised second draft Constantius's fantasy of riding in triumph—if not in the chivalry that Helena dreams of her rider, at least at the head of real troops, not a ceremonial unit, "at the heart of power, at the entry into possession . . . in his service uniform." He is at any rate not a carpet knight.

To portray their emotional and spiritual union, Waugh shifts the figure and in successive revisions elaborates and intensifies it:

> They gazed at one another, unknowing /separate/ pressing close; like rain drops on a window pane. [Cancel MS draft; continues as p. 25.]
>
> They gazed at each other, unknowing, separate, drawn together, like two raindrops on the window pane, bulging one against the other, until [Revised MS and *Tablet*; continues as p. 25.]
>
> They gazed at one another, unknowing, separate, then running together like drops of condensed steam on the ewer, pausing, bulging one against the other, until, suddenly, they were one and ran down in a single cascade. Helena trotted on and Constantius bestrode her in triumph. [p. 25.]

33. *Letters,* p. 207. This letter and others by Waugh to Betjeman are in the University of Victoria library, Victoria, B.C. See also Waugh's letter to Penelope Betjeman, pp. 217-218.

The hesitations of the final draft establish more effectively the union, and here the section ends in the manuscript. Later in the manuscript, after the bantered nicknames "Chlorus" and "Stabularia," Waugh changed scene with a white line and moved directly into Constantius's dialogue with Coel. After the *Tablet* fragment was published but before book publication, no doubt more fully aware of Constantius's coming defection, Waugh inserted the final paragraphs on pages 25 and 28 that declare forthrightly that Constantius "had fallen in love" and that, however uncharacteristic or inconvenient this may be, he deals with the situation as expeditiously as possible, thus establishing the conflict later resolved to Helena's disadvantage.

Most subsequent appearances of Constantius are substantially identical in manuscript and novel. Waugh, however, took the opportunity to insert on the back of a manuscript page the paragraph detailing his refusal to seek the higher degrees of the Mithraic mysteries (pp. 95–96), and after manuscript stage to undercut his final, triumphant appearance as Caesar and potential Emperor:

He was soon back, /resplendent/ 'Chlorus, the purple.' 'Yes, at last.'	He was soon back, resplendently, imperially overdressed. 'Chlorus, the purple.' His was not the complexion for it. 'Yes, at last.' [pp. 98–99]

He may have the office, Waugh implied, by picking up the joke about his green complexion, but he cannot really fill it.

Waugh also revised to underscore the dichotomy between station and person in the characterization of Fausta, Helena's daughter-in-law. His first impulse, as on similar occasions in the past, was to move rapidly to the situation, without nuance:

The Empress Fausta was the first (caller) /to call/. (Helena ha) She and Helena had never met and (it [illegible] very) she needed to know at once whether her mother-in-law was likely to be of any importance in the elaborate strategy of court life. Five minutes small-talk with the formidable old lady made it clear that she was someone placate [*sic*].

Theology was the craze. Things had not gone well recently with Fausta's proteges/./ (, and she needed an ally.) She was a handsome woman accustomed to getting her way. Now she felt the need (for) /of/ an ally. She must put the Empress Dowager right on the situation before anyone else got at her.

Waugh must have seen almost immediately the skimpiness of this account, for he canceled it in favor of a passage appreciably closer to the nearly two full pages of the novel version (pp. 147–49). Even here, however, Fausta was described as "(young) /youngish/ still, and /fairly/ handsome." In third draft, working from and adding to typescript, Waugh continued the process of establishing the incongruity of "the fat, (white) common, little woman, Empress of the world," adding, "Left alone, she would have been unremarkably plain, but the beauty specialists had done their worst with tweeze & tongs & (paint) /a sticky kind of paint/." The tactile image in the afterthought made her seem uglier still, but Waugh was not content. He sacrificed that image to the surer timing, firmer establishment of Helena's viewpoint, and clearer foreshadowing of Fausta's death—"like a fish on a slab"—in the final version:

> Left alone she would have been unremarkably plain, but the beauty specialists had been to work on her. She glittered and pouted, "like a great gold-fish," Helena thought. But Fausta smiled, unconscious of the impression she gave. [p. 148]

She gives the reader the impression of a woman silly and sinister at the same time. While she speaks, as Waugh informed possible translators, "ultra-fashionable 1930 slang,"[34] she uses it to condemn to death those who represent even the remotest threat. Waugh took particular trouble with the scene which causes her downfall. Having disposed of her stepson, Helena's grandson Crispus, she suggests that Helena may have known something of the supposed plot. In manuscript Waugh perhaps overindulged in authorial commentary. Only the italicized words survive in the published text:

> *It was then that Fausta conceived her one (enormous) /egregious/ mistake.* She was tired and scared. It seemed easy. It had worked before. But she should have known better. [Italics added.]

In place of this commentary Waugh inserted in the final version, after the fates of Constantine's victims—"hacked, strangled, poisoned"—the incongruously comic "one after another, in the ups and downs of twenty years of married life" (p. 185). Immediately thereafter, he altered "There is no secret about" Helena's British origin to "It was one of my father's few secrets" to justify Constantine's conclusion that Fausta has rigged the seance to condemn his mother.

Even those unsympathetic to the novel's basic themes will find Fausta's death memorable, and Waugh worked hard to make it so. He canceled a

---

34. Evelyn Waugh, "Note on Translating Helena," unpublished manuscript in the University of Texas—Austin.

tentative first draft to provide a topic sentence, "Now was the good hour," later revised and combined with its successors to form the incremental, elegant, and in effect if not in form periodic opening sentence of the scene: "At the usual time, the good time, there in the torrid room, quite alone and quited naked Fausta gazed into the unclouded mirror—for the heat was dry as the desert—and studied her round, moist, serene face, and meditated" (p. 190). The roundness of the face came only in the final draft; like the change from "an almost girlish figure" of manuscript to the subjective and illusory "deeply desirable" of the next sentence, it reinforced Waugh's altered conception of her person.

The body of the scene is essentially the same from manuscript to novel, but the conclusion, after Fausta reaches the locked door and realizes that she is doomed, moved through at least four versions as Waugh searched for the precise detail and rhythm. The first attempt drew for its concluding lines upon the witch's enigmatic song that prophesies Napoleon's fate:

/But it [the door] was locked./ Nothing moved. She beat (on) with her hands and the feeble damp thuds kept time with (the) /(her) the feverish/ blood, pulsing feverishly in her ears pulsing in her ears: the song
Left there to rot on Helena's isle
Ave atque vale Heil

This linked her fate with her machinations and established a literal rhythm, but Waugh had already alluded to the song at the end of the previous paragraph, and he soon decided to present the final view of Fausta in his own detached description:

but it was (bar) locked from the other side. She had known it would be. Somewhere, between one cushion (illegible) and the next, she had come to herself.

CANCEL	REVISION
The good hour was over. She did not push or thump. No use in now knocking or ringing; the good hour was over.	No use now to push or ring or knock. The good hour was over. (She) /The Empress Fausta/ subsided, squatted, sprawled, panted, (expired) /and at last
That was the end of the Empress Fausta; like a fish on a slab.	expired,/ like (any fish on any slab anywhere) /a fish on a slab./

The revision of this revision pays careful attention to rhythm; the first was too curt. Even, however, with extension and resulting emphasis in the last member of the series and the return to the simpler "like a fish on a slab," the final sentence needed further work. For the final version (*Month* and page

227

proof ended the chapter with "The good hour was over"), Waugh trimmed the hyperalliterative and melodramatic series of verbs, separating the remaining elements with conjunctions to make the sentence more measured and the tone more detached. Then he moved quickly to the final simile, added in revision of page proofs: "She slid and floundered and finally lay still, like a fish on a slab" (p. 183).

Constantine's fate is less dramatic but more significant thematically: busy collecting "really important stuff" at the end of the novel, he fulfills the Wandering Jew's prophecy that the search for relics will for many obscure the meaning of the Cross. Moreover, the Emperor embodies the theme of "Power without Grace" that distinguishes Rome from Jerusalem, the earthly from the heavenly city. As Waugh conceives him, he is—to borrow the phrase later applied to Pinfold—at once absurd and formidable, and as Waugh revised, he blended the two qualities more and more inextricably. Absurdity is never absent; a character introduced as "all upholstery" below the neck, wearing a green wig (the color an echo of his father's complexion) that he clutches in alarm, could never be taken wholly seriously. But Waugh exerted some effort to make him more than a comic butt. Confronting the sculptor who has completed his triumphal arch, Constantine was originally the victim of burlesque anticlimax:

> 'Have you, may I ask, ever (been) taken part in a battle?'
> 'Certainly not.'
> 'I have. Perhaps you will accept my judgment that (your battle scenes are about the worst efforts I ever saw) /you fail to convey the/ full dramatic force of a charge of cavalry. But you have been to court. You're here now. You've made a court scene with everyone standing in the same position with exactly the same expression of [*sic*] (their) /his/ face. You can't tell one from the other.'
> Here he paused and looked round the glittering semi circle. It so happened that all were standing in the same position, all with the same expression. He may have (noticed) observed this for he ended, with less force. 'Anyway I think they are dreadful.'

In revising the passage for the final version, Waugh allowed Constantine to retain the offensive and to enunciate representationalist aesthetic views very similar to his own, views consistent with the practicality of Helena, who bestows the accolade, "Spoken like a man, my son" (p. 174).

The religious service that ensues was revised on much the same principles. In first draft the Emperor speaks in "a loud, parade ground voice" the thanksgiving for "the various decisions he had made in the course of the afternoon's business," only the arch being given in dialogue. "Then he read a chapter of one of St. Paul's epistles. It was not an easy chapter and Constantine's reading though loud did not make the sense any plainer." This was canceled; the revised manuscript was close to the final version, which says that Constantine "fruitily exhorted ... in a special tone of voice which he had lately grown [MS, developed] for the occasion" and "gave thanks [MS, to God] for all the blessings of his reign [MS, It was a well detailed autobiography.] in a detailed autobigraphy," which includes, in summary, the afternoon's events (this, perhaps, an echo of his grandfather Coel's love of detailed family history). The added detail is comic, but Constantine's reading and brief exposition of the epistle are treated straightforwardly and lead to a fairly dignified and solitary exit. Later, in contrast with his reinforcement of Fausta's plainness, Waugh deleted the description of Constantine in one of his most elaborate wigs, one "of tight alternating curls of /gold and/ silver thread (& green silk)."

Although Constantine's appearance after Fausta's death was heavily revised, Waugh seems in the opening passage to have been concerned primarily to achieve colloquial rhythms characteristic of the Emperor's speech rather than to add or alter detail, as in the insertion of the three plaintive questions about orgies, dancing, and enjoyment (p. 197). Later, however, Waugh inserted the passage on the labarum—called "This magnificent piece of arts-and-crafts" in a phrase that always signalled Waugh's disapprobation—to emphasize the scale of the Emperor's comic if horrifying self-delusion (pp. 201–203), and for his final appearance, canceling a direct move to his plans for the New Rome and his immediate exit, Waugh inserted and before the final draft rewrote Constantine's dialogue to raise his megalomania to the level of comic near-blasphemy. The manuscript draft is fairly simple:

> I shall leave my bones in the East when I die ... if I die. (I suppose I shall; but) /One can never be sure/; there are quite a number of authenticated cases, are there not? When God for His own good reasons has dispensed with the /usual/ process. A chariot, perhaps, as in the case of the prophet Elias, would not be inappropriate. /It wouldn't surprise me at all/ /nor anyone else, I daresay/.

The revision, as usual, expands and elaborates:

> "I shall leave my bones in the East when I die ... if I do die. You know, one can never be sure; I've been thinking a lot about it lately and reading it up; there are quite a number of authentical cases—are there not?—when God for His own good reasons has dispensed with all that degrading business of getting ill and dying and decaying. Sometimes I feel that in His bountiful mercy He may have something of the kind

in store for me. I can't quite imagine myself dying in the ordinary way. Perhaps He will send a chariot, as He did for the prophet Elias... It wouldn't really surprise me at all—nor anyone else, I daresay." [p. 203]

The fumbling confidence in this research, the delicate rejection of specific elements of the horrid process, and the dismissal of ordinary fate lead more pompously and more humorously to the afterthought about general recognition of his exalted spiritual qualities and prepare for the further anticlimax, inserted for the final version, in which the Romans, who murdered Saint Peter and Saint Paul, "even thought of murdering *me*."

The scene of which this forms a part advances both plot and theme. By focusing upon Constantine's intention to abandon Rome to Pope Sylvester and found a new city, a great Christian capital that in successive drafts is to be dedicated first to wisdom and finally to Divine Wisdom and Peace (p. 204), Waugh not only removed the Emperor from the plot but reinforced the contrast between the ideal, abstract conception and the solid, factual event that is introduced in the novel's opening scene and from now on is very nearly the exclusive object of attention.

In the dialogue between Helena and Pope Sylvester that follows, it is the exclusive concern. In contrast to Constantine's exit scene, this one is refined, simplified, and made more direct in revision. In the manuscript draft Waugh depended upon discursive treatment. The "holy cities of Asia" that wall out imperfection are present in all versions, but whereas in the book Sylvester dismisses the notion as the invention of slaves—an echo of Helena's remark in the opening scene (p. 8)—in manuscript he expands upon the idea:

People have always liked to imagine cities like that. I daresay they always will. Sometimes it is just a trick of the mind, a figure of speech, a way of trying to understand Grace. Sometimes it is a madness. They think these places really exist in brick & stone and that Grace (can be) /is/ waiting /quite literally/ at the end of a journey on camelback. It is one of the most difficult illusions to dispel because it is so near the truth.

'I know,' said Helena, 'I understand perfectly.' She did.

'The East follows the ideal; the West the concrete. And in the Providence of God, on the exact frontier the two become one. The Word became Flesh.'

'And the cross and the nails and the spear and the crown of thorns. They were concrete objects.'

'Of course.'

'I wonder how many people really believe in them. Does the Emperor? (Does the Bishop of Nicomedia?) How could he (keep?) be what he is, if he did? /Does he (believe) //know// that Christ was crucified in just the same way as he knows Fausta was roasted in her bath? Is it just a figure of speech with him?/

Having emphasized the theme, the manuscript moves to a discussion of the contrast between the Church's heroic age and modern "technical niceties," to Helena's contrast between "hypostatic union" and *"wood,"* and finally to her decision to seek the physical cross: "It hasn't been needed before. Now it is. And I am going to find it." Here Waugh broke off, leaving a third of a page blank, and apparently began recasting. In second draft he has Sylvester contrast not merely herosim and speculation but, picking up the Mithraic theme, "a mystery-cult for a few fanatics" (in the novel "heroes") and the true conception of the Church as "the whole of fallen mankind redeemed" in accord with Helena's earlier vision of the walls of the City embracing all men (pp. 47–49).

A similar unifying passage, which presents the Magi as "patrons of all late-comers," stems from Waugh's realization on the Feast of Epiphany, 1945, of "how specially Epiphany is the feast of artists." Waugh was obviously thinking of himself when he wrote the passage, and in translating the idea that even the learned can be saved into the passage that ends Chapter 12 he may have extended it to friends like Cyril Connolly, Harold Acton, and other "Children of the Sun"[35] whom he by no means uncritically loved. But the novel itself provides sufficient reason for the passage, since it gathers, by name, in the final version, "all who are confused with knowledge and speculation" from Helena's tutor Marcias to Longinus.

According to Mrs. Waugh, her husband "thought that prayer one of the best passages he ever wrote."[36] As always, it was the result of careful labor rather than happy accident. At least four drafts were needed to bring it to final polish. The first, parallel in content to pages 238 and 239 of the novel, gives to Helena the final authorial speculation about her fame resembling that of the Magi and has her speak of them in third person. Both first and second drafts move directly from the beginning of the journey to the visit to Herod and its result; the third interpolates a version of the account of the relaxation of "the primordal discipline of the heavens" to give cosmic significance to the event.

The final draft, which follows the description of the laborious progress of their journey (in second draft the journey follows the arrival), not only introduces the conversational rhetorical question—"What did you do?"—

35. See Martin Green, *Children of the Sun: A Narrative of "Decadence" in England After 1918* (New York: Basic Books, 1976).

36. Gene D. Phillips, *Evelyn Waugh's Officers, Gentlemen, and Rogues* (Chicago: Nelson-Hall, 1975), p. 95.

bringing Helena closer to the three she later calls princes and in revision, as befits her station, cousins, but also compresses more emphatically to the single word "unended" the phrases "year after year, generation after generation, perhaps to the end of time" in the third and longest version.

The concluding petitionary segment of the prayer received similar attention in successive drafts. Originally Helena urged the Magi to pray

> for Lactantius and Marcias and the young poets of Treves and for the souls of my wild, blind ancestors. Pray for all the scholars and artists and /sophists,/ for the (over clever, the royal) /ingenious/ and the fastidious, everywhere and for ever more. Let them never be quite forgotten at the throne of God when the (poor) /simple/ come into their kingdom;

CANCEL	REVISION
for His sake, who did not disdain your exotic gifts, Amen [White line]	do this, dear cousins, for His sake who did not disdain your gold and frankincense and myrrh. [White line]

In first typescript Waugh deleted everything after "kingdom," no doubt for reasons of emphasis, and he pasted onto a later typescript the passage, picking up after "ancestors," which concludes the final version:

> ... for their sly (Ithacan foe) /foe Odysseus/ and for the great Longinus.
> "For his sake who did not reject your curious gifts, pray always for all the learned, the oblique, the delicate. Let them not be quite forgotten at the Throne of God when the simple come into their kingdom." [p. 240]

This version makes explicit in the final subordinate clause the link between the Magi and their successors, and the use of the single series instead of parallel phrases not only simplifies the rhythm but establishes more clearly than "ingenious" and "fastidious" the sincere if misdirected desire for truth on the part of "the learned, the oblique, the delicate" (p. 240).

The finding and apportioning of the Cross and other relics, except for the Wandering Jew scene, required some recasting, but as usual Waugh expended greatest effort on his conclusion. In first draft as well as the patchwork revision of typescript and revised manuscript that became the final six pages of the novel, Waugh envisioned the Invention of the Cross as the climax, stating directly that Helena's work was completed and reinforcing and reiterating the point more firmly in the final version (pp. 259-60). Since she has already "completely conformed to the will of God," the rest of the novel is anticlimactic, and in the first draft Waugh's awareness of that led him to a conclusion so huddled and abrupt that the casual observer can overlook it.[37] Waugh first traced Helena's intinerary after Cyprus, summarized her bequests to Constantine and others, and speculated on the location of her body:

> It is said that her dust now lies in the Church of Ara Coeli on whose steps [, visited? visioned?] Gibbon first conceived his great work of slander. But the people of Rhiems say that she rests with them and the people of Constantinople used to claim her, too, until the Turk came to punish them for their [illegible] foolishness.
>
> So she disappears, as she came, into that world of fairy-story which is (the love of the people. Firm ground of the love & confusion) /darkness/ to the (wise) /learned/ and (the?) clear true (lore [?] of the simple) day-light to the simple.

Waugh's impatience to finish the work of five years is understandable, but in retrospect one can see why he became dissatisfied with these last two pages of manuscript. Not only do they move from certainty about her itinerary to vagueness about her tomb and to much inflated ascription of the cause of Constantinople's downfall, but they also introduce in cursory and choppy fashion a theme contradictory to the thrust of the novel, which states and implies in every chapter that fact rather than speculation or even legend is the basis of Christianity's central doctrine.

The revision in typescript not only solved these problems but took advantage of opportunities that Waugh had missed. He retained the irony of her exploits becoming legend, but he used the ironic passage to replace the itinerary and altered the focus and tone to increase considerably Helena's stature: "the people of those abandoned shores have taken her into their hearts and made her one with all great and beneficent ladies of myth and memory. In their poetry her cargo multiplied and was enriched with all the spoils of fantasy" (p. 261 reads "fairyland"). Then Waugh moved out of legend into dramatized scene as Helena and Constantine discuss relics, and Waugh added to the original detail of the Emperor's using a holy nail for a snaffle Helena's amused "Stabularia," a link with the novel's opening scenes. This demonstration of the actions of Power without Grace is far more effective than a cursory reminder of Constantinople's destruction; it fulfills the confident prophecy by the Wandering Jew that Christians will confound themselves with false relics; and it contrasts effectively with the more solemn conclusion.

37. As does Jeffrey Heath in "Concluding *Helena*," *Evelyn Waugh Newsletter* 10 (Autumn, 1976):4–5.

That conclusion firmly established Helena's final resting place at "the church of the Ara Coeli. . . . It was within a few yards of her, on the steps of that church, that the apostate Gibbon later sat and premeditated his history" (p. 264 varies slightly). The denotation is the same as in the first draft, but "premeditated" is cooler, more judicial, and less complimentary than "his great work of slander." Then Waugh carried the resolution even further than in first draft with a paragraph on the widely varying effects of Helena's prayers: Constantine was baptized and died expecting "an immediate, triumphal entry to Paradise"; "Britain for a time became Christian"; "The Holy Places were alternately honoured and desecrated, lost and won, bought and bargained for, throughout the centuries" (p. 264).

But this is merely preparation for the real resolution, which moves beyond the fate of individuals and countries to the effect of the Cross "the world over" and "among every race." Having recast once, Waugh expended even greater effort on the novel's final lines. The revised manuscript uses generalizations to convey the theme:

Manuscript and Proof

[The Cross] found worship /devotion/ among every race. To all mankind, confused with ancestral memories, prone to every aberration of symbol and speculation, it has brought the same blunt statement of fact, in which alone is hope.

This satisfied Waugh into page proof, and the version he gave *Month* follows the manuscript-typescript draft.[38] He was dissatisfied, however, with the rhythm of the final sentence, which must have seemed too long, and, with prepositional phrase in final position, too unemphatic.

His first major revision of corrected page proof solves some of these problems: The Cross found a joyous welcome among every race.

For it states a fact.
Far from Eden, lost in desert and jungle, man beguiles himself with symbols and speculation. The voice of Helena rouses him like a hunter's horn. Like a huntsman she throws him back on the scent.
Above all the babble of her age and ours, she makes one blunt assertion. And there alone is hope.

The blunt, one-sentence paragraph isolates and emphasizes the reality of the Crucifixion, and the introduction of Eden, desert, and jungle provides, as "ancestral memories" do not, concrete contrast to "symbol and speculation."

38. *Month,* n.s. 4 (August, 1950):103.

Furthermore, the hunting metaphor—though introduced rather abruptly and in its English overtones sorting rather ill with the imagery of the previous sentence—recalls Helena's youthful love of sport that has carefully been mentioned in her conversation with Pope Sylvester (p. 209). It ends the novel with a simile, however, one that identifies men with dogs, not the fact that Waugh has promised. Judging from the ink, Waugh must have added the final paragraph almost immediately. Then, in pencil, he revised the metaphor to direct statement and inserted it as the penultimate paragraph: "Hounds are checked, hunting wild. A horn calls clear through the covert. Helena casts them back on the scent."

Despite the pains Waugh took with these and other theological polemics, they are not the most successful parts of *Helena*. As a novel it is too diffuse and sketchy, with long gaps obscuring important changes in character. As a legend it is far too chatty and colloquial. Yet *Helena*, "The American Epoch in the Catholic Church," and other religious writing of the period helped Waugh purge himself of the tendency to state his religious beliefs directly and turn back to what more than a decade earlier he had called the writer's true material—"the individual soul."[39] In writing what became *Sword of Honour*, he expressed more artfully than in *Helena* what Father Martin D'Arcy called "his own personal thesis . . . that God put man on the earth to do a special task and God took man away only when he had done what God had put him there to do."[40] The war novel, D'Arcy implied in another context, became Waugh's vision of his own appointed task.[41]

39. Evelyn Waugh, "Art from Anarchy," *Night and Day* (September 16, 1937):24–25.
40. Phillips, *Evelyn Waugh*, p. 97.
41. "Father Martin D'Arcy, who will be 80 this year, talks to Quintin Hogg," *Listener* 79 (January 18, 1968):75.

12

Men at Arms:
A Sense of Purpose

Even before the outbreak of World War II, Waugh looked forward to active duty less from patriotic than from professional motives:

> I have to consider thirty years of novel-writing ahead of me. Nothing would be more likely than work in a government office to finish me as a writer; nothing more likely to stimulate me than a complete change in habit. There is a symbolic difference between fighting as a soldier and serving as a civilian, even if the civilian is more valuable.[1]

Waugh had his wish, of course, but in light of his previous career the delay in treating his war experience in fiction is striking. He may have realized that it would underlie the major work of his maturity and his delay may have resulted from a desire to use it to full advantage. Of course, he ended the war in far different spirit and circumstances from those in which he had begun it, and his first, tentative approach dealt with the subject and mood of that end.

A year before he completed *Helena,* he told Harvey Breit that, though he was "on leave" from writing, "I suppose I do want to write a novel or two novels about the war, it would be a study of the idea of chivalry."[2] In fact, Waugh had planned and probably written "Compassion."[3] The story, written during Waugh's most active period as a Roman Catholic spokesman, has much in common with *Helena.* Although the story deals with Major Gordon's failure to evacuate all the Jewish refugees from their Yugoslavian camp and his movement toward faith as a result of his experience, while the novel presents Helena's triumphant recovery of the True Cross and assump-

1. Evelyn Waugh, *The Diaries of Evelyn Waugh,* ed. Michael Davie (Boston: Little, Brown and Co., 1977), p. 438 (August 27, 1939).

2. Harvey Breit, *The Writer Observed* (New York: Collier Books, 1961), p. 35. The interview was first published March 13, 1949. Breit's punctuation is followed. On October 24, 1946, Waugh wrote to Nancy Mitford that "I have two shots in my locker left. My war novel and my autobiography. I suppose they will see me out." *The Letters of Evelyn Waugh,* ed. Mark Amory (New Haven and New York: Ticknor & Fields, 1980), p. 238.

3. *Month* n.s. 2 (August, 1949): 79–98. The story is not mentioned in the diary at all, and in the Peters files it is mentioned only after it had already been written and sold.

tion into legend, the two narratives share the tendency to state dogma overtly—in the story, "No suffering need ever be wasted. It is just as much part of Charity to receive cheerfully as to give"—and a sense of the dichotomy between public history and private conscience. "Compassion" does not state the concept, found in *Helena,* of "Power without Grace," but it embodies it no less clearly.

By the time Waugh had finished the first volume of his war novel, he was less impressed then he had been by the "defiant assertion of the supernatural."[4] Instead of Major Gordon, the religious naïf, he placed at the center of his story Guy Crouchback, naïve about a number of things, including the true nature of the spiritual life, but not about theology, and in working out the implications as opposed to the statement of his theme, Waugh devised over the course of a decade an increasingly elaborate design. For one thing, the intention to write "a study of the idea of chivalry" had become, by the time Waugh had completed the three volumes of the war novel, "a study of Guy Crouchback's disillusion with the army. Guy has old-fashioned ideas of honour and illusions of chivalry; we see these being used up and destroyed by his encounters with the realities of army life."[5]

Men at Arms carries Guy through a complete cycle from dessication to schoolboy enthusiasm to official disgrace if not disillusion. As the novel begins, Guy lives alone in Italy, heir to the much-reduced Crouchback estates, himself without an heir because of the failure of his marriage. The approach of war gives him a sense of purpose, and he returns to England to find in the Royal Corps of Halberdiers the camaraderie he had always sought. A fellow officer, Apthorpe, serves as unconsious parody of Guy's aspirations as a military man. After many false alarms, the Halberdiers sail for action at Dakar. The invasion is called off, but Guy commands a scouting party in which Ritchie-Hook, his commanding officer and unauthorized member of the party, is wounded. Although Guy is not responsible for Ritchie-Hook's wound or—morally at least—for Apthorpe's death, he is blamed for both and returns to England in disgrace that he does not take to heart.

The composition of *Men at Arms* is difficult to trace from external sources, since Waugh kept or at least preserved no diary for the period, and his letters to A. D. Peters are relatively few and uninformative. He

4. Evelyn Waugh, "The Heart's Own Reasons," *Commonweal* 54 (August 17, 1951): 458.

5. Evelyn Waugh, "The Art of Fiction XXX: Evelyn Waugh," *Paris Review,* no. 30 (Summer–Fall, 1963): 82. Waugh is speaking of *Men at Arms.*

began his "war-novel" confidently enough—"I think it will be all right"[6]—in Chantilly, where he had gone in mid-June, 1951, planning to finish a rough draft in six weeks, return to Stinchcombe, and "expand & polish at leisure."[7] Homecoming preceded completion, but by October 19 he had finished "52,000 polished & publishable words of the novel."[8] By this time, however, it had grown on him; he spoke not of the original "novel" but of publishing in 1952 the first of three or four volumes because he foresaw that "some months"—changed from "weeks"—of writing would be needed to complete his still rather nebulous plan.[9] Accordingly, he sent Peters the typescript of "Honour" in late October and apparently continued to revise through early January, when all that remained to do was the retyping and proofreading of what had become in the interval *Men at Arms.*

Perhaps because Waugh always perceived *Men at Arms* and what were to be its two successors as essentially a single work that personal finances and publishing procedures split asunder, his treatment of the manuscript of all three volumes was for him unusual. Instead of having each or all bound, he placed the manuscript of each book, as he had done that of *Scoop*, in a specially constructed box one edge of which resembles a leather binding. Then he collated each manuscript with the text of the first English edition, inserting page numbers at the top of each corresponding manuscript page, deleting with light pencil marks material that had not survived cutting and polishing, and indicating, also in pencil, the proper location of inserted material. At the beginning of each manuscript, furthermore, he inserted a note that it had been "collated and found complete except for some changes made in proof."[10] Waugh did not record his motives for taking this trouble, but he dated his collations of the first two volumes 1961. Since *Unconditional Surrender* was published in that year, he may have compared manuscript and text of each novel to assure himself that no contradictions or significant omissions had been made in the final volume. And, of course, he grew increasingly aware of the value of the manuscripts to his heirs, took pains to add to their value, and understood the importance of authorial notes attesting to their completeness.

6. Letter to A. D. Peters, ca. June 18, 1951. For concrete information, see *Letters,* pp. 351–80 passim.

7. Letter to Peters, ca. June 24, 1951.

8. Letter to Peters, October 19, 1951.

9. Letter to Peters, received in Peters's office October 19, 1951.

10. This is in the manuscript of *Men at Arms;* that of *Officers and Gentlemen* reads the same except in "for minor changes"; that of *Unconditional Surrender* reads "for changes."

The manuscript of *Men at Arms* shows that Waugh was as businesslike in writing it as he was in later treatment of it; Waugh exhibits none of the hesitations and afterthoughts discernible in the manuscripts from *Brideshead* through *Love Among the Ruins.* The relative assurance in *Men at Arms* may be due to his awareness that his experience in the Royal Marines, from induction through the fiasco at Dakar, formed a natural unit with its own internal structure, and both his diaries and John St. John's memoir[11] contain ample evidence that fictional event followed closely the historical order. As a result, Waugh's decisions in the process of composition could be devoted to inventing details, as much of character as of incident, that would highlight Guy's fascination with military life and prepare for his disillusion with it.

In fact, the most obvious manuscript variants are not necessarily the most significant. For example, in manuscript, at the end of what is now Book 2, Chapter II,[12] Waugh included in the action devoted to the Halberdiers' training an episode in which the troops, faces blackened, board a bus to be taken on a night exercise and find it occupied by two girls who think the vehicle part of the regular service and become increasingly mystified and disturbed by the silent, blackened men. Sometime between manuscript and volume, Waugh obviously decided that the sequence was not particularly funny and that it had no relevance to the struggle between Apthorpe and Ritchie-Hook for possession of the thunder-box. He deleted it and introduced a chapter division to emphasize the fellowship of Apthorpe and Guy at the end of Book 2 and "the saga of the chemical closet" at the beginning of Book 3 (pp. 188–89), perhaps because the thunder-box episode, self-contained, involves no major shift in meaning or direction.

Nor does an even more obvious kind of revision, the restructuring of the opening of Chapter 5 (in volume form Book 2, Chapter 5) and of what is now Book 2, Chapter 7. As far as can be determined from the present condition of the manuscript, much cut, pasted, and interlinked with typescript—Waugh's pencil notes indicate that there are "Parts missing"—Book 2, Chapter 5 originally began on April 1 with Ritchie-Hook's "Gentlemen, tomorrow you will meet the men you will lead in battle," moved to Truslove and Bonnie Prince Charlie, and gave a retrospect of the four days of preparation for the arrival of the enlisted men. In revision Waugh gave a chronological account of the preparations in the body of the chapter, putting at the beginning the allusion to the film about Bonnie Prince Charlie and at the end Guy's

---

11. John St. John, *To the War with Waugh* (London: Leo Cooper, 1974).

12. *Men at Arms* (London: Chapman and Hall, 1952), p. 188. Hereafter references to this edition are given parenthetically in the text.

ruminations about Apthorpe. The beginning reinforces the mock-heroic theme; the body continues the chronological framework; and the conclusion links the new setting and action with the activities at Kut-al-Imara House. Then, in the ensuing chapter, Waugh could move to the fourth day and to a new motif: Guy Crouchback's private myth of Captain Truslove and the world of patriotic, militaristic fiction from his youth.

The section that became Chapter 7, Guy's meditation on the questions from the "Army Training Memorandum," was entirely restructured soon after first draft. Manuscript and volume orders are:

MS	BOOK
What are we fighting for?	Are you trying to make yourself
How many of your men do	competent to take over the job
you know by name and what do	of the next senior man to you?
you know of their characters?	Who runs the platoon—you or
Do you keep a notebook	your sergeant?
containing their ages, trades,	How many of your men have
and other particulars?	you marked in your mind as
Are you satisfied that your	possible candidates for a
men will come to you with	commission?
their troubles and complaints	How many of your men do you
because they realize that they	know . . . what do you know
will get sympathetic hearing	of their characters?
and good advice?	What are we fighting for?
What games do you play with	
your men? Have your men been	
warned of the danger of booby-traps?	
Are you trying to make yourself	
. . . senior man to you? Who	
runs the platoon . . . sergeant?	
Is your platoon the best in	
the battalion?	
/How many men have you	
marked in your mind as a	
possible candidate for a	
commission?/	
Do you discuss difficulties and	
compare notes with your fellow	
officers?	

In manuscript, the questions are set in the form of an examination of conscience, and the section ends in badinage among the junior officers.

Perhaps recalling that he had already linked examination of conscience with professional duties (p. 63) and more fully aware of the claims of emphasis, Waugh moved the joking to the beginning of the section and put the questions in the framework of the game "Happy Families." Furthermore, the original order of the questions is essentially aimless, and some of them and their answers are trivial. In reordering, Waugh halved their number, in the process removing details about Guy's relations with Apthorpe and other officers, and put them in logical sequence—superior officer to lowest subordinates—and ended with the question that is the key to Guy's dilemma in the trilogy as a whole. In manuscript Waugh expanded Guy's consideration of war aims in an over-page insert; in the final version the question is given emphatic final position and linked with morality and Romance, the two major determinants of Guy's character in the novel.

In this passage Waugh was not so much changing as discovering more fully his intentions. The same thing is true of the novel's external, formal structure. In manuscript it is divided into six chapters, themselves divided into no more than three sections, while the published version contains a Prologue and three books, divided into nine, nine, and eight chapters.[13] The revision accords with Waugh's usual process of dividing his material in more numerous and more clearly demarcated units as he moved from first to final draft, and the titles of the four major units—"Sword of Honour," "Apthorpe Glorious," "Apthorpe Furibundus," and "Apthorpe Immolatus"— give the reader obvious thematic and structural clues.

More important to Waugh's discovery of his meaning, however, were the many revisions and insertions, minor in themselves but having great cumulative effect in creating character, enforcing theme, and preparing for later volumes of the story. Thus, because Guy is important not only as a moral agent but as the last of a distinguished English Catholic family, Waugh took at least second thought in describing his forebears. Originally, for example, only Guy's mother had martyrs among her ancestors; sometime before publication, probably to anticipate the development of Blessed Gervase Crouchback in *Officers and Gentlemen,* Waugh altered the line to read "Forbears of both their names had died on the scaffold" (p. 1). Even more important for the trilogy as a whole was Waugh's uncertainty about the disposition of Broome, the family estate. At its first mention in manuscript and first edition, "The property was reduced ... to the house and park and home farm" (p. 13), but in the manuscript conversation about the

13. The correspondence of manuscript to book version is Chapter 1, Prologue; Chapter 2, Book 1 , Chapter 1; Chapter 3, Book 1, Chapter 5; Chapter 4, Book 2, Chapter 1; Chapter 5, Book 2, Chapters 5, 6; Chapter 6, Book 3, Chapter 1.

family between Guy and the genealogist Mr. Goodall, Guy remarks that "my father sold (the place) Croome [*sic*] some years ago." Waugh had clearly forgotten the earlier passage, which may have been at the typist's and therefore inaccessible. At any rate, the first edition reads, "My father left Broome some years ago" (p. 132), reopening the possibility of Crouchback's return to the family estate. When he wrote the Goodall section, Waugh obviously had not seen that far ahead. For local purposes, of course, it is enough that Mr. Crouchback be able to live in the memory of Broome and that Guy feel cut off from that refuge.

Still more important to *Men at Arms* is the change in Waugh's conception of Guy's mad brother Ivo. In both manuscript and first edition he dies in solitude, at first in Paris and then in the more commonplace Cricklewood, but in manuscript Waugh labors to clear the family of possible taint by contrasting the reality with the plebian fears of Arthur Box-Bender, married to Guy's sister, who helped locate Ivo:

> It was true that the post-mortem revealed a rare but entirely concrete disease of the brain. It was also true that there (were very few lunatics in the Crouchback pedigree) /was uncommonly little insanity in (among) the family./ But there was a great deal of intermarriage. In the last two centuries (the names of) a dozen /august/ Catholic (families) /names/ wove in and out inextricably in the Crouchback pedigree, and Box-Bender subscribed to the popular view that a long, recorded genealogy was, somehow, evidence of decadence. /as though the mere writing down of the names & achievements of one's ancestors tended to unsettle (the) //their// minds/.

Later in the manuscript, responding to his nephew Tony's concern over madness in the family, Guy gives nonhereditary disease as the cause of Ivo's condition.

Originally Waugh seems to have created Ivo and Guy's oldest brother, Gervase, who, in an inserted passage, was killed "fresh and clean and unwearied" on his first day in the trenches of France, as extremes of the recluse and the pure, illusioned soldier between whom Guy uneasily fits. The spirit of Gervase is kept before the reader by means of his "medal of Our Lady of Lourdes," which Mr. Crouchback originally intends to give to Tony and then bestows upon Guy. But while Ivo's name recurs, he remains inert as a symbol because of the special nature of his malady, his physical resemblance to Guy producing only Box-Bender's unjustified discomfort. Therefore, by the first edition Waugh had changed his illness to "an excess of melancholy" (p. 29) and canceled the passage about the sanity of aristocracy. Though Guy says that Ivo's madness is not hereditary, Box-Bender's concern about Guy's stability seems more plausible in the absence of authorial statement; the parallelism between Ivo's situation and Guy's—though Ivo's isolation is sought, while Guy's is imposed—becomes clearer, and the possibility of Guy's sinking into delusion remains open.

Deluded or at least distracted he is, but not by melancholia. The donnée of his character, announced clearly at the beginning, is that he "had been deprived of the loyalties which should have sustained him" (p. 5); both his political and his religious convictions have become arid and habitual. During the course of the novel, though both are prodded, neither awakens. Instead, Guy is introduced to new forms and rituals to which he temporarily attaches his emotions, only to lapse into dryness again. Though the distinctions are to some extent artificial, Guy's progress can be seen in terms of regimental ritual, private school life, the liturgical year, and the historical progress of the war. The first two occupy the foreground; the last is made to seem almost incidental. To establish these perspectives and to show the regressive nature of Guy's attachments, Waugh made recurrent and important revisions.

In first draft Guy's behavior at his London club (not until well into the manuscript named Bellamy's) while seeking wartime employment is contrasted with his former isolation: "Frustration made a change in Guy /he became/ rather garrulous and convivial. When he was not talking or drinking he wrote letters." And, "Every evening he got rather drunk." With the advantage of hindsight Waugh realized that his change would render less effective the contrast between Guy's meditation on his failure to say, "Here's how," over a drink in the final paragraph of the Prologue and his saying it in the opening line of Book 1 (pp. 44–45).[14] In revision he left the civilian Crouchback solitary and sober. Furthermore, the sharpened contrast shows the effect on Guy of regimental life.

The traditions of the Halberdiers (spelled Halbediers through most of the manuscript) are a source of innocent delight to Guy and of mordant interest to his creator. Many are present in the original manuscript, but two of the most memorable came as second thoughts. Originally, for example, the mess gives a toast to its "Colonel-in-Chief, the King," as unexceptionable as it is uninteresting. Waugh clearly thought as much, and in an over-page insertion at some later date changed the King to the Grand Duchess Elena, given the title as a young beauty in 1902, to emphasize the archaism, at once endearing and absurd, of the ritual honoring an irrelevant past. The second insertion, important through the end of *Officers and Gentlemen* as a

14. This contrast may have been introduced in revision, however: both pages are cut and then pasted on blank full sheets.

symbol of empty military ritual, valuable chiefly for its difficulty of delivery rather than of execution, is the piling-arms command. In first draft it is mentioned and then quoted in an over-page insertion. Waugh later inserted phrases from it not only in the scene where it is executed but also in Guy's examination of conscience at the section's end (pp. 53, 63), to fix in the reader's mind its absurd, labyrinthine complexity.

Of course, an army involves men as well as ritual, and Waugh labored throughout the process of composing the novel to people his world with characters who would be interesting in themselves, who would support local themes, and who would figure prominently in subsequent action. The loathsome Trimmer, for example, was at first merely "marked for disgrace," then made a professional photographer by an insertion. Perhaps later still, Waugh inserted on the back of the manuscript page the full description of his appearance, habits, and character that appears in the novel (pp. 48–49). Guy's explosion of temper at Trimmer and his remorse for his fourth-form behavior (pp. 126–27) is written on manuscript pages that, cut up and renumbered, indicate heavy revision if not insertion. Waugh apparently thought out the broad movements of the trilogy even as he wrote *Men at Arms,* and he seems to have decided that Trimmer would replace Apthorpe as Guy's ironic double. Trimmer disappears halfway through *Men at Arms,* but to fix him in the reader's mind, Waugh inserted after manuscript stage reminders of his character. During Virginia's quarrel with Guy he recalls "the brawl with Trimmer" (p. 164); and in an over-page insertion in the manuscript Guy's platoon sergeant "reminded Guy of Trimmer" (p. 218). To balance Trimmer, Waugh created Jim Leonard (changed from Lazarus) in a series of insertions that augmented his character to make him seem "made of the very stuff that constituted the Corps" (p. 70) and expanded the portrait of his anxious and carping wife—a sharp contrast to Virginia—who destroys his effectiveness as a soldier.

In one instance Waugh reversed the process of giving clearer definition to his characters. Guy's commanding officer during the chaotic dispersal and re-formation of the brigade before and after Dunkirk is in manuscript called Major Trench. By publication Waugh had expunged his name, so that neither Guy nor the reader knows it. The mystery is preserved almost to the end of *Unconditional Surrender,* when he is revealed (and then not to Guy) as the brother of the Grace-Groundling-Marchpole who throughout the trilogy adds to the "Most Secret" dossier on Guy.

By the time the novel was published, therefore, it seems clear that Waugh had conceived a least at general outline of the succeeding volumes. Waugh's treatment of Frank de Souza provides even stronger evidence of his sense of purpose. Though de Souza appears only once, and that briefly, as a picturesque, competent platoon commander in *Officers and Gentlemen,* in the final volume he emerges as Guy's commanding officer in Yugoslavia, a major contributor to Guy's loss of illusion about the war. In the manuscript of the first novel, he was a very minor figure, at first identified only as "the Cambridge man." Later, during Guy's first visit to London in uniform, Waugh canceled his encounter with two unnamed subalterns and inserted over page the meeting with de Souza and his girl, down to her complaint about his facetiousness (p. 92); the rest of the scene, including the revelation that the two live together and that Guy thinks them a "cold odd couple," is in typescript. But de Souza's morals were at this stage less important to Waugh than his competence as a soldier, since in the final volume he would have to have Guy's confidence in order to betray it. Therefore Waugh contrasted de Souza with the thoroughly incompetent Jervis and later inserted "a dull young regular named Brent" to substitute for de Souza in the ludicrous episode in which the Loamshire officers are thought to be German spies (pp. 265–69).

When Guy first meets the other Halberdiers, however, he is not burdened with responsibility. Despite the weakness of his fellow officers and the absurdities of regimental ritual, he is happy, for his first days in the Corps give him "something that he had missed in boyhood, a happy adolescence" (p. 50). In manuscript this read "happy school life"; the alteration involves a distinction important to the purposes of the novel, for Waugh explicitly contrasts "life in barracks" as "a survival from long years of peace" (an insertion in manuscript) to the atmosphere at Kut-al-Imara House, the private school commandeered for a training site. The name is taken from a battle that besieged and starving Anglo-Indian forces lost in 1916.[15] The school itself Guy recreates imaginatively on the model of "many recent realistic novels," and in manuscript Waugh added the description of patriotic history and of language classes taught by rote and rule. The basic manuscript reads: "Divinity was taught twice a week without theological bias." Only history survived final cutting. Here and in subsequent pages the tone and many of the details, especially about food, were drawn in large part from Waugh's memories of his school days in 1918:

> Everything was of necessity a makeshift—the clothes we wore, the food we ate, the books we worked with, the masters who should have taught us.
> We were cold, shabby and hungry, not in the ethos of free Sparta, but of some beleaguered, enervated and forgotten garrison.[16]

15. Thomas Harbottle, *Dictionary of Battles* (New York: Stein and Day, 1971). Revised and updated by George Bruce.

16. Evelyn Waugh, *A Little Learning* (Boston: Little, Brown and Co., 1964), p. 116.

Even the names of the rooms are taken from World War I battles; Guy settles in Passchendaele (the battle in which Alec Waugh was captured). Neither the school nor the Halberdier training group have what Dr. Fagan would call "tone," and in the summary of daily activity Waugh revised to lower the tone still further than in original conception. The eight sentences justifying, by reason of the bus service, cold, and inconvenience, a seven-hour working day were an over-page insertion, while the stale, text-parroting curriculum, added in the space between sections, was a perhaps more immediate second thought (pp. 138–39), and before the first edition Waugh capped the section by inserting, "They were to stay there until Easter—a whole term" (p. 139).

With the appearance of Brigadier Ritchie-Hook at Kut-al-Imara, the literary model changes from realistic fiction to something very like *Stalky & Company* or even the *Boy's Own Paper.* Ritchie-Hook is presented, however, not as the rather remote, omniscient, and benevolent head of Kipling's school but as himself an *enfant terrible.* As the manuscript grew longer, Waugh began formulating more clearly to himself and stating, in a series of insertions and revisions, the key to the Brigadier's character, as in:

> For this remarkable warrior the image of war was not hunting or shoot-ing; it was the wet sponge on the door, the hedgehog in the bed; or, rather, he saw war itself as a prodigious booby-trap. [p. 83][17]

This analogy, probably inserted after Waugh had worked through Apthorpe's thunder-box debacle—itself, in a revision, described as the "culminating illustration" of "the Brigadier's training methods" (p. 176)—is reinforced by the summary characterization introduced into the Brig's rebuke to the training group, who are as apprehensive as schoolboys. Originally he ad-dressed the situation directly. In revision he sends everyone on leave and pauses to smile before discussing their limitations. To extend the pause and to underscore this aspect of the Brig's character, Waugh included this passage:

> The Brigadier was no scold and he was barely one part bully. What he liked was to surprise people. In gratifying this taste he had often to resort to violence, sometimes to heavy injury, but there was no pleasure for him in these concomitants. Surprise was everything. [p. 143]

To support this theme, Waugh made important revisions and an insertion to prepare for the greatest surprise of all.

17. This passage is a three-line manuscript fragment pasted to a full sheet. Waugh's direction in red ink: "Insert p. 78, 1. 15." For the source of the Brigadier's character, see the *Diaries* on St. Clair Morford, especially p. 464 (February 26, 1940).

The Brigadier's rhino story earlier in the manuscript was revised to take account of his love of uproar. Originally, sounding like an old Africa hand, he pursued the rhino for six weeks because the beast had impaled a bearer and returned to place the reeking head on the C. O.'s desk. After a type-script stage Waugh revised the story to its present form: the C. O. "talked a lot of rot about" licenses; Ritchie-Hook fired a line of flares in the rhino's path; it charged the camp, "caught a black fellow bang through the middle," and was shot by Ritchie-Hook in the middle of very satisfying confusion (pp. 77–78).

Still later, before the climax of the thunder-box episode, Waugh took the opportunity to foreshadow the catastrophe more clearly and economically. In first manuscript draft the lecture on booby traps, given by a visiting sapper, is mentioned only after the explosion that unsettles Apthorpe's mind. Exposition after the fact was poor technique, and the sapper was extraneous. Having already passed over Ritchie-Hook's lecture in brief narrative summary, Waugh revised to give it the ominous subject of booby traps. Originally the Brig's exuberance is due solely to his having put the box's hiding place "Out of Bounds to all ranks below Brigadier"; the revision makes his glee anticipatory as well (p. 184).

In fact, Waugh apparently began to see Ritchie-Hook as a humor character, for with two exceptions he removes traces of human weakness or normal concerns from his dialogue and actions. One, offset by the comedy of Apthorpe's challenge to the signalers, is the substitution after manuscript of his return to camp, "hag-ridden by the news from France" (p. 232) for a description of him "gazing out of the window . . . trying to comprehend the unspeakable truths he had learned in London" just before the Dunkirk evacuation. The other is his dialogue with Guy about the Dakar operation, his envy of Guy's command of a company, and his rueful admission after breaching security that "I'm getting too old for courts martial" (p. 275). At the end of the same section, however, in the scene preparing for Guy's "Operation Truslove" at Dakar, Waugh canceled the dialogue of the ship's captain and Colonel Tickeridge in which they conspire to provide a coconut if Guy cannot find one because "your brigadier has had a lot of annoyance & disappointment lately. We just want to cheer him up." As finally conceived, Ritchie-Hook may be annoyed or disappointed, but never alarmed or despondent.

Nor do his methods remotely resemble those of a professional soldier. Waugh had already shown in Guy's disgrace at Mudshore firing range the textbook method of training. To make a sharp contrast and to expunge Guy's unhappy memory, Waugh inserted a second visit to the range, drawing an explicit contrast between the Army Way and the Brig's way: "The firing of a live round . . . was attended with all the solemnity of a salute at a funeral, always and everywhere, except when Brigadier Ritchie-Hook was around. The sound of flying bullets exhilarated him to heights of levity," examples of which are using his hat as a target, raising his head for another, and leading his men "on all fours in front of the targets a few inches below the rain of bullets" (pp. 173, 174). This is hardly the kind of officer Guy had envisioned in manuscript after Ritchie-Hook takes direct command of training:

> What impressed Guy was /the/swiftness with which the brigadier had appreciated the situation and made his plan. At their first meeting Guy had thought him slightly preposterous. Now he had (given) shown the stuff of his reputation. He had been at Southsand for a night and a morning. What he had learned from the guarded conversation of the staff could only be guessed. All he had certainly seen was an empty mess and a (lethargic) /listless/ class of small-arms. He had made an unreasoned conclusion, like a diagnotician [*sic*] confronted by (disease) the first vague symptoms of disease or a connoisseur uneasy in the presence of a forgery, that things were amiss at Kut-al-Imara House; and he had been right. He had decided then & there to change the whole training-plan; he had given himself the minimum of time to make the change; and he would do it. It was an expert's decision. Like any expert Brigadier Ritchie-Hook had his own mannerisms & extravagances. But here, Guy felt as countless Halbediers [*sic*] had felt before him, was a man to follow.

The Brigadier's method is too rational and Guy's response too Truslovean for Waugh's final conception of the characters, and after a typescript version he revised to show the effect on Guy's emotions rather than his reason: ". . . that evening Guy felt full of meat, gorged like [MS, a young lion.] a lion on Ritchie-Hook's kill" (p. 145).

Waugh also changed Apthorpe's response to this speech, from approval — "the right stuff" of the earlier quotation — to "He might have made it clearer that there were certain exceptions." Like the Brig, Apthorpe becomes more himself and less like anyone else as Waugh began to see more clearly his character and its function in the novel. This is one of the many occasions on which his dialogue is given the tinge of bland, obsessive certainty that makes him, as the section title "Apthorpe Gloriosus" indicates, an outstanding modern example of the humor character. Thus, in a series of telephone calls by which he thwarts Guy's seduction of Virginia, he originally explains the grounds for arresting a civilian, which, though preposterous, are more sensible than the none at all of the final version, and when Guy tells him he cannot arrest a civilian, his defensive, "That's exactly what I was afraid you'd say. It's what he says," becomes the accusatory, "That, Crouchback, is what the prisoner maintains. I hope you aren't going to take his part" (p. 164). Moreover, Apthorpe originally appeals to Crouchback—"old man" —as a friend, but in final form insists pompously that "this is an official communication. I am calling on you as an officer of His Majesty's Force." Both changes put upon Guy the guilt-by-association and render even funnier Apthorpe's bland dimissal of the incident on the following day.

Apthorpe never apologizes, but he does, reluctantly, sometimes explain, and the explanations are consistently revised to eliminate the uncertain man within and strengthen the façade. Thus Apthorpe in manuscript fears being thought too old, in print not being fit (p. 57); first he wishes to speak to the Captain-Commandant to remind him that Apthorpe exists, then to say, "Anything that crops up" (p. 59); explaining why he wears a steel helmet to use his thunder-box, he admits in manuscript that it might be called a quirk but in print attributes the habit to normal home-sickness for his topee (p. 191). Apthorpe as the insider, the survivor, the old Africa hand is emphasized in dozens of minor touches, and Waugh in-serted Guy's review of his activities in the new camp—evading inoculation, advising the Pioneer Officer, making friends with the brigade staff, setting up comfortably in his illicitly transported equipment (pp. 206–207). Still later, after a reprimand loud enough for the whole camp to hear, he ascribes it merely to "red tape," Waugh having cut in manuscript his recognition that the C. O. "put these things strongly" and added before publication the comment, "Since the loss of his thunder-box, Apthorpe was impervious to shock" (p. 228).

Like Shakespeare with Malvolio, Waugh must have discovered delightedly that there was almost nothing that Apthorpe would not do and that authority, however minor or temporary, would make him more eccentric. Given com-mand of Headquarters Company, he exults rather mildly and ignores Guy's allusion to the thunderbox, and the scene originally ended with Guy's conversation with his own company commander. On reflection Waugh realized that he had not exploited Apthorpe's self-importance, and on the back of the manuscript page he inserted the last five paragraphs of Part 2, Chapter 5, in which Apthorpe cautions Guy against further mention of "that happening at Southsand" on pain of "drastic action" (p. 213).

Promoted to captain two chapters later, Apthorpe is cocky enough in first draft and irrepressible in revision. What de Souza terms in revision "The Matter of the Captain's Salutation" receives most of its funniest de-tails in second or later draft. All versions begin the plot with Guy's joking salute of the newly promoted and tipsy Apthorpe, his subsequent collision with a night bucket when Guy does not repeat the salute, and his appeal to Guy to continue saluting him. In first draft, however, Guy asks if he can repeat the conversation, anticipating further merriment at Apthorpe's expense. In revision Waugh seems to have realized that Apthorpe was so far sunk in self-importance that the request to tell others could come from him. This part of the manuscript is more than ordinarily confused, but it seems clear that all the overt examples of the persecution of Apthorpe, including de Souza's dropping to one knee with a worshipful stare, are at least revisions of earlier attempts and perhaps insertions of additional material.[18] It is clear that Waugh compressed two drafts of respective exposition and speculation about the explosion's psychological effect on Apthorpe into the scene inserted fairly late in the process in which Colonel Tickeridge questions Guy:

> 'I'm getting the most extraordinary reports on him from all sides.'
> 'He had a rather nasty accident the morning we left Southsand.'
> 'Yes, I heard about it. Surely that could not have affected his *head?*'
> [p. 226]

As Dr. Johnson might have said, humor about the backside is an inferior mode, but within that mode there can be lesser and greater. That is certainly true of the incident that unsettles Apthorpe's mind—or rather of its aftermath:

"Nothing worth salvaging," he said, still too dazed for grief.
"Better come back to breakfast."
"I've had it ten years."
"You wouldn't have been able to take it to camp, you know."
"It would have been waiting for me after the war. I spent hours in bed last night thinking where to store it. I'd found just the place."
Guy was at a loss for words of condolence. They turned silently towards the house.

He seemed too dazed for grief. Guy was at a loss for words of condolence.
'Better come back to breakfast.'
They turned silently towards the house.
Apthorpe walked unsteadily across the wet, patchy field with his eyes fixed before him.
On the steps he paused once and looked back.
There was more of high tragedy than of bitterness in the epitaph he spoke.

18. Judging from the pagination, the material including Guy and Apthorpe's conversation, pp. 17–18 (ink numbering), is a revision in typescript of the preceding manuscript p. 8. The material containing Apthorpe's revised request to Guy, numbered 192*b*, seems to have been inserted at a later stage and blended with fragments that include the end of Chapter 8

> "It'll take years to find another   *'Biffed.'* [p. 196]
> like it. I may never find one."
>   They walked across the wet,
> patchy field. On the steps
> Apthorpe paused once and looked
> back.
> "Biffed," he said bitterly.

By moving to an earlier position (p. 194) and making speculative rather than certain Apthorpe's plans for the box, Waugh made his loss less directly affecting; by changing his bitterness to high tragedy, Waugh elevated the tone to the mock-heroic in accord with earlier references and with the section's title, later added, "Apthorpe Furibundus"; and by altering the order and amount of comment on Apthorpe's attitude, Waugh led more rhythmically up to the final, emphatic monosyllable that concedes victory to the Brigadier.

Even when moribund, Apthorpe expands. In the anticlimax of the Dakar operation, "Local leave to up-country stations was given to officers for sporting purposes. Apthorpe was one of the first to go" (p. 296). The manuscript continues, "He had returned with malaria and dysentery and lay in the hospital tent." This was obviously unworthy of his final entrance, and Waugh inserted, perhaps after completing the manuscript, the summary of Apthorpe's return, beginning with a pidgin message and ending with his return on a hammock, "looking like a Victorian woodcut from a book of exploration," arguing feebly with the bearers in a language that he insists they understand (pp. 298–99).

However, making Apthorpe talk oddly and intensifying the effect of his vagaries did not satisfy Waugh, who well into the process of composition was still finding ways to let him act preposterously. Apthorpe's obsession with boots is established at his and Guy's first meeting, but in first draft nothing came of it. Then, working on Apthorpe's feud with the signaler Dunn over inspecting Dunn's lines and Apthorpe's subsequent challenge to a signaling duel, Waugh conceived a situation that would intensify and extend the ramifications of the quarrel. He at least expanded and may have inserted Apthorpe's destruction of a soldier's boot to reveal its poor workmanship, used the incident as a climax of the quarrel, extended the result to the bitter comedy of Dunn's holding a hearing on the offense during the whole of his brief tour of duty in France (p. 261), and concluded it when, Apthorpe dead, Guy pays Dunn nine shillings to clear the books (p. 307).

Large as Apthorpe and Ritchie-Hook loom in the novel, however, they are in the literal sense incidental, providing action and anecdote but not, as

Waugh observed, affecting the theme: "the Second World War as it was seen and experienced by a single, uncharacteristic Englishman, and to show its effect on him." Of course, these and other characters are part of the effect, and the manuscript reveals Waugh's conscious and often inspired efforts to use them to set off Guy as soldier, as Englishman, and as Catholic.

At the beginning of his private crusade against "the Modern (world) /Age/ in arms" (p. 5), Guy puts himself under the protection of Sir Roger of Waybroke, the crusader who never reached his destination but who has been informally canonized by the Italian villagers as "il santo inglese." Several times during the course of *Men at Arms* Sir Roger's memory is invoked as a parallel to Guy's experience, and the manuscript reveals that Waugh introduced these references with great care. Thus, in describing Guy's loneliness in London before joining the Halberdiers, he originally concluded the paragraph (p. 23) with "Sir Roger's sword had lost its brightness." Perhaps Waugh felt that the reference came too soon after the theme was introduced or that to be effective it had to be used sparingly and at crucial moments. At any rate, he cut the sentence before publication. When occasion warranted, however, he used Sir Roger twice within ten pages, first recovering, revising, and pasting on a canceled passage comparing Guy and Sir Roger as experienced losers (p. 211) and then, after he had ceased to make changes in the manuscript itself, inserting into Guy's meditations on the justice of his cause, "But Guy's spirit was as high as on the day he had bade farewell to Sir Roger," and, to complement the moral sanction, "There was in Romance great virtue in unequal odds" (p. 220).

Sir Roger is a figure of Romance; Apthorpe is both a figure of fantasy and a means by which Guy is "diminished and caricatured by duplication" (p. 111). Less explicitly, he is both source of temptation and memento mori; his cultivated façade as professional soldier perhaps motivates Guy to cultivate the moustache and monocle that gain him new status among the temporary officers. The moustache seems to have been developed in an afterthought; in novel but not in manuscript it is casually introduced by Virginia's comments (p. 97); the passage in which it combines with the monocle to make Guy "every inch a junker" (p. 129) was an insertion; the reference to it two pages later as ending triumphantly the week in which Guy's spirits rise is inserted and specifically linked to Apthorpe's claims to distinction. The laughter of Tommy and Virginia that causes Guy to reexamine it and find it a ludicrous part of his masquerade as soldier is in the basic manuscript, but the last word about it is given to Apthorpe, in an addition to typescript, when he laments its disappearance because, "It suited you, Crouchback. Suited you very well" (p. 165).

Evelyn Waugh, Writer

Having dispensed with the outward military appearance, Guy begins to show promise as a soldier under Ritchie-Hook's new regime, whereas "Apthorpe's fine show of technical vocabulary fell flat" (p. 173), and henceforward Guy is never again mistaken for or, with one exception— the disappearance of both "Uncles" from the regiment—even linked with Apthorpe. Thus detached, Guy is not only able to savor the thunder-box campaign but to attend to the reality from which Apthorpe is increasingly and, with the destruction of the box, permanently distracted. One unfunny thing in the novel is the war, and to the original references to its progress Waugh made several important additions. To the description of the ornate ritual of the Halberdier guest night he either added or moved from an unlikely position the following passage:

> It all seemed a long way from Tony's (experiences) /excursions/ in no-man's-land, further still, immeasurably far, from the frontier of Christendom /where the great battle (was being) //had been// fought and lost; from/ those secret forests where the trains were, even then (rolling east and west day) /while (they sat bemused)/ the [illegible] Halberdiers and their guests sat bemused by wine and harmony, rolling east and west with their /doomed/ loads (of prisoners). [pp. 87–88; manuscript changes are indicated.]

This corresponds to the later passage in which Guy and the general public are shown "quite indifferent to [MS, oblivious of] those trains of locked vans still rolling East and West from Poland and the Baltic, that were to roll on year after year (with their ghastly) /bearing their innocent/ loads to ghastly unknown destinations" (p. 155). Both clearly anticipate the Jewish refugees of *Unconditional Surrender,* and perhaps Waugh substituted "doomed" for "of prisoners" in the earlier passage to make it applicable to others besides military prisoners and "innocent" for "ghastly" in the second to place the situation firmly in the moral realm.

Other major revisions expanded the frame of reference at even greater length. Some time after completing the manuscript, though he inserted corrections to it by means of penciled notes, Waugh reconsidered what is now Book 2, Chapter 8, and expanded the originally casual reference to the simultaneous elevation of Apthorpe to captain—"with effect from April 1st"—and Winston Churchill to Prime Minister. As I remarked earlier, the manuscript is more than ordinarily confused—Waugh may, most uncharacteristically, have thrown away an earlier draft—but it does indicate that the response to the new Prime Minister, Guy's unflattering description of him, Major Erskine's declaration that he "is about the only man who may save us from losing this war" (pp. 222–23), and Guy's reflection on the grim reports from Norway were all introduced at a later stage of composition. This final

254

passage was in manuscript followed by one beginning "But in recent weeks a malaise quite unrelated to national disasters, had been creeping over the camp," exposing the incompetence of the Halberdiers, an unwelcome subject from which Apthorpe's eccentricities provide distraction. This passage was canceled before publication, probably to emphasize the contrast between military disaster abroad and local foolery about "The Captain's Salutation," and thus accords with the contrast inserted at typescript stage between Apthorpe's destroying the boot and the Brigadier's conclusion that the Allied armies will need boots with which to flee the enemy (pp. 231–33).

This contrast between private idiosyncrasy and public responsibility at first moves Guy to identify with Ritchie-Hook, but Waugh indicated clearly in the senior officer's first appearance that he represented a good not simply indifferent but actively hostile to the Catholic church, for he advocates football scores instead of religion as consolation for a dying soldier and asserts that Catholic chaplains "kill hundreds just with fright" (p. 81). But in *Men at Arms*, Guy's patriotism is stronger than his Catholicism, and he fails or refuses to see possible conflicts between their claims. To emphasize the conflict and to imply that the Halberdiers represent a lesser good, Waugh made two major kinds of revision, one local, at least on the surface, and one more obviously structural.

The first occurs in Book 2, Chapter 7. Originally Guy's meditations on the Army Training Memorandum began with the question, "What are we fighting for?" and the simple answer, "To ensure the independence of Poland," which has ceased to exist. Then, in an over-page insertion, Waugh expanded Guy's consideration of the definition of a just war, an outline of Hitler's growing enormities, which "confirmed the enmity of the world," and the "comforting development for the Halberdiers" that the fall of Norway assured them that "a whole new coastline was (ready) /open/ for biffing." Waugh reorganized this chapter to secure greater emphasis, as I pointed out earlier, but he also expanded this section for the book version. After condemning Hitler to the world's enmity, Waugh added

and the punishment of God.

Guy thought of this as he lay in his hut that night. He clasped Gervase's medal as he said his night prayers. Then came a personal, comforting thought. However inconvenient for the Scandinavians to have Germans there, it was very nice for the Halberdiers. [p. 220]

Then comes the sentence about a new coastline, in effect a new playground for Ritchie-Hook and his men.

Waugh's second way of contrasting the Halberdiers and the church was to insert recurring parallels between the course of training and the liturgical year. Originally the Brigadier's rebuke and dispersal of the training cadre fell on the Feast of Saint Valentine, for whom Guy has particular reverence. Guy's conversation with Mr. Goodall comes two days later (p. 146), and in an insertion is dated by news of the boarding of the *Altmark*, a German ship carrying British prisoners, made in fact on February 17. Guy's meeting with Virginia falls in manuscript on an unspecified day in which the newspapers are full of the atrocities on the *Altmark*,[19] and the climax of the thunder-box campaign comes at the unspecified day of the end of the course. The account was chronologically correct but thematically inert. In revision Waugh inserted every reference to the season of Lent found in *Men at Arms*, all the way from the Brig's outburst on Ash Wednesday to the end of the course at Easter and to the vigil of Mr. Crouchback and Guy before the Altar of Repose that counterpoints the addition of Guy's name to the Most Secret Index in the Good Friday dawn. Apthorpe's disaster probably takes place on Holy Thursday morning, and Saint Valentine's Day is used not for the Brigadier's rebuke but, more appropriately, for Guy's humiliating attempt to seduce Virginia. Most of this is chronologically impossible—Ash Wednesday, 1940, fell on February 6; Guy's conversation with Goodall would have to fall on February 8, his assignation with Virginia on the tenth, his return to duty on the eleventh, and the end of his leave on the thirteenth— the day before Valentine's Day and four days before news of the *Altmark* was released. The shade of C.R.M.F. Cruttwell, Waugh's history tutor at Oxford, may well have exulted. Thematically, however, the revisions establish a counterpoint between sacred and secular and remind the reader, if not Guy, of the existence of a level beyond the comic hubris of Apthorpe, the pious legalism of Goodall that leads to Guy's licit but inhuman attempt at seduction, and even beyond the exuberant adventurism of Ritchie-Hook. Easter passes uncelebrated in the novel, however; Resurrection and renewal cannot take place.

Disaster and disgrace can, not only in the series of defeats inflicted on the Allied armies but also in Guy's personal world. Ritchie-Hook's lack of discipline as a soldier and Apthorpe's lack of temperance remain constant, but Waugh takes care to isolate Guy as victim of the first and to exculpate him as occasion of the second. In manuscript Colonel Tickeridge, like Guy, has been demoted and is in trouble because of the Brigadier's unauthorized expedition on the beach at Dakar, and both officers are taken off duty to attend an inquiry, giving Guy at least some company. In the novel, of course, Guy is alone in his trouble. Even in manuscript he had been alone in disgrace as cause of Apthorpe's death. There Guy acted on his own initiative, but later Waugh

19. See the *Times*, February 19, 1940, pp. 6–8, 10, for an account of the raid on the *Altmark*. Briefly, H.M.S. *Cossack* invaded (neutral) Norwegian territorial waters to free 299 British prisoners captured by the *Graf Spee*.

inserted the Brigade Major's suggestion that Guy take the bottle because "it's always done" and removed the Major's promise, made in manuscript, to speak to Tickeridge on Guy's behalf. At the end of the novel, therefore, Guy is cast out of the Halberdiers, as "deprived of the loyalties which should have sustained him" (p. 5) as he had been at the beginning. Like his creator in late 1940, he is emotionally detached from his unit, ready for a new stage in his adventures that will carry him beyond regimental pietas to a more complex and more bewildering system of private loyalties.

13

Officers and Gentlemen:
A Sense of Discovery

Having seen *Men at Arms* through the press, Waugh seemed confident that he had not lost the threads of his story. On April 19, 1952, probably having disposed of proof that had been ready for him by March 26, he announced to Peters his intention to "toil away at the war saga" instead of writing a proposed life of Saint Thomas More. Despite various interruptions characteristic of this period of his life—work with Carol Reed on a filmscript, apparently aborted; a campaign, involving letters, articles, and speeches, against Marshal Tito's visit to England; tidying up *The Holy Places* for the press and rewriting *Love Among the Ruins;* [1] traveling to Goa at year's end to escape the English winter—he resumed his task without apparent change of plan. According to his note at the end of the first edition, he actually began writing in February, 1953; judging from his diary, it was probably late in the month, since before March 4 he had already written the "first pages of novel. Very good too. White's in an air raid."[2] By November the BBC had broadcast the passage in which Tommy Blackhouse and Guy dine with Mugg, and shortly therafter Waugh had sent Peters about 25,000 words, perhaps through the plans to bring Jumbo Trotter to the Isle of Mugg.[3]

About this point the writing temporarily ceased. Waugh admitted to John Montgomery that he had missed deadlines of November 1, 1953, and January 1, 1954, and could not even predict a date for completion.[4] To John Lehmann he wrote from Cairo that he had been ill but that he hoped to complete the novel by summer.[5] The illness, of course, was the Pinfoldism de-

---

1. See my "Shaping a World: The Textual History of *Love Among the Ruins,"* *Analytical & Enumerative Bibliography* 1 (Spring, 1977):137–54.

2. Evelyn Waugh, *The Diaries of Evelyn Waugh,* ed. Michael Davie (Boston: Little, Brown and Co., 1977), p. 716. Dated March 16, but Waugh is writing about late February or early March.

3. Evelyn Waugh, *Officers and Gentlemen* (London: Chapman and Hall, 1955), p. 89. Hereafter references to this edition are given parenthetically in the text.

4. Letter to John Montgomery, January 11, 1954.

5. Letter to John Lehmann, February 9, 1954. *The Letters of Evelyn Waugh,* ed. Mark Amory (New Haven and New York: Ticknor & Fields, 1980), p. 419.

scribed in *The Ordeal of Gilbert Pinfold.* As the discussion of *Pinfold* will show, fictional and biographical chronology do not coincide, and in fact Waugh did not interrupt work on the novel in progress, as Pinfold was to do, to write the account of his delusions. Like Pinfold, however, Waugh apparently had his goal firmly in mind. Even as he fled England, he refused permission to include "Compassion" in *Tactical Exercise*, first because "this may well form part of Vol III *Men at Arms*" and a bit later because it "will appear in Vol. III"[6]

By late June, Waugh was pleased to report to Peters that "the novel is in a constant state of activity and grows in length."[7] By mid-October, Peters had seen enough of "Happy Warriors"—the title throughout the manuscript and perhaps the typescript stage—to worry about a possible libel suit from the model for Major Hound. Waugh had finished the manuscript by November 4, but since he told Peters that it was "shorter" but "rather better"[8] than *Men at Arms*—which in fact was some twenty pages shorter than *Officers and Gentlemen* in the same format—he obviously added material, perhaps before delivering typescript to Chapman and Hall three weeks later, perhaps in correcting the galley proofs in mid-January, 1955, or page proofs by the end of March, when he commented to Peters, "I must say it reads easily."[9] The new title, *Officers and Gentleman,* was apparently suggested by Little, Brown, but Waugh offered, at least to Peters, no resistance to the change.

The title was suitably ironic. Guy finds renewed purpose in the Commandos, where his superior officer is Tommy Blackhouse, another former husband of Virginia, and in the idealized figure of Ivor Claire, dandy and horseman. With the disappearance of the low Trimmer—who becomes Virginia's lover and is fabricated into a hero for the press—the Commandos seem to represent the flower of English chivalry. In the Middle East, however, discipline and morale degenerate, and the force lands in Crete only to participate in the shambles of the retreat. During the retreat a regular officer, Major Hound, collapses into gibbering cowardice, and Ivor Claire deserts his men in the face of direct orders. Guy, who knows of Ivor's desertion, is sent back to England to prevent possible disclosure of the facts. The book ends with the disillusioned Guy participating in the complex and circumstantially ironic piling-arms ritual at Halberdier headquarters.

As usual, the book read easily because Waugh had done a good deal of revising and rethinking not only to secure euphony and coherence but also to

6. Letters to A. D. Peters, January 17, January 26, 1954.
7. Letter to Peters, June 24, 1954.
8. Letter to Peters, November 4, 1954.
9. Letter to Peters, March 29, 1955.

clarify the thematic implications of the characters. His augmentation of Trimmer's role in *Men at Arms* indicated that he was to reappear, and Waugh very probably foresaw that he would become Virginia's lover. However—and this is the most interesting feature of the manuscript of *Officers and Gentlemen*—Waugh had only a general plan; the nuances and even some of the major motives of the characters he discovered only in the process of composition and revision.

One of Waugh's happier inventions was Colonel "Jumbo" Trotter, benign, placid, irresistible weaver of red tape. On the level of pure plot, Jumbo is used to enable Guy to move the enormous burden of Apthorpe's gear from Southsand to London and thence to the the coast of Scotland opposite the Isle of Mugg, where Chatty Corner accepts it, and to rout Grigshaw, the former sergeant who as quartering officer threatens to disturb Mr. Crouchback and his fellow guests at Matchett. On the mythic level, as F. J. Stopp has noted, he is the wise old man, the fairy godfather who by virtue of superior knowledge enables the hero to realize his desires.[10] Thematically he is used to effect Guy's transition from the custom-bound Halberdiers to the raffish Commandos. Himself a revered member of the Corps, Jumbo is able to move confidently through the jungle of army regulations because he knows not only the rules and exceptions but also the secret of personal appeals to those who enforce the rules. Furthermore, like Apthorpe and other doubles, he presages what Guy might becomes: more than avuncular, vaguely patriotic, and finally indifferent to all but his own comfort.

Trotter's first appearance in the novel, cheating at solitary billiards at Halberdier HQ, is probably a very late insertion, for the inserted page, uncorrected, is identical with pages 16 and 17 of the novel. It established Jumbo as both comic and sympathetic. As orginally conceived, Trotter (in second draft Baldy, probably in a revision of third draft Jumbo), was neither, being merely a convenience of the plot:

> Colonel Trotter, (gazetted (1911) /1909 [?]/ two DSOs 1914-18) [W's parentheses] had established himself in the Halberdier Barracks within an hour of the declaration of war, (He h) No one had summoned him. No one had any use for him. /No one had dared question his presence./ His age & rank rendered him valueless for barrack duties. (His) /He had found/ life from 1920 to 1939 (had been) tedious. He (had) /now/ settled into the Barracks as into a club and spent his days reading the newspapers and playing billiards. The only parade he attended was Church Parade. Now & then

10. Frederick J. Stopp, *Evelyn Waugh: Portrait of an Artist* (Boston: Little, Brown and Co., 1958), p. 169. The idea is Stopp's; the vocabulary is closer to Joseph Campbell's in *The Hero with a Thousand Faces.*

he expressed a wish to 'have a go at the Gerries.' Very often he complained of the cooking. Everyone would feel the easier for a day or two without Colonel Trotter.

Guy had left 'The Marine Hotel, Matchett,' as his address while on leave. Accordingly it was there, accompanied by an ancient servant with three ponderous leather suitcases, that the Colonel repaired bearing /buttoned in an inner pocket the/ (a) heavily sealed envelope (for Guy) marked 'Most Secret.' The contents had not been revealed to (the) him. He rather supposed they comprized the plan for the invasion of Germany.

Waugh then shifted the scene to Guy, forlorn and encumbered at Southsand, but broke off halfway down the page and canceled everything from the beginning of the passage quoted. In a second draft, also canceled, Trotter is made so agreeable that, in a passage anticipating the second paragraph of page 34, the Captain-Commandant agrees to give him an outing. Having established his character as a pleasant potterer, Waugh began to see comic possibilities in Jumbo's ponderous and inexorable movement, in which he accumulates more and more objects. A revised draft that antedates the text of pages 34 and 35 adds a car to his servant and luggage, and the final draft celebrates his elaborate and leisurely departure with the only copy of the *Times*, whose death notices he scans "before giving the order to move" (p. 35).

One object in his path is Guy, and Waugh went through a similar process of expanding on his situation. At first he showed Guy already in Southsand, having secured Apthorpe's gear in two brief sentences. Then, in two successively longer drafts, Waugh presented both the process and Guy's situation in Southsand in more and more detail, but the real exfoliation occurs when Jumbo confronts Apthorpe's gear. A typescript draft began modestly:

'Got much stuff with you?'

'A great deal.'

('I'll send my man to have) /Lets have a/ look of it.'

('I'm afraid it weighs two tons) /over a ton/, sir.'

'Ah, then we'll need a lorry. I wonder where the nearest RASC depot is' (paragraph symbol deleted) I won't ask what you've got. Something pretty important I've no doubt. Otherwise they wouldn't be sending me to fetch you like this. We'll fix everything up tomorrow.'

And fix it Jumbo did, with great simplicity. They were in London next day in time for luncheon at 'the Senior.' There Jumbo settled down in an arm chair.

'I've told the men to stand by until we know our next move. Come back here when you've had your interview.'

A second draft added a parking place for the lorry, getting to London and through lunch in three lines of manuscript. Waugh may have remembered his self-criticism a decade earlier that he tried to make everything happen at once on one page. At any rate he took second thought and elaborated some ten lines into the three pages of *Officers and Gentlemen* (pp. 48–51). In doing so, he not only added two characters, the off-stage transport officer and "Beano," the Major General who secures a parking place for the lorry, but the struggle for lunch in which Guy loses a chicken leg to a Rear Admiral. In the process Waugh characterized the offhanded self-centeredness of senior officers and instead of merely cataloguing Apthorpe's gear, elevated it to epic, indeed mythic, proportions in a passage that begins as a simple estimate of weight:

'Have you much luggage?'
'About a ton, sir.'
'Have you, by God? Let's have a look at it.'
Together they visited the baggage store and stood in silence before the heap of steel trunks, leather cases, brass-bound chests, shapeless canvas sacks, buffalo-hide bags. Jumbo was visibly awed. He himself believed in ample provision for the emergencies of travel. Here was something quite beyond his ambition. [p. 48]

All of this leads to the punch line of Waugh's joke, where, asked if he has a batman, Guy replies, "At the moment . . . I have a service car, a three-ton lorry, and RASC driver, a Halberdier servant and a full Colonel" (p. 52). The reply, in what Stephen Potter termed a "plonking tone," is even funnier: "Ah . . . you ought to be all right then." All but the full Colonel disappear during the course of the novel: the gear is delivered to Corner; the lorry is abandoned because of Tommy Blackhouse's professional instinct against overreaching. But Jumbo, besides being what Tommy will at best become, is the ideal embodiment of his hopes for "an elderly fellow who knows all the ropes and can get round the staff [MS, Generals]" (p. 89), and he joins X Commando as the competent if somewhat bemused adjutant. Special units may be formed and dispersed, but the army way endures.

But if Jumbo and Tommy represent what is most stable, professional, and in the broad sense humane in military life, two contrasting figures, "Chatty" Corner, or Kong, and Dr. Glendenning-Rees foreshadow disasters that will overtake the Commando. Kong the jungle expert is sent by caprice of higher echelons to teach mountain climbing, and not unnaturally there are a number of accidents, culminating in Tommy's causally unrelated but thematically linked fall, which takes him out of the Cretan action and leaves Major Hound in de facto command. Glendenning-Rees, the expert in emergency rations, not only furnishes the pretext for leaving Trimmer behind but, borne home in disgrace on a hurdle by the starving sappers he led into the wilderness on a demonstration, foreshadows the scenes of hungry and demoralized troops on Crete. Glendenning-Rees is certainly an afterthought; the first scene is an insertion; the longest sequence may be.[11] The first prepared for his entrance and in the process established the Commando as the natural object of attention from wandering cranks and frauds.

Chatty, alias Kong, presents a different case. Waugh established him carefully in *Men at Arms* as part of Apthorpe's claim to authentic knowledge of "the real Africa" and undoubtedly foresaw that Corner would deflate this claim. But Corner also serves as a reminder of Guy's happy adolescence in repeated references, the first inserted after manuscript (p. 18), to the Guest Night on which Guy injured his knee. Having received his legacy and helped lay Apthorpe's ghost, Kong had served his function, and Waugh canceled in manuscript a passage in which he is to be loosed on the Highlanders under Trimmer's command and omitted from the book another in which the commandos plan to kill him by drowning or explosives. Either action would have given him too large a role for Waugh's design, and he transferred the explosion to Colonel Hector Campbell of Mugg and the experiment on Trimmer and his men to Glendenning-Rees, thus trebling his roster of eccentrics and enabling him to conclude decisively the Apthorpe-Kong theme.

Judging from the greater emphasis on Trimmer in the revision of *Men at Arms,* one can assume that Waugh planned to make him the last in the series of men who supplant Guy as Virginia's lover and the fake hero who gets the medal that Guy deserves. In the course of the novel, however, Trimmer—metamorphosed into McTavish or "Son of David"—is more than a parody of Guy, for he reenacts not only Guy's desire to possess Virginia physically but also his dream, no less adolescent, of attaining military glory. Because Trimmer is surrogate and scapegoat on whom Guy's unworthy if traditional English desires are loaded, Waugh reconsidered several aspects of his character to make him less obviously unattractive and to emphasize that he is less predator on than victim of the establishment precisely because he aspires to its fringes.

In manuscript, for example, Trimmer is dishonest about money, pocketing the pay due his men, whereas in revision he has enough money because "he was not admitted to the [commandos'] gambling sessions at the hotel" (p. 90). The minor dishonesty of not signing for the drinks is made to seem not merely impudent but an attempt to edge into the society that excludes him. On the

---

11. The number 103 does not occur in the manuscript; pp. 119–23, though unnumbered, are written in the same kind of ink and on the same kind of paper as the preceding page and a half and the following pages. The lack of numbering, however, is puzzling.

other hand, Waugh denied him even lip service to conventional values. Originally, in a passage canceled in manuscript, Trimmer's motive for volunteering was ostensibly patriotic: "Our finest hour, and all that. We all had that spirit, I think, after Dunkirk." Only then does he admit that he "was rather at a loose end" (p. 64), in clear text his only motive.

Trimmer's essential aimlessness also characterizes his relationship with Virginia. Perhaps Waugh already knew that in the final volume of the trilogy she would be converted and perhaps redeemed, though not essentially changed. He was clearly aware that she would cast off Trimmer emotionally if not physically. Therefore, he took great pains to adjust the tone of their relationship, and in the process Trimmer becomes less loathsome than pathetic, another victim of the 1920s version of *la belle dame sans merci.* In Trimmer's first encounter with Virginia at the station hotel in Glasgow, Waugh revised to make her seem more pathetic and defenseless that she was in first manuscript. Thus the phrase about Virginia's "infinitely faint mist of shabbiness" is deleted, to be replaced by images from her surroundings that become an objective correlative of her situation: "the empty tank which had lately been lit up and brilliant with angel fish [changed from the commoner and less suggestive "goldfish"] the white cordings on the crimson draperies, now a little grimy, [MS, shabby] the white plaster sea-horses, less gay than heretofore" (p. 93). Originally Trimmer was less opportunistic: to Virginia's lament that her latest lover, like so many others, has disappeared without giving a destination, he is first made to brag that he too is "in something pretty hush-hush," but Waugh realized that Trimmer the lover, not the warrior, should respond, and he changes the speech to "I'm here for a week. I hope I shall be seeing something of you." This must have seemed too gentlemanly, for the novel's text captures the right note of impudence: "You've got me for a week if you're staying on" (p. 95).

Virginia is not entirely pathetic, of course; Waugh changed the circumstances of her deflowering from the manuscript's "a sordid little episode after a country ball" by one of her mother's friends to the text's "her seduction by a friend of her father's, who had looked her up, looked her over, taken her out, taken her in, from her finishing-school in Paris" (p. 97), more stylish if not more elevated. Furthermore, he changed the circumstances of her farewell scene with Trimmer to remove any traces of self-pity. In manuscript, alarmed by an encounter with the second-in-command of his battalion, Trimmer returns to the hotel room and prepares to depart, explaining only:

'I'm sorry, it's off.'
'Gustave!'
'Recalled for immediate service, my dear. I can't explain. War on, you know.'

'Oh God!' she said. 'Another of them.'
Slowly she took off her dressing-gown and returned to bed.
['Got enough for the hotel bill?'
'I suppose so.'
'Here's ten pounds.'
'Thanks. Leave (them) /it/ there.' Then she began to laugh.
'Just like a tart,' she said. 'Money on the dressing-table.']
'Aren't you coming to see me off?'
'Not on your life, Trimmer.'
'What are you going to do?'
'I'll be all right. I'm going to sleep again. Goodbye.' [p. 101]

Officers and Gentlemen, by omitting the passage enclosed in brackets, emphasizes Virginia's basic indifference to Trimmer and perhaps to all her lovers.

Trimmer is far from indifferent, and Waugh took at least three drafts to establish precisely the quality of his response to Virginia. What seems to be a first draft survives as a cancel on the verso of the third page of Book 2, Chapter 2. After mere mention of the encounter, it reverts to Trimmer's orders to report for active duty, his desire for "a little comforting chaff that evening with *les girls* behind the bar," and concludes with the vision of "a (ghost /mystery/) /stranger of unknown portent/ . . . a creature born of Atlantic spray and Tyneside fog; /something long desired, (fondly //long//) //often// imagined,/ something (with) which Trimmer did not feel up to (coping at all) that evening." A second canceled draft,[12] on the verso of the chapter's fourth page, placed Trimmer's vision of Virginia immediately after the encounter, then reverted to the call from HOOHQ and set up a transition to his meeting with General Whale. Here Virginia is "a vision of unknown portent, a creature from far elsewhere, from Atlantic spray and Tyneside fog, something long desired, often imagined; something that Trimmer did not feel up to, that evening of all evenings." The call from HOOHQ has become "the slow tortoise of War," changed from "slow mechanism," and rather than a "nasty shock" the news became "a cold wind [that] had blown through his Arcadia."

The tortoise image survives in final draft; the rest has been suppressed. Virginia's association with "Atlantic spray and Tyneside fog" undoubtedly stemmed from Waugh's memory of her welcome of Trimmer/ Gustave as "the guide providentially sent on a gloomy evening to lead her back to the days of *(dolphins) spray and dolphins,"* the italicized phrase of which was revised

12. The refinement of language is used as evidence for judging the order of successive drafts.

to avoid the rhyme, to strengthen the metrical quality to reflect her self-hypnosis, and to introduce the assonance and the implied sexuality of "wallowing"—as "sun and sea-spray and wallowing dolphins" (p. 98). But this established Virginia as victim of nostalgia; the later image links her to foam-born Aphrodite, and the reference to Arcadia identifies, though loosely, Trimmer as a satyr or at the very least as a shepherd. None of these associations suited Waugh's purpose, and final draft is deliberately prosaic:

> . . . here, at his grand climacteric, in this most improbable of places, stood a portent, something beyond daily calculation. For in his empty days he had given much thought to his escapade with Virginia in Glasgow. So far as such a conception was feasible to Trimmer, she was a hallowed memory. He wished now Virginia were alone. He wished he were wearing his kilt. This was not the lovers' meeting he had sometimes adumbrated at his journey's end.
>
> On this moment of silence and uncertainty Virginia struck swiftly with a long, cool and cautionary glance.
>
> 'Good evening, Trimmer,' she said. [p. 178]

Here Trimmer is confused rather than awed; "escapade" and "hallowed memory" strike the properly banal note; the wish for the kilt, an insertion in final manuscript draft, reminds the reader of Trimmer's protean impostures; and the buried reference to *Twelfth Night,* itself a cliché, is perhaps intended to call to mind its context, the song "O mistress mine, where are you roaming," and its audience, Sir Toby Belch and Sir Andrew Aguecheek, the song an ironic reference to Virginia's infidelities, the audience more fit company for Trimmer than nymphs and satyrs. And, of course, lowering the context makes much more logical the transition to the offhand dialogue that follows.

But Trimmer is in love or at least in thrall, and Waugh consistently revised to reveal his condition more clearly. For example, though Trimmer realized in first draft that his farewell letter to Virginia, "not so much as he had seen her, but rather as she had seemed to see him" (p. 189), would not do, he thought it "a good letter, too good to waste. It would keep for future use." This might have been characteristic of Trimmer before Glasgow, but to the Trimmer altered by what passes for love, tearing up the letter, the action substituted in manuscript, is far more appropriate. But Waugh took care to create shifting responses toward Trimmer. On the one hand, he showed that Trimmer's caddishness is ineradicable by substituting for the mild, "I know she cared for me not so long ago," the oafish, "She can't put on this standoffish turn with me" (p. 285). On the other hand, ten pages later he added to the conversation between Ian and Virginia about the affair to make the concluding, capping lines: "'Now the poor beast thinks he's in love,'" and, "'Yes, it's too indecent,'" to remind the reader that Virginia is in part responsible for her fate. The final direct view of Trimmer in the trilogy—though offstage he is Virginia's physical lover for two years because Ian insists that his morale needs bolstering—is on the tube platform, with "a sad little song in his heart" (p. 292).

As a rejected lover, then, Trimmer gains a measure of the reader's sympathy. As publicly successful soldier—his accidental invasion of France corresponds to Guy's "Operation Truslove" at Dakar and to his participation in the Cretan debacle with which Trimmer's exploit is counterpointed—he is not exactly sympathetic, but neither is he condemned. According to Alexander Pope, a cripple is not funny unless he affects to be a dancer. In these terms Trimmer stands excused: he is by no means a soldier, but Ian Kilbannock turns him, a least on paper, into a national hero. In fact, Ian is one of the trilogy's major villains. The Communists who emerge in *Unconditional Surrender* at least have a discipline, however alien and distasteful to Waugh; Grace-Groundling-Marchpole of Intelligence has a paranoid vision of interlocked complicity. Only Ian, peer of the realm and putative friend of Guy Crouchback, betrays all principles of ethics and honor for local, immediate self-interest. In *Men at Arms* he insinuates Air Marshal Beech into Bellamy's; in *Officers and Gentlemen* he fabricates the legend of Trimmer and forces Virginia to resume the unwelcome liaison; in *Unconditional Surrender* he uses the death of Brigadier Ritchie-Hook to convince the Americans that the partisans are a viable fighting force. To emphasize this betrayal, Waugh revised the account of Trimmer's "Operation Popgun" to make clearer his judgment of Ian's cold exploitation of the incident.

In first draft the number and order of incidents are much the same as in final text. Waugh later inserted details about the atmosphere in the submarine (the material between "too many" and "Ian drank," p. 188), as he had earlier about the Halberdier barracks, to specify impressions more explicitly. More important, he consistently revised to exclude Trimmer's point of view, even one shared with Ian, so that Ian is the single, albeit blurry, focus. Still more important, in first draft Ian and Trimmer shared a bottle, and it is difficult to determine where drunkenness ends and simple incompetence begins. In revising some time after the manuscript stage, Waugh decided to expunge this symbol of camaraderie and made a series of changes in which Ian retains the bottle for himself while Trimmer must stumble sober through his ordeal. However, it is hard to determine whether Waugh was motivated by the desire to establish Ian's detachment from Trimmer or to set up more effectively the punch line of the episode, in which Trimmer's susceptibility to the cold becomes the "exemplary coolness" of the official citation for the Military Cross (p. 194). All the references to cold and Ian's private joke itself are inserted in manuscript, and at least according to comic convention alcohol is a specific against the cold.

The other important revision of the episode came at the end. Originally Waugh moved directly from Ian's derisive reference to Cranmer's final speech (p. 197) to his interview with General Whale the following day and then to a version of the citation that ends with McTavish following the operation's timetable and finally to Whale and Ian's dialogue about adding color for the press releases. In revision so late that Waugh did not bother to correct the manuscript, he added the process of Popgun's return and deferential reception; Trimmer's laconic responses, which could pass for heroic modesty; and Ian's query about a medal for himself (pp. 197-98). Then, to underline the irony of Trimmer's elevation, Waugh reordered the rest of the chapter to place first the discussion about understatement for the citation and expansion for the press. Only then does he give the citation, itself preposterously inflated in view of the reader's knowledge of the facts, and the citation itself is reordered to give final emphasis to the joke about coolness. General Whale's complacent, "That ought to do it," which concludes the chapter, emphasizes the cynicism with which the episode is being exploited.

The plan is even more successful in final draft than in manuscript. Origininally Ian informs Whale that the Ministry of Information needs someone like Trimmer "to send round munitions factories and hot up the girls to work harder." In the published version, "Supply, Aircraft Production and the Foreign Office" are competing with M. I. for Trimmer "to boost civilian morale and Anglo-American friendship" (p. 206). This not only extends the effect of Ian's fraud but prepares for Trimmer's later encounter with the American reporters and his journey to America in *Unconditional Surrender.*

Like Trimmer, Ivor Claire has a Military Cross—for his action "at Dunkirk, for shooting three territorials who were trying to swamp his boat" (pp. 63-64), according to Trimmer. Throughout *Officers and Gentlemen,* Claire is apparently the anitithesis of Trimmer, and Waugh revised to sharpen this contrast, to make Claire more attractive to Guy and to the reader, and to prepare for the ultimate disillusion of both. At first called Lord Ledbury, a coronet of the Coldstreams and a steeplechase rider, Ivor is renamed in the manuscript of Book 2 and made a captain of the Blues and a show jumper. The change in avocation is easy to account for, since a steeplechaser is unlikely to fear personal injury, while a show jumper is likely to be calculating as well as precise. The change in names can be explained by the fact that Ivor means "military bowman,"[13] which has attractive connotations for Halberdier Guy Crouchback, while Claire comes from the French for "bright" or "clear";

13. Evelyn Wells, *What to Name the Baby* (Garden City, N.Y.: Doubleday and Co., 1946), pp. 248-49.

the names in conjunction run on *voir clair,* which carries the fruitful ambiguity of "to see clearly" and "to see through."[14] It is also possible that Waugh sought to avoid too close association with the person from whom some of Ledbury-Clair's characteristics were drawn. More important are Waugh's shadings of the character. In the novel's version of the conversation about the Commando, about Kerr's injury, and about Guy's getting his room, Claire is laconic and reserved, but he does, except to Trimmer, stop just short of being rude. In manuscript he was more direct, especially in announcing his delight at Guy's securing a room:

'It's (pleasant) /discouraging/
to reflect how much (good one
can do by being ((offensive))
misanthropic) /sweetness &
light a misanthrope inevitably
spreads/, said Ledbury. 'That
lazy fraud of a doctor wouldn't
have gone /to see Rifleman
Whats-his-name/ but for me. And
come to think of it, it was I got
you your room. I didn't know
you and I know the others so I
naturally didn't want *them* to
have it.'

'I'm glad you beat Bertie and
the rest to that room,' said Claire.
'Of course you can't expect it to
make you popular. But perhaps
you won't be here very long.'
[p. 62]

The revised version better prepares for the subsequent closeness between Guy and Ivor after Ivor has estranged himself from the other officers by using a bus to reach a training objective. Parallel texts show how Waugh blurs Guy's perception of the differences between them while allowing the reader to perceive them:

/As for/ Guy, /he/ had recognized from the first a certain remote kinship with this most dissimilar man, a common aloofness,

/differently manifested—
(Ledbury was?) Ledbury was
//always superior,// often
supercilious/—a common
melancholy sense of humour;
each in his way saw life
subspecie aeternitatis; each
/even deeply/ concealed

differently manifested—a
common melancholy sense of
humour; each in his way saw
life *sub specie aeternitatis.* . . .

14. *Larousse's French–English English–French Dictionary* (New York: Washington Square Press, 1969); see *clair.*

(disparate? a common)
/(somewhat) something of the
same/ sentiment—antiquated
and exalted—for (their) the
cause that had drawn them
together.

Guy's illusion is further emphasized by Waugh's revision of the climactic passage of "Interlude," titled "The Voyage Out" in manuscript, in which he contemplates with affection and pride his fellow Commandos as "The Flower of the Nation." In manuscript, after some revision, Guy thinks of Ledbury as "another pair of boots entirely: /English,/ cynical, curiously ascetic in his dandyism, curiously hopeless," a description which by the final version had become "salty, withdrawn, incorrigible." The second series has much the more favorable connotations and leads more naturally to the judgment, "Ivor Claire, Guy thought, was the fine flower of them all. He was *quintessential England,* the man Hitler had not taken [MS, counted on] into account, *Guy thought*" (p. 147; italics added). The italicized words were added after the manuscript stage and reveal both the depth of Guy's commitment and the subjectivity of his judgment.

Ivor appears for the last time as the British forces are preparing to surrender in Crete. Ordered to surrender with his troops, he questions Guy about orders and about points of honor. The structure and essential nature of the conversation are the same in manuscript and in final text, but Waugh added several passages containing motifs that create important overtones in Ivor's character and help unify the novel. The references to the commanding general's leaving the defeated troops and Napoleon's leaving his army at Moscow, which imply the justification that Ivor will later use to disobey orders, were added in manuscript, but the important motifs of Ivor's experience at Dunkirk—"Not much fuss about priorities there. No inquiries afterwards" (p. 294)—and his lament that his Pekinese will be old when he gets out of prison camp were added at a later stage. The first recalls Trimmer's story about the medal he won by preserving himself at others' cost, an action he is about to repeat. The second concludes a series of four references to the dog Freda, two (pp. 138, 295) inserted in typescript or later, and recalls Guy's first glimpse of Ivor reclining "on a sofa, his head enveloped in a turban of lint, his feet shod in narrow velvet slippers embroidered in gold thread with his monogram. He was nursing a white pekinese; beside him stood a glass of white liqueur. . . . The pictorial effect was of a young prince of the Near East in his grand divan in the early years of the century" (pp. 56–57). Throughout every change in fortune Claire is concerned only for the dog (see also p. 105), an extension, perhaps, of his narcissism, like Sebastian's teddy bear in *Brideshead Revisited.*

Though features of Trimmer and Ivor may have been drawn from living models, Waugh seems to have shaped them to support his themes. The case of Corporal-Major Ludovic is different. The manuscript provides evidence that he was probably not part of Waugh's original design for the novel and that, whenever he was conceived, he grew in depth and importance as Waugh revised the manuscript. The process was complicated by the diversity of models upon which Waugh's imagination worked. As finally conceived, he is based loosely upon two noncommissioned officers with whom Waugh served. After he returned from Crete, he discovered that the sergeant in charge of the liaison section who became Waugh's orderly-room sergeant, in peacetime " 'a commercial artist' employed by Lever the soap boilers," had been keeping, "in great detail," a diary, "written in a horrible style" and "illustrated with drawings and photographs" that "consisted of three elements, a prosaic travel narrative with descriptions of all the trees & birds & ships he saw, running criticism of the officers of the unit, and a selection from every confidential document which had passed through his hands." Unlike Ludovic, the sergeant "was a small, tubby, cheerful fellow . . . exceptionally neat & industrious," who even in Crete was "cheerful & resourceful" before being left behind and taken prisoner.[15]

Ludovic escapes with Guy, of course, and another noncommissioned officer from the intelligence section provided Waugh the information upon which this event was based:

> Pattison took refuge in a m. l. c. with an assorted party of Australians & marines; they set out at dusk with petrol for about fifty miles, some tins of water and a few tins of food. . . . An Australian private soldier took charge of the party all of whom started the voyage in extreme exhaustion. When petrol was exhausted they hoisted a sail made of blankets. They had no map or compass & steered by the sun & their memory of the map. They were nine days at sea and at the last gasp (one man had died and one shot himself) they held a religious service & sang God save the King. An hour later they sighted land.[16]

These memories came together only gradually. Originally and well into the manuscript the mysterious corporal-major was named Connolly in one of Waugh's recurrent baitings of Cyril Connolly. Waugh may have remembered belatedly that he had already used the name in *Men at Arms* for Apthorpe's thunder-box (changing it in manuscript from *Crowden's Chemical Closet*), but on a deeper level Connolly continued to inspire him. As the chapter on

15. Waugh, *Diaries,* pp. 514–15.
16. *Ibid.,* p. 510.

Helena indicates, Waugh had derided Connolly's *The Unquiet Grave* in terms repeated if somewhat softened in his *Tablet* review,[17] including the identification of one persona as a lady novelist. Ludovic is not Connolly any more than his novel *The Death Wish* is *Brideshead Revisited*, but it seems to have been Waugh's memory of Connolly's book that accounts for the fashionable *angst* that pervades Ludovic's *pensées* in final draft. In manuscript, for example, Corporal Major Connolly's first recorded diary entry, an insertion in manuscript, including "both events and pensees," reads: "*After the last war . . . ex-officers sold matches in the Strand. A fat lot I shall buy from them after this one, I don't think.*"[18] This, presumably, is in the style of Waugh's sergeant. Ludovic's corresponding entry has a much more formal and graceful style: "*Man is what he hates. Yesterday I was Blackhouse. Today, I am Crouchback. Tomorrow, merciful heaven, shall I be Hound?*" [p. 159]

As the style became more complex, so did the man. Waugh inserted an earlier reference to Ludovic to prepare for his appearance (p. 104) and expanded another passage to include speculation about his communist politics and the meager facts about his reappearance at the war's beginning (p. 144), and on these occasions and one other (p. 298) Waugh included, after he had finished working with the holograph copy, references to Ludovic's odd, sometimes pink, sometimes colorless eyes to make him seem still more alien and to contrast him with Mrs. Stitch's bright-blue gaze (pp. 140, 144, 158, 214, 298). The most significant passage characterizing Ludovic comes at the end of Chapter 5 of Book 2 (p. 272), and the manuscript shows Waugh suddenly changing the plot line and beginning to see Ludovic's full, ominous significance. After the dialogue in which he outlines to Major Hound his plan to embark under Hound's nominal command and asks whether "we might drop all that" insistence on regulations, Waugh continued, "[white line] Next day as the cruiser sped home Ludovic sat with his note book and pencil," but broke off. Perhaps he remembered the escape of the man from intelligence; perhaps he felt that Hound was getting off too easily; perhaps he realized that the sinister reversal of roles could be exploited further. Whatever the immediate cause, he canceled the line and finished the paragraph and the chapter with Ludovic's shift from "plummy" [MS, professional] to "plebian" [MS, private] and his injunction "to shut your bloody trap." After the manuscript stage, to emphasize the consequences of this reversal, Waugh added this conclusive sentence: "Suddenly, for no human reason, a great colony of bats came to life in the vault of the cave, wheeled about, squeaking in the smoke

17. Evelyn Waugh, "A Pilot All at Sea," *Tablet* 181 (November 10, 1945), pp. 225–26.

18. An over-page insert of a revised draft on the preceding page — as the manuscript is now ordered — contains an early version of the entry on p. 207.

of the fire, fluttered and blundered and then settled again, huddled head-down, invisible" (p. 272).

This passage, which moves the relationship beyond army regulations and their breach into the realm of elemental struggle, not only gives Ludovic a new dimension but culminates the collapse of Major Hound. Murdered offstage by or with the connivance of Ludovic,[19] Hound appears no more, but at this point he has already ceased to exist morally and professionally.

In fact, Waugh first conceived Hound solely in professional terms; his existence in moral terms was the result of an inspired afterthought. Originally Hound was nameless, one of a series of Tommy Blackhouse's acquisitions on his way to command of Hookforce. Then, in what appears to be a revision,[20] Hound is given a name and even more background—missing active service in Palestine because he attended Staff College—than in the final text. Moreover, in manuscript he finds the commandos puzzling rather than distasteful; Waugh increased his hostility, probably to strenghten the reader's dislike of the rule-bound precisian. The same motive may account for the insertion, after Waugh had moved beyond holograph stage, of Guy's casual report to Hound about the enemy agent (p. 174) and the change of the duty troop that confronts the commander-in-chief from the trained B Commando to the anarchic Catalans. The second revision causes Hound's immediate discomfiture; the first prepares for a mild rebuke from Tommy because he took no action since "it was not an official report" (p. 186). Waugh underlined the commandos' attitude toward Hound by changing the reason he does not come to dinner from a desire to sleep to, "It did not occur to [Guy and Tommy] to ask Major Hound to join them" (p. 216).

Hound's stuffiness and general unsuitability are further emphasized in a series of revisions and insertions in manuscript. When told that Colonel Prentice is dead, Hound is first described as unfamiliar with the idea of sudden death, then as one who might be "speaking of an aunt whom he believed to be in good health," and finally, in supreme fussiness and with faultless rhythm, as reacting "crossly as though officiously informed of the demise of an aunt who, he had every reason to suppose, was in good health" (p. 224). A bit later, having established headquarters, he is satisfied with himself. Originally his mood is presented directly: "Everything was in order, Major Hound believed. Whatever strange events were occurring round him Hook-

19. Evelyn Waugh, "Synopsis," *Unconditional Surrender* (London: Chapman and Hall, 1961), p. 3.

20. The page, two-thirds of a normal foolscap sheet, is numbered 1*b*, normally a way by which Waugh indicated later addition. The preceding page ends "collect a submarine," so that the last two paragraphs on p. 155 and the first two of p. 156, portraying Guy and Hookforce's situation, are not in the manuscript.

force was behaving correctly." The irony not only of his security but of his ultimate downfall is emphasized by the metaphor Waugh substituted: "Whatever strange tides were flowing round him, Major Hound floated [p. 231: still kept afloat] like Noah, secure in his own righteousness." His "faith in the magic of official forms," in which "In bumf lay salvation" (p. 268), is underscored by the insertion of these lines, and the passivity that leads to his destruction is more clearly foreshadowed in his encounter with the barbaric Cretan patriarch by Waugh's deletion of his wild pistol shot in favor of " . . . his finger lay damp and limp on the trigger" (p. 267). Other revisions emphasized the moral significance of his nickname, Fido, and his surname: "head" became "muzzle" (p. 250); his shaking Guy becomes "scratching and snuffling at him" (p. 251).

However attractive the canine analogy, Waugh came to regard it as inadequate and moved to create for Hound a moral crisis unique in the novel. A professional soldier, Hound has subscribed de facto to a set of rules that he has mindlessly tried to enforce and then fails to follow. Therefore, Waugh canceled a passage that excused Hound as mere automaton:

> He was not scared, /nor was he a cur/ in the sense of attaching any exaggerated importance to his own safety. He was disordered. He was not a (pugnacious /dangerous/) dog, a mechanism, rather, /devised for the specific, useful purpose of/ the accurate receiving and transmitting of orders. Given correct handling and correct fuel and he would have worked. Now he was out of order. All might have gone on working; whatever injuries were threatened now he was out of order, far from the workshops.

Linked to this in theme if not in textual history is the passage Waugh inserted earlier in the manuscript. The foodless headquarters group is joined by stragglers, who begin to eat. The original manuscript moves directly from "Fido watched" to his question about spare food, his bartering, and his withdrawing from his comrades to eat. No doubt the civilian reader cannot be expected to remember the injunction that "the men under your command come first, second and third. You come nowhere. A Halberdier officer never eats until he has seen the last dinner served" (*Men at Arms*, p. 105). At any rate, Waugh inserted the paragraph that raises the stakes beyond professional conduct:

> He craved. Not Guy nor the ragged, unshaven sergeant, (nor anyone on that fragrant hillside), not Fido himself who was dizzy with hunger & lack of sleep, nor anyone on that fragrant hillside could know that this was the moment of probation. Fido (faced a choice. On one side) /stood at the parting of the way. Behind him/ lay a life of blameless professional

progress; before him (lay the choice between) /the high road of/ duty, honour, /authority/, self-respect (on one hand and) /and the low road of/ sensual appetite (on the other. Fido fell. The false step once taken would require /demand/ a lifetime's expiation. Fido barely gave the matter a thought He fell.) It was the first great (decis) temptation of Fido's life. He fell.

To the manuscript of the chapter's final paragraph Waugh added the phrase "the price of his shame" and the climactic "and his lost soul" further to emphasize Hound's collapse. The phrase about "a lifetime's expiation" may have been deleted because Waugh, in developing the confrontation between Ludovic and Hound, decided that Hound was to have no future.

No other character in the novel faces this kind of moral crisis. Ian Kilbannock, Ivor Claire, and finally Julia Stitch cannot be accused of betraying public codes of morality, one might argue, because they subscribe to none. Like characters in earlier Waugh novels, they are beyond or beneath public codes, and in fact Waugh uses the last two characters and the professional perspective of Tommy Blackhouse to confront Guy once more with the possibility that public codes are irrelevant. Tommy is concerned to advance his own career, protect the reputation of his unit, and prosecute the war, more or less as equal objectives. For example, when X Commando and Headquarters are forced to delay their landing on Crete, Tommy originally signals Prentice of B Commando to put his unit "at the disposal of the garrison commander." To underscore Tommy's professional myopia, Waugh canceled the passage and inserted over page the order to Prentice that "his main job is to keep the brigade intact as a formation" (p. 214).[21] Later Waugh revised heavily to adjust the tone though not the content of Tommy's speech to Guy about Ivor's misconduct, changing "made a Christ Almighty bloody fool of himself" to "put up a mighty poor show," and the inserted, "I shouldn't be keen to serve with him a second time," to the consciously superior, "You won't find me applying for him a second time"; and, "There's nothing anyone could do except court martial him for desertion in the face of the enemy. You can get shot for that," to the legalistic and comfortingly remote, "He might have to stand trial for desertion in the face of the enemy. They shot people for it in the last war" (p. 316). Guy's analysis of Tommy's attitude further emphasizes his professional detachment: his "constant guide" is, first, "never make trouble unless absolutely necessary," in revision "never kick up a stink" and finally made it

---

21. The revision is consistent with the orders two pages later in clear manuscript, corresponding to p. 219 of the printed version.

"never cause trouble except for positive preponderant advantage." Tommy's judgment of Ivor's behavior is first the inserted "a matter of honor not expediency" and then the softer, "Nothing was in danger save one man's reputation."

Julia Stitch's response is even simpler: "An old friend is in trouble. Rally round" (p. 319). But her rallying is less in ordinary human terms than in the unaccountable fashion of a Greek goddess protecting a favorite hero, and Waugh revised consistently to elevate if not apotheosize her. He began preparing for her entrance when he revised *Men at Arms* by inserting the cow in the underground stable that is to serve as the password by which Julia recognizes Guy. His memory of the incident was inserted sometime after manuscript (*Officers and Gentlemen*, pp. 124-25). In addition, Waugh revised to clarify or expand the allusive aura that surrounds her. He changed the name of her yacht from *Nimbus* to *Cleopatra,* perhaps because direct reference to an aura prepares less effectively than its substitute for her emergence in Egypt as fascinating and capricious. Waugh revised the direct description of "her great blue eyes" to the allusion to Saint Mary Magdalen in "her eyes, her true [this inserted after MS] blue, portable and compendious oceans" (p. 166), and to typescript he added the final line devoted to her in the novel: "Her eyes were one immense sea, full of flying galleys," a paraphrase, as Stopp has noted, of Hérédia's sonnet on Cleopatra.[22]

Waugh also took considerable pains in shading the tone of Julia's conversation with Guy about Ivor. The order she invents to account for Ivor's departure from Crete was changed from "all fighting troops were to take priority" to "for Hookforce to embark immediately," and Waugh inserted the simile "as though at repetition in the schoolroom" to emphasize the falsity of the line (p. 314). Her disquieted evasiveness is much clearer in response to Guy's question about X Commando escaping—"I don't think there were actually any of the others" (p. 312)—than in the original, "I think Ivor was the only one of them," and Guy's inserted question, "What was Ivor doing?" makes the story sound even thinner.

Guy's bewilderment and growing resistance to Julia's leading questions are shown more clearly in the progression introduced in revision:

'I imagine everything was pretty complete chaos.'
'Yes.'
'And everyone too tired and hungry (they don't) /to/ remember anything (clearly).'

22. Stopp, *Evelyn Waugh,* p. 177.

CANCEL	INSERTION
'Yes.'	'More or less everyone.'
'Exactly what I've said all along.'	'No one making much sense.'
'Everyone behaving pretty	'Not many.'
barmily.'	'No one with much reason to
'Some people.'	be proud of themselves.'
	'Not /a great/ many.' [p. 313]

The revised responses, especially the distinction inserted in the last line, lead more logically and by clearer stages to Guy's revelation that he has written orders that make perfectly good sense and demolish Julia's story.

Aware of the fact, Julia arranges Guy's return to England, out of reach of Ritchie-Hook, who, unlike Tommy, would bring Ivor up on charges. Ironically, Guy has decided, as a result of the Anglo-Russian alliance, to destroy the evidence, and to underscore his shift in attitude, Waugh inserted the retrospective passage about Guy's response in *Men at Arms* to "the Russo-German alliance, when a decade of (confusion /chaos/) /shame/ seemed to be (emerging into) /ending in/ light and reason, when the Enemy was plain in view, huge and hateful, all disguise cast off: the modern age in arms" (p. 320). This illusion is ended, and Guy is "back after /less than/ two years' pilgrimage /in a Holy Land of illusion/ in the old ambiguous world, where priests were spies and gallant friends proved traitors (and the whole blundering might of his country) and his country (blundered into disaster and dishonour) /was led blundering into dishonour/" (pp. 321–22).

Julia does not know this, of course, and has Guy transferred. Though devious, this is not criminal, and the manuscript left the matter there, ending with Guy's plea to her to arrange for him to stay in Egypt and her refusal to interfere because doing so would displease her husband. In revising typescript, Waugh added an overt criminal act. Guy gives her, without telling her what it contains, an envelope containing the unknown soldier's identity disk to forward to headquarters. In all three manuscript versions of the added material she notes the address, kisses Guy, and waves the envelope in farewell; the Hérédia allusion concludes the passage. Between typescript and final draft, so late that the addition was not made in the American edition.[23] Waugh decided that implication of criminal activity was not enough and describes her disposing of the envelope.

Mrs. Stitch's intensely personal attitude toward the war is complemented in the Epilogue by Ian Kilbannock's smugness at his promotion, by the

---

23. *Officers and Gentlemen* (Boston: Little, Brown and Co., 1955), p. 330. I am indebted to Joseph Dickens for pointing out this variant.

captain-commandant's recommendation that Guy participate in drill because "people forget everything on active service" (p. 333), and finally by the piling-arms command. The sergeant's repeated, "All right?" does not require an answer, but the narrator supplies it at the novel's end: "All right, Halberdier Colour-Sergeant Oldenshaw. All right" (p. 335). It is not all right, of course; it is even less right than Guy knows.

Waugh may have been anticipating the mood of these final chapters when he wrote that John Betjeman was not a satirist because "Scorn is the essence of satire. Mr. Betjeman is moved sometimes to vexation, most often to sorrow, by the nastiness which all around him, of which he is intensely conscious."[24] At any rate, these chapters create a diminuendo effect that helps justify Waugh's assertion that "these first two books constitute a whole" because "*Men at Arms* began with its hero inspired by illusion. *Officers and Gentlemen* ends with his deflation."[25] Moreover, in the echoes about the Modern Age in arms and the Halberdier ritual, he had given what he knew to be the illusion of unity. Neither the diary nor the Peters files mention Waugh's decision to represent the two volumes as a unit, but in the final stages of production, probably in May, he obviously decided to protect himself against charges of stringing out a supposedly completed tale as well as a relapse into Pinfoldism, a fear obscurely hinted at in, "If I keep my faculties I hope to follow the fortunes of the characters through the whole of the war." Though he kept his faculties, with various degrees of impairment owing to age, ailments, and the effects of sleeping draughts and alcohol, and though in the intervening years he was active as a writer, he was to realize these hopes only six years later.

24. Evelyn Waugh, "Mr. Betjeman's Bouquet," *Sunday Times,* July 11, 1954, p. 5.
25. Dust-jacket flap of *Officers and Gentlemen.*

14

Prerogatives
of the Artist:
The Ordeal Of Gilbert Pinfold

Even before *Officers and Gentlemen* was published, Waugh notified Peters that he had "fully formed in my mind an account of my lunacy,"[1] and after several desultory months enlivened by the annoying visit of an American television crew and a passage at arms with Lord Noel-Buxton and the *Daily Express's* Nancy Spain,[2] Waugh settled at Folkestone to begin what he himself called, in quotation marks, his "novel."[3] Judging from his diaries, he may have worked intermittently on the book, but he had new distractions: finding a house to replace Piers Court, which he left in the autumn of 1956, helping plan his daughter Teresa's debutante ball, and writing what for him was a relatively new kind of journalism: brief memoirs and appreciations of recently deceased elders and contemporaries. Not until September, 1956, did he resume serious work on *The Ordeal of Gilbert Pinfold,* and by mid-October he was well into stride. He had completed two-thirds of the first draft by November 10.[4] Two weeks later he sent Peters a rough manuscript to offer for serial rights and promised "the final shooting script,"[5] with repetitions eliminated and the final polish given, in three weeks. In late January he rewrote the last two pages of the novel.[6]

There are few external incidents in the novel: Pinfold grows feebler; seeks to escape English winter by taking ship for Ceylon; begins to hear voices abusing him and plotting against him; leaves the ship in Egypt and flies to Ceylon; continues to hear the voices; flies home; threatens to expose his tormentors; ceases to hear the voices; and, after telling the story to his wife, sits down to write the title of the novel and of the first chapter.

1. Letter to A. D. Peters, March 29, 1955.
2. See Evelyn Waugh, "Awake My Soul! It is a Lord," *Spectator* 195 (July 8, 1955): 36–37 and subsequent correspondence.
3. Evelyn Waugh, *The Diaries of Evelyn Waugh,* ed. Michael Davie (Boston: Little, Brown and Co., 1977), p. 770 (October 28, 1956).
4. Letter to Peters, November 10, 1956.
5. Letter to Peters, November 24, 1956.
6. To John Montgomery, ca. January 20, 1957.

Waugh's repeated assertion that *Pinfold* was "a confessedly autobiographical novel" [7] is obviously true, but it cannot be accepted without qualification. Both Frances Donaldson and Christopher Sykes testify that the novel differs from the account each heard from the Waughs, and close examination of Waugh's letters and diaries and of the manuscript itself undermines Waugh's claim, implied on the final page of the novel, that he simply sat down and transcribed his experience. Sykes the critic forgets, as he does so often, what Sykes the biographer has recorded, asserting that "in the main plot of *Pinfold* Evelyn seems to have not only drawn heavily on his raw material but to have left it raw."[8] In fact, Waugh retained the prerogatives of the artist not "to leave any experience in the amorphous, haphazard condition in which life presents it; and putting an experience into shape means, for a writer, putting it into communicable form."[9]

The basic experiences that went into *Pinfold* are easily outlined. On September 23, 1953, the BBC recorded Waugh's appearance on "Frankly Speaking" at Piers Court. In January he had two unsettling experiences: his delusion about a nonexistent ornament in the wash-hand stand given him by John Betjeman [10] and the appearance of "Mr. Stopp the Cambridge critic who is going to write my 'life.' " Because the second event is not recorded in *Pinfold,* it has never been thought significant, but it seems likely that the ensuing "Portrait of the Artist in Middle Age" was a response to the outsider's attempt at biography. Late in January, paralyzed by the cold, Waugh took ship for Colombo, Ceylon, on the *Staffordshire.* He returned by air in March. Except for Stopp's visit, all these events occur in *Pinfold.* Waugh did not confine the novel to these experiences, however. He had known Shakespeare very well since his school days, but seeing productions of *Titus Andronicus* in August, 1955, and *Lear* in February, 1956, may have prompted him to allude to them in fact or spirit when he wrote Chapter 3, and it is clear from his diary entry of February 29, 1956, that he is recording a very recent memory of the Box, which in the final version of the novel plays a large part

7. Evelyn Waugh, "Anything Wrong with Priestley?" *Spectator* 199 (September 13, 1957):328–29; a reply to J.B. Priestley, "What Was Wrong with Pinfold," *New Statesman* 54 (August 31, 1957):224.

8. Christopher Sykes, *Evelyn Waugh: A Biography* (Boston: Little, Brown and Co., 1975), p. 367. See also Frances Donaldson, *Evelyn Waugh: Portrait of a County Neighbor* (Philadelphia: Chilton Book Co., 1968), pp. 54–70.

9. *Ninety-two Days* (New York: Farrar & Rinehart, 1934), p. 5.

10. Waugh, *Diaries,* p. 722 (January 2, 1954); *The Ordeal of Gilbert Pinfold* (London: Chapman and Hall, 1957), pp. 20–21. Further references to the novel are given parenthetically in the text.

in Pinfold's paranoid reasonings.[11] Waugh's defective memory of Lord Curzon's tomb, recorded a month later, may have been an echo of an earlier incident; if not, it is further evidence that chronology did not determine the selection of incidents for the book. Furthermore, though Waugh says that Pinfold leaves a manuscript half-finished in order to write about his ordeal, Waugh's composition of *Officers and Gentlemen* was interrupted only by his illness, and he finished it at least three months before announcing his intention to write *Pinfold*.

Waugh would undoubtedly have abhorred the chart given below, but it gives a brief and I hope lucid summary of the sequence of biographical fact and of the incidents and events—to adopt Walter O'Grady's useful distinction between objective, external and subjective, internal elements of narrative[12] —as ordered first in the manuscript and finally in the opening and closing pages of the published novel.

DATE, EVENTS IN WAUGH'S LIFE	MANUSCRIPT	BOOK
9/28/53 BBC Interview	Pinfold's status as writer	Pinfold's status as writer
1/2/54 Illusion about stand	Social and poltical life	Social and political life
February–March, 1954 Trip. Checks on "Mr. Black" at BBC; consults Fr. Phillip Caraman and Dr. Eric Strauss, a psychiatrist	Manservant; boredom	Bruiser and Box
11/4/54 Finishes *Officers*	Roman Catholicism	Roman Catholicism
3/29/55 Mental plan for *Pinfold*	Abhorrence of present	Friendships; Roger Stillingfleet
8/1/55 To Folkestone to write	Pinfold not mild; drill sergeant	Drill sergeant

11. Waugh refers to the box, owned by Diana Oldridge (nicknamed Tanker) in letters to Laura of February 8 and February 12, 1954. *The Letters of Evelyn Waugh*, ed. Mark Amory (New Haven and New York: Ticknor & Fields, 1980), pp. 418, 420. In view of the diary entry, it is possible that Waugh's memory had not ceased to play tricks upon him.

12. Walter O'Grady, "On Plot in Modern Fiction: Hardy, James and Conrad," *Modern Fiction Studies* 11 (Summer 1965): 107–16.

8/18/55 Sees *Titus Andronicus*	Public reputation, hope for libel	Public reputation
2/25/56 Sees *King Lear*	Freedom from angst	Lack of manservant; boredom
2/29/56 Laura and Box	Physical status	Physical status
3/4/56 Lord Curzon's tomb	Insomnia	Insomnia
ca. 11/15/56 First two-thirds of MS is obsolete	Visit to tomb	Mr. Hill
1/20/57 Rewrites last two pages	Mr. Hill	News of suicide
	BBC—Mr. Andrews	Freedom from *angst* (end of Chapter 1)
	Status of novel	Status of novel
	Cold	Progress of winter
	New pills	Wash-hand stand
	Books passage	Christmas
	Insert: missing Mass Bruiser and Box	New pills
	London	Booking passage
	Climbs aboard *Caliban*	London
	End of Chapter 1	To cabin and to bed
	To cabin, bed	End of Chapter 2

In writing the opening chapter, which, as the chart shows, became two chapters after at least one typescript version, Waugh was faced with two related problems: what to reveal about his character—the pun is inevitable—and in what order to reveal it. For once, he did not attempt to conceal his own personality and, in fact, toyed in the second paragraph of the manuscript with the idea of using present tense to gain further autobiographical immediacy. He obviously felt, however, that certain passages needed adjustment to achieve the proper tone. Contrasting Pinfold's Catholicism with the Communist sympathies of his peers, Waugh added, "Unlike them Mr. Pinfold remained steadfast." The novel then turns to the church's attitude toward his art. In manuscript, however, Waugh discoursed at greater length on Pinfold's religion:

...the experiences of each succeeding year confirmed him in his skepticism of all other philosophic systems; he felt an (increasing) /a deepening/

loyalty toward the body which he had joined on very slight acquaintance; more than this he became /from time to time/ increasingly aware of a process operating without conscious effort of his own, drawing him outside himself into a communion which owned a remote (/recognizable/) cousinship to the prayers of the /holy (devout)/. But Mr. Pinfold did not pass as pious. /His trade (was is one that is) by its nature (liable to shock the susceptible) is (open) //liable// to condemnation as, at the best frivolous, at the worst corrupting./

While this may have been true of Waugh himself, it obviously came to seem inappropriate for Pinfold. For one thing, it posits a line of development that Waugh did not intend to pursue—Pinfold is not clearly a better man for his experiences—and for another it gave Pinflod a link with humanity that the rest of the novel takes pains to preclude. In fact, Waugh probably added the passage about ecclesiastical distrust of Pinfold's trade to make the reader regard him at least as much as artist as human being and to prepare for Pinfold's triumphant conversion of experience onto art. Furthermore, the passage about the correctness of Pinfold's views must have seemed unduly polemic, especially when used of a man whosè estrangement from the hierarchy is to be described immediately.

The motive was somewhat different for canceling the following passage:

For there was nothing mild about Mr. Pinfold. /Much of/ the foregoing description is delusive and might fit someone totally unlike him, a diffident, fastidious creature; a (st) tall, stooping person with whispy hair, with a beard, even, a silky colourless beard, a tie-ring and wet, myopic eyes. But Mr. Pinfold was not tall; his manner was (challenging and) dogmatic, his style of appearance rigidly coventional and the eyes with which he surveyed his contemporaries were like those of a drill sergeant inspecting an awkward squad, bulging with wrath that was half-facetious and with half-simulated incredulity; like a drill-sergeant he was at once absurd and formidable.

This passage, itself a revision, embodies two rather elementary faults in characterization: definition by negation and overspecification of detail. Like many other literary characters, Pinfold is given physical embodiment not by the author but by the reader, who develops a conception of the outer shell based on the inner person revealed. In revision Waugh moved directly from the simile of the movie camera to that of the drill sergeant, more effectively preparing for the later image of "a front of pomposity mitigated by indiscretion, that was as bright and antiquated as a cuirass" (p. 9).

Other details about Pinfold's drug taking and allergic reaction to the mixture of alcohol and barbiturates were probably omitted because they were overspecific, but Waugh's motive in deleting the passage describing Pinfold's search through press cuttings in hope of finding grounds for libel suits was more practical than aesthetic. As the novel was nearing publication, Waugh's libel suit against Nancy Spain and the *Daily Express* was decided in his favor, but a further suit was being contested, and even Waugh could see that the manuscript admissions of *Pinfold* would be ill-advised. Accordingly, he sent revisions of the offending pages to A.D. Peters on March 7, 1957.

Manuscript and book diverge in various other details of Pinfold's character, most notably in the inserted detail about frequenting brothels in *Pinfold* (p. 133), but no startling details have been suppressed for publication. Far more interesting to the student of Waugh's art were the pains he took in disposing his materials effectively. As the chart shows, he had particular trouble in doing so in the opening pages.

One source of difficulty was that the introductory pages deal less with events than with habitual states unamenable to chronology and requiring conceptual structures of emphasis. In the original draft Waugh presented first the static aspects of Pinfold's character and then the events—the lapses of memory and the Hill and BBC episodes—that accompanied or revealed its change. Then he moved back to rather static exposition of Pinfold's attitude toward Christmas and the lack of progress of his uncompleted novel before turning to events once again, carrying Pinfold through embarkation on the *Caliban.*

By the time he received a typescript, Waugh had detected flaws in the construction of this long first chapter, and with scissors, paste, and a clearer sense of purpose he sorted it into the two chapters that now begin the book. In manuscript-typescript he was concerned chiefly with the new second chapter, but before publication he had made further additions and adjustments in the first. It now begins and ends on high notes: Pinfold's reputation as a novelist and, salvaged from an unemphatic position in mid-chapter, his freedom from angst. The two external events, which seemed trivial at the time, the affairs of Hill and the BBC, are retained in the first chapter because they have no immediate repercussions and because they do little to disturb Pinfold's drug-induced equanimity, to which they are juxtaposed. Therefore, the canceled title "Portrait of the Artist in Middle Age," now justified, could be retrieved.

Its replacement, "Collapse of Elderly Party," taken from generations of *Punch* cartoons, could be shifted to the new second chapter. Two kinds of revision reflected the process in the title's first word. First, Waugh canceled the static opening at Christmastide. Instead, he began the new chapter with Pinfold in idleness, his novel unfinished, then moved gradually, through the cold of October to the drug-induced allergies of November to the alarming—and internal—events of the tomb and the wash-hand stand to the "dread week" of Christmas, when "he made copious use of wine and narcotics and his inflamed face shone like the florid squireens depicted in the cards that littered the house" (p. 21). Then, in a clear transition, when Pinfold "was gathering himself as it were for a strenuous effort at reformation," he falls prey to aches that call for a new sort of pill, which Pinfold adds "to his bromide and chloral and Crême de Menthe, his wine and brandy, and to a new sleeping-draught which his doctor, ignorant of the existence of his bottle, also supplied." The equanimity of the first chapter is totally dispelled.

Considerations of point of view as well as emphasis seem to have dictated Waugh's revision of the end of the new second chapter and the beginning of the third. The original first chapter had ended as Pinfold "painfully climbed aboard" the *Caliban*. The material that follows on pages 29 to 31 of the novel—telephoning his mother, conversing with the stewards, ordering brandy, and going, "prayerless" (this added in manuscript), to bed—follows what is now the opening paragraph of Chapter 3 (p. 32). In revising, Waugh moved to climactic position in Chapter 2 Pinfold's benumbed, stumbling efforts to telegraph to extend still further the process of his degeneration. Then, at the beginning of Chapter 3, he could begin with an objective description of the ship and follow it with Pinfold's clearer perception of his surroundings, foreshadowing the physical regeneration that accompanies the increasingly complex hallucinations.

With one exception Waugh had little difficulty in dividing the remaining chapters. That exception was the break between Chapters 6 and 7. In manuscript the former carries over the nonclimactic seduction scene with Margaret through the next morning to the voices' mocking commentary on Pinfold's cable and ends with his gratification that his tormentors

> had put themselves outside the law. Immediately after breakfast he would lodge a formal complaint. From then on his life /in the Caliban/ would be (undis) untroubled.
>
> This was not exactly the outcome of his morning's action. He did, however, make a huge advance toward the centre of the mystery.

Chapter Seven The Scientists

'Captain Steerforth, may I speak to you for a moment?'

Between manuscript and final version Waugh significantly altered the emphasis of Chapter 6. As originally titled—"The Gossips"—its conclusion with a new way of invading Pinfold's privacy was suitable. But as previous chapters had demonstrated, Waugh had a lively appreciation for the anticlimactic effect; furthermore, he had begun attaching new and greater significance to Margaret's role. Accordingly, at some stage before publication, he added to Goneril's taunts of Pinfold's impotence the reply, "It was Glover snoring," said Mr. Pinfold, but nobody seemed to hear him" (p. 137), and ended the chapter. He also changed the title to "The Human Touch," partly to signal a return to the direct attack on Pinfold's supposed failings in contrast to the elaborate "International Incident" and partly to signal Margaret's emergence from a subordinate to a major role, a process that continues until she disappears in the last chapter. The new beginning to Chapter 7, Pinfold's resolve to change tables and cabins, is followed by the mockery of his wireless messages. The anticipatory remark at the end of the manuscript of Chapter 6 is transmuted into the new title of Chapter 7: "The Villains Unmasked—But Not Foiled."

The development of Margaret's role is one of the most interesting features of the manuscript and its successors. Waugh seems always to have intended her to be the one sympathetic voice among Pinfold's tormentors, but as Waugh's conception developed, the intimacy grew ever deeper. For example, when Waugh first dealt with Pinfold's attitude toward Margaret after she failed to come to his cabin, Waugh originally wrote:

> Mr. Pinfold could not help liking Margaret. He was sorry to be leaving her. But she /Margaret/ kept bad company—and after the embarrassments of the night (he) /Mr. Pinfold/ would never (feel quite at ease with her) trust her, (but he was sorry to be leaving her so abruptly.)

Almost immediately Waugh canceled the passage for one that left much more problematic the degree of Pinfold's estrangement from her:

> Poor waif, Mr. Pinfold thought, she has kept bad company and been corrupted. After the embarrassments of the night Margaret had forfeited his trust, but he loved her a little and felt it unmannerly to be leaving her flat. [p. 145]

Labeling her a waif—a positive word for Waugh in *A Handful of Dust* and *Scoop*—and thinking of manners is not the act of one who really hopes to sever connections.

Later, during Pinfold's long-distance dialogue with Margaret as he flies from Cairo to Colombo, Waugh inserted on the back of the manuscript page the motive of Margaret and her family for remaining with him permanently: the rest hate him; she loves him (p. 175). As Pinfold returns to London, Margaret attempts to persuade him to tell no one of the voices. Originally her plea went uninterrupted:

> 'Gilbert, you must never tell *anyone,* promise. You can imagine what this means to me. I've so loved being with you.'

By publication Waugh had altered the passage:

'Gilbert, you must never tell *anyone,* promise, especially not Cousin Reggie.'

'And you, Meg,' said Mr. Pinfold in bantering but fond tones, 'are you going to leave me alone too?'

'Oh, Gilbert dearest, it's not a thing to joke about. I've so loved being with you.' [p. 176]

Both passages lead into her plaint that "if my brother switches off it will be a kind of death for me," presaging the revelation that Pinfold himself is the source of the voices and the extinction of them all. Once more Waugh significantly alters the passage. The manuscript was little more than functional:

'It's perfectly true, darling,' said Margaret. 'I'm afraid it's the end of *me*. Goodbye. . . Love . . .' and her voice trailed away into silence.

In revision Waugh not only introduced a stronger note of intimacy in the final image but created, primarily by means of the series at beginning and end, a more effective dying fall to Margaret's exit lines:

'It's perfectly true, darling,' said Margaret. 'I never had a brother or a sister-in-law, no father, no mother, nothing . . . but I do love you, Gilbert. I don't exist but I do love...Goodbye...Love...' and her voice too trailed away, sank to a whisper, a sigh, the rustle of a pillow; then was silent. [p. 186]

In all versions the voices end more suddenly and more dramatically than they did for Waugh, who heard them well into the first night he spent in London.[13]

The longest and perhaps most important augmentation of Margaret's character is linked to a whole web of themes and incidents introduced into the novel at relatively late stages. First in the process of composition was the Bruiser and his Box, which Pinfold comes to believe is the mechanism by which his tormentors are able to communicate with him. Not until page 73 of the eighty-three page manuscript is the Box mentioned in the basic manuscript, which supports the inference that Waugh decided to use the device early in 1956. Whenever he seized upon it, he apparently lost no time in adding, probably to first or subsequent typescript, references that would prepare for it. The first addition makes the Box's owner a Miss Grant-Batchelor—according to Donaldson[14] a real neighbor whose name Waugh invoked to terrify his tormentors—and the second, which records her Sunday visit to

13. Donaldson, *Evelyn Waugh,* p. 60; Sykes, *Evelyn Waugh,* p. 365.
14. Donaldson, *Evelyn Waugh,* p. 65.

Lychpole for the customary glass of sherry, introduces Pinfold's fear that the Bruiser and her Box will interfere with his life waves (p. 25), an extension toward paranoia new in his mental aberrancy that is repeated in his suspicion, added after the manuscript stage, of the young man from the travel agency (p. 26). The Box is prominently featured in the manuscript in Pinfold's first letter to his wife, but the resolution of the plot, "No Box?" just before the voices die was a later addition.

Even later than the Box was Waugh's inspiration about the possibilities for evil of the BBC man who interviews Pinfold at the beginning of the novel. He inserted on the back of that manuscript page the scene in which the suicide of the next interview subject is announced, probably to make the incident more memorable and more threatening to Pinfold, but throughout the manuscript the man's name is the commonplace "Andrews." Between manuscript and novel, of course, Waugh changed it to "Angel." The inspiration may have been occasioned by the insertion, on the back of the manuscript page, of Pinfold's second letter to his wife, in which he wonders "*whether it is not literally the Devil [MS, that is after me] who is molesting me*" (p. 171). If so, the addition, after he had stopped working with the manuscript, of Margaret's accompanying Pinfold to Mass (pp. 173–74) was intended to dispel this notion—she makes the responses and urges Pinfold to pray for her brother and sister-in-law—to demonstrate that the voices were at worst morally neutral and to strengthen still further the intimacy between Margaret and Pinfold, whose ability to pray is an important issue throughout the novel.

Margaret and the Box account for the most pervasive revisions between first draft and published novel, but others, more local, reveal Waugh's concern to fashion a smoothly finished work as well as to emphasize his themes, or, as he wrote to Peters, "to tidy it and polish it into a respectable novelette."[15] Of course, Waugh was aware of these concerns at all stages of composition. On two occasions he inserted dialogue in which Pinfold comments to his fellow passengers about things he thinks he has heard[16] to deepen his sense of isolation and persecution and to give the reader clues that the voices have no objective reality. In other instances Waugh introduced what he had earlier called "the masked buttresses, false domes, superfluous columns . . . all the subterfuges of literary architecture,"[17] as in the passage on the old peer at Bellamy's (based on the wartime behavior of "Ran" Antrim)[18] who kept

15. Letter to Peters, November 24, 1956.
16. These passages deal with the servants' language (p. 42) and with Clutton-Conforth's morbidity (p. 71).
17. Evelyn Waugh, *Work Suspended* (London: Chapman and Hall, 1942), p. 2. This passage does not appear in later printings of the fragment.
18. Waugh, *Diaries*, p. 549 ("Written on 23 Sept.," 1943).

up a running commentary on the fellow members and the family of "bright, cruel girls,"—Mitfords undoubtedly—who stuck out their tongues on the periphery of the guest's vision (pp. 120-22). Besides being funny in themselves, these paired memories give Pinfold a false sense of familiarity and therefore of security with what he thinks is an elaborate practical joke, and in turning away from the mild pathology of the Earl to the practiced malice of the girls Pinfold avoids, as he has done at the end of the "International Incident," the possibility that he is deluded or mad.

This contrast of youth and age may have prompted another series of revisions that significantly augmented the role of the "generals." In the basic manuscript they are at first civilian fathers of the bright young people whose music and threats torment Pinfold. By the time of the international incident they have become colonels. Waugh's imagination continued to work, probably as a result of the nonclimactic seduction scene of Chapter 7 in which the father becomes the stock soldier using, as Waugh later realized, the voice of Lady Chatterley's father,[19] and in correcting typescript he added Pinfold's visualization of two major generals (p. 56). Apparently at some later stage, since no trace of the revision survives in the manuscript, he decided to use them rather than the ship's officers as principals in the plot to hand Pinfold over to the Spaniards. At any rate, the page augmenting their description is misplaced in the bound manuscript, immediately after the conference at which the plan is formulated. Originally the older men were allowed to fulminate against Spanish piracy and to hear the Captain's opinion of Pinfold—far more contemptuous than in the final version (pp. 105-106)— but are not allowed to hear the secret plan. Before publication the role of the other officers had dwindled—their conversation about the Captain's allowing the ship to be wired for the plot against Pinfold[20] was removed, probably because they seemed to resolve Pinfold's doubts about the Captain—and one of the generals is told the Captain's plan. Manuscript and book versions of the plan itself are identical in detail, but the first is far thinner:

'Pinfold is going to be very useful to us. He's going to be pushed into the corvette. I've got all the papers made out. They'll be put into his pocket at the last moment. The Spaniards will think they've got the man they're after and they won't bother (about) us any more after that. It will take them days, weeks probably, to find their mistake. It won't hurt Pinfold to sober up in prison. When they do find out who he is, they'll probably be all over

19. *Ibid.*, p. 777 (March 24, 1961).
20. In the novel these conversations would come at the bottom of p. 85; after the first sentence of the last paragraph, p. 86; and at the end of the antepenultimate paragraph on p. 87.

him—he's a Roman Catholic and a fascist. I believe he's done some spying for them in his time. They'll be quite pleased to see him. Whether they ever let him back to England again, I don't know and I frankly don't care.'

In the novel (pp. 106–108) Waugh took the opportunity to allow the principals to reveal themselves in questions about and elaborations of the plan. Captain Steerforth's animus is converted to professional objectivity about the suitability of Captain Pinfold for the mission and the necessity for keeping it a secret from him. This revision makes more plausible Pinfold's scruples about sabotaging the plan and his decision to participate willingly—a movement, as both versions clearly indicate, away from his isolation.

Perhaps the most interesting revisions serve Waugh's sense of craftsmanship as well as his theme. Both manuscript and novel establish the presence of the dark little man who eats at the separate table that Pinfold covets and finally takes and whom the Captain identifies as the secret agent for whom Pinfold is to be substituted. In manuscript the final reference to the man is the Captain's identification of him as Mr. Murdoch, whose destination, in manuscript alone, is Port Said. Originally Pinfold disembarks at Port Said alone, secures the necessary papers from a variety of sources, and is taken to dinner by a journalist. Some time before publication Waugh obviously found this sequence of events and characters unsatisfactory. Not only was the carefully established double, Murdoch, allowed to drop out of sight, but a set of faceless characters had been introduced. In a series of revisions, Waugh had Murdoch disembark with Pinfold and serve as companion and guide throughout the Egyptian sequence.

In both manuscript and book the voices are silent from the time that Pinfold disembarks until he mentions the name of Simon Dumbleton at the end of Chapter 7. The introduction of Murdoch gives the respite a point beyond coincidence. Pinfold had envied the other's solitude, but only in his company is he temporarily freed from the voices. This unobtrusive companionship contrasts quietly but distinctly with Pinfold's memory of his parachute jump, a rapturous experience in which he "felt himself free of all human communication, /the sole inhabitant of a private, delicious universe/. . ./one with hashish-eaters and Corybantes and Californian gurus, high on the back-stairs of mysticism/."

Except for the two inserted phrases, the parallel passages in *Unconditional Surrender* (pp. 128–29) and in Waugh's diary, in which he describes his first jump as "the keenest pleasure I can remember,"[21] might obscure Waugh's

---

21. Waugh, *Diaries*, p. 556 (December 30, 1943). See also Waugh's comment to Lady Dorothy Lygon: "For one who values privacy there is no keener pleasure than the feeling of isolation as you float down. . . ." *Letters*, p. 181.

ambivalence toward the experience. Pinfold's isolation and inability to communicate are at least symptoms if not actual causes of his problem, and only when he is able to communicate, first by cable, then by letter, and finally by direct disourse, is he able to quell the voices that beset him. Like his public personality, the vision of solitude is a prison.

However, the conclusion of the novel presents not a moral but a professional resolution to Pinfold's ordeal. The first draft was typically perfunctory: the voices, he announces, are

'Gone for good.'

'I think you'd better see a doctor, you know.'

'Certainly not. I've had quite enough psycho-analysis. I say what very odd things I said to myself.'

'Feel like taking the tea-train home?'

Mr. Pinfold was still a little puzzled. 'I must tell you all about it,' he said.

The narrative extended over two days as new [illegible] incidents came to mind.

'You know,' said Mr. Pinfold, 'I very nearly accepted Andrews' offer. If I had, and if the voices had stopped, I should all my life have believed that (he really had his) /the/ infernal box /existed/. I should always have had to fear that someone was listening to me. That the whole thing might start up again at any moment. I consider it was rather (brave) /courageous/ of me to turn the offer down.'

'(Yes, dear, very brave) /Heroic, darling/.'

'And what's more I shouldn't have been able to write a book about it.'

'That would have been a pity,' said Mrs. Pinfold.

The End.

Stinchcombe-Pixton-Chagford. Autumn 1956.

This contains most of the necessary motifs, but only in outline. Waugh's second attempt, added to a typescript, picked up at "Gone for good" and with the over-page addition describing the sharpness of the memories and Pinfold's questions about why the voices' indictment was not blacker, resembles pages 180 to 183. Then, introducing the Bruiser and Pinfold's reluctance to talk about the Box, Waugh elaborated the literary theme:

He (looked at the) took from the drawer the pile of half finished manuscript. That story was still clear in his mind. He knew what had to be done. He would do it in his own good time. Meanwhile there was a more urgent theme; something on his mind; a load of experience which had to be unpacked (repacked, sorted) searched for rubbish, repacked and deposited in its proper place. First things first. While the Bruiser sat across the hall sipping his sherry, Mr. Pinfold took his pen and at the head of a new sheet of foolscap wrote: *'The Ordeal of Gilbert Pinfold "Chapter One":* *Portrait of the artist in middle-age'*

He heard the Bruiser take his leave. He went back to the drawing room. 'I've begun /to/ work again,' he said.

/'The old novel?'

'No, an account of my barminess/ 'It hasn't got very far as yet but I think it ought to amuse a certain number of people. To judge by (the statistics in the papers jolly) /what the papers say very/ nearly half the inhabitants of the (co) kingdom are more or less barmy at one time or another.'

'Oh dear,' said Mrs. Pinfold, 'Have you thought of the fan mail?'

The End

And finally, as serial rights were being offered in late January, 1957, Waugh rewrote the transition from the Bruiser to the library and then, in a maneuver unusual for him, compressed the passage and moved from Pinfold's sense of triumph even in mortality to his decision to write and then to the emphatic and circular closing words of the novel's title page:

> As the wood crackled and a barely perceptible warmth began to spread among the chilly shelves, Mr. Pinfold sat down to work for the first time since his fiftieth birthday. He took the pile of manuscript, his unfinished novel, from the drawer and glanced through it. The story was still clear in his mind. He knew what had to be done. But there was more urgent business first, a hamper to be unpacked of fresh, rich experience—perishable goods.
>
> He returned the manuscript to the drawer, spread a new quire of foolscap before him and wrote in his neat, steady hand:

The Ordeal of Gilbert Pinfold
A Conversation Piece
Chapter One
Portrait of the Artist in Middle-age

And that, as far as Waugh was concerned, was the end not only of the novel but of the experience. The fan mail was apparently as large as Mrs. Pinfold had feared, since Waugh allowed a version of the novel to be broadcast by the BBC on the condition that all letters sent to him in care of the network be returned to sender.[22] He did not seem to fear a recurrence

22. Letter to John Montgomery, March 16, 1960.

of his "pinfoldism," a word he added to his vocabulary, but writing about his delusions seems to have been analogous to writing about macabre details of the mortician's trade in *The Loved One:* having exhausted the literary possibilities, he had no further interest in either subject.[23]

23. See Waugh's Preface to *The Loved One* (London: Chapman and Hall, 1965), p. 8.

15   *Unconditional Surrender:* A Sense of Vocation

Despite Waugh's assertion on the dust-jacket flap of *Officers and Gentlemen* that his war novel was complete, he later confessed that he "was not quite candid. I knew that a third volume was needed. I did not then feel confident that I was able to provide it."[1] By 1957, however, he was assured enough to tell Thomas C. Ryan that he had merely put aside his "trilogy on the war" to write *The Ordeal of Gilbert Pinfold.*[2] External evidence from before and after this date reveals that he had a clear idea of three major plotlines for the third volume: he refused in January, 1954, to include "Compassion" in *Tactical Exercise* because it would be used in the war novel; he consulted Ann Fleming on August 8, 1955, for "some particulars about abortions in wartime for my next volume"; to Sir Maurice Bowra he outlined major events in the next novel "if there is a next time";[3] and he reminded himself to ask experts about the effect of senility upon prayer for his "treatment of Mr. Crouchback in the final volume or volumes of work in progress."[4] The last two entries came after Waugh had tried to begin work on *Pinfold,* and thus in spirit *Unconditional Surrender* is the novel in progress that Pinfold sets aside to write of his ordeal.

Once shelved, the novel was not easy to continue. Negotiating the sale of the film rights to *Scoop* and seeing *Pinfold* through the press and the reviews occupied the first half of 1957, and when it became obvious that Ronald Knox would soon die, Waugh decided to write the biography and in late June received Knox's permission.[5] Furthermore, he had in 1950 been

---

1. Front flap, dust jacket, Evelyn Waugh, *Unconditional Surrender* (London: Chapman and Hall, 1961). Further references are given parenthetically in the text.

2. Thomas C. Ryan, "A Talk with Evelyn Waugh," *Sign* 37 (August, 1957):43.

3. Evelyn Waugh, *The Diaries of Evelyn Waugh,* ed. Michael Davie (Boston: Little, Brown and Co., 1977), p. 736 (August 8, 1955). Letter to Bowra, *The Letters of Evelyn Waugh* (New Haven and New York: Ticknor & Fields, 1980), p. 444.

4. Waugh, *Diaries,* p. 743 (October 2, 1955).

5. Evelyn Waugh, *The Life of the Right Reverend Ronald Knox* (London: Chapman and Hall, 1959), p. 13.

named Knox's literary executor, and myriad details concerning permissions and posthumous publications occupied Waugh's attention almost exclusively for some time. The biography itself embodies the only original research Waugh ever did—the Rossetti and Campion books admittedly recast, however gracefully, the work of others—and he did not finish it until January, 1959. Eight months earlier he wrote to Peters refusing to write for the Cities of Enchantment series because "while I have an [sic] capacity left for original work I ought to avoid hack-work. As soon as Knox is done, I must start a novel—get it done while I have inventive strength left."[6] The long effort had wearied him, however, and he accepted an offer from the Union Castle line to travel to Africa at their expense and write an account of the trip. The result, *Tourist in Africa*,[7] a book that Waugh regarded with considerable distaste both in writing and in retrospect—he consistently referred to it as "the pot-boiler"—was finished in mid-December, 1959, and, to escape the English winter, he accepted another commission, this from the *Daily Mail*, for a series of articles on the Mediterranean. He returned to England in mid-March, 1960.

According to the date at the end of *Unconditional Surrender*, he began the final volume of the trilogy almost immediately. Only in May, however, did he inform Peters that he was writing. By August he had written about thirty thousand words of "Conventional Weapons" and hoped to finish in January.[8] By November the book was still progressing "slowly and to my own satisfaction."[9] Christmas interrupted compostion, and Waugh resisted or deferred various tempting commissions, incuding one for an essay on sloth, which coincided with one of the novel's major themes, in order to push through to a conclusion. In February he discovered that Jocelyn Brooke had prior claim to his working title and subsequently decided on *Unconditional Surrender*.[10] He finished a manuscript draft early in April, 1961, but confessed to Peters that he did not "think the last 1/3 as good as the first 2/3."[11] Two weeks later, while finishing the article on sloth, he provided a long list of alternate titles for the American edition, including "Uncle Tom's Cabin and the Seven Dwarfs," which was not used, and "The End of the Battle," which was.[12]

6. Letter to A. D. Peters, April 18, 1958.

7. Evelyn Waugh, *Tourist in Africa* (Boston: Little, Brown and Co., 1960).

8. Letter to Peters, August 30, 1960.

9. Letter to Peters, November 16, 1960.

10. Letter to Jocelyn Brooke, February 18, 1961. Brooke's novel was published by Faber in May, 1961.

11. Letter to Peters, April 4, 1961, *Letters*, p. 564.

12. Waugh also suggested "Quixote in Modern Dress" and "Honour comes a pilgrim grey." Letter to Peters, April 19, 1961. *Letters*, p. 565.

The novel begins with Guy in a meaningless office job from which he is rescued by a computer, which delivers his name as uniquely suited for a mission. Although Communist conspirators thwart these plans, he is sent for parachute training, where he encounters Ludovic, now a major. After Guy is injured in a jump, he is approached by Virginia, pregnant with Trimmer's child, who wants to remarry him. In order to perform a task that no one else can, he does so and then leaves for Yugoslavia. There he learns of Virginia's death in a V-1 raid and encounters a group of Jewish refugees, whom he tries to move to safety. To one of them, Mme Kanyi, he confesses that he too wanted war as a means of escaping from his personal shortcomings. When she and her husband are unjustly executed because of her association with Guy, he loses all faith in official justice. In the Epilogue, which takes place six years after the end of the war, Guy is happily married to a girl from an old Catholic family, living on his family estate, content at last.

In composition and especially in revision Waugh confronted a problem shared by all writers of sequence novels: the large and complex web of events and relationships built in the earlier novels had to be conveyed as gracefully as possible to remind old readers and to acquaint new ones with the necessary information. Waugh felt that the new book would be "unintelligible to a new reader,"[13] and a few months later decided that a preface summarizing previous action would be necessary.[14] In the manuscript stage, however, Waugh chose not to worry about these matters and concentrated not on retrospect but on new events. In revising, mostly at a typescript stage, he turned his attention not only to the needs of his audience but to the coherence of his work. Most simple but most significant for the trilogy as a whole were the brief insertions recalling earlier events and themes. The reference inserted in manuscript to Guy's sailboat at Santa Dulcina (p. 70), like the inserted comparison of the olive groves of Crete to those of Guy's Italian home in the previous volume (p. 274), economically provides a synchronic perspective in which to view Guy's change or lack of change. Similar purposes are served by the inserted comparisons: of the falling leaves to Ludovic's notebook entry on Guy as a ball of lead that in a vacuum falls no faster than a feather (*Unconditional Surrender,* p. 82; *Officers and Gentlemen,* p. 215); of the innocent biffing of early Halberdier training to the sloppy and cynical operation in which Ritchie-Hook loses his life (p. 283), inserted in manuscript; and of the Air Force yard to the Halberdier barracks (p. 147)—this inserted after manuscript. Important thematically are the various references to Sir Roger of Waybroke, whose crusade ended in futility

13. Letter to Peters, August 30, 1960.
14. Letter to Peters, November 15, 1960.

and whose mission Guy hoped to fulfill by combating "the Modern Age in arms" (*Men at Arms,* p. 5). The two placed in strongest points of emphasis, near the beginning and the end of the novel, serve to reinforce the theme and to mark stages in Guy's development. The latter is a revision at manuscript stage. Originally Waugh wrote: "Guy had come to the end of the road he had taken in 1939. His war was over." This was both flat and hackneyed, and Waugh substituted, "Guy had come to the end of the crusade to which he had devoted himself at the tomb of Sir Roger. His life as a Halberdier was over" (p. 301). This not only reinforces a major theme but provides a frame for the trilogy as a whole.

The first reference to Sir Roger, which does not occur in manuscript, was part of a major reshuffling of material in the opening pages of the novel proper. In the final version, after summarizing Guy's two years in England and showing his comfortable circumstances at the transit camp, the Prologue concludes, "But it was not for this that he had dedicated himself on the sword of Roger of Waybroke that hopeful morning four years back" (p. 13). The manuscript, however, opens with the description of Westminister Abbey and the solemn procession past the Sword of Stalingrad. Then, on what is now page 19, Guy is introduced on his way to a birthday celebration at Ruben's. This is followed by the survey of Jumbo's activities (now on pp. 11–13) and by an account of Guy's two years since returning to England (pp. 5–7), by a version of Guy's final meeting with his father (pp. 7–10), and by Guy's interview with the legless major who tries to find him work and Tommy Blackhouse's choice of Guy as liaison officer (pp. 11–13). The manuscript then moves directly to the end of lunch and the meeting with Kerstie Kilbannock and Lieutenant Padfield.

Although the first draft began with action rather than summary, it built up very little momentum before the necessary summary began. Furthermore, it buried in the middle of the long flashback the thematically crucial scene with Guy's father. After the manuscript had been typed, Waugh conceived the idea of a Prologue to replace the flashback.[15] Though much shorter than the published version, dealing as it does only with Guy's military duties, it placed the emphasis upon Guy as soldier and immortal soul rather than upon the atmosphere of London and allowed the scene at Ruben's to move forward uninterrupted.

An obvious way to bring together and dispose of characters as well as themes from earlier volumes was the end of the novel, but Waugh was no more inclined to expend undue effort on the first draft of the ending than

15. See the second title page of the manuscript, headed "Conventional Weapons," which is part manuscript, part typescript.

he had been in writing *Decline and Fall.* The manuscript contains an Epilogue and the inserted title "Festival of Britain," but it focuses almost exclusively on Guy. The only mention of other characters is the remark of Job, porter at Bellamy's club, to Arthur Box-Bender that "Mr. Crouchback's here tonight, sir. First time he's been in for more than a year. There's a commando dinner upstairs for General Blackhouse—Mr. Claire, (Captain) /Sir Angus/ Anstruther Carr, /Lord Luxmore/ all of them and quite a few guests." In the final version, the analysis of the condition of England in 1951 (1950 in manuscript) is followed by plans for a commando reunion, in the course of which Tommy's and Ivor's careers are traced and Trimmer's disappearance reported. Also added by the time of publication were references to Air Marshall Beech's memoirs and Lieutenant Padfield's new job as "Ludovic's factotum." By this means incidents from all three novels are recalled and major characters appropriately disposed of.

Late enough in the process that the title in manuscript is *Unconditional Surrender,* Waugh wrote the Synopsis. The manuscipt version—judging from the cut-and-pasted second page, itself a revision—is flat and factual. The manuscript begins, "The story opened in summer 1939 when Guy Crouchback, aged 35, returned to England from the family villa in Italy where he had been living, to take part in the war which was imminent," and moves to a somewhat flat version of what is now paragraph three (p. 1). Waugh did insert in manuscript the sentences about Grace-Groundling-Marchpole's suspicions of Guy and Ludovic's belief that Guy knows what he has done to Hound (pp. 2, 3), but the first draft ends with the account of Virginia and Trimmer. The only mention of the trilogy's major theme is the last sentence of the penultimate paragraph, "For Guy the alliance with Russia has nullified the honour of the cause for which he is fighting," hardly an emphatic statement or position. In revision, of course, Waugh began the Synopsis with the dramatic quotation from *Men at Arms* about "the Modern Age in arms" and the authoritative, "What follows is the story of his attempt to find his place in that battle." Waugh ended the Synopsis with a quotation from *Officers and Gentlemen* about the end of Guy's sojourn in the "Holy Land of illusion" and his return to "the old ambiguous world" in which "his country was led blundering into dishonour."

The revision accurately reflects Waugh's assertion on the dust flap of *Officers and Gentlemen* that "*Men at Arms* began with its hero inspired by illusion. *Officers and Gentlemen* ends with his deflation." The reference to "the descent into the nether world of Crete," however, is an obvious allusion to the conventions of epic. Specific parallels to the *Aeneid* and the *Odyssey* cannot be pursued here, but the structural pattern invoked implies that the hero will return to the surface and attain his destiny. This may have been Waugh's way of letting the subtle know that *Officers and Gentlemen* would not be the end of Guy's crusade. In any case, in *Unconditional Surrender* he returns Guy to the ambiguous world not to have him languish in the spiritual sloth of the Santa Dulcina period but to have him combat the public betrayals of honor and justice with private acts of charity—in its full sense as a theological virtue—which lead to his reconciliation with the world and with himself.

In writing and especially in revising the final volume, Waugh consistently strove to augment characters and motifs which support the themes of public betrayal and private reconciliation. The first encompasses both political betrayal—by Americans through invincible ignorance and by the English through duplicity—and aesthetic betrayal. The second involves both the reconciliation of Virginia with Guy and with his church, and with the reality that crusades are now and perhaps always were foredoomed, that they are unworthy of the just man's interest, and that qualitative rather than quantitative judgments operate in the moral sphere.

Conscious political subversion of what Waugh regarded as England's interests in favor of international Communism plays a major role in *Unconditional Surrender.* Waugh does not trace the inner workings of the conspiracy; the sole mention of higher levels couches in passive voice the decision to abandon the Yugoslav royalists for the Communists.[16] The highest Waugh goes is Sir Ralph Brompton, renamed from Anglesea,[17] and he revised carefully to make the character both fatuous and dangerous. Even before he was fleshed out, Waugh conceived him as a double agent in plot as well as in politics, for his previous connection with Ludovic helps account for the latter's sophistication and his influence at and above HOOHQ enables him to send Guy and later Ian Kilbannock to Yugoslavia. In first draft, corresponding to page 27, he is introduced almost in afterthought, entering the scene during a hiatus in the conversation with very equivocal purpose:

> Either for his curls or his communism Susie had a frequent visitor in Sir Ralph Anglesea who at that moment dropped in.
>
> 'I just dropped in,' he said, slightly put out to see Guy there, 'to see if you are getting the Foreign Affairs Summary.'

Only after the insistence that all ranks should read it is he described:

---

16. Waugh's anger at British policy was voiced in letters to the *Times* in 1945 and continued through his agitation against Tito's visit to England in 1953-54.

17. Donald Greene, "Sir Ralph Brompton: An Identification," *Evelyn Waugh Newsletter* 8 (Winter, 1974):1-2; see also Auberon Waugh's response, Spring, 1975, p. 6.

> Sir Ralph was a retired (diplomat) /ambassador/ still, despite clothing restrictions, (slightly) dandified in appearance. /his post was that of diplomatic adviser; his task (internal propaganda) something very modern for so old a hand—'indoctrination'/ He was known /in the office/ as 'the commisar'; (his task, propaganda).

This was functional, but no more. In revision, Waugh made him the interlocutor in Susie's conversation about the Sword of Stalingrad and introduced him as "a tall, grey civilian dandy who stood nonchalantly posed beside him twirling a single eye-glass on its black cord. . . . He seemed a figure of obsolescent light comedy rather than of total war" (p. 27). Other insertions at various stages establish his attitude toward Guy as politically unsympathetic and as candidate first for a coffin and then for a firing squad. Moreover, Sir Ralph's mission to Susie was rendered political rather than sexual by the addition to his reminder of the evening's meeting the line announcing his own absence. And Waugh emphasized the contradiction between his style and his political conviction by changing Susie's remark after he leaves from a jocular threat of political reprisal to the comment that Sir Ralph is "a bit of a bourgeois at heart for all his fine talk" (p. 28).

In writing and revising the next episode in which Sir Ralph appears, Waugh carefully reinforced his dandyism and his "fine talk," adding, of the tea he gives his housekeeper, the precious "bartered in what strange eastern markets I know not" (p. 36) and a detail about his elegant dress (p. 33). More extensive were the revisions of his final scene. Waugh inserted over page the contrast between Sir Ralph's former aversion for secret work and his new relish for it and, more memorable, the sharp contrast between Sir Ralph, natty in out-of-season "light herringbone tweed" and "brilliant black brogue shoes," smoking "a Turkish cigarette," and the Communist general, frumpish in readymade uniform, dull buttons, and cloth belt, holding a pipe insecurely between false teeth (pp. 180-81). The two, made sharply incongruous by the additions, are arranging the practical details of "liaison with Balkan terrorists" — changed in manuscript from "revolutionaries" — and the immediate fates of Guy, who is not sympathetic but potentially useful as a screen, and Frank de Souza and Gilpin, solid party members.

Like Sir Ralph, de Souza is "a bit of a bourgeois at heart." A Cambridge man, he is attractive to Guy in *Men at Arms* because of the cynical wit he trains on the absurdities of army life. In fact, the first draft of the synopsis leading into *Unconditional Surrender* explicitly links him with Ivor Claire, who is his "aristocratic simulacrum." In revision Waugh apparently decided that the comparison was better implied than stated, but he did insert in manuscript the detail about de Souza's "ribbon of the MC" (p. 121), a decoration Claire and Trimmer also wear. And while de Souza's speculations on the character of Ludovic, whom in an insertion he names Dracula, recall the first volume of the trilogy, Waugh took pains to show his subordination to Gilpin. In manuscript de Souza comments on Gilpin's background before changing the subject, but in revising the manuscript, Waugh shifted the material to make de Souza respond to a direct question rather than volunteering information about his superior (p. 122). Moreover, to the manuscript's conversation between Gilpin and de Souza Waugh added Guy's conclusion that "de Souza was attempting to justify himself" and later revised it to show him "with uncharacteristic humility . . . attempting to justify himself" (p. 120). Gilpin's contempt for the Halberdiers is emphasized by the revised material inserted on pages 121 and 198, the second after manuscript stage, to demonstrate that he is not only faithless, like de Souza, but churlish as well.

Gilpin's active rejection of social amenities is further emphasized in his dealings with Guy in Bari. His professional suspicion of non-Communists is strongly implied in the inserted grudging and indirect admission that Guy's fellow Halberdier is "in a way . . . in command when the Brig is away" and in the inserted question about Guy's gear, as if fearing "what it might contain of a subversive, perhaps explosive nature" (p. 199). And to the message announcing the "bath" of Virginia's baby and Gilpin's inserted rebuke in the name of the Brigadier, Waugh added a second error, "birch," a second rebuke, the correction to "birth" and, in contrast to Gilpin's churlishness, the congratulations of the Brigadier (pp. 237–38).

Finally, however, the spirit of Gilpin triumphs in Bari. In the scene in which he reveals the fate of the Kanyis, whom Guy had attempted to befriend, Waugh reordered the speech to put first the unfounded charge of Guy's affair with Mme Kanyi and finally her and her husband's fate in Gilpin's comment: "They were tried by a People's Court. I don't have to tell you what that means, do I?" This may have sounded too triumphant and personal for the drab, fanatical Gilpin, for Waugh revised the second sentence to the impersonal certitude of, "You may be sure justice was done" (p. 305).

The activities of Sir Ralph, Gilpin, and de Souza cannot be called treason, for they influence rather that contravene British policy, and, while morally they may do evil, they act according to coherent plans that are not self-serving. Waugh judges far more severely the betrayals of principle, political and aesthetic, which have no motive beyond immediate personal aggrandizement. The most serious of these betrayals, and the most pervasive in the trilogy, is Ian Kilbannock's. Having driven Air Marshal Beech distracted "from social inferiority" (*Officers and Gentlemen,* p. 127), invented Trimmer as a national hero, and impressed Virginia into service to keep up his morale, Kilbannock looks in the final section of *Unconditional Surrender* for broader scope than he finds at HOOHQ and plots his abandonment of General Whale, now virtually powerless, for a position as special correspondent in the Adriatic. First, however, he is given the problem of dealing with Trimmer, a failure in his tour of America, and with Ben Ritchie-Hook. Judging from the manuscript, which gives the issues in greater detail than does page 241, Waugh briefly considered sending Trimmer with Ritchie-Hook to Yugoslavia, but this is no more than initiated. In fact, neither in manuscript nor in the book is the immediate fate of the two announced, for Whale, possessed by the wish to die, turns the matter over to Ian.

Trimmer was not mentioned again until Waugh revised the Epilogue, but Ritchie-Hook and Ian are both in the party sent to observe the partisan battle exercise laid on to impress the visiting Americans. Their general, later named Spitz, is accompanied by a photographer, Sneiffel, whose odd appearance and antics are emphasized by a series of insertions that prepare for the bizarre scene in which Ritchie-Hook, accompanied, according to German reports, by a midget or a small boy, makes a "single-handed attack on a fortified position" (p. 288). Ian is jubilant at the success of the demonstration, for, despite the failure of the attack, Ritchie-Hook's death has persuaded Spitz that the Americans should back the partisans. In manuscipt Ian is fully aware of the deception in which he participates:

MANUSCRIPT	REVISION
Ian was soberly confident. ('It's an odd thing that) /You didn't miss much/, Loot,' he said. (That's) /It's an odd thing. In all this war I've/ only twice (in this war have I) had any part in an operation. Both were (bogus) /futile/. Both have turned out stories of heorism [*sic*]. (General Spitz has decided that) /Respect for a gallant brother officer is the key note of General Spitz's report/. Ritchie-Hook died leading a charge of partisans. That is to be the story. Air co-operation is to be played down. The arrival of the German relieving force played up. All the	Ian was soberly confident. 'You didn't miss much, Loot,' he said, 'but the object of the exercise has been attained. General Spitz is satisfied that the partisans mean business and are skilled in guerrilla tactics. He was rather skeptical at one moment but Ritchie-Hook changed all that. A decision of the heart rather than the head perhaps. It's an odd thing. In all this war I've only twice had any part in an operation. Both have afforded classic stories of heroism. You wouldn't have thought, would you, that Trimmer and Ritchie-Hook had a great deal in

garrison of the block-house are to be German.

common?' [p. 289]

'You wouldn't have thought would you? that Trimmer & Ritchie-Hook had much in common.'

In revision Ian seems wholly unconscious that he has perverted the truth. By making the change, Waugh decreased or removed the sense of Ian as a moral agent and made his behavior consistent throughout the trilogy. Like characters in some of Waugh's early novels, he seems beneath morality, virtually soulless, so that he can be rejected or despised but not condemned.

The betrayal of literary values Waugh embodied in the figure of Everard Spruce (originally Kenneth Willoughby, then John Spruce) and his quarterly *Survival* (originally *Endurance*). Character and journal were closely modeled on Cyril Connolly and *Horizon*.[18] Perhaps because he had a clear model, Waugh needed no significant alterations to the manuscript introduction of the character (he did change the room adjacent to the site of the party from Spruce's bedroom, filled with the clothing and toilet articles inherited from a deceased friend, to the shabby, cluttered office of p. 46). However, the summary of *Survival*'s contents was consistently revised to denigrate both journal and editor. In first, canceled draft Waugh had something to say in its favor:

/Part was silly, part was meaningless and part was plain, flat dull, but, apart from the illustrations,/ It made better (reading) /value/ than the squadron-leader's 'comics.' /his draughtsmen were superior every time./ . . . Everard Spruce's taste in graphic art was not what Lieutenant Padfield would call significant; it stopped short in the [illegible] of the E. J. Coney & Frankie chose the art, —

This comparison may have been just, but it did not seem satisfactory to Waugh, for he broke off, canceled the passage, and substituted the contrast found in the novel that gives the comic book laurels for text as well as pictures (p. 156). He also changed Spruce's taste in art from negative to a positive "preference for Fragonard over Léger," which he conceals behind the assertion of an indifference which "the Workers" share. First Waugh decided to make this dissembling painful: "Coney and Frankie's choice of

18. See Frances Donaldson (who was the original for the Frankie of the novel), *Evelyn Waugh: Portrait of a Country Neighbour* (Philadelphia: Chilton Book Co., 1967), pp. 110–12. In view of her revelations, Waugh's assurances to Connolly that Spruce is not a caricature of him seem disingenuous. *Letters*, p. 578.

illustration found weak spots in his aesthetic armour & hurt him more than anyone knew." This, however, gave Spruce a conflict almost creditable, and Waugh struck it in favor of the final version, in which the Ministry of Information supports nonrepresentational art as antifascist, a judgment to which "Spruce submitted without demur," making him still more a time-server. Another revision, substituted for "a 'Canto' by the pacific Parsnip" which, in contrast to the illustrations, "seemed to mean something," Parsnip's essay comparing Kafka and Klee (p. 156). This reading, which does not occur in manuscript, indicates not only that Guy is deficient in knowledge but also that Spruce has allowed false taste in illustrations to corrupt the text of the "magazine devoted 'to the Survival of Values' " (p. 42).

In composing and revising Spruce's final appearance, Waugh took pains to show that in fact he was symptomatic of the decay of values. Originally, describing Spruce's interest in high society, Waugh wrote, "lately in the confusion of war he had come to know some of these figures of oppression and frivolity." In revising the manuscript, Waugh substituted "decline of social order" for "confusion of war" to make the change permanent, and in typescript or afterward he changed "came to know" to "met on friendly terms" to emphasize even more clearly the lowering of standards and Spruce's fantasies about his past (pp. 257–58). The decay of order, however meretricious, in Spruce's own house is underlined by the paragraph, inserted in manuscript, describing the effect of V-1 bombs on the girls and on Spruce, who "was like a school master who fears that a rag is brewing" (p. 258). To defend himself against the reproaches of Frankie and Coney not only for paying attention to frivolous people like Virginia but also for actually giving her a salmon and, even worse, a lemon—this Waugh's afterthought— from their meager stores, he launches into a eulogy of Virginia as the last of the line of heroines originated by Aldous Huxley's Myra Viveash.

This eulogy begins the process of deluded characters turning Virginia into literature. On a symbolic level Guy is freed from her spell by seeing her as a real, limited woman.[19] Trimmer falls in love with a version of her past social self and impregnates her, and she turns to Guy not as an enchantress but as a woman in need of help. Spruce turns her into a literary cliché. While he may quote approvingly Huxley's description of Myra's walk, "as

19. Virginia's affair with Tommy, which leads to her divorce from Guy, is anticipated in "The Man Who Liked Dickens," where Mrs. Henty desires to marry a captain who, like Tommy, is in the Coldstream Guards. The similarity leads one to suspect a source in Waugh's experience. See *Letters*, p. 84 and n.2 for resemblances between the situation of Tony Last and Lord Brownlow. See also his description of a "heroine . . . straight from the 1920's—elusive, irresponsible, promiscuous, a little wistful, avaricious, delectable, ruthless," in "Love Among the Underdogs," *Night and Day* 1 (October 7, 1937):29.

though . . . treading a knife edge between goodness only knew what invisible gulfs," Waugh was less impressed. Rereading *Antic Hay* not long after he had finished *Officers and Gentlemen,* he recalled her supposedly limitless power:

> . . . power which, I must confess, has never much impressed me. She was 25 when I was 20. She seemed then appallingly mature. The girls I knew did not whisper in 'expiring' voices and 'smile agonizingly' from their 'death beds.' They grinned from ear to ear and yelled one's head off. And now thirty years on, when women of 25 seem to me moody children, I still cannot weep for Mrs. Viveash's tragic emptiness.[20]

In revising for the final text, Waugh took care not only to add the line placing the heroines "between the two world wars" but also to emphasize by repetition the phrase "the exquisite, the doomed and the damning, with expiring voices" and to reinforce the final phrase by adding it to Frankie's link of the series to "the heroine of Major Ludovic's dreadful *Death Wish*" (p. 250). Spruce's defiant and willful immersion in romantic, nostalgic delusion is further emphasized in the cancellation of the passage on the left and the substitution of that on the right:

'You aren't going to say "the mould has been broken" are you, Everard?'
    'Yes, dammit, I am,' said Spruce.

'We shall never see anyone like her again in literature or in life and I'm very glad to have known her . . .'
    'Perhaps you are going to say "the mould has been broken," ' said Coney.
    'If I wish to, I shall,' said Spruce petulantly. 'Only the essentially commonplace are afraid of clichés.'

Like Spruce, Ludovic is symptomatic of the decline of aesthetic values, but Waugh did considerably more work on this character because he had to bring him from the phantasmagoric underworld of Crete, where he was enigmatic, sinister, and omnicompetent, to the prosaic daylight world of England. The themes of aesthetic and political betrayal Waugh links through Ludovic's homosexual liaison with Sir Ralph Brompton as his valet and secretary, an association that accounts for his ability to speak upper-class English and

---

20. Evelyn Waugh, "Youth at the Helm and Pleasure at the Prow," *London Magazine* 2 (August, 1955):52.

for the intellectual interests that accrued to his character in its metamorphosis from Connolly to Ludovic in *Officers and Gentlemen.* In *Unconditional
Surrender,* Ludovic first appears at Westminster to view the Sword of Stalingrad. On the pretext of establishing his past, Waugh describes a fashionable
wedding of 1931[21] at which Ludovic served as corporal of the guard of
honor and at which he attracted Sir Ralph's notice. As Waugh's manuscript
revisions show, he was also establishing a contrast between the crowds of
1931 and 1943. After manuscript stage, he canceled a brief description of the
bride and fragments of dialogue from the crowd and replaced them with a
much longer description of the guard, the whole line of the wedding party
and guests, and the generalized but thematically more pointed "cheering,
laughing London crowd" (pp. 32–33). Turning to a summary of the relationship between Brompton and Ludovic, Waugh inserted in manuscript Ludovic's zest for psychology and distaste for specifically Marxist books on economics before describing Ludovic's current meeting with Sir Ralph for the
purpose of advancing his literary career. Waugh's only major alteration of
Ludovic's role was to insert the title passage for Book 1 in which Ludovic
identifies his ceremonial weapon as a "state sword." Even shorter but far
more important was the revision of the authorial comment that "at heart or
in a part of his heart" to "at heart, or rather in some vestigial repository
of his mind" Ludovic had been a romantic (p. 39).

By denying him a heart, and therefore an emotional life, Waugh denies him
a soul. Ludovic does have an unconscious mind, but his psyche is so fragmented that he does not even dream, though he does fear that Guy will
expose his misdeeds. Waugh inserted his subordinates' attribution of his
logomania to religious obsession; the appearance of Guy's name on the list
of those to be sent to his station is called, in an insert, an evil omen (p. 108).
After Guy's minor accident, however, the symptoms of Ludovic's relief
expand in strange and ludicrous ways. The first, clearly an afterthought, is
his acquiring a dog. Earlier in the manuscript Waugh had compared his rooms
in the nurseries of the converted villa with those of Mr. Crouchback at
Matchet, excepting the smells of dog and pipe tobacco. Unchanged in manu-

21. The name Perdita suggests that Waugh was thinking of the wedding of Captain the
Hon. William Jolliffe of the Coldstream Guards and Lady Perdita Asquith, reported in the
Times, January 15, 1931, p. 15. That wedding, however, took place not at St. Margaret's,
Westminster, but at the Brompton Oratory (a source of Waugh's change of Sir Ralph's
name from Anglesea to Brompton?), and Jolliffe's name was not "familiar on advertisement
hoardings and the labels of beer bottles" (p. 32). The name of Bryan Guinness was, however;
his marriage to the Hon. Diana Mitford, a much more lavish affair than the Jolliffe-Asquith
wedding, took place on January 30, 1929. See *Times,* January 31, 1929, p. 15. Also, of
course, the Guinnesses were later divorced; the Jolliffes, Roman Catholics, were not.

cript is, "Ludovic did not smoke and he detested dogs." After Waugh had conceived the idea of a dog like Claire's Pekinese who bore Fido Hound's nickname, it was simple enough to change the second half of the compound to "had never owned a dog" (p. 105). Ludovic's first announcement of his plan to acquire the beast is brief and rather flat. For example, the dialogue with Captain Fremantle lacks the pace and timing of the final draft:

'I think I should get a dog.'
'Yes, sir. Jolly things to have about.'
'I don't want a jolly dog . . . I want an affectionate one. Where can one get an affectionate dog?'
'You want to start with a puppy.'
'Yes, yes (and where can I get a puppy) I think I should like a Pekinese puppy,' and then /as though impatient of a discussion on which his mind was already decided/ he rose from the table . . . .

'I think I shall get a dog.'
'Yes, sir. Jolly things to have about.'
'I don't want a jolly dog.'
'Oh, no, I see, sir, something for protection.'
'Not for protection.' He paused and surveyed the stricken staff-captain, the curious and silent diners. 'I require something for love.'
No one spoke. A savoury, rather enterprising for the date, was brought to him. He ate it in a single, ample mouthful. Then he said: 'Captain Claire had a Pekinese.' After a pause he added: 'You would not know Captain Claire. He came out of Crete, too /—/ *without a medal.*' Another pause, a matter of seconds by their watches; of hours in the minds of the hearers. 'I require a loving Pekinese.' [pp.134–35]

By prolonging the suspense, Waugh achieves a startling climax to the sequence, and he made even greater comic capital from the inserted reference to Claire's dog and exit from Crete. De Souza's earlier speculations about Ludovic's bizarre behavior added to the alarm of the station staff, and Waugh disconcerted them further by inserting after the manuscript stage Ludovic's overheard song, "Father won't buy me a bow-wow-wow-wow" (p. 135). The scene in which Ludovic is discovered fussing over the dog was augmented after manuscript by the detail that the dog has "eyes as prominent as Ludovic's own" and by the angle of vision on Ludovic's "khaki trouser-seat, like Jumbo Trotter at the billiard-table; a figure from antiquated farce, 'caught bending,' inviting the boot" (p. 144). Finally, having written the report that he hopes will send Guy to his death and apparently struck by an association of ideas, "with the puppy *on his heart*" (p. 152; italicized words—my emphasis—added after manuscript), he announces its name: Fido.

Allied to though less obviously funny than Ludovic's descent from the cynicism displayed in *Officers and Gentlemen* to the sentiment lavished on Fido is his rake's progress as man of letters. As Spruce observes of him, ". . . very few of the great masters of trash aimed low to start with" (p. 262). At first, though "an addict of that potent intoxicant, the English language" (p. 41), he is to some extent in control of himself as he polishes his journal into the *pensées* that excite Spruce and other followers of the avant-garde. However, Ludovic is committed to language, not to form or content; as he says of his proposed sonnet for the *Time and Tide* competition, "I just like writing. . . . In different ways about different things" (p. 38). To illustrate obsession and release and to reinforce the theme of Ludovic as lapsed romantic, Waugh added to typescript the passage at the end of Book 1, after the view of the empty abbey and unattended sword (added in manuscript), which contrasts Ludovic's sonnet with the winning entry (p. 61).[22] Later in the manuscript Waugh inserted the simile of Ludovic sifting through the dictionary like a prospector and added to one of his nuggets, "Coke-upon-Littleton," his speculation about occasion to use it in conversation.

Climax and end of his career as writer is his absurd but popular novel, *The Death Wish.* No longer in control of his medium, writing automatically and without correction or self-criticism, Ludovic displaces and perhaps dispels the personal anxieties evident in the *pensées* and in the sonnet. However, Waugh is less interested in Ludovic's psychology than in broader themes. *The Death Wish,* which provides the title for the final book of *Unconditional Surrender,* was named fairly late in the manuscript stage, for it is consistently inserted to replace more general terms. The phrase itself was applied to Guy twenty-six pages before Ludovic adopts it (p. 244) in a passage not present in manuscript, and by strong implication it applies to General Whale and to Virginia. By writing the novel, Ludovic helps exorcise Virginia not only from Guy's imagination but from Waugh's, for, as many have pointed out, *The Death Wish,* completed in June, 1944, is a conscious travesty of *Brideshead Revisited.* In composing and revising the description of Ludovic's novel, Waugh heightened and exaggerated its excesses. Thus after manuscript stage he inserted "almost gaudy" to the description

22. Waugh quotes accurately the second quatrain of the winning sonnet by "Denvil" entitled "The Sword of Stalingrad (On View in the Art Gallery)." See *Time and Tide* 24 (November 6, 1943): 912. Waugh asked Joan Saunders to do research on the Sword of Stalingrad. See *Letters,* pp. 532, 539.

of it as "a very gorgeous, almost gaudy, tale of romance and high drama," and for flat statement and allusion he substituted in manuscript more direct description:

> (Plot and counterplot were absurd). /The plot was Shakesperean in its improbablity./ The dialogue might have been written by Disraeli, the scenes of passion by Elinor Glynn [*sic*].

> The plot was Shakespearean in its elaborate improbability. The dialogue could never have issued from human lips, the scenes of passion were capable of bringing a blush to readers of either sex and every age. [p. 242]

The addition in manuscript of "Transept" to "Lady Marmaduke" makes even more ludicrous as well as reckless the naming of the heroine, and the two-sentence paragraph describing the novel's melancholy tone (p. 243) was inserted after manuscript to give a focus to the following paragraph. In that paragraph, moreover, Waugh augmented the manuscript's analysis of Lady Marmaduke as "extravagantly beautiful, clever, doomed" with the additional qualities and the startling reversal of

> . . . passionless only towards Lord Marmaduke; ambitious for everything except his professional success. If the epithet could properly be used of anyone so splendidly caparisoned, Lady Marmaduke was a bitch. [p. 243]

Nor did Waugh spare himself, for he revised the passage describing himself and his colleagues to emphasize their failures of imagination and taste:

. . . half a dozen other English writers sickened by the austerity of the regime and apprehensive of the threatened changes of peace, were even then severally and secretly composing books which would turn from the proletarian alleys of the thirties into the odorous gardens of transforming memory and imagination.	. . . half a dozen English writers, averting themselves sickly from privations of war and apprehensions of the social consequences of the peace, were even then severally and secretly, unknown to one another, to Everard Spruce, to Coney and to Frankie, composing or preparing to compose books which would turn from the drab alleys of the thirties into the odorous gardens of a recent past transformed and illuminated by disordered memory and imagination.

"Privations of war" and "drab" are more precise because more generalized than the terms they replace; "social consequences" is more precise because more specific than "threatened consequences," while the expanded description of the mental process not only places the responsibility upon the individual rather than upon external events but attains the sense-supporting chime of "odorous"-"disordered."

Aesthetic betrayal, however, was a secondary if important theme. Throughout his career Waugh associated public activity, including writing, with fraud and sometimes considerably worse crimes, and characters like Paul Pennyfeather and William Boot retreated into private, nostalgic refuges that were themselves objects of Waugh's humor. *Unconditional Surrender* adopted but significantly modified this pattern, for, unlike the Boots of Boot Magna, eccentric, willful, decaying, the Crouchbacks embrace positive values and become reconciled with their place in the world.[23] The thematic center of these values is Guy's father, Gervase Crouchback, and in revising the manuscript Waugh inserted and repeated his injunction to his son that is the novel's major point: ". . . quantitative judgments don't apply." Even before he reordered the opening pages to begin with the reprise of Guy's activities and then move to Guy's visit to his father, Waugh realized that the first draft of their encounter needed work. For one thing, it went on too long—Guy thinks of his father's speech as a "homily"—to accord with what the reader knows of the elder Crouchback's character. Waugh must half-consciously have realized this, for he commented three times on Mr. Crouchback's persistent development of the topic. The force of the conversation is also vitiated by its placement, for it is followed by the mild comedy of the boarding house proprietors' new obsequiousness to their guests. Finally, the diction and syntax of the scene were too loose and imprecise for a central thematic statement.

Waugh solved all three problems by scrapping the first draft and salvaging phrases and themes for two separate scenes. The first scene, now page 8 of the novel, announces but does not develop the theme of the church's role in the world, underlines Guy's disillusionment with the justice of the Allied cause, and reaffirms Mr. Crouchback's affection for his son. The second is Mr. Crouchback's letter to Guy. Placed at the end of the chapter, it receives proper emphasis; separated from dialogue, it obviates the need for reply that made the first draft seem rather rambling; presented as written rather than

23. In Northrop Frye's terms, Waugh has moved from the pattern of low-norm satire to comedy. See Northrop Frye, *Anatomy of Criticism* (Princeton: Princeton University Press, 1957), pp. 226—27.

oral discourse, it became more precise and pointed, as a comparison of material from the first and the final draft shows. The first follows Mr. Crouchback's initial rebuke to Guy's shallow mockery of the fall of the House of Savoy and equally shallow regret that the Lateran Treaty was signed: "That isn't at all what the Church is like. It isn't what she's *for*" (p. 8); the second comes from the letter that contains his reflections:

Manuscript

'You are talking nonsense, you know. Just like your uncle Peregrine. Worse. Like (your) /our/ cousin Flavia Gonfalconi. But I don't suppose you remember her. She was very "black." ' It was many years since Mr. Crouchback had rebuked Guy. Now he added. 'I'm sorry. I suppose it is working as a schoolmaster makes me talk like this. /Of course in the seventies & eighties every decent Roman was "black" just as every decent Frenchman now is against the Germans. They'd been invaded. But to go on sulking year after year—/

But really, you know, That isn't at all what the Church is like. It isn't what she's for . . . to stand on dignity and make dramatic gestures. There have been vulgar popes, of course, just as there have been wicked popes, but the Church herself can never be vulgar or wicked. She is part of the Mystical Body. You must remember that.'

'Yes, I suppose I must.'

'Always. It's the most important thing.'

Revision

'Of course in the 1870s and 80s every decent Roman disliked the Piedmontese, just as the decent French now hate the Germans. They had been invaded. And, of course, most of the Romans we know kept it up, sulking. But that isn't the Church. The Mystical Body doesn't strike attitudes and stand on its dignity. It accepts suffering and injustice. It is ready to forgive at the first hint of compunction.

'When you spoke of the Lateran Treaty did you consider how many souls may have been reconciled and have died at peace as the result of it? How many children may have been brought up in the faith who might have lived in ignorance? Quantitative judgments don't apply. If only one soul was saved that is full compensation for any amount of loss of "face." ' [p.10]

The revision gets rid of the specialized slang "black," corrects the erroneous label of the church as *part* of the Mystical Body of Christ,[24] cancels

24. The Mystical Body of Christ, as defined in Waugh's time, consisted of the Church Militant (souls in the physical body on earth), the Church Suffering (souls in purgatory), and the Church Triumphant (souls in heaven).

the irrelevant and in part snobbish comment that puts vulgar and wicked popes on the same level, and, in substituting "compunction" for "penitence" makes the Church much readier to forgive.[25] Furthermore, Waugh expands considerably the positive effects of the Lateran Treaty.

The key phrase, "Quantitative judgments don't apply," does not occur in the manuscript revision. By the time Waugh composed the description of Mr. Crouchback's funeral, however, he had formulated the phrase and assigned it to his letter. During the funeral, Waugh originally wrote " 'I'm worried about you,' his father had written in his last letter. With an effort Guy recollected that he was not there to worry about himself." Then Waugh turned to Arthur Box-Bender. In insertion and over-page addition, Waugh added the material now on pages 80 and 81, elaborating on Guy's apathy in making prayer "a mere act of respect," a reporting for duty. Then, apparently struck by the theological possibilities, Waugh added to the insertion a key paragraph:

'I don't ask anything from you'; that was the deadly core of his apathy; his father had tried to tell him, was now telling him. That emptiness had been with him for years now even in his days of enthusiasm and activity in the Halberdiers. Enthusiasm and activity were not enough. God required more than that. He had commanded all men to *ask.* [p. 80]

This prepares for Guy's change of heart and, after a repetition of, "Quantitative judgments don't apply," his prayer at the end of the insertion: "Show me what to do and help me to do it."[26]

On two later occasions Waugh repeated the key phrases in Guy's recollections from the letter. The first was apparently inserted almost immediately. Waugh canceled Lieutenant Padfield's interruption of Guy's brooding "about /the antithesis between the acceptance of/ sacrifice and the will to win" and continued with the speculation that the subject is relevant to Guy and with his rereading the letter (which, like the receipt for Apthorpe's gear, he carries with him) and concluded the chapter with, "There was a congress at Terhan at the time entirely occupied with quantitative judgments" (pp. 161-62). The second (pp. 193-94) is in a passage that carries on over page without apparent interruption through the end of Book 2, Kerstie's assertion that Guy is mad to marry Virginia, pregnant by another, and Guy's answer, "This is just one case where I can help. And only I, really." His mental

25. See *Penitence, Webster's Seventh New Collegiate Dictionary* (Springfield, Mass.: G. & C. Merriam Co., 1965). Compunction involves the action of conscience; penitence involves the later stage of conscious regret. Waugh would probably have scorned the source but accepted the distinction.

26. See Waugh's diary at the beginning of his Pinfold period: "Church again. My prayer is now only, 'Here I am again. Show me what to do; help me to do it' " (p. 722; January 3, 1954).

response, in which he accepts without rancor or shame the worldly judgment of his marriage to Virginia, concludes with him rereading the key phrase of the letter.

Waugh took considerable pains to show that Guy's decision to remarry Virginia is not based solely on theology. In *Men at Arms,* prompted by Mr. Goodall's account of a "blameless and auspicious pseudo-adultery" (p. 148), Guy had attempted to seduce Virginia and had been called, with varying degrees of justice, a "wet, smug, obscene, pompous, sexless lunatic pig" (p. 164). In *Unconditional Surrender,* commenting upon Virginia's situation, Waugh revised heavily, first to establish more clearly and emphatically her predicament, then to make her renewed relationship with Guy depend upon human kindness and mutual comfort as well as desperate need and the higher reaches of charity, and finally to indicate that in marrying Virginia Guy may have saved more than one soul.

In the initial stages of the novel Waugh revised to isolate Virginia both socially and psychologically. Her revelation about her brother and his death and of her unsympathetic stepmother, inserted after manuscript, emphasizes her financial plight, and to the manuscript Waugh added Kerstie's and Virginia's condemnation of the disgusting Mr. Troy to close off hope of a reversal of the divorce decree (pp. 50–51). After Virginia discovers that she is pregnant by the departed Trimmer, she seeks an abortionist and discovers Dr. Akonanga, now turned witch doctor for HOOHQ. She comes upon him as he is casting a spell while beating a tom-tom, and after finishing the manuscript, Waugh remembered the lyrics of "Night and Day" crooned by Trimmer in *Officers and Gentlemen* and inserted Virginia's memory of them and the comparison of the color of the doctor's eyes to "Trimmer's cigarette-stained fingers" (p. 102). At the end of the scene Waugh canceled the doctor's moralizing about the need for babies in order to insert the reference to the sadistic *No Orchids for Miss Blandish,* to isolate and emphasize the doctor's task of "giving Herr Von Ribbentrop the most terrible dreams," and to sharpen the comparison with Virginia's dream in which, like the cock, "she was extended on a table, pinioned, headless and covered with blood streaked feathers." To strengthen the Trimmer motif and to emphasize Virginia's sense of doom, Waugh later added, ". . . while a voice within her, from the womb itself, kept repeating: 'You, you, you' " (p. 104).

Ironically, two of the men largely responsible for Virginia's plight direct her to Guy. Lieutenant Padfield, the "loot," has gathered divorce information for Mr. Troy and then informed her of Guy's inheritance from his father (p. 97). Ian Kilbannock, who forced her to continue the liaison with Trimmer, suggests the idea of her remarrying Guy if she can't get into a home "for unmarried factory girls" of the kind, Waugh added in manuscript, that Trimmer had visited (pp. 110–11). We are not shown either her decision to follow this advice or the advice itself. But the process by which she carries out her plan is considerably expanded in revision in order to make it more plausible, to make Virginia less devious, and to show, by means of her relationship with Guy's Uncle Peregrine, that, far from being the literary stereotype envisioned by Ludovic and Spruce, she is human.

In first draft Waugh seemed to be ruled by the impulse he had noted in 1944 to make everything happen at once. At first he intended to move from Peregrine's fascination with Virginia (p. 169) directly to his inviting her to dinner. Then he inserted details about the symptoms of the fascination but put the invitation on the next day. He also included Guy and Virginia's expansion of the topic of his inheritance. Not until typescript did Waugh decide that matters were moving forward too rapidly, and to slow the progress of Virginia's designs and make her a bit less precipitous, he inserted the description of their habitual activities and set the invitation on her tenth visit.

Waugh also elaborated considerably on the relationship between Peregrine and Virginia, partly because of the comic possibilities and partly because Peregrine, fascinated and curious as Guy cannot be, brings out her pleasant qualities in a context separate from her designs on Guy. Even in his reconciliation with his wife Guy has a double. His brother Ivo had represented his melancholy side, his brother Gervase futile chivalry. Peregrine embodies "the indefinable numbness which Guy recognized intermittently in himself" (p. 157). The first mention of Peregrine in the trilogy as "a bore of international repute whose dreaded presence could empty the room in any centre of civilization" (*Men at Arms,* p. 9) was an afterthought. In *Unconditional Surrender* he is mentioned as an acquaintance of Lieutenant Padfield's (p. 22), and on his reappearance Waugh took pains to underline his possibilities by revising, "During the first World War Uncle Peregrine had served as ADC to a colonial governor," to the more complex and comically distressing, "In 1915 Uncle Peregrine contracted a complicated form of dysentery on his first day in the Dardanelles and was obliged to spend the rest of the war as ADC to a colonial governor /who (constantly)//repeatedly but vainly// cabled for his recall/" (p. 157).

Precisely because he is an unlikely suitor, Peregrine sets off Virginia's qualities. He first encounters her with the same expression that Churchill and Roosevelt turned toward the Sphinx, and Waugh added after manuscript the observation that "Uncle Peregrine was never really disconcerted but sometimes, when a new and strange fact was brought to his notice, he took a little time to assimilate it" (pp. 163–64). This accords with Waugh's extension of the time between their meeting and his proposing the dinner engagement.

At dinner, Virginia questions Peregrine about his life, which to her means his sex life, and Peregrine is flattered by the interest, even when asked if he is a homosexual. Waugh took several tries to get his response just right. At first he simply says "Oh, no, I assure you. What an extraordinary idea" and begins reminiscing about the unnamed Sir Ralph Brompton (p. 173). In revising after manuscript, Waugh has him find "Virginia's frankness . . . childlike and endearing" (p. 173) and, with characteristic pedantry, correct her pronunciation.[27] The joke about his heterosexual experiences—he has had two, twenty-five years apart, with the same woman—is set up slightly better in revision (Virginia has to ask him to continue his account), and the effect on Virginia is magnified in revision to emphasize her attractiveness: for the simple "Virginia sat back in her chair and laughed" Waugh substituted, "Virginia's spontaneous laughter had (always) /seldom been heard in recent years; it had once/ been one of her chief charms. She sat back in her chair and gave full, free tongue," and added, "Sympathetic and envious faces were turned towards her" (p. 173). Personally and socially she is enhanced and Peregrine gratified.

Having placed Peregrine beyond the claims of morality, Waugh had to exercise some effort to return him to moral reality. In manuscript, "not afraid to spoil his triumph with expatiation" (p. 174), Peregrine is given a motive for continuing:

> He had never before spoken to a woman, or indeed to a man, about such matters but he /instinctively/ recognized in Virginia, as many others had done, (someone) /a child of nature/ to whom (all subjects were natural) to whom nothing was (indecent) /improper/.

Betrayed by momentum into an earlier manner, into the moral climate of *Decline and Fall,* where, socially, Waugh seems to have lived a good part of his life, he later realized that this characterization would undermine the moral theme of the trilogy and struck it out. In revising a later passage, he moved back to the theological view in canceling Peregrine's confession that he found the idea of an affair with Virginia "highly exciting" and insert-

27. In the copies in his library, now at the University of Texas, catalogued AC-L W357L W357u, copies 1 and 2, Waugh deleted, "It comes from the Greek not the Latin" and substituted "as in homeopathic." In Evelyn Waugh, *Sword of Honour* (London: Chapman and Hall, 1965), p. 681, it became "as in homogeneous," following Waugh's correction of the Penguin edition, p. 136.

ing his statement that it would be "Very Wrong indeed. I did not seriously entertain it" (p. 177). Then he repulses her attempts to enlist his aid in remarrying Guy.

In an insertion after manuscript stage, Guy is made to feel annoyed as well as amused by "the departure of this oddly-matched couple" (p. 171), but for the most part his attitude toward Virginia is reserved but uncensorious. More important, Virginia is by a series of revisions made less devious and more frank, if not penitent, about her situation. Her oblique confession of the liaison with Trimmer (p. 165) was inserted over page in manuscript. Later in the manuscript Waugh inserted first her song about "a little broken doll" and then the pair's laughter, which leads to her confession of need and finally, just after the break that ends the scene, of, "Then she informed him, without extenuation or plea for compassion, curtly almost, that she was with child by Trimmer" (p. 189).

The reconciliation of Virginia with Guy and her conversion to Catholicism are presented briefly but effectively. The generalized description of her lovemaking (p. 254) was added to the manuscript in a revised insertion, perhaps to satisfy the reader's curiosity, which has been provoked by Kerstie's speculation (p. 244). The contrast between her new family piety and her previous actions is underlined by Waugh's insertion of her desire to have the baby named Gervase, with Peregrine as godfather (p. 206) and the substitution of "Little Trimmer" for "the child" in the analogy with Ludovic's novel (p. 207). The final judgment about Virginia was added to Angela Box-Bender's letter of condolence to Guy. In manuscript it ended with her wish that Mr. Crouchback could have known about the baby. Enough later that he was no longer working with the manuscript, Waugh added Angela's eulogy of Virginia:

> I wish you had seen Virginia these last weeks. She was still her old sweet gay self of course but there was a difference. I was getting to understand why you loved her and to love her myself. In the old days I did not understand. [p. 253]

Unlike Spruce or Ludovic, Guy has escaped his obsession with what Virginia represents and, leaving her to heaven, is free to live and act.

First, however, he must make an act of will, for his reconciliation with Virginia is "a time of completion not of initiation" (p. 254). Waugh established the psychological state before describing it in Guy's confession as he prepares to leave for Yugoslavia. Prompted by a remark about his death wish, Guy confesses that he wants to die. Waugh expanded the priest's question from, "Despair?" to, "To want to die is quite usual today. It may even be a very good disposition. You do not accuse yourself of despair?" In response to Guy's statement that he is, rather, presumptuous because he is unfit to die, the priest was given after manuscript the line, "This is mere scruple" (p. 220). Later, describing Guy's state of mind at the mass he has requested for Virginia, Waugh originally perpetuated his sense of self-doubt:

> How could one think of, say, the finding of Christ in the temple, ask for Mary's prayers at the hour of death, and commit Virginia's /soul/ to the mercy of God all in one single action? He tended to talk to God as though he were talking to himself. Was he?

Then Waugh described the Communist interpreter watching Guy and indicated the end of the scene with "[White line]." On second thought, he canceled the break and added the dialogue that includes, " 'I don't require an interpreter to say my prayers,' said Guy. But later he wondered, did he?" (p. 257). This indicated the possibility of change as the original formulation of his spiritual state had not, and in later revision Waugh focused more clearly on Virginia's nature and reduced doubt to irony in:

> He committed Virginia's soul—'repose,' indeed, seemed the apt petition— to God in the colloquial monologue he always employed when praying; like an old woman, he sometimes ruefully thought, talking to her cat. [pp. 256–57]

In fact, by marrying Virginia and saving the child's life, Guy has already begun to emerge from his apathy, and though on the human level his marriage is an end in itself, on the spiritual level his act of charity has, in the terms Waugh would have been familiar with, gained him *actual* grace, which in turn prompts him toward further good action. The occasion for that action has already been established in the plight of the 108 Jewish refugees who look to Guy for help, and three manuscript pages before the doubt-ridden prayer, Waugh had already written, ". . . he felt compassion; something less than he had felt for Virginia and her child but a similar sense that here again, in a world of hate and waste, he was being offered the chance of doing a single small act to redeem the times" (p. 248).

The Jews had been on Waugh's mind for more than a decade. His diary records that about thirty Jews occupied Randolph Churchill's attention in Topusko, but, aside from noting that they complained about their lot, Waugh seemed to give them little further attention,[28] spending most of his off-duty time in recording "the plight of the Roman Catholic Church in Croatia."[29]

---

28. Waugh, *Diaries,* pp. 579, 586 (September 16, 18, October 24, 1944).

29. Evelyn Waugh, "Church and State in Liberated Croatia," dated May 17, 1945, R5927/1059/92, Foreign Office Archives.

Later, before July, 1949, he wrote "Compassion."[30] So clear in his mind were events and themes that eleven years later he could paste pages cannibalized from the *Month* into his manuscript; the account of uncertain progress of the Jews toward Italy and the execution of the Kanyis, including the quantitative question, "What do two [Jews] more or less matter?" is almost identical to that in *Unconditional Surrender.*

In the novel, of course, the evacuation of the Jews is set in a complex series of events extending through five years, and Guy must experience a change of heart far more complex than Major Gordon's incipient conversion. Thus Gordon's first movement of concern for the Jews is fairly simple:

> The Jews were numbered, very specially, among his allies and the partisans lapsed from his friendship. He saw them now as a part of the thing he had set out hopefully to fight in the days when there had been a plain, unequivocal issue between right and wrong. Uppermost in his conscious mind was resentment against the General and Commissar for their reprimand. By such strange entrances does compassion sometimes slip, disguised, into the human heart. [*"Compassion,"* p. 89.]

Guy's response, quoted earlier, takes into account both his increase in charity and his earlier crusading fervor. As he becomes more and more involved with the plight of the Jews, he fashions for himself a new image, no longer Sir Roger of Waybroke but instead a deliverer, a Moses.

Waugh had some difficulties with the context of this passage. In manuscript, no doubt recalling Randolph Churchill's struggles to read the entire Bible on a bet,[31] he has Guy read, in early October, the Authorized Version of the Old Testament for the first time; then rather clumsily he links official permission to evacuate the Jews to Guy's "reading about Pharoah and Moses. It seemed highly appropriate." Then he elaborated:

> He was not well versed in Old Testament history. The (stories of Pharoah and)/bullrushes, the burning bush/ the plagues of Egypt belonged in his mind to very early memories, barely distinguishable from Grimm and Hans Andersen, but the Pass-over was deepset in his every Holy Week— *Est enim* Phase (*id est transitus*) [Waugh's parentheses] *Domini*—and Moses stood before his eyes, preposterously striking water from the rock near the Grand Hotel in Rome, majestically laying down the law (near the Piazza Barberine) /in St.-Peter-in-Chains/. That day (he) /his/ cuckold's horns (acquired) /were transformed and took on/ renaissance dignity. He was Moses leading a people out of captivity.

30. *Month,* n.s. 2 (August, 1949):79–98.
31. Waugh, *Diaries,* pp. 591–92 (November 11, 18, 1944).

The mock-heroic use of horns and the fairy-tale element of the Old Testament were salvaged from this tangle for the revised passage, which ends, "That day Guy's cuckold's horns shone like the patriarch's, when he came down from the awful cloud on Sinai" (p. 293). Probably at the same stage of revision Waugh expunged Churchill's baleful influence. In "Compassion" the evidence of Mme Kanyi's espionage was "a lot of foreign propaganda publications" (p. 97), which were in fact English magazines and agnostic apologetics that Gordon had sent her. When Waugh reached this stage in adapting his story, he realized the value of the detail and inserted a similar passage into his manuscript. Then, perhaps in typescript, he changed Guy's Bible to "a huge bundle of illustrated American magazines, mostly of distant date" (p. 292), perhaps to underscore the mischief caused by America's uninformed intervention in political affairs.

In "Compassion," Gordon is near despair on learning that the Kanyis have been executed and is unmoved when the priest tells him, "You mustn't judge actions by their apparent success. Everything you did was good in itself." He is, however, struck by the question, ". . . don't you think it just possible that *they* did *you* good? No suffering need ever be wasted. It is just as much part of Charity to receive cheerfully as to give" (p. 98). In recasting the story for the novel, Waugh transmuted this relatively easy consolation into Guy's admission to Mme Kanyi that he was one of those who "thought their private honour would be satisfied by war. They could assert their manhood by killing and being killed. They would accept hardships in recompense for having been selfish and lazy" (p. 300). By this admission Guy recognizes his complicity in "a will to war, a death wish," abandons even nostalgia for his crusade against "the Modern Age in arms" and the perfect cause, and accepts his place in humanity even after he learns that his efforts to save the Kanyis have come to nothing.

The effects of Guy's movement toward charity are shown clearly if indirectly by the Epilogue, which provides a sharp contrast with the Guy of 1939, physically and spiritually isolated at Castello Crouchback. In the action he is part of the boisterous group of Commandos; in the summary he is modestly prosperous, he has returned to Broome, if to the Lesser House rather than the manor, and he is suitably and apparently happily married to Domenica Plessington, descendant of another Catholic recusant family. Thus far Waugh's purpose was constant, but in another significant respect his intention wavered. Both in manuscript and in the first English and American editions he indicates with two lines—"Domenica all right, and the children?" and "Now they've two boys of their own"—that Guy has genetic offspring by Domenica as well as legal offspring by Virginia via Trimmer. Between April and the book's publication in October he had second thoughts. He tried to correct Anthony Powell's impression that the ending was "happy" and confessed that he had failed to realize his intention by "allowing Guy legitimate offspring . . . . I thought it more ironical that there should be real heirs of the Blessed Gervase Crouchback [*sic*] dispossessed by Trimmer but I plainly failed to make that clear. So no nippers for Guy & Domenica in Penguin."[32] Marking "Errata noted before publication, October 1961" and adding "errata noted by readers 1962" to a personal copy, Waugh made sixteen minor corrections and part of a major one. Overlooking Box-Bender's question about the children, he deleted the statement about the boys and the supporting "when Domenica isn't having babies" and added the sentence, "No children of their own, but that's not always a disadvantage."[33] Both the second English edition and the Little, Brown "fourth printing" of *The End of the Battle* (pp. 318-19) contain the anomaly. A second annotated copy does nothing to resolve it; marked only on page 311, it does not contain the line about the lack of disadvantages in having only one child but adds, "A pity they've no children of their own," which in slightly varied form makes its way into *Sword of Honour*, where the contradiction is finally resolved.

However erratic Waugh's attempts to remove Guy's genetic family, Waugh thought it significant enough to mention to Randolph Churchill: "The second edition of *Unconditional Surrender* has an important change. The hero is allowed no children of his own."[34] According to Mrs. Waugh, whose agricultural proclivities were much like Domenica's, Waugh made the change "because he wanted to reinforce the fact that Guy had married Domenica as an act of generosity, to provide a home for her and for Virginia's child."[35] While interesting, this hardly seems conclusive, for nothing in the text supports the assertion, and in fact Waugh added after manuscript Box-Bender's assertion that Domenica's mother is responsible for the marriage— "I think Eloise deserves some credit in arranging it" (p. 311)—which reinforces the earlier offer to take Gervase because "It would be an interest for Domenica," who is an obvious worry to her mother (pp. 260-61). Bogaards argues that "once [Guy] and Domenica are denied a family, little

32. *Letters*, p. 579.

33. *Unconditional Surrender*, Humanities Research Center copy, AC-L W357L W357u, copy 1. Judging from the note, "To be returned to Combe Florey House, Taunton," this copy was used to set the second edition of the novel, which contains the anomaly. See Winnifred M. Bogaards, "The Conclusion of Waugh's Trilogy: Three Variants," *Evelyn Waugh Newsletter* 4 (Autumn, 1970):6-7.

34. Letter to Randolph Churchill, August 28, 1962, "Evelyn Waugh's Letters (and Post-Cards) to Randolph Churchill," *Encounter* 31 (July, 1968):12.

35. Gene D. Phillips, *Evelyn Waugh's Officers, Gentlemen, and Rogues* (Chicago: Nelson-Hall, 1975), p. 137.

Trimmer takes on far greater significance as the means which divine providence, no respecter of rank and wealth, has chosen to provide an heir for a devout Catholic couple who would otherwise be barren."[36] This gets the process backward, since Waugh had always planned to have Guy acknowledge Trimmer's child as his own, and the law of primogeniture and the carefully explained position of younger sons (p. 172) makes Gervase the bearer of the Crouchback name whether or not Guy and Domenica have children. The Epilogue already has enough "prizes, pensions, husbands, wives, babies, millions, appended paragraphs, and cheerful remarks."[37] Moreover, the question of whether or not Guy has children of his own is irrelevant to the central themes of the novel: the acceptance of moral reponsibility in place of the comforts of illusion and of the Christian duty of charity in place of personal egotism. Waugh undoubtedly deleted Guy's children in the final version of the novel because he wished to leave him with his virtuous acts as ends in themselves.

36. Bogaards, "The Conclusion of Waugh's Trilogy," p. 7.
37. Henry James, "The Art of Fiction," in *The House of Fiction,* ed. Leon Edel (London: Rupert Hart-Davis, 1957), p. 27.

16   The Magnum Opus: *Sword of Honour*

In the same letter informing Peters that *Unconditional Surrender* was finished, Waugh said that he did not plan to write another novel for at least five years.[1] Five years and six days later he was dead. In the intervening time, though he continued to plan new projects, the chief results of his activity were retrospective. Most important was *A Little Learning*, the first of three projected volumes and the only one completed, which begins, "Only when one has lost all curiosity about the future has one reached the age to write an autobiography."[2] During the winter of 1961-62, as the result of a return to British Guiana (Guyana) with his daughter Margaret—on the *Stella Polaris*, on which he had sailed during his first honeymoon—he wrote an article on English tourists[3] that sounds like a reprise of his "In Defence of Pleasure Cruising," written thirty-two years earlier.[4] Also in 1962 he pronounced on "Manners and Morals" for the *Daily Mail* as he had done for the same paper in 1930.

In the latter article he maintained that

> In normal civilizations it is the old who are the custodians of the tribal customs. It is their duty to transmit them. The young can enjoy flouting them until they themselves age, when they will find they revert to the conventions they were first taught.[5]

Relationships between young and old occupied much of his attention: he was writing about his own father, who had suffered from Evelyn's anarchic

---

1. Letter to A. D. Peters, April 4, 1961. *The Letters of Evelyn Waugh,* ed. Mark Amory (New Haven and New York: Ticknor & Fields, 1980), p. 564.
2. Evelyn Waugh, *A Little Learning* (Boston: Little, Brown and Co., 1964), p. 1.
3. Evelyn Waugh, "Here They Are, the English lotus-eaters," *Daily Mail,* March 20, 1962.
4. "In Defence of Pleasure Cruising," *Harper's Bazaar* (London) 2 (May 1930):36-37, 99-100.
5. Evelyn Waugh, "Manners and Morals," *Daily Mail,* April 12, 1962, p. 12.

behavior, and his favorite daughter was soon to be married.[6] Recalling his younger self and anticipating the loss of his daughter, he wrote *Basil Seal Rides Again.* Finished a month after the chapter on Arthur Waugh for *A Little Learning,* the story brings up to date the careers of many early characters and in its main action shows Basil first reacting in apoplectic impotence to and finally routing the young man who in looks and manners is identical to his younger self.

More important than the story in terms of Waugh's career was his attention to what became the final authorized edition of his novels. *Brideshead* had already appeared in 1960; uniform with it, containing prefaces briefly explaining the circumstances of composition and incorporating some textual emendations, were *Decline and Fall* and *Black Mischief* (1962), *A Handful of Dust* and *Scoop* (1964), *Vile Bodies* and *The Loved One* (1965), and *Put Out More Flags* (1967). Most important after *Brideshead* were the revisions of the war trilogy into *Sword of Honour.*

In 1964, probably in midyear,[7] Waugh began the process of converting the war trilogy into the "magnum opus"—the singular must be emphasized—he had planned from the beginning. His principles in revising were clearly stated: In the process of publishing three separate volumes in ten years, he had introduced various "Repetitions and discrepancies . . . which, I hope, are here excised. I have also removed passages which, on rereading, appeared tedious."[8] In making the revision, he used the cheapest and most expedient means. Penguin editions of the three novels were used for copy text; corrections, deletions, and a few additions were made in red ink.[9]

Waugh's motives for local revisions, as for most of his structural revisions, are fairly obvious. Many deletions make the narrative more direct, paring away extraneous material like Tony Box-Bender's appraisal of chemical warfare as "the end" and Guy's memory of initiation customs in regiments other than the Halberdiers (*Men at Arms,* pp. 30, 44). Also cut were anticipations of later, historical events irrelevant to the novel, such as the authorial com-

6. Christopher Sykes, *Evelyn Waugh: A Biography* (Boston: Little, Brown and Co., 1975), p. 436. Sykes did not know that the story was finished before the wedding, which took place on October 26, 1962.

7. Waugh used the back of two typescript pages of his broadcast-article on Alfred Duggan for the manuscript of the Dedication and the transitional passage into what had been *Unconditional Surrender.* The piece was broadcast on July 2; it was then published as "Alfred Duggan," *Spectator* 213 (July 10, 1964): 38-39.

8. Evelyn Waugh, *Sword of Honour* (London: Chapman and Hall, 1965), p. 9.

9. The three copies, stripped of covers, front matter, and irrelevant material like the synopsis preceding *Unconditional Surrender,* are in the Waugh collection at the Humanities Research Center, University of Texas—Austin. Page references in the text are to the Penguin editions of the three novels.

ment on the introduction of army psychiatrists too late to detect Apthorpe's mania (p. 183) and Guy's subsequent reading of *The Heart of the Matter* and reflection that he might have gone, though in fact he did not go, to confession to Father Rank (p. 232). Perhaps on the theory that the one-volume version would have more than a Russian plethora of proper names, Waugh disburdened the text of minor characters in the Cretan debacle by canceling the names of Roots, Slimbridge, and Smiley and identifying them solely by their military functions (*Officers and Gentlemen,* pp. 170ff.) and by removing altogether B Commando and its fanatical Colonel Prentice and the fruity-voiced officer whom Guy suspects of being a German spy (pp. 117, 157, 172–73). In the Bari episode he deleted Sir Almeric Griffiths and General Cape's nurse (*Unconditional Surrender,* pp. 156, 169–70). Other characters had, on reconsideration, exfoliated beyond necessary limits, and thus Waugh deleted most of the description of Sergeant Soames, preserving only his likeness to Trimmer (*Men at Arms,* p. 172), and some of the details about Uncle Peregrine's war work and his activities at Christmas (*Unconditional Surrender,* pp. 125, 143–45).

Incidents as well as characters were cut, notably Air Marshal Beech's embarrassing rhyme about Elinor Glyn, Ritchie-Hook's extended game of housey-housey, the false alarm in which Guy suspects the Loamshires of being German agents (*Men at Arms,* pp. 125, 138–40, 209–13), and the summarized war of nerves between the Commandos and the Navy, including the Brigadier's nickname, "The widow Twankey" (*Officers and Gentlemen,* pp. 108ff.), though a holograph insertion restored the phrase characterizing the captain as "the booby on the roof." Personal references are also deleted: Everard Spruce's inherited clothes (*Unconditional Surrender,* p. 40) do not survive, nor does the reference to Winston Churchill as "a master of sham-Augustan prose" (*Men at Arms,* p. 176). The elaborate description of the Rising of '45 over which Waugh had labored so hard in writing *Men at Arms* was suppressed; so was the recurrent reference to Captain Truslove, foe of the Pathan, whose activities in a boy's book are compared to Guy's (pp. 165–66 and elsewhere), perhaps because Guy's renewed adolescence is clear enough without it, perhaps because Waugh wished to make him less ridiculous. Later Waugh cut much of the description of Ludovic's *The Death Wish,* including the judgment that "The dialogue could never have issued from human lips, the scenes of passion were capable of bringing a blush to readers of either sex and every age" and the characterization of Lady Marmaduke Transept (and her last name) with its sudden drop from "splendidly caparisoned" to "bitch" (*Unconditional Surrender,* pp. 187, 188).

Most of these revisions affect plot and theme very little. Others seem to represent Waugh's clarification or change of intention. For example, he changed Ian Kilbannock from a "sporting journalist" to a "gossip columnist" (*Men at Arms,* p. 25; *Officers and Gentlemen,* p. 9; *Unconditional Surrender,* p. 185) to place him even lower in the journalistic scale, and besides deleting de Souza's Military Cross he gave him two of Trimmer's more sensible lines (*Men at Arms,* pp. 88, 89), as well as the disastrous reply to Ritchie-Hook about biffing (p. 115), perhaps to make de Souza seem less omnicompetent. Waugh also inserted the sentence "The great explosion which killed Mugg and his niece was attributed to enemy action" at the end of the Isle of Mugg episode (*Officers and Gentlemen,* p. 104; *Sword of Honour,* p. 380) to clarify an allusion several pages later. Most important, however, is the passage that resolves the fragmentary plot concerning the activities of Colonel Grace-Groundling-Marchpole:

> Colonel Grace-Groundling-Marchpole, like General Whale and Mr. Churchill and many other zealous fellow countrymen, was at that time becoming a smaller and smaller bug. But he had no sense of failure; rather of triumph. Everything was turning out as he had long ago expected. Every day he closed a file. The pieces of the jig-saw were fitting together and the whole was taking shape.
>
> Crouchback, Box-Bender, Mugg, Cattermole—fascist, nazi, scottish nationalist, communist—all were part of a single, intelligible whole.
>
> That morning he had resigned the Crouchback file to the cellars. [p. 762]

Elsewhere, in a series of cancellations, Waugh removed sympathetic comments about the Yugoslav partisans, including Joe Cattermole's explanation of their hostility on the grounds of country and race (*Unconditional Surrender,* pp. 163–64), General Cape's admission that they have good reason to be suspicious (p. 166), their solicitude for the public gardens (p. 178), the partisans' anxiety "to do what was right" in offering to let the village priest conduct a funeral service for the dead Englishmen (p. 224), the singing of the *Te Deum* (p. 228), and the comment that the people making trouble for the Jews have "no coats and boots" (p. 229).

Undoubtedly aware of the charges of snobbery frequently made against his postwar novels, Waugh deleted some material that critics might have used to support their charges. Mr. Goodall's speech about Guy's connections dispersed under "the usurper George" (*Men at Arms,* p. 110) was deleted, as was the description of Mr. Crouchback as member of a class of "Jobs" brought low by the modern age (p. 34). The potentially more inflammatory paragraph ending with, "Regular soldiers were survivals of a happy civilization where differences of rank were exactly defined and frankly accepted" (*Officers and Gentlemen,* pp. 70–71) was deleted, and later all references to

General Miltiades were expunged, so that Ludovic's journal entry about Guy's desire to believe that gentlemen are fighting the war was rendered irrelevant (p. 186) and cut.

Several important deletions affect the reader's response to Guy. In writing *Men at Arms,* Waugh had revised and elaborated the paragraph on the justice of the allied cause in morality and in the conventions of romance (p. 174), emphasizing Guy's mixed motives. Perhaps because he wished to make Guy less self-righteous, he deleted the passage for *Sword of Honour.* Also removed was the much later summary of Guy's activities that includes references to "il santo inglese," to his brother Gervase's medal, which he now wears (in an insertion for *Sword of Honour,* probably in proof, Waugh has Guy note its disappearance [p. 526]), and to his brother Ivo's despair, which Guy now begins to feel (*Unconditional Surrender,* pp. 168-69). In the single volume Waugh must have felt that the summary was needless, and in any case the references to limbo and to Guy's passive wish for death are not related to despair. One other deletion removes an error. In *Officers and Gentlemen,* Waugh wrote of the day of Guy's escape from Crete: "He had no clear apprehension that this was a fatal morning, that he was that day to resign an immeasurable piece of his manhood" (p. 221). Besides being melodramatic, the passage seems to be untrue. Nothing in the context bears out the judgment: unlike Ivor Claire, Guy has not been ordered to surrender; he displays almost uncharacteristic enterprise in boarding the boat; and there is nothing dishonorable about seeking to evade capture in order to fight again. Whatever his purpose in writing the passage, Waugh decided not to include it in the final version.

These local revisions have a subtle cumulative effect; the structural revisions are more obvious, as the outline indicates:

Men at Arms	*Sword of Honour*
Prologue "Sword of Honour"	Chapter 1 (title the same)
Book 1 "Apthorpe Gloriosus"	Chapter 2 (title the same)
Book 2 "Apthorpe Furibundus"	Chapter 3 (title the same)
Book 3 "Apthorpe Immolatus"	Chapter 4 (title the same)
	Officers and Gentlemen
Book 1 "Happy Warriors"	Chapter 5 "Apthorpe Placatus" (sections 1-7 of Book 1 of *Officers and Gentlemen*)
Interlude	Chapter 6 "Happy Warriors" (sections 8-10 of Book 1 as

329

	sections 1–3 of Chapter 6; Interlude as section 4)
Book 2 "In the Picture"	Chapter 7 "Officers and Gentlemen"
Epilogue	Chapter 8 "State Sword" (part of Epilogue is used)

Unconditional Surrender

(Synopsis of Preceding Volumes)	Omitted
Prologue "Locust Years"	Chapter 8, sections 2–3 (part)
Book 1 "State Sword"	Chapter (9) /8/, sections 3–6
Book 2 "Fin de Ligne"	Chapter (10) /9/ (title the same)
Book 3 "The Death Wish"	Chapter (11) /10/ "The Last Battle"
Epilogue "Festival of Britain"	Chapter 11 "Unconditional Surrender"

The renumbering in the first half of what had been *Officers and Gentlemen* is explained by Waugh's admission after he had finished the trilogy: "Originally I had intended . . . *Officers and Gentlemen* to be two volumes. Then I decided to lump them together and finish them off. There's a very bad transitional passage on board the troop ship."[10] *Sword of Honour* deals with the problem by using as a structural principle an idea first stated on the dust-jacket flap of *Officers and Gentlemen,* which, Waugh said, "begins with the placation of [Apthorpe's] spirit, a ritual preparation for the descent into the nether world of Crete." Thus Book 1 of *Officers and Gentlemen* is divided for the final version. The first seven sections resolve the Apthorpe bequest, introduce the characters who are to dominate Chapters 6 and 7, and seal the friendship between Guy and Tommy Blackhouse. The new Chapter 6 includes the serious training and embarkation of the Commando and the enclosed minor action of the affair between Trimmer and Virginia.

The transition between the second and third volumes required a bit more ingenuity. As the discussion of *Unconditional Surrender* indicated, Waugh was quite aware of the difficulties he posed for his reader. He had ended *Officers and Gentlemen* with Guy's return to England in order to impose temporary and artificial two-volume unity: the first book ending in illusion, the second in disillusion. To emphasize the structural pattern of the magnum opus, he combined in Chapter 8 of *Sword of Honour* the Epilogue of

10. Julian Jebb, "The Art of Fiction XXX: Evelyn Waugh," *Paris Review,* no. 30 (Summer–Fall, 1963):83.

Officers and Gentlemen, the Prologue, its beginning revised, of *Unconditional Surrender,* and, after some hesitation, Book 1 of that novel. Waugh's first impulse, to preserve "State Sword" as a separate chapter, may have been purely mechanical. On reflection—judging from the Penguin copy's substitution of "10" for "Epilogue" and subsquent shift to "Eleven," as in the proof copy of *Sword of Honour,* that reflection came before proof stage—he must have decided that all of the material preceding "Fin de Ligne" was transitional.

In hindsight, his decision clarified the structure of the resulting volume. Chapters 1 and 11, containing the exposition and resolution, form, without using the terms, prologue and epilogue. The nine remaining chapters form a triad. At the end of each, Guy prepares to return to England, having experienced the death or disgrace of a character who embodied an illusion that blocked his progress toward grace and truth. In Chapter 4, that character is Apthorpe, the "brother-uncle" whose efforts to become the good soldier parody Guy's. In Chapter 7, it is Ivor Claire, the symbol of "quintessential England," the gentleman-soldier whom Guy admires and rather pallidly imitates. In Chapter 10, three deaths—Virginia's, Ritchie-Hook's, and Mme Kanyi's—deliver Guy from sexual and military versions of romantic illusion and from the illusion that a just cause necessarily prevails in the secular world.

The other obvious revision came in the titling of the chapters, a matter that Waugh always considered an aspect of structure. The change of "In the Picture" to "Officers and Gentlemen" deletes the rather facile irony of the second volume's title for Book 2 and preserves and emphasizes the deeper irony involved in the behavior of Trimmer, Hound, Claire, and others. Waugh's motives for altering "The Death Wish" and "Festival of Britain" are more difficult to account for. Waugh may have felt that he had leaned too heavily on the formula from psychology, a field he professed to despise, and therefore decided to let the characters' desire for death carry the theme without comment. In positive terms, "The Last Battle"—a variant of the third volume's American title, *The End of the Battle*—emphasizes not capitulation but honorable striving, and there may be a connection between the title and Waugh's deletion of Sir Almeric Griffiths, whose only obvious purpose in *Unconditional Surrender* was to label Guy as possessing "the death wish." Though Guy's confession that he wishes to die is preserved in *Sword of Honour,* its appearance in isolation emphasizes that he and perhaps he alone may have "a very good disposition" (p. 718) toward death. The title of the next chapter, "Unconditional Surrender," preserving like Chapter 7 the title of a book in which it originally appeared, is still more difficult to explain. As the title of a book its confession of defeat is largely vitiated by the time the reader arrives at the resolution of the action, in which "things have turned out very conveniently for Guy." As the title of the final chapter, the words seem to emphasize more firmly the capitulation to the modern world and its standards. One could argue that the title contains an even deeper and more palatable irony: Guy, in giving up his crusade and accepting the consequences of his charity toward Virginia and her child, including the passing of Broome to Trimmer's offspring, is able at last to live happily in the world, his imagination free of the false romanticism that immures Ludovic in Castello Crouchback.

With the final adjustments made to *Sword of Honour,* Waugh's career as a writer essentially came to an end. In the time remaining to him, Waugh the private man became increasingly embittered by changes in the liturgy of the mass and the statements of ecumenicists to the point that, in his final diary entry, he prayed that he would not apostasize and concluded, "I shall not live to see things righted."[11] But Waugh the novelist had solved a major structural problem in what he regarded as his major work. A few years earlier, when asked, "Are there any books which you would like to have written and found impossible?" he pronounced what as writer and self-critic could serve as his literary epitaph: "I have done all I could. I have done my best."[12]

11. Easter, 1965. See Sykes, *Evelyn Waugh,* Chap. 26, for a fuller account of Waugh's last years.
12. Jebb, "The Art of Fiction XXX: Evelyn Waugh," p. 85.

17   Conclusion

Near the end of his career Waugh testified that the processs of writing a novel took longer as he grew older: six weeks for the early ones, a year for *Men at Arms,* and, as we have seen, still longer for others. The problem, he continued, was that "one's memory gets so much worse. I used to be able to hold the whole of a book in my head. Now if I take a walk whilst I am writing, I have to hurry back and make a correction, before I forget it."[1] The various chronological accounts testify independently that the process became more difficult, but the objective evidence does little to bear out Mrs. Waugh's view that her husband "made increasingly more corrections and alterations as he grew older."[2] Although Waugh obviously had different intentions in writing *Unconditional Surrender* from those he had for writing *Decline and Fall,* the same kinds and degrees of meticulous revision are present in both manuscripts. And while details in the composition of the novels are more interesting than abstractions from more than thirty years of practice, the manuscripts do reveal fairly consistent, if artificially demarcated, kinds of concern, all the way from the phrase to form in the broadest and most obvious sense.

Waugh's view that "Writing [is] not . . . an investigation of character, but . . . an exercise in the use of language"[3] is, with some qualifications, obviously borne out by the manuscripts. Again and again—far more often than could be indicated in this book—they reveal him searching for just the right rhythm, tone, and shade of meaning and settling on a pattern that is unique and yet impervious to parody because all idiosyncrasy has disappeared. On the other hand, he confessed that "it is drama, speech and events that interest me";[4] this implies that his presentation of character, as opposed to

1. Julian Jebb, "The Art of Fiction XXX: Evelyn Waugh," *Paris Review,* no. 30 (Summer–Fall, 1963):78.
2. Alfred Borrello, "A Visit to Combe Florey: Evelyn Waugh's Home," *Evelyn Waugh Newsletter* 2 (Winter, 1968):2.
3. Jebb, "The Art of Fiction XXX: Evelyn Waugh," p. 79.
4. *Ibid.*

"investigation" of it, is intimately connected with language. Many of his characters, from Mrs. Beste-Chetwynde and Mrs. Grimes in *Decline and Fall* all the way through Ludovic in the last two volumes of the trilogy, were discovered as he composed his novels, and most of the characters were enlarged, heightened, and made more individual not so much because of what they do as because of what they say. For Apthorpe, as for Grimes, the style is the man, and throughout his life as novelist Waugh's revisions helped the characters become more themselves and less like anyone else.

Frequently, as in *A Handful of Dust,* allowing characters to reveal themselves involved revision to give them the literal last word in a scene. In manuscript Waugh tended to skimp endings, whether of scenes, chapters, or whole books, and again and again, in looking over what he had written, he took the opportunity to augment. Very rarely does he add action much beyond stage business; instead, he uses his own and the characters' rhythms of language to encapsulate theme and character. The manuscript of *Decline and Fall,* for example, ended, "So Peter went out, and Paul settled down again in his chair." In revising for the printed version, Waugh added:

> So the ascetic Ebionites used to turn towards Jersualem when they prayed. Paul made a note of it. Quite right to suppress them. Then he turned out the light and went into his bedroom to sleep.

The added business emphasized, with help from the false parallelism of "So," the author's and character's lack of moral differentiation between the dynamic Peter and the static Paul and concludes the novel with an unmistakable finality of rhythm and action. In revising *Unconditional Surrender,* Waugh exhibited the same concern for rhythm in concluding the crucial scene. When Mme Kanyi describes men who thought "they could assert their manhood by killing or being killed," the manuscript continues:

> "Did none in England?"
> "God forgive me," said Guy, "I did."

This must have come to seem too curt, and the book reads:

> "Were there none in England?"
> "God forgive me," said Guy, "I was one of them."[5]

The revision subtly alters content as well as rhythm, for not only are the two halves of Guy's speech more equally balanced, but Guy places himself in a human context instead of insisting—as he had done at the beginning of the trilogy—on his isolation.

5. Evelyn Waugh, *Unconditional Surrender* (London: Chapman and Hall, 1961), p. 300.

For a writer who said that in his youth he could "set a few characters in motion, write 3,000 words a day, and note with surprise what happened,"[6] the manuscripts reveal surprisingly few changes in basic conception. Waugh said that he had "very little control" over his major characters and that "I start them off with certain preconceived notions of what they will do and say in certain circumstances but I constantly find them moving another way." His example is Angela Lyne in *Put Out More Flags:*

> I had no idea until halfway through the book that she drank secretly. I could not understand why she behaved so oddly. Then when she sat down suddenly on the steps of the cinema I understood all and I had to go back and introduce a series of empty bottles into her flat.[7]

This account accords with the evidence of the manuscripts discussed in this book. For the most part, the sudden inspirations or revelations and subsequent changes in a character's fate occur with secondary characters like Mrs. Grimes, Sambo the parrot, and Major Hound. The major action, theme, and pattern seem to have been fairly clear in Waugh's mind—the theme of art in *The Loved One* is a notable exception—and in the novels after *Helena* all three elements seem to have been clearer in Waugh's mind before he began than they had in earlier novels. This does not mean that the process of composition was easier; it does mean that in all of his work, and especially in later work, Waugh devoted most of his attention to highlighting his themes by introducing or altering the actions of secondary characters.

The broadest if not the final concern in Waugh's revision for publication was structural. Day-to-day revisions and intermediate reconsiderations established the network of correspondences and allusions that hold the novels together from within, but like many writers more obviously committed to modernist experiment, Waugh took great care to guide his readers by means of external form. As the manuscripts of *Decline and Fall* and *Brideshead Revisited* show, he was sometimes torn between the claims of physical and thematic symmetry, and in the second novel he struggled through several principles of division before finding one that satisfied both. In other cases, as in *A Handful of Dust,* he completed the manuscript before settling on an external structure that would support and reveal his theme. In still others—notably *Scoop* and *The Loved One*—he went back and introduced new scenes (for Mrs. Stitch and Sir Ambrose Abercrombie) to balance earlier actions and to emphasize elements of the theme that had been neglected or underemphasized in first draft.

6. Evelyn Waugh, "Preface," *Vile Bodies* (London: Chapman and Hall, 1965), p. 7.
7. Evelyn Waugh, "Fan-Fare," *Life* 20 (April 8, 1946):56, 58.

This aspect of Waugh's habits of composition reveals what textual study, by its concentration upon particulars, inevitably obscures: the novels are organic wholes, analyzable but indivisible. Waugh clearly stated this principle on at least two occasions. On the first, contrasting journalism with fiction, he asserted:

> The value of a novel depends on the standards each book evolves for itself; incidents which have no value as news are given any degree of importance according to their place in the book's structure and their relation to other incidents in the composition, just as subdued colours attain great intensity in certain pictures.[8]

Seven years later, admonishing Cyril Connolly, he denied that isolated passages could reveal much about style because

> the style is the whole. . . . writing is an art which exists in a time sequence; each sentence and each page is dependent on its predecessors and successors; a sentence which he admires may owe its significance to another fifty pages distant.[9]

When he was no longer "able to hold the whole of a book in my head"—if he did not exaggerate his youthful powers—he depended on increased diligence and a longer process of composition.

The major difference between Waugh and most of his modernist predecessors was that he regarded himself as a popular writer and grew increasingly impatient of technical innovations.[10] He knew a good deal about those innovations, however, and as he told Connolly in concluding the passage just quoted, ". . . even quite popular writers take great trouble sometimes in this matter." Waugh wanted to sell books; more that that, he wanted to have them read and understood, and, as this book has attempted to show, he always took great trouble in these matters.

---

8. Evelyn Waugh, *Remote People* (London: Duckworth, 1931), p. 52

9. Evelyn Waugh, "Present Discontents," *Tablet* 172 (December 3, 1938): 743.

10. See my "Evelyn Waugh on the Art of Fiction," *Papers on Language and Literature* 2 (1966):243-52.

Index